On the Road North of Boston:
New Hampshire Taverns and Turnpikes,
1700-1900

On the Road North of Boston:
New Hampshire Taverns and Turnpikes, 1700-1900

DONNA-BELLE GARVIN   **JAMES L. GARVIN**

New Hampshire Historical Society
Concord, New Hampshire

This book was funded in part by grants from the National Endowment for the Humanities, a federal agency.

Library of Congress Cataloging-in-Publication Data

Garvin, Donna-Belle.
  On the road north of Boston.

  Includes index.
  1. Hotels, taverns, etc.—New Hampshire—History—18th century. 2. Hotels, taverns, etc.—New Hampshire—History—19th century. 3. New Hampshire—Social Life and customs. I. Garvin, James L. II. New Hampshire Historical Society. III. Title.
GT3810.N4G37 1988   394.1′2′09742   88-34478

ISBN 0-915916-19-3

Published by the New Hampshire Historical Society, Concord, New Hampshire
Designed by Cyndy M. Brady
Printed by Northlight Studio Press, Inc., Barre, Vermont

COVER: *The South West Prospect of the Seat of Colonel George Boyd at Portsmouth, New Hampshire, New England, 1774*, oil on canvas. Built about 1745, this imposing estate was acquired in 1771 by shipbuilder George Boyd. The dwelling, warehouses, and tidemills, called the ''white village,'' were located on the principal road leading north from Portsmouth. Leading to the new settlements of New Hampshire, this road supplied the hinterlands with trade goods from the coast and carried the raw materials of the province to the mercantile and manufacturing center of Portsmouth.

Courtesy, The Lamont Gallery, Phillips Exeter Academy (Gift of Thomas W. Lamont, Class of 1888)

Preface

THIS BOOK HAD ITS beginnings in the 1970s with the suggestion by John F. Page, then director of the New Hampshire Historical Society, that the Society mount an exhibit of tavern-related materials from New Hampshire. With the help of several volunteers, Page had assembled a list of artifacts, centering on a number of colorful tavern signs, which hinted at the richness of tavern life in northern New England. An interpretive display, which would offer a look at a lost and largely forgotten world, became a challenging possibility. Page rightly suggested that the Society was not yet ready to do full justice to his idea, but the staff added the idea of an exhibit and accompanying catalogue to its list of future projects.

The first step toward realization of Page's idea came late in 1984, when the Society was awarded a planning grant from the National Endowment for the Humanities. The decision to seek NEH aid carried with it several commitments. First, the catalogue assumed primary importance, becoming a potential vehicle for carrying out a complex interpretation that would express the purposes of the Endowment and would make a permanent contribution to the recorded history of New Hampshire and northern New England. Second, the planned emphasis of the catalogue was broadened considerably to include a full exploration of the conditions of travel in New Hampshire before the age of the automobile. Third, the exhibit began to assume a separate role, one to be funded largely by non-NEH funds.

The NEH planning grant permitted the Society's small staff to be supplemented for three months by three assistants who helped to gather the vast quantities of information required to undergird a study based on the humanities. David C. Boyle, a former staff member, was employed to free James L. Garvin, then curator, to carry out research and direct the efforts of two researchers. Trustee Charles E. Clark suggested the first of these researchers, Susan Noard. A graduate student in history at the University of New Hampshire, Noard was entrusted with a search of both primary and secondary sources. Concentrating much of her time on the untapped richness of the State Archives, recently made accessible through the organizing efforts of its director, Frank C. Mevers, Noard uncovered a wealth of information on the role of the tavern in early New Hampshire and on early road-building in the province. The second intern was Quentin Blaine, also a recent graduate student in history at the University of New Hampshire and, in 1985, a law student at the Franklin Pierce Law Center in Concord. Blaine also located primary and secondary information and pursued and arranged a vast body of material on the legal and legislative underpinnings of the tavern and of highway construction before 1900.

At this stage, the Society relied once again on a volunteer researcher who had already demonstrated her skill and persistence in the largely thankless task of searching secondary sources, especially town histories, for their crucial but often obscure references to the subject at hand. Sandra Burt tirelessly combed histories and photocopied materials to provide an extensive file of the relevant comments and invaluable recollections of earlier writers.

Other volunteers assisted in a similar manner, notably Portsmouth historian Raymond A. Brighton. On his own initiative, Brighton proceeded to search eighteenth- and nineteenth-century newspapers for references to taverns, hotels, and travel, greatly augmenting the newspaper research carried out by the Society staff. W. Dennis Chesley gave the fruits of years of work when he provided the authors with his unpublished scholarly papers on the First New Hampshire Turnpike and the Piscataqua Bridge. John Preston shared his long-term research on the Third Turnpike. Dr. Dorothy M. Vaughan offered her files on the Old Bonney Tavern, accumulated in preparation for an article on that building in 1941. Robert A. Whitehouse provided a variety of materials from his research and collections on Dover history; Joan R. Watts made a similar contribution for Chester, including the identification of the early daguerreotype of the Manchester-Haverhill stage outside the Central House. Barbara Bullock Jones of Charlestown and Robert H. Leavitt of Lebanon shared a wealth of information on the taverns of their two towns. Gerald D. Foss provided encyclopedic information on Freemasonry and its connection with various taverns.

By the time the work funded under the NEH planning grant was completed in September 1985, several things were evident. First, what had been conceived of as an exhibit catalogue had now grown in concept to a book, a volume which had the potential to be the Society's first recent effort at narrative scholarship. Second, this book could be based largely upon the wealth of primary sources discovered by the team of researchers, thereby making an original contribution to scholarship in northern New England. Third, the book could be amply illustrated, enriching the reader's understanding as words alone could never do.

With these principles in mind, and with the encouragement of Dr. R. Stuart Wallace, then the Society's director and a social historian in his own right, the staff applied for and received a National Endowment for the Humanities implementation grant in 1986, and began work on the book. When James L. Garvin left the Society for other employment in the spring of 1987, he continued his work on a voluntary basis. Donna-Belle Garvin, the Society's museum cataloguer and a participant in the project since its inception, assumed full co-authorship of the book while continuing to assist other staff members with preparations for the accompanying exhibit. The completion of both book and exhibit were overseen by John L. Frisbee, who assumed directorship of the Society in 1987.

In addition to those already mentioned, a great number of individuals enthusiastically offered their time, knowledge, or collections. Society staff members who were crucial participants in fulfilling the requirements of one or both NEH grants include Barbara E. Austen, Douglas R. Copeley, William Copeley, Stephen L. Cox, Heidi Gitelman, Mary Ann Gundersen, and Jan McCoy.

Many institutions and individuals contributed illustrations, which are credited throughout the book. Others assisted in a variety of ways, each making an important contribution to the volume: John P. Adams, Charles W. Allen, Joann W. Bailey, Donald Baker, Janet Ball, Georgia B. Barnhill, Ronda Berchuk, Ronald P. Bergeron, Kenneth A. Berry, Colette Bouchard, Nan Esseck Brewer, Mary Pat Brigham, Raymond A. Brighton, David S. Brooke, Ernest B. Brown, Helene Carol Brown, Edward C. Brummer, Charles E. Buckley, Charles L. Bullock, Sandra Burt, Mrs. Crawford J. Campbell, Peter and Dawn Carswell, June Brundage Cater, Gardner A. Caverly, Gilbert S. Center, Gordon A. Chamberlin, Marian Chase, W. Dennis Chesley, Charles E. Clark, H. Nichols B. Clark, Ruth Hilton Cleland, Christopher W. Closs, John J. Collins, George S. Comtois, Lorna Condon, Rebecca Courser, Kenneth C. Cramer, John O. Curtis, Ellen S. Derby, Nancy Druckman, John H. Dryfhout, Pamela Drypolcher, Philip F. Elwert, Ralph Esmerian, Colleene Fesko, Nat Figuers, Henry C. Ford, Gerald D. Foss, Compton E. French, Cynthia Gabrielli, Guy Gosselin, J. Kevin Graffagnino, Mr. and Mrs. Cyrus Gregg, Frederick S. Hall, Stanley A. Hamel, Rosalind P. Hanson, Mrs. Stillman Hobbs, Dorothy Imagire, Grace Jager, Timothy Johnson, Barbara Bullock Jones, Susan Jukosky, Frank Kelly, Ellen Koenig, Michael Komanecky, Gregory H. Laing, J. Larsen, Robert H. Leavitt, Ruth A. Lepovsky, Elizabeth Lessard, Laurence Libin,

George Lindsey, Gary Thomas Lord, Sally Loring, Rosetta B. Lowe, Jean E. Mansell, Thomas Marsh, Nancy C. Merrill, Patricia Merrill, Frank C. Mevers, Pauline H. Mitchell, Laura V. Monti, Nancy C. Muller, Anne M. Murphy, Margaret J. Nagy, M. P. Naud, Shirley H. Nemiccolo, Chester H. Newkirk, Christina O'Sullivan, David L. Ottinger, Jeanne E. Palmer, Charles S. Parsons, Heather Pentland, Faith Learned Pepe, Ann Marie Powers, John Preston, Malcolm Purington, Robin S. Reynolds, Patricia Riley, Marion R. Robinson, Steve Robinson, Shirley Roehrs, Michael Rounds, Alan F. Rumrill, Beverly and Ray Sacks, Roland Sallada, Dorothy Sanborn, David Sanderson, Helen Sanger, Winthrop T. Sargent, Dorothy W. Sears, Jr., Holly K. Shaw, Ernest L. Sherman, Helene Smith, Julie Solz, Esther Munroe Swift, Nicholas Sysyn, Ida Taggart, Andrew S. Taylor, Norma C. Thibodeau, Matthew E. Thomas, Edward Thulin, Charles D. Townsend, Jo Anne Triplett, Theodore Turgeon, Richard F. Upton, Dr. Dorothy M. Vaughan, William L. Warren, Joan R. Watts, Melvin E. Watts, Mr. and Mrs. Glynn Wells, Robert Wester, Robert A. Whitehouse, George Williams, Barbara W. Wood, Mary Baker Wood, Rawson Wood, Mr. and Mrs. Robert K. Wood, Mary Yusko, and Roberta Zonghi. In addition, officers and staff members representing libraries and historical societies around the state assisted by conscientiously completing detailed survey forms requesting information on their tavern-related collections.

The book owes much to the care of its two principal photographers, Bill Finney and Ernest Gould. Invaluable photographic reconnaissance was undertaken by long-time volunteer Michael Rounds. The text has been vastly improved by the faithful and judicious work of editor Linda Landis.

Some may be disappointed that this volume does not offer a complete list of every New Hampshire tavern and tavernkeeper. The completion of such a list proved impossible because of the great numbers of houses that were licensed as taverns over two centuries. The town of Amherst alone, for example, is known to have supported some sixty taverns, and many others are doubtless still undiscovered. The Society's research files on taverns, developed under the NEH planning grant and organized by town, are available to the public at its headquarters at 30 Park Street in Concord. They will continue to be augmented with new information as it becomes available, and contributions from readers are warmly solicited.

The authors hope that this volume, relying as it does largely on original materials and on the words of early travelers, will provide the reader with a comfortable understanding of life on the road in times far different from our own. Although the book concentrates on the province and state of New Hampshire, the authors also hope that the insights offered by the volume will prove valuable to those interested in the broader fields of New England and American history.

Contents

Photograph, Albert W. Russell's New Hampshire Central House, Goffstown, N.H., circa 1865. Located at the center of a busy village, the Central House was a typical small hotel, advertised in 1866 as standing ''in one of the most pleasant and healthy situations in New England.'' The bustling activity recorded in this photograph reflects the central role played by small country inns within the community.
NHHS Collections

THE TAVERN IN SOCIETY

CHAPTER 1

UNTIL THE MID-NINETEENTH CENTURY, the tavern served the diverse needs of a society with few specialized institutions. It provided hospitality, food, and drink to neighbors as well as strangers. It provided shelter to the traveler and his animals in an age when distances seemed vast and when transportation was slow and hazardous. It provided a meeting place for the local electorate and for social organizations. On occasion, it substituted for the meetinghouse, the school, the courtroom, the store, and the hospital. Its yard doubled as military training field, sports arena, stockyard, and fairgrounds. By its very nature, the tavern was also a place of comfort, relaxation, and gossip, a home away from home, a place where people congregated at times of celebration or play. The tavern offered fellowship, enhanced by the bottle, the pipe, the shared and dogeared newspaper, and the diverting spectacle of the passing world. The tavern was truly a public house, its door open to all.

It is small wonder that one nineteenth-century English visitor found taverns "so large an institution, having so much closer and wider a bearing on social life than they do in any other country, that [one is] bound to treat them . . . as a great national feature in themselves."[1] Envisioning the ideal New Hampshire community in 1792, historian and minister Jeremy Belknap specified both "roads and bridges in good repair" and "a decent inn for the refreshment of travellers, and for public entertainments."[2]

Of all its roles, the tavern's hospitality to strangers was seen as the most important. As long as transportation was restricted to the pace of man or animal, a house offering accommodation for "man and beast" remained an essential landmark every three or four miles along each major highway. A French visitor around 1795 found "the number of inns in America . . . out of all proportion to that in Europe"; as if to confirm this, one late-nineteenth-century local historian recalled "twenty-two [taverns] flourishing at one and the same time, between Concord and the Centre Road village of Salisbury, a distance of twenty miles."[3]

Because of its central function in the local community and in society at large, the tavern was subject to close governmental supervision from the days of earliest settlement. The tavern was watched and regulated at both the local and provincial levels. The people of Londonderry petitioned the New Hampshire Assembly in 1758, asking that innholders be placed "under such Regulations, in Respect to Travellers, Towns-Men, Sabbath-Days, & every night, as in your Great Wisdoms you think . . . most Conducive, to Incourage Virtue & Discourage Vice."[4] In response to such concerns, the Assembly gradually instituted general laws for licensing, regulating, inspecting, and taxing taverns and "tippling houses." The complexity of the resulting legislation is clearly indicated in a 1782 law entitled "An Act

Newspaper advertisement for Stephen Huse's Greenland Hotel, New-Hampshire Gazette, 1810. Huse chose to use the newly fashionable designation "hotel" for his tavern, advantageously located at a busy intersection of post roads. Although not an exact likeness of this Federal-period tavern, the woodcut clearly indicates a large building (in this case with a second taproom door) and a tall signpost.

NHHS Collections   Photographer, Ernest Gould

for reviving an Act intitled an Act in addition to an Act intitled to repeal Sundry Acts of this State relating to Taverners. . . ."[5]

Despite numerous modifications through the years, the basic provisions for regulating taverns remained constant from the seventeenth century. All tavernkeepers were required to obtain a license, as were "retailers"—storekeepers who could sell liquor in bulk but who were forbidden to mix or sell individual drinks or to allow drinking on their premises.

The first step in seeking a tavern license was a petition, often to the governor (or lieutenant governor) and Council, explaining the need for a tavern and the applicant's qualifications as a taverner. Around 1675, Joseph Purmort of New Castle, for example, requested that, "having a wife and family of Children to maintaine and at the present all trading being very dead, [he be granted] licence to keep a publiqe house of entertainement there being at present but one on yᵉ great Island and that very inconvenient for strangers and travellours in theire journeying through the country."[6]

The next step was approval by the town selectmen, both for the initial license and the necessary annual renewal. These officers frequently presented written support or opposition of an applicant to an appropriate court. Daniel Gilman's application in 1765 failed, for example, when leading Exeter citizens accused him of having kept "a Disorderly House and Suffar[ing] people to Spend their Time and Substance in gitting Drunk to the Common hurt and Disturbance of the Neighbourhood."[7]

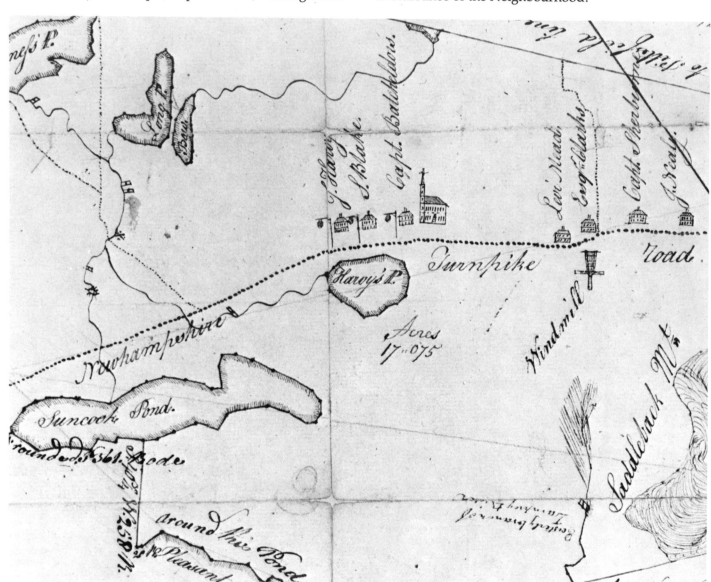

Plan of the town of Northwood, 1805, (detail). Made in compliance with a law of 1803 requiring each town to submit to the New Hampshire Secretary of State a map detailing its natural and man-made features, this manuscript map of Northwood shows the section of the First New Hampshire Turnpike near Harvey's Pond, with three taverns and the town meetinghouse nearby.
Courtesy, New Hampshire Division of Records Management and Archives   Photographer, Bill Finney

ON THE ROAD NORTH OF BOSTON

Competition for licenses could be intense, since provincial law set a maximum number to be granted for any town. Portsmouth was allowed as many as six taverns by a law of 1715, but most New Hampshire towns were permitted no more than three.[8] While New Castle was successful in gaining "the privilege of another publick house" in 1717, other towns of the same period, seeing "the evil Effects of an extream Multiplicity of Taverns," sought a reduction in the number of their licenses.[9]

As late as the 1820s, this tradition of strict governmental regulation limited the average number of taverns in New Hampshire towns to 2.2. Yet communities located along major highways, having a legitimately greater need for taverns, might have as many as eleven at the same period. At the junction of several turnpikes leading through New Hampshire and Vermont, Lebanon had more than twice as many taverns as adjacent Hanover, a town with greater population but fewer highways.[10] Since traffic was a key justification for the granting of licenses, applicants often emphasized that their house stood where two "great roads" intersected. A typical newspaper advertisement of a "tavern stand" for sale might highlight, for example, its "unrivalled" location "at the intersection of the stage road from [Exeter] to Concord, and the great eastern road from Portland to Boston."[11]

Before the construction of major bridges, ferry landings were regarded as appropriate sites for taverns. Stephen Chase of Nottingham West (now Hudson) was successful in obtaining a tavern license in 1749 because his house stood near Hardy's ferry on the Merrimack River. John Neal's location at the "ferry house" in Stratham guaranteed the renewal of his license from 1753 until he moved to New Market in 1761. William Fellows' Portsmouth tavern was a favorite stopping place on the road from Boston to Maine during the early 1700s "by reason of its nighnesse to the fferry" across the Piscataqua River.[12]

Waterborne traffic along the coast or on New Hampshire's major rivers also required convenient taverns. In 1764, Joseph Pattinson's house at Ragg's Point in Newington was found "very convenient for those going up and down the [Piscataqua] river." On a branch of the same river, "sloopmen" and those coming upriver for rafts of logs patronized Benjamin Quinby's Somersworth tavern in 1747. An applicant for a tavern license at Derryfield (now Manchester) on the Merrimack River in the 1750s emphasized the need for a tavern at Amoskeag Falls to serve workers floating mast trees downstream.[13]

New Hampshire seafarers likewise depended upon coastal and harbor taverns. In 1682, Henry Russell of New Castle applied for renewal of the "permission formerly

Dover Landing, *Dover, N.H., 1845-48, oil on canvas, by William Stoodley Gookin. Distinguished by its signpost, the Cochecho House (known from 1800 to 1843 as the Ela Tavern) stood near Dover's public landing, in a location convenient for serving both river and road traffic. River traffic retained its importance in the industrial era until the coming of the railroad.*
Courtesy, Thomas C. Dunnington, Jr.

☞ New-Hampshire Hotel.
☞ PORTSMOUTH.

JAMES A. GEDDES, most respect-
fully informs his Friends and the Public, that
he has taken that elegant and commodious House
known by the name of the Newhampshire Hotel,
where Boarders, Select Parties, Fire-Societies, Particular Associations, and transient Travellers may
always be accommodated with excellent Provisions,
good Liquors, capital Beds, or any thing else which
they may please to order.

J. A. GEDDES begs leave specially to
observe that the situation of the Hotel, from its o-
ponness to the water line of the town, will always
be the most convenient place, for the Merchant,
ship-owner, Captain, Mate and Mariner, to meet at,
transact business in, and use as a Boarding House ;
and he pledges his honor to those Sons of old Nep-
tune, that they may always command the full-flow-
ing bowl ; tip the Saturday night's can, and enjoy an
oyster-supper in all its perfection.

N. B. The one half of the late Man-
sion House of the late JOHN STAVERS, to let, en-
quire as above.
JAMES A. GEDDES.
Portsmouth, October. 12.

Newspaper advertisement for James A. Geddes' New-Hampshire Hotel, Portsmouth, N.H., Portsmouth Oracle, *1805. Boasting a location at the end of Portsmouth Pier long favored by seafarers and merchants, Geddes' brick tavern was originally a dwelling built by Samuel Penhallow in the late 1600s. Operated as a tavern during the eighteenth century by the Sherburne family, the building was remodeled in 1797 and destroyed by fire in 1813.*
NHHS Collections   Photographer, Ernest Gould

[granted him] to entertaine ffisher men and Seamen with Diet and Lodging at [his] house."[14] A century later, Portsmouth innholder James Geddes assured his customers that his tavern, "from its openness to the water line of the town, will always be the most convenient place, for the Merchant, ship-owner, Captain, Mate and Mariner to meet at, transact business in, and use as a Boarding House."[15]

The tavern played a special role in relation to the unheated meetinghouses of the eighteenth and early nineteenth centuries. People attending Sunday services or town meetings needed warmth and refreshment, and the licensing of a tavern near the meetinghouse was seen as essential. When Moses Leavitt of Hampton applied for a taverner's license in 1703, he gave as his reason "the desire of severell persons of this Town that Lives Remote from the publick worship . . . that I would keepe a cup of drink and cakes for their Refreshment."[16] The selectmen of nearby Greenland licensed Enoch Clark in 1734 because there was no tavern near the meetinghouse, "the want of which we find

hurtful on manny accounts."[17] In Newington, Samuel Nutter was licensed about 1746 because the town was "Destitute of a house of Entertainment for the Accomodation [sic] of strangers as also the inhabitance on Sabbaths Days."[18]

The commerce of thriving villages also attracted taverns. Tavernkeepers in such locations often advertised their houses as standing "in the centre of business," "only one mile from the Market," or "amidst a number of Stores."[19] Construction of the capitol building in Concord in 1819 gave rise to a "rich display of hotels" which impressed even the foreign visitor.[20]

Rural centers required taverns as well. In 1768, aspiring tavernkeeper Jacob Currier stressed the need for an inn at Crawley's Falls in Brentwood because of mills and an iron works there. Agnes Russell, living in Portsmouth at Islington, where a stream enters the North Mill Pond, claimed that the "grist and fulling mills there drew large numbers of people."[21] If frequented by workers, even open country might be deemed appropriate for an inn. When the Hampton selectmen recommended Rachel Freese as a tavernkeeper about 1730, they took into account her nearness to the marshes where local farmers came to cut salt hay, recognizing the "hard Labour and Toile that many of our men have in hay time" and noting that the harvesters "many times are from their houses twenty-four hours att a time and many times want refreshment."[22] Seasonal runs of fish and eels, attracting scores of fishermen to the Merrimack River, similarly prompted the approval of Samuel Patten's application for a tavern on the "Island of Ammosquage Falls" in 1765.[23]

Having proven himself to the proper authorities as "a fit person" to keep a tavern, a license holder next had to guarantee his adherence to the law by posting a bond for faithful performance of his duties. In 1683, Richard Webber of Portsmouth gave bond to "wel behave himself in yᵉ Alehouse to which he is licensed, without suffering any unlawful games or meetings or other disorders," and likewise bound himself to "put into every barrel of beer he shall brew two bushels of good malt, during yᵉ s[ai]d License," and to sell no liquor to Indians.[24]

As Webber's bond suggests, tavernkeepers were closely regulated in what they sold, to whom, in what quantities, and at what hours. During the seventeenth century, when malt liquors were popular and when tavernkeepers were often brewers, the laws were concerned with the quality of domestic beer, requiring that no molasses, coarse sugar, or other inferior materials be substituted for "good Barley Malt."[25] The law also stressed that no license holder should fail to keep an adequate stock of alcoholic drink, considered sustenance and stimulant. In 1721, the legislature required that "all licensed houses w[i]thin this Province shall constantly be provided w[i]th beer or Cyder for the refreshment of travellers, under penalty of paying ten shillings for every defect so often as they shall be found two days w[i]thout it. . . ."[26]

ON THE ROAD NORTH OF BOSTON

Engraving, Front Street, Exeter, N.H., circa 1840. At the far left is the elegant Swamscot Hotel, a four-story brick structure built in 1837, and next to it is Colonel James Burley's tavern; both buildings stood near the commercial center of town, with the Granite Bank and First Parish meetinghouse opposite.

Courtesy, Exeter Historical Society   Photographer, Ernest Gould

Photograph of original drawing (now lost) showing brick meetinghouse and Darrah's tavern, Charlestown, N.H., circa 1830. Built in the eighteenth century, Joseph Darrah's was one of the most prosperous of Charlestown's several taverns, benefiting from its location adjacent to the town's wooden meetinghouse and its elegant brick successor. The tavern porch was a nineteenth-century addition.

Courtesy, South Parish Unitarian Church, Charlestown   Photographer, David S. Putnam

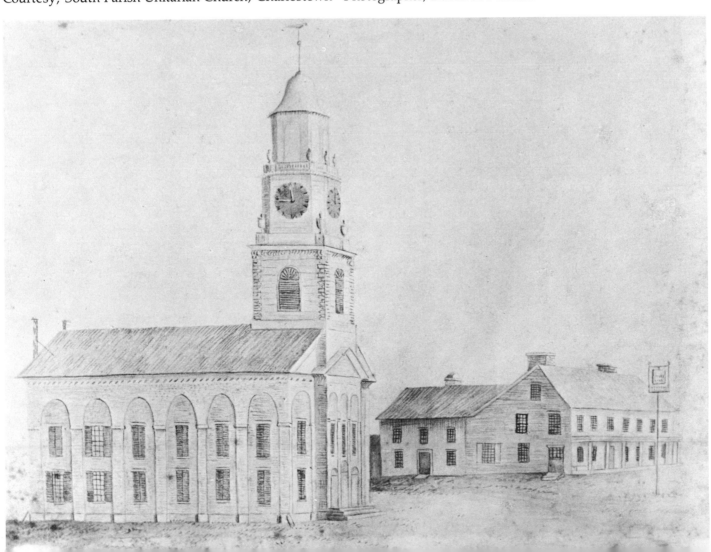

Daguerreotype of the Notch House, Crawford Notch, circa 1840. Built in 1828 by Ethan Allen Crawford and kept as a hotel by Thomas Crawford from 1829 until 1852, the Notch House became one of the most famous of the White Mountain taverns. It stood at the Gate of the Notch, below the ledge called Elephant's Head. The ledge and notch are seen in the center of this reversed image, one of the earliest known American photographs.

Courtesy, Private Collection   Photographer, Dr. Samuel Bemis

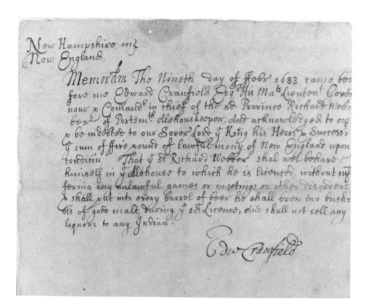

Manuscript tavernkeeper's bond for £5 from Richard Webber of Portsmouth, N.H., 1683. The bond required Webber to prevent "unlawful games or meetings or other disorders" in his alehouse, specified that he must use "two bushels of good malt" in each barrel of beer he brewed, and forbade him to sell liquor to Indians.

Courtesy, Private Collection   Photographer, Bill Finney

The Coachman and Farmer's TAVERN! ISAAC MARSH

Informs the public that he has lately erected and opened a House of Entertainment at *Dunstable Harbor,* for the purpose of commoding travellers, who will favor him with their custom. His conveniences and accommodations need no recommendation. They are sufficient to entertain twenty gentlemen and ladies, and sixty horses and oxen; and he can house fifteen carriages and loaded waggons, where they will be dry and secure.

Oct. 26, 1805.   6e52.

Advertisement for Isaac Marsh's Coachman and Farmer's Tavern, Dunstable Harbor (Nashua), N.H., Farmer's Cabinet (Amherst), 1805, (detail). Although the law required tavernkeepers to maintain a certain level of accommodation, most taverns in busy communities, such as Marsh's tavern (also known as the Dunstable Hotel), far exceeded the minimum standards.

NHHS Collections   Photographer, Ernest Gould

The law also governed other essential aspects of the tavern. Tavernkeepers were required at all times to "be furnish'd with suitable Provisions and Lodging, for the Refreshment and Entertainment of Strangers and Travellers; Pasturing, Stable-room, Hay and Provender for Horses; on pain of being deprived of their License."[27] Such fundamental controls were often necessary. In 1746, for example, one aspiring tavernkeeper in Dover sought to be licensed in place of another who had not "kept a Sufficient Supply of necessaries for the Refreshment . . . of Strangers." In 1760, Sandown selectmen accused Moses Blake not only of lacking a barn, but also of purchasing his liquor "by singal galons."[28] Such shortcomings remained common enough that by the nineteenth century, the legislature provided selectmen with a printed form to use when it became necessary to "deprive a Taverner of his license" for lack of provisions or accommodations.[29]

Despite government regulation, legend suggests that New Hampshire tavern bars, larders, and stables were sometimes not even minimally stocked. The appearance of a satirical poem, entitled "A New-Hampshire Tavern," in a popular New England almanac of 1821, did nothing to enhance the reputation of the state's hospitality. In it, an exasperated traveler, successively denied oats, corn, gin, brandy, rum, cider, beer, and even water, finally demanded, "What keep you but yourselves and sow?" To this the shiftless hostess indignantly replied, "What do we keep? why we — *keep Tavern, Sir.*"[30] That this rhyme had some basis in fact is suggested by an incident in Dunstable, Massachusetts, in 1797. There, just south of the New Hampshire border, a party stopped for dinner at a house "which hung out a sign informing us that it was an inn . . . but [where we] could get nothing either for ourselves or our horses."[31]

Yet most New Hampshire taverns were places of ample welcome. In 1788, a French visitor found the people of Massachusetts and New Hampshire "more hospitable than the inhabitants of any of the other New England and Central states." A Massachusetts traveler in 1801 proclaimed that "no town in New England ever did come in competition" with Portsmouth's warm reception of visitors.[32] A traveler from the South visiting New Hampshire and Maine noted that "as you recede from the great commercial towns . . . the people become more friendly and hospitable," remarking that by the time she reached Charlestown on the Connecticut River the people virtually "vied with each other who should bestow the most pains to render [the traveler's] visit pleasant."[33] Arriving at a rustic tavern in the White Mountains in 1797, a group of visitors found themselves greeted "with as much good will as if we had been near friends of the family."[34]

Some of those who enjoyed the hospitality of New

Engraving, Squawm [*sic*] Lake (New Hampshire), *published 1839, engraved by G. K. Richardson after sketch by William Henry Bartlett, 1836-38. This view from Red Hill in Moultonborough illustrates the scenic beauty that increasingly attracted tourists to New Hampshire's lake and mountain region in the nineteenth century.*
NHHS Collections   Photographer, Bill Finney

Hampshire taverns in the decades after the Revolution were foreigners, traveling for pleasure, health, or curiosity about the new nation. Many of these visitors remarked on the beauty of the countryside; in 1796, the Duke de la Rochefoucault praised the landscape as "an uninterrupted garden."[35] Others remarked on the freedom and cheapness of travel in America. One visitor characterized Americans as "the most restless and energetic people under the sun"; another noted that by the 1830s, the people of the United States had already begun to show their characteristic "mania for travelling."[36] In 1824, a traveler could journey "from Maine to Georgia . . . at a price which . . . is infinitely below the cheapest rate of travelling in any part of Europe."[37]

Still others were astonished at the lack of official constraint upon the traveler. In 1798, a Polish visitor marveled at the open border as he entered New Hampshire:

A few miles beyond the Marimak river the boundary of New Hamschire [sic] begins. One has to inquire for it, since there is nothing to point it out. There are no eagles, nor customs, nor sentries, nor do they stop nor ask who one is, whence one came, and for what purpose. They do not inspect nor put their seal on trunks. A traveler goes a thousand miles in America and nowhere will he be held up nor inspected nor tormented. In Europe one can not travel a score of miles without being exposed to all this unpleasantness.[38]

Although most New Hampshire people traveled within a limited radius, many nevertheless ventured away from home for pleasure. While such travel was limited before the early nineteenth century, and even then was probably undertaken more to visit relatives and friends than to gratify a general curiosity, some New Hampshire people made frequent use of the road and the tavern. A contemporary description of New England society in the 1820s described "journeys taken for pleasure [as] a very favorite object," and visiting as one of the "principal amusements of the inhabitants."[39] By the time she was ten years old in 1828, Lavinia Bailey Kelly of Northwood had visited nineteen New Hampshire towns, recording in her diary overnight stays in Lee, Durham, and Deerfield.[40]

Not all New Hampshire residents were equally free to travel and enjoy the hospitality of the tavern. Beginning in the seventeenth century, the legislature and courts had seen the tavern as an institution with a potential for ill as well as good, and had sought to limit its use to those deemed responsible for their own behavior. Early laws prohibited Indians, blacks, servants, apprentices, and children from visiting taverns without permission from their masters or guardians.[41] Formal indentures which gave a master legal control over his apprentice specifically forbade the latter from "haunting Ale Houses, Taverns, or play Houses."

The tavern's temptations posed especially acute problems in Hanover, where Dartmouth College was chartered in 1769. Despite Governor John Wentworth's insistence that "no taverner or retailer should be licensed within three miles of the College," President Eleazer Wheelock soon reported at least one "disorderly" tavern in the vicinity.[42] A decade after its founding, the college was compelled to insist "that no student board at a tavern or sit at a tavern unless when on a journey or with express leave. . . ." Yet the penalty for violating this regulation was light: a "public admonition" for "any one being convicted of a breach of this law four times within the space of six weeks." As the college grew, students boarded in taverns as a matter of course, but their use of "ardent spirits" under such inviting circumstances remained a perennial problem.[43]

Violations of good order in taverns resulted in punishment both to the customer and the tavernkeeper. A law of 1679 decreed a heavy punishment for drunkenness:

whatsoever persons shal be found drunk at any time, in any Tavern, Ordinary, Ale-house, or elsewhere in this Province, & be legally convicted thereof; HE or they shal for the first offence be fined ffive shillings, to the use of the Province; ffor the Second offence Ten shillings: And if he or they will not, or cannot [pay] the fine; Then to be set in the Stocks, not exceeding two hours: And for the third transgression, to be bound to the Good behavior. AND if he shal transgress a ffourth time; To pay ffive pounds, or be publicly whipp'd.[44]

Further legislation stipulated "That the Select-men in each Town shall cause to be Posted up in all Publick Houses . . . within this Province, a List of the Names of all persons reputed Drunkards, or common Tiplers, mispending [sic] their Time and Estate in such Houses."[45] As for the innholder himself, the same statute levied a fine on "every Keeper of such House . . . that shall be Convicted before One or more Justices of the Peace, of Entertaining or Suffering any of the persons named in such List to drink or tipple in his or her house."

Later laws also discouraged the common practice of allowing customers to accumulate large tavern bills on credit. A statute of 1791 placed the risk of sales on credit squarely upon the innkeeper, providing that "no taverner shall be entitled to recover [at law] more than twenty shillings on any account for spirituous liquors sold to any inhabitant of the town or place, and drank in such taverner's house; notwithstanding such taverner may in the trial prove the sale and delivery of spirituous liquors to more than that value and amount."[46]

Tavernkeepers were as closely regulated in the hours during which they could open their bars as in the clientele they could serve. A law of 1715 forbade a license holder to "suffer any Inhabitant of such Town where he dwells, or [anyone] coming thither from any other Town, to sit Drinking or Tipling after Ten a Clock at Night, in his or her House, or any of the dependancies [sic] thereof, or to continue there above the space of Two Hours," although exceptions were made for "Travellers [from a distance], persons upon business, or extraordinary occasions."[47]

The law also regulated tavern operation on the Sabbath.

"Frequenting Ordinaries in time of public worship" was forbidden, and only "Strangers or Lodgers" were permitted to patronize taverns between sundown on Saturdays and Monday mornings.[48] When the widow Mary Frederick of New Castle applied for a license renewal in 1746, she was accused of having allowed on at least one occasion "a blacksmith, a fisherman, and two mariners to drink in her tavern and idly spend their time on a Saturday after the sun had set."[49]

Other aspects of the law, however, guaranteed good tavern patronage by "Strangers" on the Sabbath. A law of 1700 specified that "noe Traveller, Drover, Horse Courser, Waggoner, Butcher, Higler, or any [of] their Servants shall Travaile on that day, or any part thereof Except by Some adversitye they were belated, and forced to Lodge in the Woods, Wildernesse or high wayes the night before, and in Such Case to Travaile no further than the next Inn or place of Shelter."[50] Travelers' diaries frequently mention tarrying "over the Sabbath" at some tavern. One tavern guest of 1774 in the Haverhill area, for example, simply noted:

A[u]gust 30   Being Sabbath Continued our Lodging
       31   Being Munday we paid our Lodging[51]

Petitions to the legislature during the 1780s suggest that people were beginning to find such restrictions burdensome. Many travelers apparently ignored the law. The selectmen of Windham complained in 1784 that "the Lords Day is very much prophaned by persons traveling with and without Loads which is a sin henious [sic] in the Sight of the Supreme Being."[52] Such conservatism ensured that stagecoach lines were unable to operate on Sundays well into the nineteenth century. Even when revised legislation removed the restriction against Sunday travel in 1842, one English visitor noted that in northern New Hampshire as late as 1860, the railroad "cars do not run on Sundays."[53]

In addition to governing tavern hours and clientele, the law also sought to guarantee fair value to each customer.

The tavernkeeper was required to have and use standard measures. For liquids such as spirits, he used a set of graduated metal vessels ranging from a half-gill to a quart; for dry commodities such as oats, he employed wooden measures ranging in capacity from a quart to a bushel. All such measures were to be taken annually to a town sealer of weights and measures for testing. If proven accurate, the tavernkeeper's containers were marked with a symbol representing the town.[54] In Warren, New Hampshire, for example, the town sealer stamped "WN" on the measures he approved.[55]

At less frequent intervals, town measures were compared against a set of standard measures owned by the province or, in later years, by the counties. "Town standards" found accurate were marked with the seal "P.N.H.," denoting provincial approval.[56] In 1766, it was found necessary to stipulate

That when and so often as the Sealer of Weights & measures in any Town or parish within this Province, shall have probable Cause of Suspicion that any Inhabitant has two Sets of Weights and Measures, according to one whereof (being legal) the said Inhabitant buyeth, and with the other (being lighter, or smaller) he selleth and secreteth the latter, or produceth not the same to the Sealer, It shall and may be lawful for the said Sealer verbally to warn the said Inhabitant to appear before the next Justice of the Peace . . . so the Fraud (if any there be) may be detected.[57]

Similarly, all liquor sold in quantity was required to be measured by "a sworn Gager" of casks, who branded the amount on the vessel's head with an iron.[58]

Emphasis on accuracy protected both the customer and the taxpayer. All liquor, whether sold in quantity or by the drink, was subject to either an impost or excise tax. Innkeepers and retailers were required periodically to submit a record of the liquor they had sold and to testify under oath (if required) to the accuracy of their figures.[59] On the basis of such figures, Enoch Clark of Greenland, for example, was taxed on 810 gallons of spirits and 5 barrels of cider sold during the year beginning in September 1760; Susanna Johnson of Charlestown was taxed on 376 1/2 gallons of spirits and 6 barrels of cider; and Thomas Lucas of Pembroke on 53 gallons of spirits.[60]

Set of five graduated liquid measures (copper), each stamped "P.N.H.," circa 1750. The stamp indicated that these vessels, owned by a New Hampshire town, had been tested against a standard set maintained by the Province of New Hampshire. Approved town measures, in turn, were used to validate sets used by tavernkeepers in selling alcohol.

Courtesy, Private Collection   Photographer, Bill Finney

Wantage rod, made by Thomas Salter Bowles, Portsmouth, N.H., circa 1815. This rule computes the wantage or empty portion of a partly filled cask, and is graduated for use with barrels, hogsheads, pipes, puncheons, and tierces. It would have been useful to tavernkeepers in gauging their stock of liquors.

NHHS Collections   Photographer, Bill Finney

Clandestine "tippling houses . . . that privately sell strong drink without license" were clearly "much to the Detriment and Discouragem[en]t of Such persons as do pay Excise." A strong law of 1721 required

> That every Justice of the Peace within this Province be impowered to summon all such persons as they shall have information of, that do at any time drink strong drink in any of those houses, and put them to their oath whether they pay for it either directly or indirectly; and upon refusal to take such oath, to be sent to his Majesty's goal [gaol], there to remain until they take the oath. . . .[61]

Such laws, generally enforced by local justices of the peace, helped to ensure that tavernkeepers honored the regulations under which they held their licenses. Town officials known as "tythingmen" served a rudimentary policing function, being sworn to "duly inform some Justice of the Peace of all Persons who shall sell Wine & other Spirits contrary to Law, of all disorders & misdemeanors in licensed houses, of all retailers who shall sell mixed liquors . . . & of all other breaches of [tavern and Sabbath] Law & of the peace."[62]

Upon taking his oath of office, each tythingman was issued "a Black Staff of Two foot long, tip'd at one End with Brass or Pewter . . . as a Badge of his Office." The burdens of this appointment were not always welcomed, and those who refused to serve were fined.[63] The general sentiment toward tythingmen was graphically shown when one such official interfered with some "resolute" teams trying to pass through Lebanon one Sunday at noon. Three days later, tythingmen throughout New Hampshire mysteriously received a cartoon showing one of their fellow officers being carried to his just reward in the claws of the Devil.[64]

The tavern filled many roles in addition to those required by law. As a building open to all and visited by many, the tavern was a natural place for the exchange of information, for formal and informal meetings, and for business contacts with the wider world. Dr. Alexander Hamilton described the excitement which greeted the arrival of a fresh newspaper at Ann Slayton's Portsmouth tavern in 1744: "I returned to my lodging att eight o'clock, and the post being arrived, I found a numerous company . . . reading the news. Their chit-chat kept me awake 3 hours after I went to bed."[65] Portsmouth innkeeper and coachman John Stavers emphasized the role of his tavern in providing news when he advertised in the New-Hampshire Gazette that "through Heat and Cold, Rain and Snow Storms," he had "push'd forward, at Times when every other Conveyance fail'd, to bring and carry his Passengers, as also the Mails of Letters and News Papers."[66]

Expanding upon their natural role as delivery points for the mails, many taverns doubled as post offices. Some tavernkeepers, like Cummings Pollard of Nashua, Edward Langmaid of Hampton Falls, and Major Josiah Richardson of Keene, eventually secured appointments as postmasters. The Amherst tavern of Dr. Samuel Curtis served both as local post office and as the focus of a network of post riders.[67]

The tavern barroom often served as a community bulletin board, either by custom or by vote of the town meeting. The taproom wall of David Bean's tavern in Moultonborough was the official posting place for public notices, and the walls of Levi Jones' tavern in Milton often displayed warrants for town meetings, newly passed legislation, ballots for forthcoming elections, notices of road reroutings, auction advertisements, and notices of lost animals or articles. The signpost outside William W. Poole's Hanover tavern was a posting place for town-meeting warrants or agendas.[68]

The tavern also provided a temporary office for itinerant officials such as probate judges, or for businessmen whose affairs were spread throughout New Hampshire. Ozias Silsby, a Chester post rider whose routes extended from Exeter to Charlestown, used the New-Hampshire Gazette of 1801 to publish a lengthy list of taverns where he would make himself available at stated times "for the purpose of settling [accounts] with his friends and customers"; on some busy days, Silsby promised to be in attendance at no less than three taverns in different towns.[69]

Most taverns could provide rooms suitable for private meetings, and many offered large halls which could accommodate sizeable numbers. These large chambers often served as Masonic lodgerooms during the eighteenth and early nineteenth centuries. The first Masonic lodge in New Hampshire, St. John's of Portsmouth, held its earliest recorded meeting in 1736 in the brick waterfront tavern kept by Henry Sherburne. The building most intimately connected with New Hampshire Freemasonry was the Earl of Halifax (later William Pitt) Tavern in Portsmouth, kept by John Stavers, a member of the fraternity. In 1768, shortly after the building was constructed, St. John's Lodge moved to the "long room" on its third floor, as did the Master's Lodge, the only Masonic body then capable of conferring the third degree. At other times, St. John's Lodge met in Portsmouth taverns kept by James Stoodley, John Goatam, Isaac Williams, and Zachariah Foss.[70]

The Grand Lodge of New Hampshire was founded in the long room of Stavers' tavern in July 1789, and met there regularly in the years following. On occasions when a still larger chamber was needed or a procession was planned, the Grand Lodge sometimes marched from Stavers' to the Portsmouth Assembly House, later returning to the tavern lodgeroom to close their meeting.[71] After moving their lodgeroom to a commercial building in 1805, the Grand Lodge nevertheless adjourned regularly to the tavern of fraternity member John Davenport for an "elegant dinner."[72]

Freemasons in country towns likewise met in taverns. Vermont Lodge in Charlestown first met in Abel Walker's tavern in 1781, and Blazing Star Lodge in Concord was founded in Benjamin Gale's tavern in 1799. The hospitality of the tavernkeeper was highly valued at the conse-

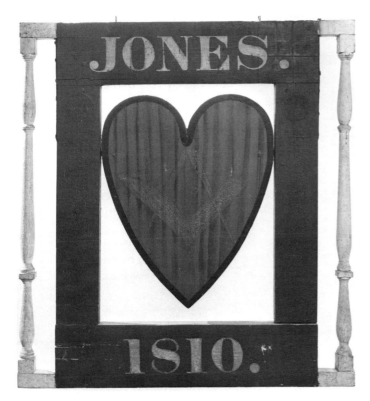

Sign from the tavern of Levi Jones, Milton, N.H., 1810. Hidden under later paint is the Masonic symbol of the square and compass, possibly painted over during the anti-Masonic fervor of the late 1820s. On the opposite side of the sign are crossed keys, apparently symbolizing Jones' office as lodge treasurer.

Courtesy, The Currier Gallery of Art
  Photographer, Bill Finney

Newspaper advertisement for Mark Spinney's American House tavern, New-Hampshire Gazette, 1846. The American House, formerly the Pound Tavern, stood near the junction of Middle and South roads, close to the main routes leading south and west from the center of Portsmouth. Like the tavern at Portsmouth Plains, still farther out of town, this tavern included bowling alleys; both provided hospitable settings for parties.

NHHS Collections   Photographer, Ernest Gould

cration of new Lodges. When Morning Star Lodge was constituted in the Moultonborough tavern of George Freese in 1805, "a rich repast was served up, in a style magnificent and splendid," by the innkeeper, "accompanied with those ebullitions of wit, those effusions of humor, which wine and mirth inspire, furnish[ing] a feast of reason and a flow of soul."[73] After consecrating the new Sullivan Lodge in the Deerfield Parade tavern of Benjamin Butler, the celebrants "partook of an excellent dinner," and, "having sufficiently refreshed and regaled themselves, the Grand Lodge closed in due season, and every Brother was satisfied."[74]

Although the Freemasons were the most numerous and extended group to make use of the tavern, smaller organizations, especially those with no permanent office of their own, found the hospitality of the inn indispensable to their affairs. In an age when the modern corporation had not appeared in New Hampshire, private business associations used the tavern as a regular meeting place. Of these, by far the most important was the Masonian Proprietors. In 1746, this group of about twenty wealthy merchants, mostly from Portsmouth, purchased a proprietary claim to New Hampshire from the heirs of Captain John Mason, the seventeenth-century recipient of the royal grant. The Pro-

prietors thus secured title to some two million acres within a great arc with a radius of sixty miles from the sea. The dividing of this territory into townships required decades, and had an influence on the shaping of New Hampshire second only to that of the provincial government itself.

Despite the momentous nature of their business, the Proprietors conducted their affairs, drew their plans, and met prospective grantees of new townships in a series of Portsmouth taverns. Of the seven inns where they met, those of Ann Slayton and James Stoodley were the favorites, the latter providing their primary meeting place between 1757 and 1775.[75]

The State of New Hampshire began to charter corporations in the late 1700s, and many of these businesses continued the tradition of meeting in taverns. Among them were the proprietors of most of the New Hampshire turnpike roads and private toll bridges of the early 1800s.[76] Large manufacturing corporations likewise had their beginnings in taverns; the proprietors of the Peterborough Cotton Manufacturing Corporation, for example, met in Asa Evans' tavern in 1810, while those of the Dover Cotton Factory met at the inn of Lydia Tebbets in 1812.[77]

Shrewd tavernkeepers were quick to see the profit in entertaining such groups. When James A. Geddes of Portsmouth became the proprietor of the New-Hampshire Hotel (formerly Henry Sherburne's tavern) in 1805, he offered "excellent Provisions, good Liquors, [and] capital Beds" to "Boarders, Select Parties, Fire Societies, Partic-

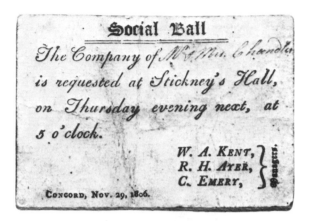

Printed invitations to balls held at Concord taverns (top) and taverns in Atkinson and Unity (bottom). Many invitations were printed on the backs of playing cards, frequently the only available paper stock with the required stiffness for such tickets.
NHHS Collections   Photographer, Ernest Gould

ular Associations, and Transient Travellers'' alike.[78] Geddes had learned about the profitability of entertaining fire societies from the experience of his father-in-law, John Stavers, who had routinely billed the town of Portsmouth for the entertainment of the ''Engine Men'' at the Pitt Tavern between 1784 and 1790.[79] In the same tradition, fire societies met in taverns in Dover, Keene, Amherst, Concord, and elsewhere in the early 1800s.[80]

Among the ''Particular Associations'' which met in taverns were many with cultural or educational purposes. In 1770, the trustees of Dartmouth College and President Eleazer Wheelock convened their first meeting at Wyman's tavern in Keene, thus beginning the operation of the school.[81] The New Hampshire Medical Society regularly met in Exeter, Portsmouth, and Concord taverns after its founding in 1791, and its various district chapters patronized still other inns.[82] The New Hampshire Historical Society held formative meetings in 1823 in taverns in Exeter and Portsmouth.[83] The Central Musical Society met at J. S. Kelley's tavern in Warner in the same year, filling the house with the sound of psalms and anthems.[84]

The tavern was home to celebration and revelry, and thus to music. By the mid-eighteenth century, dancing was one of the great social pleasures of the New Englander, and by the 1760s, coastal New Hampshire taverns began to include ''long rooms'' for dances and other gatherings. Inland taverns followed suit by the early 1800s, often providing a raised platform or seat for musicians at one end of the hall.

By 1792, the Reverend Jeremy Belknap noted without disapproval that at ''seasons of public concourse, the young people amuse themselves with dancing.''[85] Twenty years earlier, dancing master St. George de Viart had offered the youth of Portsmouth formal instruction in minuets, French jigs, hornpipes, rigadoons, and English country dances, and shortly after the Revolution many other instructors began to provide similar classes. De Viart sought to persuade New Hampshire people that dancing was more than a pleasant pastime, claiming that it imparts ''to every Motion of the Body a certain attractive Grace which never can be sufficiently admir'd, gives a free and open Air in the Gait; a happy Address in Company, and adds the finishing Embellishments in the Sexes, to every Species of polite Education.''[86]

In 1828, the elegant Grecian Hall of the Eagle Coffee House in Concord was the scene of a ball ''more splendid than any other exhibition of the kind that ever took place in the interior of New-England.'' Ostensibly given to commemorate Andrew Jackson's victory at New Orleans four-

Printed announcement of a Thanksgiving ball at Ashuelot House, Hinsdale, N.H., 1852.

NHHS Collections   Photographer, Ernest Gould

Portrait of William B. Chamberlin, 1835, pencil and watercolor on paper, attributed to Joseph H. Davis. Chamberlin was the son of Brookfield, N.H., tavernkeeper Trueworthy Chamberlin. This portrait shows the son playing a violoncello or "church bass" most likely in the father's tavern hall.

Courtesy, Private Collection

teen years earlier, the dance was actually intended to rally support for the General in the presidential election of that year.[87] The same year saw the addition of Washington Hall to the older Washington Tavern on Concord's Main Street to accommodate a ball honoring President John Quincy Adams, running for reelection. Four hundred attended this event.[88] Beginning in 1837, Concord's Grecian Hall was the site of the annual stagemen's ball each January, an event that brought up to 150 stage owners and drivers and their wives from as far away as Quebec.[89]

Occasionally dances were accompanied by musical interludes, as in 1800 when "the Principal Musicians from Boston" offered to hold a ball at the New-Hampshire Hotel in Portsmouth, with a concert of vocal and instrumental selections. The offerings included concertos for French horn, clarinet, violin, hautboy, and forte piano, with several songs for women's voices and a finale "Composed by Hayden."[90]

Other popular forms of entertainment were held in the long rooms and halls of taverns. Lectures on curious subjects, always advertised as enlightening and educational,

were a favorite diversion from the eighteenth century onward. In 1766, the State-House Tavern of Zachariah Foss in Portsmouth was the scene of two lectures by David Mason on "that Instructive and Entertaining Branch of natural Philosophy, called ELECTRICITY," with demonstrations of "Mr. Muschenbrock's wonderful Bottle," a Leyden jar. Three years later, the well-known English actor David Douglass delivered "a lecture on Heads, Coats of Arms, Ladies Head-Dresses, &c., in three parts" in John Stavers' "large room."[91] At the height of the phrenology craze in 1841, A. Peabody offered a "general description of the character and talents" of those who would pay him to examine the shape of their heads at Portsmouth's Bell Tavern, "warranting correct examinations or no charges," and offering cash "for skulls of all kinds."[92]

Douglass' "Lecture on Heads" of 1769 was actually a dramatic reading disguised as an anatomical discourse, and illustrates the deception to which actors sometimes resorted in the face of a strong New England prejudice against the theater. Yet theater openly arrived in New Hampshire in November of the same year, when John Stavers provided his third-floor room for a performance of

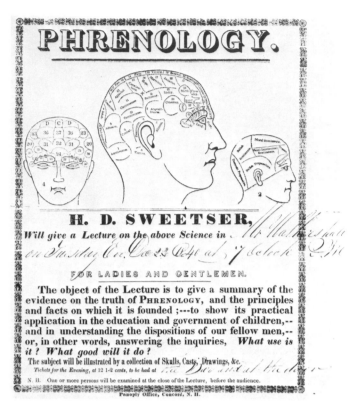

Broadside advertising a lecture at William Walker's Eagle Coffee House, Concord, N.H., circa 1840. Promoters of the pseudoscience of phrenology, popularized by Orson Squire Fowler in his book, Phrenology Proved, Illustrated and Applied (1836), and his periodical, the American Phrenological Journal, claimed that a person's character could be analyzed by studying the contours of the skull. Traveling lecturers on the subject were among the most common attractions in tavern halls during the 1830s and 1840s.

NHHS Collections   Photographer, Ernest Gould

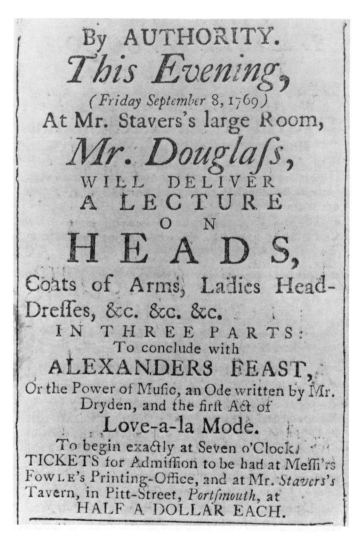

Newspaper advertisement for a reading by David Douglass at Stavers' tavern, Portsmouth, New-Hampshire Gazette, 1769. This well-known English actor probably gave more of a dramatic performance than a lecture. The earliest plays and musical recitals in New Hampshire were performed in Stavers' tavern.

NHHS Collections   Photographer, Bill Finney

Love in a Village, the first opera ever presented in the province. Its sixty-nine songs were sung by a single unnamed person (possibly Mr. Wardwell, an itinerant English actor) "who has Read and Sung in most of the great Towns in America." The performance was followed a week later by the presentation of Sir Richard Steele's *The Conscious Lovers*.[93]

These performances passed with little opposition, but when another actor, William Sampson Morgan, arrived in Portsmouth in 1772 and showed every intention of staying and building a playhouse, some sixty citizens, led by the local clergymen, petitioned the Assembly for a law to prohibit theatrical exhibitions.[94] This put an end to theater in New Hampshire until about 1800. When actors reappeared in the early nineteenth century, they usually had to rely on a local tavern as the only building that could offer a room large enough for a performance. In 1808, English actor John Bernard appeared before unsympathetic audiences in taverns in Concord and Walpole. In 1819, "a detachment of the Boston company of Comedians" used the hall in Lock's tavern in Dover for an entertainment. In 1821, the hall of Holland's tavern in Keene became the theater for the tragedy *Douglass* and the comedy *The Village Lawyer*. In 1827, an indifferent audience watched *Othello* in the Grecian Hall of the Eagle Coffee House in Concord, but the following year the company of Gilbert and Trowbridge successfully reintroduced *Othello*, as well as *The Honey Moon*, *She Stoops to Conquer*, *The Heir at Law*, and *Timour the Tartar* in the same hall.[95]

The New Hampshire tavern was often the site of another sort of drama. One of the greatest occasions for celebration in early New England was the ordination of a new minister. Ordinations brought friends, well-wishers, and other clergymen from afar, provided ceremony and procession, offered the community a holiday (especially in the years before 1800, when most towns had only one church), and usually ended in enthusiastic merrymaking in which the tavern played a prominent role. Tavernkeeper Benjamin Gale estimated that Asa McFarland's ordination as minister of the Congregational Church in Concord on March 7, 1798, brought some 1,200 sleighs onto Concord's Main Street as people gathered from twenty miles around to witness the event. The celebration ended with a splendid ball at William Stickney's tavern.[96]

The completion of a new meetinghouse offered equal opportunity for celebration. The dedication of Canaan's new meetinghouse in 1796 was commemorated by a banquet at Dr. Caleb Pierce's tavern.[97] After the Toleration Act was passed in 1819, the Congregational or "Orthodox" Church lost its exclusive right to town meetinghouses, and local parishioners often decided to build a separate church. Other denominations, freed from paying taxes for support of the Congregational Church, often found that they too could afford new buildings of their own.

The common method of reimbursing church building committees was through the sale of pews, which until after 1800 were privately owned boxlike enclosures. Local taverns often provided the site of the "vendue" or auction of such pews. Such an auction was held, for example, at Alexander Ralston's tavern in Keene in 1785.[98] According to stories repeated in many towns, the molded caps that extended across the upper rails of pew walls and doors were nailed down as single pieces of wood and left unsawn, sealing the pew door, until the pew was "bid off." After the rebuilding of the Hopkinton meetinghouse in 1789, "some of the more thoughtful and *dry* ones" at the auction "suggested that no person who bid off a pew should have his pew door sawed open until he walked over to Major Isaac Babson's tavern and paid for the toddy for the company."[99]

The tavern was also the most common site for more general auctions, providing large rooms or yards for the sale as well as food for buyers and their animals. Among the commodities most often advertised at such sales were land, buildings, animals, vehicles, vessels, prizes brought home by privateers in wartime, and entire households with their accumulated possessions. Occasionally slaves were sold, as in 1767, when an auction at James Stoodley's in Portsmouth offered a black man of about twenty, who had "been with the English about Two Years," together with a girl of seventeen, or in 1773, when "three likely strong Negro Men" and a girl ten or twelve years old were offered at Jacob Tilton's.[100] The auction might also provide a way of keeping up with current European or urban fashions. A vendue at John Stavers' Portsmouth tavern in 1760 offered "sundry suits of cloaths London made, a blue cloth cloak, good silk jackets, velvet breeches . . . [and] beaver hats"; another sale held in Stavers' long room in 1771 included "a variety of womens wearing apparel, consisting of silk gowns, hatts, caps, ruffles, laces, petticoats, cloaks, [and] linnen."[101]

Even more impressive were the land auctions commonly

Engraving, actor John Bernard as Jack Meggot in The Suspicious Husband, *frontispiece of Bernard's posthumously published* Retrospections of America, 1797-1811 (1887). *The Englishman Bernard became one of the first theatrical impresarios in America, giving performances in Concord and Walpole, N.H., taverns in 1808.*

Courtesy, New Hampshire State Library
    Photographer, Ernest Gould

held at New Hampshire taverns. Much of New Hampshire's land was owned by speculators, many of whom had acquired lots in remote townships from the Masonian Proprietors or through a governor's grant. In hard financial times, absentee proprietors frequently defaulted on their tax payments, and their holdings were often confiscated and offered for resale at public auctions. The *New-Hampshire Gazette* in 1801, for example, listed sales at a number of taverns for confiscated lands in Moultonborough, Middleton, Brookfield, Hillsborough, Rumney, Wolfeboro, Henniker, and Warren. In June 1810, fully one-fourteenth of the township of Paulsbourg (later Milan), amounting to 2,150 acres, was offered at auction at William Stickney's tavern in Concord.[102]

Holidays and local festivities brought business to the tavern. Before the Revolution, when most celebrations focused on the royal family, festivities were mostly confined to government officials. On June 4, 1761, for example, members of an elite "club" celebrated the birthday of newly crowned King George III at John King's tavern at Portsmouth Plains, consuming bread and cheese, seventeen bowls of punch, and five decanters of port, malaga, and other wines.[103]

After the Revolution, the Fourth of July became the most enthusiastically celebrated American holiday, one that usually began with an early-afternoon parade or procession that formed at a tavern and was frequently led by local militia companies. The marchers then proceeded to a meetinghouse or other hall for a reading of the Declaration of Independence and the delivery of an oration, sometimes with interludes of music. The celebrants then returned to the tavern for refreshments, toasts, and sometimes a full meal. The evening often ended with a ball.

The Amherst *Cabinet* described such a celebration in Francestown in 1803. The "Independent Company of Francestown, in complete uniform," performed "military exercises and evolutions in a very soldier-like manner till 3 o'clock, [then] escorted a procession of respectable citizens to the Meeting House, where a very ingenious and patriotic Oration was delivered by the Rev. Matthew Taylor," followed by music and toasts.[104] A similar observance took place in Bow in 1810, drawing people from Concord, Pembroke, Dunbarton, and Chester. Having no hall large enough to hold them, the throng marched "to a bower on the bank of the Merrimack River, where they found a table furnished by Esquire [Benjamin] Noyes with all the luxiries [*sic*] of the country." Their feast was followed by sixteen toasts, the first dedicated to Temperance![105]

The tavern's prominent role in local festivities made it the natural location for the town fair. Beginning with the chartering of Londonderry in 1722, many New Hampshire towns were specifically granted the privilege of holding two fairs each year. Tavernkeepers were quick to recognize the benefits that local fairs would bring to their businesses; in 1734, Hampton Falls innkeeper Benjamin Brown led his fellow townsmen to petition for two annual fairs, to be held at "the now most noted Publick house," Brown's own Georges Tavern.[106] When William Blair sold his Londonderry tavern in 1762, he noted that the building had served as an inn since the town's settlement and that it was "where the Fairs in Londonderry are held."[107]

In addition to the displays of produce and livestock, a wide variety of rural sports attracted many to fairs. Horse races were common, often with "a treat for the Company" being offered instead of cash wagers.[108] Tests of marksmanship were also popular. The most common of these was the turkey shoot, in which the tavernkeeper tied live

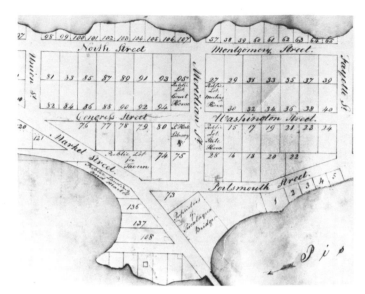

Manuscript ''Plan of the City of Franklin,'' (detail), circa 1797, by Benjamin Dearborn. Laid out in 1797 on Cedar Point in Durham, at the northern end of the Piscataqua Bridge and at the beginning of the First New Hampshire Turnpike, Franklin City, although never built, was intended by its proprietors to become the political and commercial capital of New Hampshire. Reflecting the central role of the tavern in society, its planners reserved lots not only for a State House, court house, public hall, library, and meetinghouse, but also for a tavern to be located at the busiest intersection, opposite the public landing and market.
Courtesy, Thomas C. Dunnington, Jr.
  Photographer, Ernest Gould

birds to a post as targets for riflemen who paid a certain amount for each shot; the man who killed the bird took it home. In 1806, Timothy Kendall of Amherst advertised a "Grand Shooting," in which "between sunrise and sunset, will be exposed for marksmen . . . above *one hundred* Turkies and Geese."[109] Sometimes a paper target was substituted for live game and bigger prizes were offered. Tavernkeeper John Parry held several target matches at Portsmouth Plains in 1761, offering the best marksmen a yoke of oxen, a gun, and a silver watch.[110]

Throughout the eighteenth century and into the nineteenth, the tavern assumed a multitude of roles in New Hampshire society. Its original purpose of providing food and shelter to the traveler always remained its central and indispensable function. But over the years, the tavern assumed a much larger place in daily life. It became an institution with few limitations, expanding its role to serve the changing needs of those who entered its always-open door.

THE TAVERN BUILDING

CHAPTER 2

THE TAVERN WAS truly a "public house." The tavern of every stylistic era, from the seventeenth century to the nineteenth, duplicated the form and construction of nearby dwellings. In tidewater New Hampshire of the 1600s, when the ideal dwelling was a central-chimney house with a massive decorated frame, the tavern was such a house. In those newly settled parts of eighteenth-century New Hampshire where most dwellings were small framed cabins or log houses, the tavern was likewise small and rude. In Portsmouth or Exeter, where the large dwelling of the eighteenth century was a double-chimney house with a gambrel or hipped roof, the traveler found entertainment in such a house. When changing fashion favored a three-story height and perhaps walls of brick, the tavern became such an imposing building. When the ideal was a house that suggested a Greek temple, expansive colonnaded porches were added on to taverns to evoke that popular image.

To accommodate the public and fulfill the functions assigned to it by law, the tavern required a few special features. The tavern needed a place to mix and sell liquors. This could range from a simple closet to a bar of impressive opulence. The tavern needed a place to prepare and serve food. This could be nothing more than a farmhouse kitchen or could be a dining room seating over a hundred. The tavern needed beds for the traveler. These could range from bearskins spread before a fireplace to luxurious feather beds in private rooms. To take its rightful place as a political and social center, the tavern needed a hall for meetings and dances. This could be nothing more than a finished attic, or could be an imposing ballroom with a platform for speakers and musicians and with adjacent retiring rooms. As society changed its expectations, the tavern changed to meet those expectations, yet it always remained akin to the private dwelling, and often hardly distinguishable from it.

Little is known in detail of the interior appointments of New Hampshire's seventeenth-century taverns. One such building, the inn of John West of New Castle, was inventoried in 1695. The rooms listed in this document suggest a two-story, center-chimney dwelling with a hall or large room on one side of the first floor, a bedroom opposite, and a kitchen behind the chimney. Partitioned off from the

first-floor bedroom may have been the "shop," with a few dry goods for sale, and the "barr," furnished with a settle, four chairs, and three tables. Upstairs were two sleeping chambers and, perhaps over the kitchen, a "Shuffleboard Chamber." The house was filled with chairs of many sorts, beds and bedsteads, and many joint stools, one of the most common forms of seventeenth-century seating furniture. In keeping with the seventeenth-century love of malt beverages, there was a separate "brew house" containing a "copor or furnace." The kitchen also contained several casks of wine, rum, and molasses, and no less than twenty barrels of cider.[1]

One tavern of this general era survives in Exeter. The Gilman log house, dating from the late seventeenth century, was many times licensed as a tavern both before and after the turn of the eighteenth century. Remarkable today

Lafayette House, Franconia Notch, N.H., 1845, pencil and watercolor on paper, by James Elliot Cabot. Like many taverns, the Lafayette House was no different from a private dwelling in appearance and size; a rectangular sign fixed between two sturdy posts identified the building as a tavern. The first tavern in the Profile Lake region, the Lafayette House was completed about 1835.

NHHS Collections   Photographer, Bill Finney

Photograph, Gilman log house, Exeter, N.H., circa 1895. The left-hand portion of this house, built of squared logs and once fortified as a garrison, served as a licensed tavern during the late 1600s and early 1700s. The right-hand wing was added during the eighteenth century; its store front dates from about 1865.

NHHS Collections   Photographers, Halliday Historic Photograph Company

as the earliest surviving example in New Hampshire of a dwelling built of sawn logs, the Gilman house has undergone many changes which have erased any distinctive features that may have reflected its use as an inn. A license granted to Gilman in 1678 to "keep ordinary at Exiter" for this or an earlier building is unusual in permitting the tavernkeeper to sell "wine and liquor, beer and cider . . . to strangers and travellers only, forbidding him in any way to give entertainment or sell wine, liquor or any sort of drink to any inhabitant of Exiter."[2] Both the building and its special hospitality to travelers are reminiscent of Colonel Peter Weare's Hampton Falls tavern, described in 1732 as "Bu[i]lt with Logs, after the manner of a Garrison, and on purpose for a publick hous[e] of Entertainment for travellers &c."[3]

Details of the New Hampshire tavern become clearer in the eighteenth century. A tavern built by Portsmouth carpenter John Lowe at the turn of the century stood until around 1970 on Deer Street in Portsmouth. This was a two-story, center-chimney house with somewhat larger rooms on the east side of the chimney than on the west, perhaps similar in its slight asymmetry to West's tavern in New Castle. Like West's tavern, Lowe's house was supplemented by a separate "Malt House." The tavern had lost most of its original features over the years, but its demolition revealed that it had been a forward-looking house with rudimentary Georgian detailing.[4]

The Portsmouth tavern of Dr. Thomas Packer, erected in the late 1600s and enlarged to accommodate the provincial Council and courts by about 1705, had both a "Great Room" and a "Wainscot Room," the latter undoubtedly a well-paneled room of the type that began to appear in the more affluent Portsmouth houses in the years before 1715. Perhaps these two rooms were those in which Council and courts met; in any case, both had fireplaces and were furnished formally with a dozen chairs, several tables, and large looking-glasses.[5] In 1731, this tavern was further embellished with an elaborate "beaufait" or corner cupboard.[6] Still later, in 1764, Thomas Packer, Jr., the provincial sheriff, wrote to Boston to find a carver to decorate the still-growing house, noting that "my housewright informs me [that] I have as much worke to do as will employ a man of that business one month."[7]

Despite its frequent additions and remodelings, the house seems to have remained impressive; one visitor to Portsmouth in 1787 called it "an elegant house kept by Mr. Brewster for entertainment," and two years after that, the house was selected above all others for the accommodation of George Washington, probably because it was unique among Portsmouth's inns in being able to offer "such Gentlemen as wish for *private Lodgings*," rooms where they might "be as retired and free from interruption, and be entertained with as much elegance . . . as in any *private House* whatever."[8]

Another famous Portsmouth tavern survived until 1867. This was the Marquis of Rockingham, later renamed the Bell Tavern. Built in 1743 by Paul March, and acquired in 1770 by Jacob Tilton, this building demonstrated the close resemblance between tavern and private home. Like many dwellings of its era, the structure was originally two stories tall, covered by a gambrel roof, and had two chimneys. Entrance to the building was gained through a "broad entry"; in this spacious center hallway, the notorious New Hampshire criminal Henry Tufts was disarmed by General John Sullivan and Colonel Joseph Cilley as he sought revenge against two soldiers who had "knocked me down with a club, striking out two of my foreteeth and leaving me for dead in the street."[9] Despite its location close to other houses and shops, Tilton's tavern was described by John Adams as having "a spacious Yard, good stables, and an excellent Garden, full of Carrotts, Beets, Cabbages, Onions, Colliflowers &c."[10] According to an advertisement of 1833, the yard was more than 200 feet deep and the stable was a brick edifice forty by seventy feet and two stories high.[11]

Many Portsmouth taverns were built by the area's best craftsmen. The Marquis of Rockingham was framed by Hopestill Cheswill, a housewright who constructed many fine private homes. When Zachariah Foss built his inn, marked by "The Sign of the State-House," in 1752, he employed two of the leading joiners of Portsmouth, Michael Whidden II and his son, Michael III. Father and son constructed a fine "frontispiece" or doorway and worked for 152 days in finishing the structure.[12] Like Tilton's nearby tavern, it was built on a constricted urban lot; so close was it to another house that the neighbor complained of Foss that "I am greatly plagued by him & his customers who I believe light their fires at my woodpiles."[13]

Despite alterations, one surviving Portsmouth tavern offers impressive evidence of the elegance of some public houses. Stoodley's tavern, built in 1761 after a fire had leveled its predecessor, is a two-story house with the same "broad entry," twin chimneys, and gambrel roof as the old Marquis of Rockingham. An inventory of 1780 reveals that the building was well furnished with walnut, mahogany, cherry, and maple chairs and tables, Windsor chairs in the entry, Chinese porcelain and English earthenware, silver holloware and flatware, and seven beds, including one shared by two female slaves.[14] The building itself gives evidence of well-paneled walls and wainscoting throughout, heavy molded cornices, hinged interior window shutters, and a wide and elegant staircase comparable to those in the best private dwellings of the same style and period. On the third floor, somewhat constricted by the pitch of the roof but extending the full forty-foot length of the house, is the ballroom.

Not all taverns, even those in Portsmouth, aspired to architectural elegance. One of the largest and most popular public houses, for years the terminus of the Portsmouth-to-Boston stage line and the meeting place of Freemasons, was that of John Stavers. Studied in detail since 1964 and carefully restored in 1987, this is a three-story house with its chimneys placed against the outer walls for the most flexible possible floorplan. Stavers' third-floor "long room," popular for social gatherings and as a Masonic lodgeroom, extends along the entire front of the building and is warmed by fireplaces at opposite ends. At one point, this room was subdivided by a shifting partition—probably a hinged wall which could be folded upward or against a wall.[15]

Despite its three-story height and special arrangements, however, Stavers' Earl of Halifax (later William Pitt) Tavern is extremely simple in its finish, some features resembling those of a contemporary meetinghouse. Its entry, unlike those of Tilton's and Stoodley's taverns, is not impressively "broad," and its cramped stairs, moved far to the rear of the house to avoid crowding the third-floor hall, pose a distinct danger to the head of a careless lodger. Perhaps it was for these reasons that the Spanish traveler Francisco de Miranda complained in 1783 that "this tavern is not the best possible," while John Adams confided to his diary after discovering the virtues of Tilton's tavern, "I will call no more at Stavers's."[16]

Despite its ample accommodations, even Stavers' tavern could not offer the privacy that some desired. Foreign visitors to the United States often complained about the cramped conditions of the relatively small American tavern. In 1795, one French visitor indirectly registered his impression of Portsmouth's taverns when he described his discovery of a different sort of house, the Berwick Inn kept by "Mr. ROGER, a Quaker." Here, the guests were "not promiscuously mixed together; each different company has its separate sitting, eating, and sleeping rooms . . . this inn was a kind of phenomenon of which I never yet saw the counterpart [in America]."[17]

If some eighteenth-century urban taverns offered travelers less than opulent accommodations, country taverns were usually less inviting, especially in new settlements on the frontier. Since taverns generally reflected the norms of private homes in their neighborhood, travelers to the interior of New Hampshire could expect to fare no better than the settlers of those regions. Even as late as 1790, according to Jeremy Belknap, New Hampshire's early historian, many of those settlers

erect a square building of poles, notched at the end to keep them fast together. The crevices are plastered with clay or the stiffest earth. . . . The roof is either bark or split boards. The chimney a pile of stones; within which a fire is made on the ground, and a hole is left in the roof for the smoke to pass out. Another hole is made in the side of the house for a window, which is occasionally closed with a wooden shutter. . . . By these methods of living, the people are familiarized to hardships; their children are early used to coarse food and hard lodging; and to be without shoes in all seasons of the year is scarcely accounted a want.[18]

The terms imposed on grantees of new lands usually stipulated that settlers build a dwelling within a year. Most of these houses were initially small; many land grants specified the minimum acceptable size to be sixteen feet square and one story high.[19] The documentary record makes it clear that log construction as described by Belknap remained a common frontier practice in New Hampshire until the late eighteenth century and that travelers to new settlements saw many log houses alongside framed dwellings. A 1770 inventory of Moultonborough lists twelve log houses and six framed; a contemporary list for Camden (Washington) enumerates thirteen log houses and seven framed.[20]

Engraving, A View Near Conway, N[ew] Hampshire, *by Fenner Sears & Company, 1831, after a painting by Thomas Cole, circa 1828. Cole's sketches include several renderings of the once common New Hampshire log house, showing such frontier structures to have been built of round or roughly squared logs, with roofs of peeled bark weighted down with poles.*
NHHS Collections   Photographer, Ernest Gould

Travelers seeking accommodation often encountered such houses licensed as taverns. Traveling to the White Mountains in 1797, Timothy Dwight described Eleazar Rosebrook's tavern, north of Crawford's Notch, as "a log hut, in which he has entertained most of the persons travelling in this road during the last eight years."[21] Such a house might be regarded with disdain by a traveler accustomed to something better; one writer described the road between the Notch House and Conway as having "here and there a log-house . . . in the midst of a clearing, its wood chimney, and mud-plastered sides, and windowless holes, looking cheerless enough."[22]

Yet to a weary and famished traveler like Stephen Burroughs, caught at midnight in a November snowstorm in 1782, a glimmer of light "through a small cranny of an old log hut was attended with those effusions of pleasure which a miser never feels when hoarding up his treasures." Entering the cabin, Burroughs found the building "about twenty feet square; a large fire being built in the midst, the family lay around it on the ground [presenting] a subject fit for the pencil of Hogarth. Inquiring how far it was to a public inn, I was informed that one was kept there." Taking "the bed kept for travellers, as the best piece of furniture in the house," Burroughs slept for about two hours before awakening "from the complaints which my

bones uttered" and deciding to travel another five miles in the dark to a better inn with a softer bed.[23]

Other inns, especially those in or north of the White Mountains, might be equally crude even if framed rather than built of logs. As late as 1829, Asa McFarland, a Concord youth returning home through the White Mountains, stopped at "an unpainted one-story house, in front of which was an old-fashioned sign swinging upon a dilapidated post, near the present Profile House, where pigs and fowls enjoyed the freedom of the bar-room." Here McFarland and his friends were "treated to bread, cold beef, honey, and cigars of the variety then known as 'long nines.' Our fare, coarse though it was, would have been eaten with relish but for the presence of those animals. . . ."[24]

The legendary Willey House, perched beneath an ominous mountainside in the very heart of Crawford Notch, was another such tavern. Although sometimes vacant during the summer (there being little to attract an aspiring farmer to such a desolate location), the house was occupied during the winter by a family "to keep a fire, lodgings, and a little food, for travellers and wagoners, who might otherwise perish."[25] Here, "those few [travelers] were kindly welcomed: and the cheerful host and hostess, and their comely children, were always well spoken of."[26] So infused with the spirit of kindness had this little outpost

The Willey House, *Crawford Notch, N.H., 1845, pencil and watercolor on paper, by James Elliot Cabot. Before the landslide of 1826, the Willey House offered shelter during the most inclement seasons. Several artists later painted the house as it had appeared before the slide and before a later owner annexed a large hotel to the original dwelling.*

NHHS Collections   Photographer, Bill Finney

Stereograph, "Furniture Belonging to the Willey Family," circa 1870. For some years after the landslide of 1826, the Willey House remained unoccupied but furnished as it had been left by the ill-fated family. Some of the relics of the house were displayed by later owners, and some were eventually sold at auction.

NHHS Collections   Photographers, Clough & Kimball

become that it was an event of widespread horror and dismay when in 1826 an avalanche descended on the house and swept away the panic-stricken family. The irony of the deaths of the Willey family was made still more bitter when rescuers found that the family had been destroyed as they fled the house, while the house itself, protected by a giant boulder behind it, had been left unscathed.

During the years between the Revolution and 1800, monumental changes occurred in New Hampshire. The changes were certainly social and political ones; but there were also changes in wealth, in manners, and in the material reflections of stability and prosperity. Historian Jeremy Belknap noted that during this period the population of New Hampshire increased by nearly 4,000 people each year, so that the state's inhabitants grew from an estimated 82,200 in 1775 to 142,018 in 1790.[27] The same pace of growth continued almost unabated for the next few decades, partly through natural increase among families already within the state, and partly through a continuing migration from neighboring states to an area "where land is cheap, and the means of subsistence may be acquired in such plenty, in so short a time as is evidently the case in our new plantations."[28]

These same decades saw the transformation of much of New Hampshire from a raw frontier with scattered cabins and small clearings into a mature pastoral countryside in which most worthwhile land was cleared and brought into production. Travelers consistently remarked how the small houses of the first settlers were being speedily supplanted by larger dwellings. This transformation affected the public house equally.

Timothy Dwight, who had been grateful for the shelter of Eleazar Rosebrook's "log hut" in 1797, had noted with admiration how the intrepid settler had already "subdued a farm of 150 or 200 acres and built two large barns," and was then planning to build a sawmill, a gristmill, and a proper house. Returning to the White Mountains in 1803, Dwight "found Rosebrook in possession of a large, well-built farmer's house, mills, and various other conveniences, and could not help feeling a very sensible pleasure at finding his industry, patience, and integrity thus rewarded."[29]

Much the same transformation impressed other early-nineteenth-century travelers from the seacoast to the mountains. The advent of the new Federal style in architecture around 1800, combined with the increase in prosperity and population, brought about a wholesale rebuilding across much of New Hampshire. By the early 1800s, there was no appreciable gap of style or building technology between the older coastal towns and more prosperous inland trading and farming regions, so that substantial houses or taverns anywhere in the state might display many of the same amenities. Many inland towns, moreover, had become productive cabinetmaking centers, so that the coast no longer held a monopoly on sophisticated furniture of the most current style.

The Federal style called for large and convenient buildings of two or three stories, often with low-pitched hipped

Photograph, Ezekiel Porter Pierce's tavern, Chesterfield, N.H., circa 1900. Unusual because of its stone construction, the Pierce tavern, erected in 1831, is marked by elegant details around its doorways and in the Palladian windows in its gables. The building is also unusual in retaining its bar, its ballroom with fiddler's stage, and a series of cubicles with box-like platforms providing spartan accommodations for teamsters and drovers.

NHHS Collections

roofs. Such a house is the tavern Benjamin Pierce built in Hillsborough Lower Village in 1804, with spacious and well-finished rooms and a hall extending across the entire front of its second floor. Many Federal period taverns gained still more flexible floor plans than that of the Pierce tavern by having their chimneys placed against the outer walls. Window openings were often large and were glazed with large panes, a product of New England's own glass manufacturers. Doorways were often surrounded with sidelights and fanlights. Staircases were often curved rather than angular. Moldings were light, delicate, and cut to complex new curves.

Now, too, a new fashion for brick architecture began to spread throughout New England. Residents of this region had long harbored a prejudice against brick dwellings, believing them to be, as Washington wrote, less wholesome than wood "on account of the fogs and damp" of the climate. By the early 1800s, however, a series of great fires had devastated several New England cities, including Portsmouth. Newspapers, such as the *Portsmouth Oracle*,

began to run articles on the obvious advantages of brick buildings in retarding the spread of flames.[30] The fashionable brick houses of Boston architect Charles Bulfinch also became known throughout New England, and those aspiring to the full elegance of the Federal style, even in the country, often turned to masonry construction.

Portsmouth had long had a brick tavern: the late-seventeenth-century Penhallow house, remodeled as the New-Hampshire Hotel in 1797. This ancient structure, probably the first brick house in New Hampshire, was ironically destroyed in the great Portsmouth fire of 1813. John Davenport, another Portsmouth tavernkeeper whose house was burned in that fire, quickly moved in the spring of 1814 to "that elegant and spacious four story brick stand" built some years earlier by Langley Boardman on Congress Street.[31] Later known under other tavernkeepers as the Portsmouth Hotel and General Stage House, this tavern became the terminus for stages to Boston, Portland, and Concord, and set the standard for taverns throughout northern New England.[32] In 1819, owner Boardman added

ON THE ROAD NORTH OF BOSTON

Photograph, Franklin Hall (center) and Portsmouth Hotel and General Stage House (left), Congress Street, Portsmouth, N.H., circa 1873. Built in 1819, Franklin Hall had a spring floor; on the upper story was a Masonic lodgeroom. The four-story brick hotel next door became one of the busiest stage stops in New Hampshire.

Courtesy, Strawbery Banke, Inc., Patch Collection

yet another brick structure to the complex: the elegant Franklin Hall, which boasted a spacious ballroom on the second floor and a Masonic lodgeroom on the third. Together, these buildings showed northern travelers what a modern tavern could be.[33]

Tavernkeepers in smaller towns were quick to emulate the style and appointments of such buildings. The flourishing Connecticut River valley soon had taverns which rivaled those of the seacoast. Among the best of these was the Eagle Hotel in Charlestown, one of the largest towns in western New Hampshire. Built in 1814 by Stephen Hassam, an ingenious and prosperous clockmaker, this building was originally two stories high (a third story and high-pitched gable roof were added about 1850). With its facade rendered more impressive by a blind arcade which framed its windows, the tavern established a style for brick buildings which spread to other Connecticut River towns. The Eagle was advertised in 1816 as "that elegant Tavern stand . . . containing a large Brick House with numerous rooms and an elegant Hall, with large and commodious Stabling for 60 or 80 horses."[34] A local resident later recalled that "coaches from Keene, Brattleboro, Woodstock and Hanover met here at noon and there were usually four or six horse coaches standing in front of the door. . . . I once counted thirteen which went through the town in one day."[35]

George Sparhawk of Keene built his Phoenix Hotel in 1822 on the site of a tavern that had burned down earlier that year. This three-story brick structure measured fifty-two by fifty-six feet and had a hall extending the length of its front, eighteen bedrooms, a large dining room, and a bar. The windows on its facade, like those of Hassam's tavern, were recessed within a blind arcade which extended from the granite foundation to the eaves.[36] Keene also had an Eagle Hotel, a three-story brick structure built as early as 1804. In January 1836, this building housed a party of 178 revelers from Walpole, who arrived at its door in sixty-six sleighs.[37]

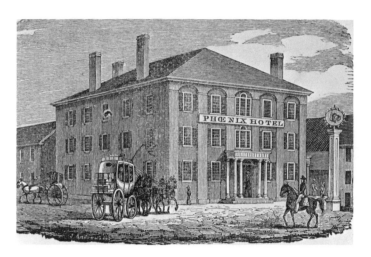

Wood engraving, Phoenix Hotel, Keene, N.H., from the Keene Directory, *1831, after drawing by J. Andrews. Built in 1822 by George Sparhawk, this impressive hotel exemplified the Federal style in its brick construction, three-story height, and low, hipped roof.*

Courtesy, Historical Society of Cheshire County
  Photographers, Cheshire Color Service

Yet another Eagle Hotel survives in Newport. Built in 1826, it copied its Charlestown predecessor in having a large carved eagle which served both as symbol and weathervane, and in having walls decorated with a blind arcade. George Sparhawk, formerly the landlord of Keene's Phoenix, became the manager of the Eagle upon its completion.[38] Upriver in Haverhill Corner stands another three-story brick tavern, the Grafton Hotel, built about 1815. Much like a large coastal house in appearance, the Grafton has a dramatic spiral staircase and woodwork of great delicacy and refinement.[39] Still farther north, in Bath, stood the imposing brick Bath Hotel, destroyed by fire in 1872, a large square structure with a wooden wing that provided stables on ground level and a spacious hall above.

Such taverns as these routinely provided amenities that only a few of their eighteenth-century predecessors could have displayed. Older taverns had only a few bedchambers, and a crowded house often required strangers to share a single bed. Stavers' William Pitt Tavern, the largest in Portsmouth, had four chambers on the second floor and four more on the third when the shifting partition temporarily subdivided the "long room." In these eight rooms were thirteen beds and bedsteads, including "turn up" bedsteads, which could be folded against the wall to save space, in almost every chamber.[40] Most of Stavers' bedsteads were low-posted and had canvas or "sacking" bottoms that did not require elaborate lacing and tightening of cords with a bed wrench. Although Stavers' tavern had hinged inside window shutters in every room, not every tavern was so equipped. Foreign visitors to the United States often complained of curtainless low-post bedsteads and unshuttered windows which allowed the summer sunrise to awaken them at too early an hour.

By contrast with crowded eighteenth-century sleeping arrangements, Keene's Phoenix Hotel of 1822 had eighteen bedchambers. Concord's own Phoenix, built in 1818, had eight chambers and four more rooms in the garret; in its enlargement in 1830, this tavern gained an additional eighteen chambers.[41] Even in the finer taverns, lesser accommodations were sometimes offered to teamsters and drovers, who were accustomed to simple hospitality. In the

Photograph, Bath Hotel, Bath, N.H., before 1872. One of the most imposing taverns in the upper Connecticut River valley, the early-nineteenth-century Bath Hotel was identical in size and appearance to the large Federal-style brick taverns and houses of the seacoast. The wooden wing behind it was evidently an older house; the chimneys in the huge stable indicate a heated ballroom on the second story. A large barn stood at the far right, beyond the stable.

Courtesy, Mr. and Mrs. Joseph I. Girardi

Bar in taproom of Israel Huckins' tavern, Province Road, Strafford, N.H., 1804. A rare survival of a once-common feature, this bar is separated from the larger room by a screen or wicket of wooden slats, and has a small sliding door in the wicket through which liquor was passed to customers. The side and rear walls are lined with shelves for bottles and decanters.

Courtesy, Mr. and Mrs. E. W. Huckins   Photographer, Bill Finney

THE TAVERN BUILDING

Pierce tavern of Chesterfield, for example, the finer rooms were apparently reserved for genteel travelers. Teamsters slept in small cell-like cubicles with built-in box bunks on which a simple mattress or even the teamster's ever-present bear or buffalo skin might be spread.

In many eighteenth-century taverns, the bar was merely a closet from which liquors were served over a half-door. The surviving Barnes tavern of Hillsborough Center, completed by 1775, has such a bar in the closet beside one of its two chimneys, as does the Wilson tavern of Peterborough, built in 1797. Other taverns had projecting enclosures within their taprooms, sometimes protected by movable or fixed wickets of wood. Although such fixtures were commonly removed by later occupants of former taverns in order to gain useful floor space, bars survive in the central-chimney Huckins tavern, built in 1804 on the Province Road in Strafford, and in the larger Federal-style Pierce tavern in Chesterfield, built in 1831 of local stone.

The taprooms associated with these simple early bars were often sparsely furnished. That of David Horney of Portsmouth, for example, was inventoried in 1757 and contained a large maple table, a dozen "Common flagg chairs," and a settle, recalling the similar furnishings of John West's tavern in New Castle in 1695.[42] The barroom of Stavers' Pitt Tavern also contained a dozen "flag bottom chairs" and a few tables in 1797. By contrast, the proud but waggish 1832 advertisement of John P. Gass, proprietor of the Eagle Coffee House in Concord, conjures up an image of opulent splendor:

The BAR is furnished with the choicest liquors and wines of every description. As an architectural ornament to the House, the Bar stands unrivalled in beauty, and will continue to *stand*, an object of *Corinthian* elegance, when those who make too frequent applications to its contents shall lose even the sober simplicity of the *Door*-ic order, and mingle with the dust.[43]

Tavern halls, like the "long rooms" of Stoodley's and Stavers' Portsmouth taverns, also improved in elegance with the passage of time. Many such rooms continued to employ hinged partitions, folding up against the ceiling or in accordion fashion against the walls, to subdivide large rooms into usable bedchambers when not needed for dances. Such movable walls remain in place in many New Hampshire taverns, including the Barnes tavern in Hillsborough Center, the Wilson tavern in Peterborough, the French tavern in Gilmanton, the large three-story Federal-style tavern owned by Stephen Huse in Greenland, and the similar Pearson tavern in Epping. Sometimes halls were not subdivided, but were merely filled with bedsteads when not otherwise occupied. The traveler C. W. Janson recounted an instance in 1809 when he "retired to bed, and had my choice of half a dozen, in a room the full length of the house, being fortunately the only guest for the night."[44]

Many taverns built after 1800 began to include specialized ballrooms with distinctive appointments. Many had permanent benches around the walls, as seen in the Bullock

Fiddler's throne from the ballroom of the Mack tavern, Deerfield, N.H., circa 1810. Originally set into a plastered wall with stenciled decoration, the fiddler's throne was flanked by doors leading into a ballroom extending the full length of the house. Its cornice probably matched mantelpieces in the same room.

Courtesy, The Society for the Preservation of New England Antiquities   Photographer, Richard Merrill

tavern in Grafton and the Davis tavern in Davisville (Warner). The ceilings of some halls were plastered in the form of a low vault, as in Pierce's tavern in Chesterfield, both for impressive effect and for good acoustics. Some of these ballrooms had a low platform or dais for musicians, frequently surrounded by an ornamental balustrade like that in French's tavern in Gilmanton, or by a low-paneled wall like that in Pierce's tavern. One remarkable survival, perhaps originally with counterparts elsewhere, is the fiddler's "throne" removed from the Mack tavern in Deerfield in the early twentieth century. Here the musician sat upon a paneled drum-like platform placed before a niche in the wall. Over his head rose a cornice supported on reeded pilasters, recalling the form and detailing of many Federal-period mantelpieces.

One remarkable feature found in many of these old ballrooms was the spring floor. Framed with supple joists, these floors were intended to flex and bounce beneath the feet, and their exhilarating effect was long remembered by

Ballroom in Coburn Tavern, East Pepperell, Mass., circa 1800; wall painting attributed to Rufus Porter, circa 1825. A man of many talents, Porter (1792-1884) was the best-known of many itinerant New England muralists of the early nineteenth century. At times a dance fiddler as well as a painter, Porter gave special attention to the imaginary landscape that enlivens the plastered walls around the musician's platform of this imposing brick tavern.

Courtesy, George G. Hayes   Photographer, Bill Finney

enthusiastic dancers of the early nineteenth century. When spring floors were built within a finished tavern, it was necessary to provide a double set of joists for the hall, the uppermost for flexibility, and the lower to support the rigid plastered ceiling of the room below. Many halls, such as those in the Colburn tavern in Temple and the Davis tavern in Davisville, were built above service wings or stables where the undulation of the floor would break no plaster, and where the noise of dancing feet would be heard only by the creatures housed below. The celebrated Grecian Hall, a thirty-two by sixty-four-foot room, was built above the seventy-five-foot-long stable wing of Concord's Eagle Coffee House.

Many of these ballrooms (and often other rooms as well) were decorated with colorful wall painting in lieu of wallpaper. Some of this decoration takes the form of stenciled designs. Although the most celebrated stencilers were itinerant craftsmen like Moses Eaton and the still-unidentified "Borderer," there were many other anonymous local prac- titioners. Several New Hampshire ballrooms, also used as Masonic lodgerooms, bear the symbols of Freemasonry among the purely decorative motifs used elsewhere.

Still more striking are the freehand scenic murals often found both in taverns and private homes. Rufus Porter is the best-known mural painter; having traveled widely before he began mural work around 1824, he combined familiar local scenes with exotic motifs.[45] Less widely tra- veled but equally imaginative was John Avery, who worked in the Wakefield-Middleton-Wolfeboro area. As with stencilers, there were also a number of anonymous local mural painters.

As taverns grew larger, guests were provided with new comforts as well as with increased privacy. By the 1820s or 1830s, even the most fastidious European or American trav- eler to New Hampshire's larger towns would find little to complain about. In 1823, Concord's John P. Gass an- nounced that his Columbian Hotel offered fifty new beds of feathers pulled from live geese and promised "the weary traveller every accommodation for sweet and undisturbed repose.''[46] In 1832, having become landlord of the Eagle Coffee House, Gass boasted of sixty-four sleeping rooms with ''124 elegant Feather Beds and Hair Matrasses.''[47]

But Gass, a Falstaffian figure in his own right, prided himself on more than his bedchambers. At the Columbian, Gass offered a dining hall big enough to seat 125 people at one immense table. At the Eagle, outdoing even himself, Gass provided three dining rooms, one of them sixty feet long, and nine parlors where visitors could withdraw for polite conversation and reading. Occasionally, tavernkeepers devised still more exotic arrangements. The giant elms which once shaded many taverns were sometimes provided with elevated platforms or ''tree houses'' in which food or drink might be served amid cool breezes. Concord's Washington Tavern had such a platform, as did the Pollard tavern in Nashua. Sometimes, more formal dinners were provided alfresco; regular guests, Freemasons, and Fourth of July celebrants were treated to outdoor meals at the Lafayette Hotel in Lebanon during the 1820s, and Asa Barton, proprietor of the Junction House in Hanover, provided meals for 1,200 guests beneath a mammoth tent at the Dartmouth College centennial in 1869.[48]

Dining rooms on the scale being attained by the second quarter of the nineteenth century required kitchens of a hitherto-unknown capacity. The eighteenth-century tavern kitchen was exactly like that of a home, having a cavernous fireplace for roasting, an iron crane above the fire for boiling, and a brick oven or two for baking. Some taverns, such as Horney's, Slayton's, and Stavers' in Portsmouth, were equipped with the single labor-saving device known to early cooks: a weight-driven ''jack,'' which slowly turned a spit suspended on hooks attached to the andirons or held within a tinned reflector oven. Refrigeration was provided by the ice houses that belonged to the better taverns from the early 1800s.

We can assume that some taverns of the first decades of the nineteenth century, like the better homes of the era, began to be equipped with ''Rumford works''—roasting ovens and cooking pots set into massive brick stoves with small, separate fire chambers to conserve fuel and reduce heat in the kitchen. Many public houses of the era, like Piper's tavern in Northwood, had at least one simple derivative of the Rumford apparatus: the cauldron or ''set kettle,'' a capacious iron vessel set into a brick ''arch'' or firebox with its own separate flue, and mostly used to heat large quantities of water for washing.

However simple the means at hand, cooks of the early nineteenth century could work miracles. It is related that a party of fifteen or twenty guests arrived at the Hatch tavern in Greenland expecting dinner. Finding the larder empty, Mary Hatch directed her son to drive home the sheep from a pasture half a mile away. Killing a lamb, the hostess cooked parts of it, baked bread, and boiled vegetables for the hungry crowd, all within the space of two hours.[49]

Stereograph, tree house (band stand) under a white pine, at the Winslow House, Andover, N.H., circa 1870. Several early New Hampshire taverns offered similar platforms, where guests could seek shade and a cooling breeze, and sometimes could be served food or drink.

NHHS Collections
  Photographers, E. & H. T. Anthony & Co.

By the 1830s, many kitchens in both tavern and home began to use a cast-iron cooking range, either a ''set'' range, standing on a brick hearth and partly built into the brickwork of a chimney, or a ''portable'' range, a free-standing unit connected to the chimney by a funnel or stovepipe. Even Lucy Crawford, in a tavern so remote that her husband had to haul his chimney bricks twenty-one miles, had a cooking stove in her kitchen shed by 1824.[50] But it was John P. Gass, the self-styled ''good portly man i'faith and pleasant'' of Concord, who introduced one final refinement in tavern cookery. Playing upon his own unusual name, Gass announced in 1832:

Every one at all conversant with the modern discoveries in Chemistry, is aware of the many useful purposes to which GAS has been applied; but the individual who now addresses the public, is not informed that any one, *save himself,* has hitherto availed himself of this important agent in carrying to perfection the art of COOKERY. He, however, in his exertions and anxiety to accommodate the taste . . . of the public, early discovered that a proper application of this substance to culinary purposes, added both to the flavor and delicacy of every viand submitted to its operation. . . .[51]

The former manager of the Broadway House in New York, Gass accomplished this feat a full twenty years before Concord's first public gas-lighting system went into operation.

Although many American taverns were otherwise well-equipped by the nineteenth century, most still lacked convenient methods for providing water for washing and cooking. Some taverns had wells dug in their cellars, some had basement cisterns for holding rainwater collected from the roof, and by the late 1700s, a few in towns like Portsmouth and Exeter were supplied with spring water through aqueduct pipes of hollow logs. Traveling to Keene in 1793, William Bentley of Salem, Massachusetts, found Richardson's tavern furnished with piped spring water—a "convenience hardly imagined till it is seen."[52] Despite Bentley's astonishment, a number of New Hampshire taverns advertised such conveniences, for stable as well as house, by the early 1800s. But in most taverns, as the traveler Niemcewicz complained, guests were forced to "wash themselves and comb their hair outdoors which, especially in the winter, is not at all pleasant."[53]

The importance of a tavern's water supply was forcefully demonstrated in the fall of 1798, when the *New-Hampshire Gazette* reported that seventeen people had suddenly been taken sick at Colonel Robert MacGregor's tavern at Amoskeag Falls in Goffstown. "They were at first seized with violent vomiting, then purging of blood, with almost total debilitation, weakness, and insensibility, so that they were obliged to be carried from the place of labour." While some suspected that the victims had been deliberately poisoned, others eventually concluded that the dire sickness had been caused "by water taken from a well which had stood useless during the summer, and from which they had that morning drew, in consequence of the water in their usual family well having failed."[54]

Since bathing was rare until the nineteenth century, most travelers did not expect bathrooms either in home or tavern. By 1805, however, Portsmouth had a public bathhouse, and thereafter public expectations began to change. By 1827, the Piscataqua Bridge Hotel on Goat Island in Newington offered "a SHOWERING BATH and Dressing Room," located "on the extremity of the Island," and when Samuel Wyatt's New-Hampshire Hotel in Dover was offered for sale in 1846, its basement was equipped with "Shower, Hot and Cold Water BATHING ROOMS, fitted up in good style."[55]

Bathing was greeted as a healthful novelty in the early 1800s, but taverns remained tempting homes to older and less wholesome amusements. Gaming of every sort was frowned upon in New England and strictly prohibited by law in taverns from the 1640s. Apprentices were forbidden in their indentures to play at "cards, dice or any unlawful game." A note in the *New-Hampshire Gazette* in 1769 expressed the common attitude toward the dangers of such pastimes:

Gaming is an amusement wholly unworthy [of] rational beings, having neither the pretence of exercising the body, of exerting ingenuity, or of giving any natural pleasure; . . . [it is] the cause of infinite loss of time, of enormous destruction of money, of irritating the passions, of stir[r]ing up avarice, of innumerable sneaking tricks and frauds, of encouraging idleness, of disgusting people against their proper employments, and of sinking and debasing all that is truly great and valuable in the mind.[56]

A writer in the same paper in 1774, concerned about the vitiating effect that such amusements might have on a nation on the brink of war, urged boycotting any tavern permitting games and shunning any person who indulged in gaming.[57]

A law of 1694, amended and expanded several times, listed some of the games which were prohibited in public

Painted checkerboard, originally owned by Hollis Bunker of Barnstead, N.H., 1832. Although gaming was considered a waste of time and a danger to the character, some New Hampshire taverns contained checkerboards and backgammon tables, probably indicating a tolerance of these relatively harmless pastimes.

Courtesy, The Currier Gallery of Art

houses: dice, cards, nine-pins, tables, bowls, shuffleboard, and billiards.[58] Despite such warnings, Americans were irresistibly attracted both to board and card games and to games of dexterity, including bowling, shuffleboard, and billiards. John West's New Castle tavern contained a shuffleboard chamber in 1695. Several eighteenth-century Portsmouth taverns contained checkerboards and backgammon tables. Despite the popularity of card games (attested to by the great numbers of card tables that survive from the eighteenth and early nineteenth centuries), games which directed a missile against a target proved especially seductive to human nature.

By the late 1700s, prosperity had evidently increased to the point that several New Hampshire tavernkeepers could afford the space and equipment needed for the most elaborate of these games. A group of Dover citizens petitioned in 1791 for a law to prevent both tavernkeepers and private citizens from having billiard tables, by which "the Husband is induced to spend not only long evenings, but [also] nights & days at those resorts of iniquity, leaving his solitary wife . . . the son is tempted to leave his home in stealth . . . [and] the apprentice is inveigled to leave his master's service & spend his time & *master's* money in preparing himself for a pest, instead of a valuable member of society."[59] Despite this public outcry, a Dover newspaper in 1793 warned the selectmen that "a Billiard Table has been set up in a licensed house" in town.[60]

Bowling was an equally great temptation. Since the New England climate did not favor lawn bowling, tavernkeepers sometimes constructed separate bowling alleys. Beginning in 1814 and for decades thereafter, the Globe Tavern at Portsmouth Plains was famous for its "six Bowling Alleys in three separate houses, erected for that purpose"; the Ingersoll or Sanger tavern at South Charlestown on the Connecticut River had a similar building.[61] Yet as late as 1852, a moralistic editorial in the *Portsmouth Journal* looked

back with self-righteousness on the fate of those who had frequented the alleys of the Globe: "Those who were not soon cut down with intemperate habits lost the confidence of the community, and are not now to be accounted for with any pleasant recollections." Refusing to continue to run an advertisement for bowling alleys and billiard rooms, the editor of the *Journal* warned any young business apprentice or mechanic: "if it is known that he is familiar with the Bowling Alley or the Billiard Room," that fact alone "is enough to stamp his fate in the mind of any business man who has a situation worth possessing."[62] New Hampshire law did not permit the licensing of billiard halls and bowling alleys until 1878.

The tavern was home for beast as well as man, and the well-appointed tavern lavished much attention on the shelter of animals. Some stables were grander than the houses themselves; Portsmouth's wooden Bell Tavern eventually acquired a brick stable, while the Mansion House, a temperance hotel, had a stone stable described by one visitor as "the finest one I ever saw, much handsomer . . . than some of the Meeting-houses."[63] Many well-appointed taverns had barns or stables measuring thirty or forty feet in width and fifty or sixty feet in length, and these buildings could accommodate from fifty to a hundred horses or oxen. In 1805, Isaac Marsh's Coachman and Farmer's Tavern in Dunstable could "house fifteen carriages and loaded waggons where they will be dry and secure"; the following year, Jacob Coffin of Londonderry advertised a stable "open to receive carriages which may pass through without unharnessing . . . twenty sleighs can be accommodated in case of a storm."[64] The brick Milliken tavern in Jaffrey had three capacious barns and, like many of the best taverns, also had a blacksmith shop for the shoeing of animals or the repair of vehicles.[65]

Tavern yards were also prized assets, often including large fenced lots for impounding animals being driven to

Old Crawford's, [Crawford] Notch, White Mts., *circa 1845, pencil and watercolor on paper, by James Elliot Cabot. Abel Crawford's tavern, later known as the Mount Crawford House, is shown with its many barns and other outbuildings, and with a fine young orchard.*

NHHS Collections   Photographer, Bill Finney

Photograph, Wheeler/Sawyer tavern, West Keene, N.H., circa 1900. This building complex was operated as a tavern from the early nineteenth century by the related Wheeler and Sawyer families; the wagon sheds and barn were attached to the main building, with a convenient field for grazing on the opposite side of the road.

Courtesy, Historical Society of Cheshire County

Wood engraving, Eagle Hotel, Keene, N.H., from the Keene Directory, 1831. *Keene's imposing Eagle Hotel was identified by an equally imposing sign suspended between two square posts topped by urn finials. The elaborate signboard, painted by Charles Ingalls, depicted the hotel and its neighboring buildings. The gilded eagle above was carved about 1827 by Amos Holbrook.*

Courtesy, Historical Society of Cheshire County
    Photographers, Cheshire Color Service

Sign from the tavern of William Yeaton (also spelled ''Yeton''), Epsom, N.H., 1813. This sign, depicting a stylized sun, retains the style of the eighteenth century in its turned side columns, high curved pediment, and flame finial. The Yeaton tavern stands at the intersection of the First New Hampshire Turnpike and a once-busy local road leading from Deerfield to Pittsfield.

Courtesy, Charles B. Yeaton   Photographer, Bill Finney

market. Gardens and orchards were of crucial importance, allowing the tavern to supply its own larder. Stephen Hassam's Charlestown tavern had a five-acre lot "with an Orchard sufficient to make 15 or 20 barrels cyder" in 1816; the Globe at Portsmouth Plains had a hundred apple trees, sixty or seventy of them having "grafts of the first rate fruit"[66] The Hatch tavern in Greenland had not only an apple orchard, but also grapevines, cherry trees, and currant bushes.[67]

To assist travelers, even the earliest of taverns displayed a sign in a prominent position. A law of 1646 required licensed houses to post an "inoffensive Sign, obvious for direction of strangers," and penalized with loss of license any house not displaying a sign.[68] These signs were not hung at eye level; from an early date, perhaps for greater visibility at a distance, they were hung from an arm extending from a post as high as the eaves of the house itself, sometimes twenty-five feet or more off the ground. Occasionally, especially after 1800, such signs might be suspended between two such posts. On rarer occasions, as with the Eagle hotels of Concord and Keene, the sign might take the form of a sculptural carving mounted on or near the building, or, as with the Eagle hotels of Charlestown and Newport, might be mounted on a spindle to turn as a weathervane.

Tavern signs frequently depicted a simple motif easily recognized even by the illiterate traveler, such as the Golden Ball Tavern in New Castle and the White Ball in Plaistow. Other simple but popular motifs for tavern names were bells, ships, globes, and both exotic and native birds and beasts: eagles, phoenixes, lions, tigers, deer, moose,

foxes, horses of many colors, and honeybees. For Freemasons, there were squares and compasses and crossed keys worked into the designs; there were suns and hearts, also with hidden Masonic meaning. Heraldry figured in the signs of taverns named the King's Arms, the Masons' Arms, and the Wentworth Arms; other taverns were named after famous individuals, such as the Marquis of Rockingham, the Earl of Halifax, William Pitt, General Wolfe, George Washington, and even Napoleon. To emphasize the bar, bottles, decanters, wine glasses, and punch bowls were depicted; and, occasionally, lists of the bar's offerings would be posted on the sign. Sometimes the tavern's own neighborhood and the tavern building itself would be colorfully painted on signs to attract passersby.

The tavern sign evolved with changing taste. Few signs from the eighteenth century survive, but a Georgian style

Figure of eagle, used as the sign of the Eagle Hotel, Newport, N.H., unidentified wood with gesso and gilt, carved by Stephen Hassam, Charlestown, N.H., circa 1827. Sculptural tavern signs were extremely rare. This is one of two surviving eagles carved by the ingenious Charlestown clockmaker Stephen Hassam; the other eagle was originally used in front of his own tavern, the Golden Eagle, established in 1820. These eagles were said to have been mounted to revolve as weathervanes.

Courtesy, Denver Art Museum

Newspaper advertisement for John Davenport's tavern, The Mason's Arms, Portsmouth, N.H., Portsmouth Oracle, 1814. John Davenport chose as his tavern sign the Freemason's arms, a shield bearing a superimposed square and compass forming a chevron separating three towers. Davenport was an ardent Mason, and Portsmouth lodges often enjoyed dinners at his tavern.

NHHS Collections   Photographer, Ernest Gould

Sign from the Stickney tavern, Concord, N.H., probably 1790s. This sign, perhaps depicting one of the legendary sachems of the Merrimack Valley, identified the tavern opened by William Stickney in January 1791 and operated by his son John from 1827 to 1837.

NHHS Collections   Photographer, Bill Finney

is evident among those preserved from the late 1700s and early 1800s. The painted boards of such signs tend to be supported between turned shafts, and to have a shaped pediment above, sometimes with a turned finial at its center, and a skirt or pendant below. During the Federal era, oval signs became popular, often surrounded with a filigree of fanciful wrought-iron scrolls and spears. Instead of being hung from an arm, these signs were sometimes fixed by long iron spikes in their bottoms to the top of clas-

sical columns or turned poles standing in front of the tavern. Still later, as innkeepers sought to shed the old-fashioned tavern image in favor of that of the city hotel, signs were changed to large but sedate boards affixed to the front of buildings, often with gilt letters set off against backgrounds of black sanded paint.

It is clear that a new standard inspired tavernkeepers as the nineteenth century progressed. More and more after 1800, we find the old terms "tavern" and "inn" replaced with the grander word "hotel." This change began during the Federal era, and became almost universal as the Greek

Photographic postcard showing sign from tavern of Joel Howe, Warner, N.H., circa 1900. Many Federal-period tavern signs departed from the old style of a hanging board. This sign, surrounded by wrought iron scrolls similar to those often used on weathervanes of the period, was attached to a single post or column by a long spike at its bottom.
Courtesy, Henniker Historical Society

Sign from the tavern of Alexander Watkins, Walpole, N.H., 1795. The Federal eagle, a favorite motif in the early republic, here bears in its beak a banner inscribed "Peace To America." The sign's oval shape was a favorite at the turn of the century.
Courtesy, Town of Walpole, N.H.
Photographer, Ned Goode; photograph courtesy of Historic American Buildings Survey, Library of Congress

amenities of the older Exchange Coffee House, doing so with a far more convenient layout and with the most modern Greek Revival detailing, but also added interior water closets and plumbing.[70]

New Hampshire tavernkeepers tried to imitate the new standards, both in decoration and amenities. The Greek Revival style was well adapted to the needs of the hotel.

Revival style became dominant from about 1830. The change was partly inspired by a new respect for temperance and a desire to shun an image that recalled the heavy-drinking habits of the eighteenth century. But the term "hotel" also promised new amenities and new standards of size, comfort, and privacy.

The model for New Hampshire hotels of the early 1800s was set in Boston. There, in 1809, was constructed the immense Boston Exchange Coffee House. A brick structure of unparalleled size, the building rose seven stories and contained a merchant's exchange covered by a dome, coffee rooms, reading rooms, dining rooms, parlors, a ballroom, and a hundred bedchambers; in short, it was a giant prototype for the many hotels built throughout New Hampshire in the following years.[69] In 1829, the architect Isaiah Rogers completed the Tremont House in Boston according to "the established principles of Grecian Architecture." Immediately recognized as unequaled in the United States, this granite building not only offered the

View of the Lafayette Hotel, Lebanon, N.H., circa 1858, watercolor on paper. Like many older taverns which differed little from private houses, the Benton tavern was modernized and made recognizable as a fashionable hotel through the addition of a porch supported by a row of Doric columns in the Greek Revival style.
Courtesy, The Society for the Preservation of New England Antiquities

Photograph, City Hotel, Keene, N.H., circa 1885. The three-tiered porches of this large hotel, built in the 1830s, were meant to suggest the appearance of a Greek temple. Painters have changed the white Greek Revival decoration of the office at the right to a darker Victorian color, and are shown in the process of doing the same to the main building.
NHHS Collections   Photographer, Jotham A. French

Almost any building could suggest the new style through the application of Grecian detailing, and one of the easiest methods of applying such detailing was through the addition of porches supported by Doric columns. If the building could be oriented with a gable end facing the street to suggest the pediment of a temple, the illusion was complete.

During the 1830s and 1840s, New Hampshire gained many such structures, of great size and with multi-tiered porches, especially in the rapidly growing manufacturing towns. Concord had its American House, standing next to the capitol. Keene had the Cheshire House and the Keene Hotel, the latter wrapped on two sides by its Doric porches. In Nashua stood the Indian Head Hotel and the huge American House. Goffstown had its New Hampshire Central House, Laconia its Cerro Gordo House, and even Orford had its Orford Hotel, a large wooden building with a three-tiered porch beneath a projecting pediment. One of these Greek Revival hotels, Thayer's in Littleton, survives to give some sense of the many that have been lost.

Many of these large buildings, perhaps the majority, had a new feature. Americans of the 1830s and 1840s had begun to hunger after a new view of the world: the picturesque. Influenced by aestheticians like the English writer William Gilpin, Americans became increasingly interested in enjoying scenery and views for their own sake. This desire for

the picturesque brought painters and sketchers to the White Mountains during this period, and the same interest in the landscape required that a well-appointed tavern or hotel have a vantage point for the enjoyment of the surrounding area, even if that scene was largely populated with buildings.

Hence, most hotels began to follow the lead of Boston's Exchange Coffee House and Tremont House in having cupolas or observatories on their roofs. In 1831, the inimitable John P. Gass of Concord, being the proprietor of both the Columbian Hotel and the Eagle Coffee House, thought it necessary to mention the view from each. Apologizing for the lack of a cupola on the Columbian, Gass noted that "although the view from the *top* is not quite so extensive as from some other houses, the *indoor* prospect, which people of *taste* value more highly, shall be such as to please the most fastidious."[71] Gass needed to make no such apologies for the Eagle, where the cupola afforded "every facility to travellers who would examine the Capitol and State Prison, or take a birds eye view of the Village and natural scenery around it."[72]

This same interest in the picturesque would shortly give rise to an entirely new phenomenon: the resort hotel of the mountains or the seashore. Built to an unprecedented scale in hitherto unfrequented places, these grand hotels marked a new chapter in travel. Constructed as an end in them-

Lithograph, Eagle Coffee House, Concord, N.H., circa 1832, by Annin, Smith & Co. A small city hotel constructed in 1827 and enlarged in 1832, the Eagle offered not only large, well-furnished rooms and spacious porches, but also, as proprietor John P. Gass boasted, extensive views to be enjoyed from its large cupola.
NHHS Collections   Photographer, Bill Finney

selves rather than merely as public houses, these resorts encouraged travel for pleasure and refreshment rather than for business or other necessity.

The emphasis on travel for pleasure did more than render the old-fashioned tavern inadequate to the needs of a new type of visitor. The demand for ease and comfort also forced a reappraisal of New Hampshire's highways. Rutted and muddy wagon roads, adequate for the stolid farmer, were too primitive for the traveler accustomed to the city street. The development of New Hampshire's potential as a source of recreation would require the transformation of a road system which had evolved slowly since the first settlement of the land, and which in many cases retained the roughness of those early days.

Photograph, Walpole bridge under construction, circa 1870. Showing the construction of the bridge over the Connecticut River between Walpole, N.H., and Westminster, Vt., this early photograph reveals the simplicity of the Town lattice truss. The road in the right foreground is typical of New Hampshire highways before the Good Roads movement of the late nineteenth century.

Courtesy, Walpole Historical Society   Photograph courtesy of Closs Planners, Inc.

THE ROAD SYSTEM

CHAPTER 3

THE DIFFICULTY OF BUILDING roads in a post-glacial wilderness like New Hampshire, using only the muscular power of men and animals and the simplest of hand tools, can hardly be imagined today. New Hampshire's land in the first decades of the eighteenth century, when settlements first began to move beyond the bounds of the original coastal townships, was covered by a thick growth of forest. That part of the forest not already harvested for pine masts and lumber was composed of northern hardwoods which sprouted vigorously when they were felled, quickly choking newly cleared areas. Under-foot lay a terrain alternately composed of bogs and marshes or else of hillsides strewn with the rocky debris of glaciers, here and there scraped bare by the ice to reveal the solid underlying ledge. Frozen and covered with snow for much of the year, the earth turned in the spring to mud so deep as to halt all travel for weeks. This was a mountainous territory, made more irregular by long hills of glacial gravels which furrow the earth in parallel deposits. The glaciers had also left countless lakes, ponds, and swamps, a few large rivers, and a myriad of small streams, all of them a hindrance to travel.

Timothy Dwight, president of Yale College and a man of letters, was also an inveterate traveler who appreciated the herculean labors that had gone into building the roads he used. Writing in 1803 from the notches of the White Mountains, Dwight was able to see firsthand the daunting challenge that had faced all new settlers for the past hundred years:

> The forests they could not cut down; the rocks they could not remove; the swamps they could not causey; and over the streams they could not erect bridges. Men, women and children ventured daily through this combination of evils, penetrated the recesses of the wilderness, climbed the hills, wound their way among the rocks, struggled through the mire, and swam on horseback through deep and rapid rivers by which they were sometimes carried away.[1]

Dwight added one more hazard: "In the silence and solitude of the forest, the Indian often lurked in ambush near their path, and from behind a neighboring tree took fatal aim, while his victim perhaps was perfectly unconscious of danger." Yet it was the Indian who first provided the set-

tler with a way into the wilderness. New Hampshire's native people were a migratory race, moving from season to season between various hunting and fishing stations and their winter villages. The Indians had marked the terrain with a number of footpaths which provided routes for raiding parties from the north to descend upon coastal settlements, but also provided white soldiers and settlers with routes extending northward toward Canada.

The rivers, too, provided avenues into the wilderness. The settlements around the Piscataqua River and Great Bay were first connected by waterborne traffic, and the tributaries of the Piscataqua furnished water power which was exploited by some of the first sawmills in North America. The Merrimack River was explored early in the seventeenth century, and the rich intervales or flood plains at Penny-cook were claimed by the Sewall family of Massachusetts as early as 1695. Seventy years later, as military rangers followed trails north to Canada, the still broader and more fertile meadows of the Connecticut River were discovered at the Upper and Lower Coos. Once these rare alluvial lands began to attract settlers, they became magnets for the roads that began to be blazed through the surrounding wilderness.

The method by which a ranging or scouting party reconnoitered the wilderness in preparation for building roads and defensive outposts is revealed in a report of 1744 from Jonathan Chesley to recently appointed Governor Benning Wentworth:

> I marched, with the forty men under my Command, from Durham . . . in the road which leads to Canterbury. I removed the Windfalls, &c, in the way. When I came to Suncook River, I searched to find out a convenient place for a Bridge; which I found about half a Mile below the way which is cleared. . . . After two days stay at Canterbury, I marched with my Men to Winnepissoccay Pond . . . I went to Merry-Meeting [Alton Bay]; & about two miles from there I joined Capt. Tibbetts, who arrived there before me, & had been down the Pond, & had found a convenient Place for a Blockhouse, & had Marked a Way from [there]. . . . I assisted Capt. Tibbetts in marking the way from the Place where I met him, to Rochester.[2]

It is likely that the "way" that the ranging party marked

from Alton Bay to Rochester became the main road which was later used for much of the commerce between Winnipesaukee and Rochester.

The method used by rangers, timber cruisers, surveyors, and settlers alike in laying out new paths through the woods was by the simple blazing of tree trunks with an axe. As New Hampshire's historian Belknap described the process, "First, a surveyor and his party, with the compass and chain, explore the country, and where they find the land suitable for a road, the trees are spotted, by cutting out a piece of the bark, and at the end of every mile, the number is marked on the nearest tree."[3] This is the process recorded in the 1741 journal of surveyor Walter Bryent when he marked the boundary between New Hampshire and Maine. As Bryent's account shows, snow was no deterrent to explorers on snowshoes, and in fact could allow them to cross intervening ponds with ease:

> Crost the head pond which was a mile over, and at two hundred rods distance from sd head pond was another which lay so in my course that I crost it three times. . . . At the end of every mile I mark'd a tree. . . . Went over a mountain from the summit of which I plainly see the White Hills and Ossipa Pond. . . . I also crost the River which comes from the East and runs into said pond, & campt, had good travelling to-day & went between seven and eight miles.[4]

Belknap described the shelter used by surveyors as a simple lean-to constructed of hemlock or spruce bark which was peeled with an axe and laid as shingles for a roof, with a bed of twigs from the same tree. "Before the open side of the hut, is made a large fire, toward which the traveller places his feet, and being wrapped in a blanket, he passes the night very comfortably, though, if the wind be unfavorable, he may be somewhat incommoded by smoke."[5]

It was often many years before the blazed trails marked by surveyors became cleared roads. When the Canterbury settlers laid out the road traveled by Chesley in 1744, they needed to plead for help from the province in completing it: "The Proprietors have with considerable expence cut a way from Durham up into the Country upwards of twenty miles . . . which if cut thro' will be of Great advantage not only to [Canterbury] but to the Province in General and which they are not able to Effect . . . & without which the Settlement will necessarily go on heavily & Slowly as it has hitherto done."[6] In 1793, William Bentley talked to a man who had settled in Orford on the Connecticut River twenty-eight years earlier, and was told that "they entered by marked trees, & for seven years there was no road for any carriage whatever."[7] Dwight related the hardships of settler David Page, who lived at the Upper Coos (Lancaster) in 1766: "For several years after he came to this spot, he carried all his bread corn to Charlestown (124 miles) to be ground." Not only was there "not a single road in the neighboring region," but Page could not even float his cargo down the Connecticut River until he had walked twenty miles to a point below the Fifteen Mile Falls.[8]

Given such hardships, it is small wonder that New Hampshire did not attempt to plant new towns beyond the "head line of Dover" for a century after the first settlements along the seacoast. By 1722, when the first new townships were laid out beyond the original towns, the provincial government and its surveyors had devised a method of settlement that would ensure the steady subduing of the wilderness and would lead to an orderly method of laying out roads in trackless lands. The proprietors or landowners of these new townships met initially in a tavern in Portsmouth or in the town where the majority of proprietors lived. There, with the help of scouts and surveyors who knew the new territory and who had marked out its corner bounds in the woods, the proprietors devised maps of lots to be divided among themselves. At an early stage, usually without having visited the newly granted territory, the proprietors drew lot numbers from a hat, taking their chances that the land they acquired would be cultivable and not located on a ledgy mountaintop or in a swamp.

The plans drawn by the proprietors of the first series of new townships varied widely. Two of the new townships, Chester and Nottingham, had compact villages with small lots grouped "in as defensive a posture as the land will allow" at crossed roads which extended off into the woods for later settlement.[9] A third township, Rochester, dispensed with the idea of a "defensive" village and was planned with a grid of medium-sized farmsteads of sixty acres each. A fourth township, Barrington, was a great rectangle laid out from border to border with lots in regular tiers or "ranges," each tier separated from its neighbors by straight "range roads." Barrington would provide the prototype for the division of outlying lands in the neighboring townships as well as for most future town plans in New Hampshire. When the next tiers of townships were granted in 1727, all were laid out as range townships, with a regular checkerboard plan of large, separate farms connected by a rectilinear grid of range and cross range roads. The same plan would be followed in most new townships granted by the New Hampshire government throughout the colonial period.

In 1740, the boundaries of the province were adjusted by the King in Council to include all of present-day New Hampshire, with a vague western limit which Governor Benning Wentworth chose to define as encompassing most of present-day Vermont. Then, in 1746, the Masonian Proprietors purchased the old royal grant of the Mason family, amounting to some two million acres. The stage was thereby set for unprecedented grants of land both by the New Hampshire government under Wentworth and, within a more constricted but still vast area, by the Masonian Proprietors. Both the government and the Proprietors chose as their model for town planning the range township which had proven successful in the earlier grants of the 1720s.[10]

Settlers in these frontier lands faced two problems in road-building. First, they had to clear a route to the new townships—initially a footpath and, as soon as possible, a cartpath or wagon road. Second, they had to begin to clear

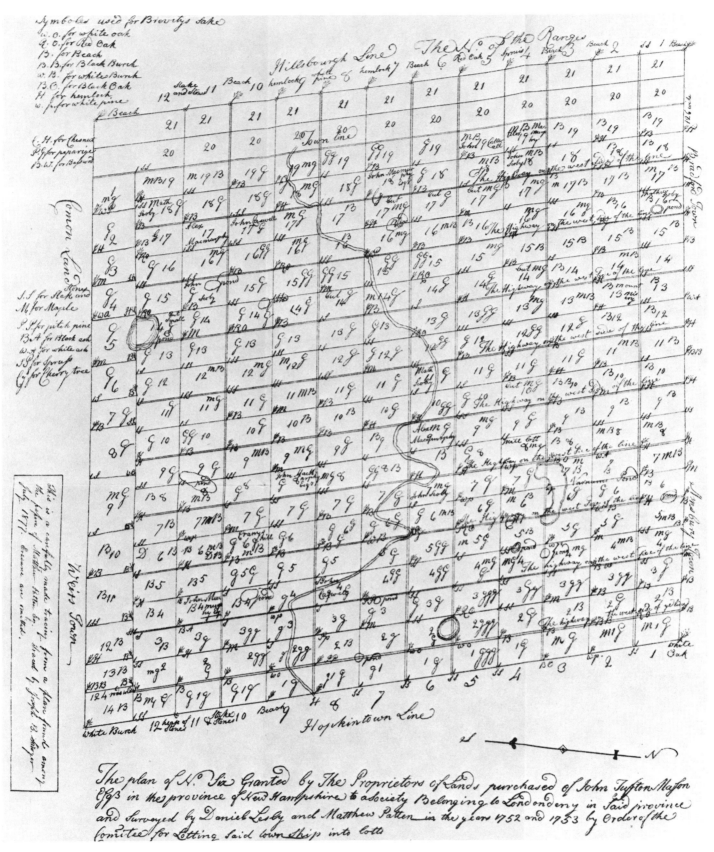

Proprietor's Plan of Henniker, N.H., surveyed by Matthew Patten and Daniel Leslie, 1752-53, copied by Joseph B. Sawyer, 1877. This map shows the grid of rectilinear lots characteristic of townships planned by the Masonian Proprietors and the straight range roads that crossed the grid. Coded letters indicate the species of "witness trees" at the southeast corner of each lot.
NHHS Collections   Photographer, Bill Finney

the range roads that divided and provided access to their individual lots. The topography of the land was often an obstacle. The proprietors of Nottingham, for example, first had to construct a "Great Bridge across Lampereel River" and a road from the coast to their new holdings, just as the proprietors of Canterbury had to span the Suncook River at the place chosen by Wentworth's scout, Jonathan Chesley. The Canterbury proprietors pointed out that roads leading to new settlements offered a "Public advantage . . . Especially in time of War," and that "as Every Town is in some degree benefited thereby, [a new road] ought not to be the burthen of the town to which it leads only, but of every Town."[11] In 1743, the House of Representatives agreed, designating part of the interest on treasury funds to be "appropriated for Cutting Roads, &c."[12]

While a road leading to a new township could take the most convenient route, the roads within the township itself were supposed to follow the straight lines drawn on the town plan. Recognizing that swamps and ledges required detours from a perfectly straight line, proprietors routinely followed the example set by the Nottingham proprietors when they voted in 1727 that "whare thare [sic] are Steep hills or other difficult Places in sd Streets . . . they are to Shun them by Turning the way round them and coming [back] to sd Streets with the way again."[13]

The key figure in laying out routes, whether from the coast to the frontiers or within townships, was the surveyor. Eighteenth-century surveyors used simple but effective tools, accomplishing remarkable results through extreme care in their craft and through their own indifference to the discomforts of the woods. The surveyor's first need was to establish direction in a trackless wilderness. For this, he used a compass, a pivoted and magnetized steel needle mounted in a wooden "box" above a "card"

Photograph, surveying party in front of Clark's Hotel, Third Turnpike, New Ipswich, N.H., circa 1875. Equipped with sophisticated instruments, including a transit, level, and steel tape, this party was engaged in more than the usual rural surveying job; they may have been rerouting the turnpike.

Courtesy, New Ipswich Historical Society   Photographers, Fisher & Foster

ON THE ROAD NORTH OF BOSTON

Brass azimuth or surveyor's compass, circa 1850, made by Abiel Chandler, Concord, N.H.; owned by civil engineer and surveyor George Plummer Hadley of Goffstown, N.H. Working on the same principle as older wooden compasses, this brass instrument, with silvered card, was somewhat more accurate. Such compasses, equipped with peep sights, have been used for common surveying jobs from the days of first settlement down to the present.
NHHS Collections   Photographer, Bill Finney

showing the 360 degrees of a circle. By peeping through wooden sights in which horse hairs were stretched, the surveyor could maintain a true course of direction with only slight error. Surveyors of the 1700s understood that the magnetic needle fluctuated in direction from year to year, and compensated for this by finding the declination of the needle through astronomical observation. When Walter Bryent laid out the boundary between New Hampshire and Maine in 1741, for example, he "set . . . course, being North two degrees West, but by the needle North Eight Degrees East."[14] Not all surveyors were equally skilled, and it was once proposed in the House of Representatives that "durable monuments should be erected in convenient places, on a true meridian, by which all surveyors should be obliged to regulate their compasses," but the proposal was rejected.[15]

The surveyor also needed to establish distance. In an age before the development of steel measuring tapes, the surveyor used a "Gunter's chain," composed of one hundred wire links which individually measured 7.92 inches and together totaled sixty-six feet. These odd measurements had a purpose: eighty chains equal one mile, and ten square chains equal one acre. Like the compass, the chain required careful use, and surveyors resorted to makeshifts to overcome its cumulative error. As Belknap recounted, some surveyors added one chain in every thirty to compensate for the sag of the chain, and added the length of a man's arm to every half chain when rough terrain prevented the chain from being stretched in a perfectly straight line.[16] In laying out a route, surveyors spotted trees along the way, and many proprietors' maps indicate the species of each of these "witness trees."

Once a route had been surveyed, as Belknap noted,

then follow the axe men, who clear away the bushes and fell the trees . . . cutting them as near as possible to the ground, that the stumps may not impede travelling. . . . In wet land, the trees thus felled . . . are formed into causeways and bridges. Rocks are either turned out of the road, or split by gunpowder or heated by fire and then softened by water. Roads are not brought to perfection at once, especially in rocky and hilly land; but after the first operations, they are passable for single horses and teams of oxen. As the earth is opened to the sun, many wet places are dried, and brooks are contracted; and as the land is more and more cleared, smaller streams disappear.[17]

Even more than rocks, tree stumps were an obstacle in the construction of new roads. Many stumps were burned on the spot with an abundance of fuel provided by the felled trees. The buttressing roots of others were cut with axes, and the stumps were wrenched out of the ground with chains and oxen. This method was not always possible; sometimes, as Dwight noted in 1803,

The roots . . . being interwoven with each other, render it impossible to obtain earth sufficient for the purpose of covering the stones, or to make drains for drying the sloughs. The earth which can be obtained in most places is nothing but vegetable mold; and this is so spongy, imbibes the water so easily, and retains it so long that in seasons not absolutely dry the inconveniences . . . are only increased.[18]

All writers agree that year-round mud was a problem when roads were not cleared to a width of eighty or a hundred feet to let the sun dry the soil. When haste in construction made it impossible to clear so broad a swath, trees beyond the immediate path of a road were undoubtedly girdled with the axe so that they would die. As Dwight complained, however, dead trees were liable to be blown over by storms, and many accounts attest to the continual labor of clearing windfalls from new roads.

After being cut, trees were disposed of in several ways. Intertwined treetops made acceptable temporary fencing for newly cleared fields; Governor John Wentworth enclosed a deer park at his Wolfeboro estate in this manner.[19] Most trees, however, were burned on the spot, so that the air in newly cleared areas was constantly hazy with acrid smoke. The ashes so produced were of immediate value as fertilizer in new fields. After 1750, moreover, the British government began to encourage Americans to use their enormous wealth of hardwood ashes in the production of potash. This alkali, produced by leaching ashes with water and by boiling the resulting "liquor" in great

Photograph, logging road, Lincoln, N.H., 1905. Although dating from relatively recent times, this photograph provides a record of the difficulty of laying out highways in the wilderness of New Hampshire. At the right is a crude stringer bridge of the type used since the first days of settlement.

NHHS Collections

iron kettles, could be further refined into pearlash by prolonged heating in an oven. Great quantities of both the refined and unrefined products were used in the making of soap both for domestic use and, on a larger scale, for use in the rapidly expanding British textile industry.[20]

Because of New Hampshire's topography, a road with any degree of straightness will encounter brooks and boggy areas within a short distance. These were overcome in the eighteenth century by the same method used since the 1600s to build wharves in tidal marshes and inlets. Belknap described such a "causey" or causeway as "built of large logs, on which they . . . lay rocks, so as to sink the logs into the mud, and form a durable road."[21] Small streams were crossed by fording or were spanned with bridges. The best bridges were stone culverts, utilizing flat slabs to span the distance between abutments built of rocks. Larger bridges were built of log stringers, laid from abutment to abutment, and covered by shorter logs laid transversely. Such bridges were treacherous, not only because they were slippery

under a horse's hooves, but also because "when they appear still to be sound, sometimes yield suddenly to the foot, and hazard the lives both of the horse and his rider."[22]

Until engineering skill provided alternatives in the late 1700s, the largest streams could be crossed only by ferries. Most ferries were pulled across streams by a rope, or propelled by oars or poles. After 1800, a few "horse boats" began to appear on rivers and on lakes like Winnipesaukee. These boats were propelled when the horses walked on a horizontal cog wheel or on a wooden treadmill which in turn moved the paddles.[23]

The building of roads and bridges placed a heavy burden on the people of New Hampshire. In most instances, however, this burden was not seen as one to be borne by all the people of the province. The New Hampshire government was generally inclined to compel all road and bridge costs to be paid by the taxpayers of incorporated towns or the proprietors of newly granted lands, and to agree to some public responsibility for these improvements only upon the

Bridge at Jackson, *N.H., 1879, oil on canvas, by Frank Henry Shapleigh. Shapleigh delighted in depicting the old stringer bridges which survived near White Mountain villages until late in the nineteenth century. Having no railroad, Jackson was one of many rural towns served by the stagecoach until 1900 or later.*

Courtesy, Private Collection   Photographer, Robert Swenson

Engraving, The Ferry (On the Androscoggin), *by William Wellstood after a painting by Albert Fitch Bellows, probably 1860. A typical flat-bottomed ferry, carrying a wagon and horses, is being pulled across the stream by a cable or rope. A horn for summoning the ferrykeeper from his cabin hangs from a tree limb at the right.*

Courtesy, Douglas A. Philbrook

approval of their work. In 1743, for example, the legislature sent a committee "to goe up to Chester & Londonderry to View a high way formerly Laid out." Only after the committee reported the road to be "the most Conveniente high way for Accommodation of Both Towns and Travellers in General" did the legislature proclaim it "the Kings highway and . . . a Publick road."[24] Similarly, when competing bridges had been built above and below Cochecho Falls in Dover in 1770, interested parties contended strenuously to have their favorite bridge declared "the Kings and Countrys Bridge" and thus to be maintained at town expense.[25]

A certain amount of public funding was made available in 1742 when the government borrowed £25,000 by mortgaging lands. Although most of the income from this loan was designated for the repair of forts, a portion was earmarked for cutting new roads. The settlers of Canterbury were permitted to receive some reimbursement from this fund for building a bridge over the Suncook River, but only after they had constructed the span at their own expense and guaranteed to maintain it for a full ten years.[26] It was similarly voted in 1752 that a portion of the income was to be used in building a road up the Connecticut River from Fort Number 4 (Charlestown) to the rich and newly discovered Coos country, and from there back to Canterbury. The cautious House of Representatives voted, however, that none of this money should be available until four hundred men had actually been settled at Coos.[27]

Throughout the first half of the eighteenth century, the legislature passed a series of progressively stronger laws giving the provincial government the power to force towns and unincorporated places to build roads as the government might direct. In incorporated towns, these laws were enforced by locally elected surveyors of highways, who were given the authority to impress men, teams, and equipment to the extent required by the job at hand. Under the most elaborate of these laws, passed in 1754, "all Male persons from Eighteen years of age" were made "liable to the Duty of Labouring on the High Ways." All those who owned teams of horses and oxen were required "to take their turn to work with such Team and implements thereto belonging," and were given credit for this work "according to the Strength of Such Team." Heavy fines, doubled under a law of 1760, were imposed on those who avoided road work.[28] In unincorporated places, where no local government existed, the legislature assessed charges for road building on the proprietors or owners of the land. In areas of New Hampshire where lands remained ungranted, the provincial government had no one upon whom to impose the burdens of road construction.

Considering the burdensome and punitive requirements placed on private citizens in building and maintaining roads and bridges, it is small wonder that New Hampshire's road system remained both fragmentary and primitive even long after settlers in considerable numbers had moved into the western townships. The need to provide communication between the Connecticut and Merrimack

rivers and the seacoast was recognized immediately after New Hampshire's boundaries were established by the King in 1740, and a number of tentative surveys of such routes were carried out through the 1750s. Nevertheless, little actual work toward opening a well-planned system of internal communication was done until the 1760s.

The first of the province highways was the road leading from the seacoast northwest to Lower Coos. Scouts who had been active during the Seven Years' War had seen and appreciated the rich alluvial lands or intervales that lay at present-day Plymouth (at the confluence of the Baker and Pemigewasset rivers) and at Lower Coos (now Haverhill) on the Connecticut River. Utilizing the services of surveyors Jacob Bayley and John Hazen, Governor Benning Wentworth had laid out a number of townships on both sides of the Connecticut River during the 1760s. In 1763, Bayley and Hazen petitioned the Governor and Council "to have a road from the Settled part of this Province to Cooss," because "we together with a Number of other People are making a Settlement at Cooss," and the rich produce of that country "must of course go down the River [to Massachusetts] unless a Road is kept open this way."[29] By the end of the year, the government had passed a law requiring such a road. The highway was to be constructed by "the Proprietors of Each Township at their own cost," and an additional law in 1765 allowed the province to confiscate land from proprietors who failed to "cause the said way to be cleared and be made passable for Teams thro their respective Grants."[30]

From 1766 to 1769, notices appeared in the *New-Hampshire Gazette* warning landowners along the route that "if any of the Proprietors or Grantees shall neglect to perform this Order" longer than six months, "so much of the Common Land of the delinquent Proprietors will be sold as will raise Money sufficient to defray their respective Share or Part of said Charges."[31] Since the committee to mark out the route did not report to the legislature that its work was done until the summer of 1768, these newspaper warnings appear to have been mostly bluster.

The province road system as finally planned and constructed was largely the work of New Hampshire's last royal governor, John Wentworth. A young and well-educated man, Wentworth was eager to undertake many internal improvements which had been contemplated as early as 1742 but never acted upon—especially the improvement of roads. Moreover, Wentworth set a personal example of inland improvement when he began to clear land in Wolfeboro in 1768 and a year later raised the frame of a dwelling that was to be the largest and best furnished in New Hampshire. But even Wentworth, with his visionary and persuasive arguments for an interconnected provincial highway system, was forced back upon the old and largely ineffectual method of requiring local residents and town proprietors to assume the heavy burden of road-building.

The House of Representatives went on record as "intirely

in [agreement with] your Excellency's sentiments, relative to . . . convenient ways for transportation." During the late 1760s and early 1770s, the House passed several laws empowering the creation of a good highway network. These laws authorized a road from Boscawen to Charlestown, the former Fort Number Four, in 1769; a road from Wolfeboro to Upper Coos at Northumberland in 1769; a road from the Governor's house to the newly founded Dartmouth College in Hanover in 1771; and a road from Conway to Upper Coos at Lancaster in 1772. Under laws of 1768 and 1772, the town of Rochester was required to build roads through the little-settled northern portions of the township, thus providing access to other roads leading through Middleton and Wolfeboro to the Governor's house, and then to Conway.

The prospect of so many new routes to the rich western part of the state excited much comment in the *New-Hampshire Gazette*. An editorial in 1770 pointed out that "the Richness and Fertility of some of our Northwestern Lands, can be no Ways better known than by letting the Public know, that at Haverhill, at the lower Cooss, one Mr. Hazzen raised more than 700 Bushels of Wheat from 30 Acres of Land." Given this bounty, the writer thought that Portsmouth "may shortly hope to see WHEAT as cheap in this Town, as in the City of Philadelphia," which sat in the midst of America's eighteenth-century breadbasket.[32] The following year a writer applauded a newly opened connection between Moultonborough on Winnipesaukee and the road to Coos, noting that a new wharf and warehouse on the lake would "shortly be supplied with Salt, Rum, Fish" and other trade goods from the seacoast, and in return would supply the coast with "Wheat and Flour . . . Pot Ashes [and] Pearl Ashes." "In a few Years," the writer predicted, "we shall be able to supply ourselves with *Wheat, Flour,* and Provisions much cheaper than to import them."[33]

Despite the good intentions behind the highway laws, each act required that the expense of opening and maintaining the roads should be borne by the towns through which they passed. For this reason, work on all these roads progressed slowly or not at all. As late as the autumn of 1773, a writer, calling himself "Benevolus," was still using the *Gazette* to argue "for some Plan to make public Roads from the Principal Towns on Connecticut River, to Merrimack River," as if nothing of consequence had yet been accomplished. Benevolus warned that "the Government of New-York are determined to get good Waggon Roads from Connecticut River to Hudson's River," and that Portsmouth would shortly be cut off forever from the riches of its own hinterland.[34]

Benevolus had good cause for concern. The slowness of the proprietors of Middleton in building a road around their own Moose Mountain, for example, was a particular irritation to Governor Wentworth, who found both his Wolfeboro house and all the roads leading northward from it to be blocked by this stretch of wilderness. Finally, in May

1769, the exasperated Governor took the matter into his own hands. Noting that "the sordid indolence and retrograde advance of a few unjust people" had led to "the dishonor of the province in having such an impassable tract in the center of the government," Wentworth declared that

I am determined no longer to suffer those grievances, and . . . on Thursday morning 18th May, 1769, I shall send my overseer with twenty able men and eight oxen to cutt, bridge, and make the road effectually . . . and I will petition the proprietors of the patent for all the land unsettled in said town, to be sold at public auction within four weeks of this day to repay the expence —provided, nevertheless, that if a body of men at least twelve, and a team of at least six good oxen actually

Engraving, The Gap of the White Mountains, *by Abel Bowen after John Kidder as a vignette for Philip Carrigain's map,* New Hampshire by Recent Survey *(1816). The exaggerated topography of this scene conveys the awe felt by travelers passing through Crawford's Notch. The road was a frightening and dangerous route before the construction of the Tenth Turnpike through the cleft.*

NHHS Collections   Photographer, Bill Finney

"Getting a Team Up [Crawford] Notch at the Rocks," 1859, *drawing on woodblock, by Marshall M. Tidd. Intended for an illustrated edition of Lucy Crawford's* History of the White Mountains, *this and other blocks were never engraved for printing. At a time when the road through Crawford's Notch was barely passable, this scene shows a "car," described by Lucy Crawford as "two poles . . . the smaller ends serving as thills for the horse to draw by and the largest ends dragging on the ground. . . ."*

Courtesy, Dartmouth College Library

come to work and continue thereupon untill the road is effectually and wholly finished . . . that then, and only then, I shall desist.[35]

Despite this threat, the Governor finally had to use his own crew, and to provide pickaxes, shovels, hoes, axes, a crowbar, a "Grindstone wore out & Spoild in the Service," and a pound of gunpowder "Us'd in blowing Rocks." The work required some 1,500 man-days, and to pay the charges, the Masonian Proprietors finally confiscated those lots upon which little improvement had been made.[36]

Similar conditions prevailed on many of the other new roads. When Governor Wentworth journeyed from Wolfeboro to Dartmouth College to attend the first commencement in 1771, he was apparently forced to abandon the route of the still incomplete "College Road," take the Coos Road to Haverhill, and then journey downriver to Hanover.[37] Sometimes even those roads which were cut with tremendous labor and hardship were left barely passable or were allowed to deteriorate. When the first road was

opened through Crawford Notch, the cleft was barely twenty feet wide and very steep. Lucy Crawford recalled that when the first horses were brought through the notch, the drivers "managed to get to the top, and by taking a zigzag course, as much as possible, got down: but in doing this there was danger of the horse tipping over—the hill was so steep. And when they returned, they would tie a rope around the horse's neck, to keep him from falling backwards."[38] In 1784, Jeremy Belknap recorded the condition of the road through Pinkham Notch, which had been authorized only twelve years earlier as "a Road from Conway to Connecticut River, on the East Side of the White Hills." Belknap found "the old Shelburne road," untraveled for years and "grown up with bushes and filled with wind-falls, the bridges broke, and the mires deep."[39] He and his party were obliged to follow behind a "pilot," who cleared the growth with an axe.

The Revolution naturally slowed progress on any road not needed for military purposes. In 1780, the residents of

Upper Coos expressed fear that "an Enemy may at some time & Probably this Summer make an attack on Connecticut River"; because Crawford Notch remained "an almost inaccesable [sic] pass," these settlers would be cut off from retreat or aid. Accordingly, the legislature passed a law requiring the road to be repaired. Instead of taxing the hard-pressed settlers, however, the legislature voted to fund the work through the public sale of "one thousand Acres of confiscated lands of [loyalist] William Stark Esqr adjoining to Conway."[40]

Following the war, New Hampshire turned with renewed energy to road-building, much of it spurred by petitions from isolated settlers. In 1787, a group of petitioners claimed "that the road (commonly called the Province Road) laid out from Durham to Cohos is in some part thereof so incumbered with hills Rocks &c as to be almost impassible [sic] for loaded Waggons which hath occasioned the produce of the Northwestern part of the state to be transported into the Massachusetts."[41] They requested permission to build a new road to bypass the section that led through Barrington. In 1789, inhabitants of Rochester and of the rapidly growing town of Gilmanton complained that "the road from Rochester-line through New-Durham and New-Durham-Gore [Alton], to Barnstead-line, is exceeding bad and unsafe for travellers, that the road through said Gore is not laid out, as said Gore is not incorporated . . . that said road through New-Durham is but two rods [33 feet] wide, and that the selectmen of said town refuse to make it wider." Noting that this "was the country road from the upper part of the state to *Dover*," the petitioners asked that it be fully "laid out and made passable."[42] In the same year, residents of Moultonborough and Sandwich complained about "the road called the college road through Tuftonborough." Despite the efforts of Governor Wentworth eighteen years earlier, a portion of this road only a few miles north of the Governor's former estate was "so bad it cannot be passed with waggons or other carriages, nor with horses without great danger."[43]

Concerned about the difficulties of transportation and communication, the legislature gave high priority to the reestablishment of a reliable postal service. While the mails had been carried to and from strategic points in New Hampshire since the late seventeenth century, the newly formed state needed a far more extensive postal system to serve the burgeoning population in areas previously occupied only by scattered cabins. Concord's steadily growing stature as a transportation center was recognized by the authorization of several new roads. Laws passed in 1784, 1786, and 1787 required the first of these roads to connect Hanover and Dartmouth College with Boscawen, just north of Concord, bypassing the now-obsolete route from Wolfeboro. Another law passed in 1791 established a road from Concord to Durham, with a spur extending south from the new route to Newmarket. Another law of 1795 authorized a road southwest from Dover to join the new Concord-Durham route in Northwood, taking advantage of a section of the old Province Road through Barrington.

Meanwhile, the legislature was busy establishing regular postal routes. Three routes laid down in 1786 were great circuits focusing on Portsmouth. One led northwest as far as Hanover; the second went west to Amherst; and the third extended north to Conway. A shorter fourth route went from Amherst to Charlestown and back.[44] When the postal routes were reestablished by law in 1791, newly built roads had begun to reinforce Concord's growing stature. Only two of these routes began and ended at Portsmouth. Two others extended from Concord west to Claremont and northwest to Haverhill. The law required that "Each Post rider shall perform his rout[e] weekly (Extraordinaries Excepted)."[45]

By the 1790s, then, the battles of a quarter-century earlier between Governor John Wentworth and the obdurate New Hampshire terrain seemed to have been won. The state had been crossed and recrossed with an adequate network of roads, many of which remain in use today. Wentworth's ambition of shifting the center of commerce and population inland had also been realized—though Concord, not Wolfeboro, had emerged as the focus of the growing network of highways. But the American obsession with speed and efficiency was about to cause the map of New Hampshire to be redrawn again. Now the speculative investment of private capital, rather than the coercion of hard-pressed settlers, would work changes that governed travel until well into the twentieth century. The 1790s would see the beginning of the turnpike era in New Hampshire, as elsewhere in the eastern United States.

Secretary of the Treasury Albert Gallatin summed up the purpose of turnpike roads in 1807 when he described such highways as "shortening the distance, diminishing the ascent of hills, removing rocks, levelling, raising, and giving a proper shape to the bed of roads, draining them by ditches, and erecting bridges over the intervening streams." On the least-expensive turnpikes, "the natural soil of the road" was used, while on the more carefully built highways, known as "artificial" roads, the roadbed was covered "with a stratum of gravel or pounded stones."[46] Depending on the care used in their construction and the terrain they traversed, Gallatin calculated that turnpikes could cost anywhere from $1,000 to $14,000 a mile. This considerable expense, which could exceed a half-million dollars on the more ambitious projects, was borne by corporations chartered by state legislatures. Because such corporations faced the necessity of carrying out their work through the territories of many townships, they were invested with the power of eminent domain. Turnpike companies thus could take land with fair compensation in the same manner as government bodies, and could not be blocked by some recalcitrant property owner along their route. The companies could likewise take over former town roads that coincided with their planned routes.

Turnpikes were toll roads, with gates every few miles,

and the funds collected from travelers had to yield a profit in order for the venture to succeed. Profits varied widely, however, even in the heady first years of turnpike development. Gallatin noted that the famous Newburyport Turnpike, connecting Boston with the northernmost port in Massachusetts, yielded a profit of only two percent in 1807.[47] For a variety of reasons, most turnpikes ceased to be profitable long before the railroad era. Since this result was not anticipated in the early 1800s, New Hampshire, like all the other New England states except Maine, was in time crossed by a network of toll roads. New Hampshire eventually became home to eighty-two turnpike corporations, a few of the later ones founded to encourage the tourist trade.[48]

Because most New Hampshire turnpikes were laid out along new rights of way rather than on existing roads, the corporations often took private land and sometimes, in the interest of a direct route, bypassed already-established town centers. These factors naturally aroused opposition among those who stood to lose land or business. For this reason, New Hampshire newspapers of the early 1800s often contained letters from turnpike supporters arguing against selfish interests and for the greater public good. A writer in the Walpole *Museum* in 1799 offered arguments that any turnpike supporter in New England might have echoed:

> Roads will be laid out in the best possible places, and those who suffer private injury for public good will have their damages equitably appraised and paid; . . . the inhabitants of each town through which a road passes will be privileged to pass gratis, except when on journeys or going out of town. . . . Who would object to paying the toll of a good bridge rather than to cross a ferry; and who will object to paying the small toll of a Turnpike, when it will expedite his journey to that degree, that it will be more than saved in his tavern expenses? Add to this the saving of time, the safety and convenience attending a journey, and we presume there will not a reasonable objection arise. . . . The waggoner may add one-fourth to his load, perform his journey in three-fourths the time, and he will find by experience that his team will last twice as long.[49]

A writer of 1800 urged the connection of Portsmouth with the Newburyport Turnpike, noting that the distance by road to Boston would thereby be shortened from sixty-seven to forty-nine miles. If a similar road were extended eastward to Portland, the writer calculated, a stagecoach traveling at the common speed of eight miles an hour could travel from Boston to Portland in the time then required to go from Boston to Portsmouth.[50]

Others predicted a social benefit from improved communication. A Walpole writer in 1801 declared that on turnpike roads "with ease and safety we travel . . . through those rugged districts, which had been nearly impassable. They bring the remote parts of a country, as it were, near to each other; and, while they greatly improve commerce, they equally facilitate social intercourse and the speedy and extensive dissolution of intelligence."[51] Traveler Timothy Dwight seemed to concur with this view when he noted that one of New Hampshire's chief "evils" was the lack of a common viewpoint across the state: "Those in the eastern counties are apparently little connected with those in the western, and those in the middle of the state still less perhaps with either."[52]

Those who doubted the visionary predictions of turnpike promoters were satirized as people of little imagination, whose objections to a new road might be "that it will not go by uncle Josiah's barn; or cousin Joseph's pigsty; or may possibly spoil sister Tabathy's potatoe yard—or that the Col. or Capt. (whose *childer* loves mightily to see the fine folks ride along in their *chronicles* and *phaesantons*) may object, because the road does not go by their houses."[53]

Occasionally the parties interested in promoting a turnpike or bridge were unable to raise sufficient funds to begin work. In such cases, especially in the construction of bridges, the New Hampshire legislature sometimes authorized a lottery to tempt wider public support for the venture. Such practices began before the Revolution; when the Stratham-New Market Bridge was built in 1775, the provincial government held a series of lotteries to fund its construction.[54] Soon after the war, in 1785, the legislature authorized the same funding technique for construction of the "Lottery Bridge" over the Sugar River in Claremont.[55] Lotteries were established in 1790 to build a bridge from Portsmouth to New Castle, and in the early 1800s to support the Piscataqua Bridge at the eastern end of the First

Advertisement for Peirce's lottery office, Portsmouth, N.H., Portsmouth Oracle, 1806. Promoting the sale of tickets for the second Amoskeag Bridge lottery and the Harvard College lottery, this woodcut illustrates the "wheels" or drums employed at the office of C. Peirce, who boasted that "his little boy above, has surely kept a good look-out as yet, and done WELL," having selected four winning numbers from five drawings.

NHHS Collections   Photographer, Ernest Gould

New Hampshire Turnpike.[56] In 1807, the Sixth New Hampshire Turnpike Corporation was likewise funded by a lottery in its rebuilding of the bridge over the Connecticut River at Hinsdale.[57] Most lotteries offered cash prizes, but when a road at Dixville, in the sparsely settled northern tip of New Hampshire, was funded by an 1808 lottery, some winners received not only handsome cash prizes but also parcels of one thousand acres of land.[58]

Approval of the seemingly painless method of raising money for public works by lottery was not unanimous. Outraged by the New Castle Bridge lottery of 1790, the *New-Hampshire Gazette* highly approved of an act of the legislature requiring the permission of selectmen in any town where corporations might "attempt to set on foot this *canker-worm* to the morals of our rising youth." In May 1791, the paper applauded the disapproval by the Portsmouth town meeting of the scheme, which "has of late proved very injurious to the morals of the youth," but noted that despite a warning visit by the high sheriff, the lottery office continued to "pursue their present iniquitous plan, in defiance of the town."[59]

Photograph, tollgate and tollhouse, Cheshire Bridge, Charlestown, N.H., 1896. Although taken at the end of the nineteenth century, this photograph captures a scene which might have been observed fifty years earlier. The light, two-horse coach ran between Charlestown and Springfield, Vermont.
NHHS Collections

The New Hampshire legislature permitted turnpike corporations to begin collecting tolls on their roads as soon as at least six hundred dollars had been spent on each mile of road between tollgates. Tolls were levied on the basis of miles traveled, so that the corporations were free to set up "gates or turnpikes" at any intervals they wished; there would be no unfairness if, for example, a company decided that it needed closely spaced gates at some point to be sure that traffic did not turn off at some by-road and thus escape its proper payment. The practice of detouring around tollgates was common and posed a serious threat to the legitimate profits of corporations. In an effort to deter the practice, the directors of the First New Hampshire Turnpike Road voted in 1805 to prosecute six men who had been detected going "around the Toll gates to avoid paying the Toll."[60]

Gates were sometimes moved from one strategic point to another as occasion might dictate; when John Drown was appointed tollkeeper on the First Turnpike in 1803, he charged $2.33 for "halling Turnpike Gate from Hoits up to my house and setting it up."[61] Tollhouses were probably much like the one constructed at the Stratham-New Market Bridge in 1807—a one-story hip-roofed building measuring thirteen feet by eleven, with clapboard walls painted white and the wood-shingle roof painted brown. The interior was neatly plastered or sheathed with wood, and had a corner fireplace for comfort.[62] Outside the house was the gate itself: a long pole or pike which could be turned aside by the tollkeeper or, in later and more elaborate versions often seen at toll bridges, a portcullis-like gate which could be lifted between two upright standards.

In the brief eight-year period between 1796 and 1804, the major components of New Hampshire's turnpike system were laid down by legislative charter. In the years that followed, most of the projected roads were actually built. Merchants in Portsmouth and Concord seized the initiative in 1796 when they petitioned the legislature with an argument that echoed the vision of John Wentworth: "Communication between the Sea-coast and the interior parts of the State might be made much more easy, convenient and less expensive by a direct road from Concord to Piscataqua Bridge, than it now is, between the Country and any commercial Sea-port." And these petitions offered a mechanism that had been unavailable to Wentworth. Recognizing that "an undertaking of this kind, however useful to the community, would burden the Towns through which it may pass," the petitioners asked to be made "an incorporated company, who might be indemnified by a Toll for the sums that should be expended by them" in building the road.[63]

It is ironic that this private-enterprise scheme to channel New Hampshire's inland wealth to the state's only port spurred equally imaginative plans which had no such ambition. The turnpike map of the state shows a number of routes channeling New Hampshire's commerce toward the very place most feared by the merchants of eighteenth-

Brass seal used by Third New Hampshire Turnpike Corporation, circa 1800. Only 1¼ inches in diameter, the seal depicts double tollgates hinged upon columns.
NHHS Collections   Photographer, Bill Finney

century Portsmouth: except for the First New Hampshire Turnpike, most of the new roads led toward Boston.

The Second New Hampshire Turnpike, chartered in 1799, set the pattern by striking a direct line from the rich Connecticut River at the Lottery Bridge in Claremont through the Contoocook River valley to Amherst, where it eventually connected with the Middlesex Turnpike in Massachusetts. The Third Turnpike, incorporated in the same year, channeled the wealth of lower Vermont from the great bridge at Bellows Falls "toward Boston, to the Massachusetts line." The Fourth Turnpike of 1800, planned by out-of-state investors, traveled from Lebanon (where it connected with Vermont turnpikes) to Boscawen. After 1804, with the incorporation of the Londonderry Turnpike, traffic could continue from Boscawen to Concord, and then along a direct route to a connection with the Essex Turnpike of Massachusetts at Andover Bridge. The Cheshire Turnpike of 1804 carried traffic from Charlestown, not east to Boscawen as in provincial days, but south to connect with the Third Turnpike and Massachusetts. The Grafton Turnpike of the same year passed from the rich Coos country at Orford southeast to join the Fourth Turnpike. While the Fourth and Grafton turnpikes, leading to Boscawen, had the potential of feeding commerce to Portsmouth via the First Turnpike, much of the traffic reaching Boscawen continued southward to the far-larger Boston market. Even the Tenth New Hampshire Turnpike, which finally made Crawford Notch passable with a widened and leveled road, denied Governor Wentworth's old dream by channeling commerce east to Portland rather than south to Portsmouth.[64]

Wherever they might lead, New Hampshire's turnpikes were governed by legislation that evolved quickly between the chartering of the First and Second turnpikes in 1796 and 1799. While details varied from road to road, almost all New Hampshire turnpike charters required that the highway right-of-way be four rods (66 feet) wide; that disputes over compensation for land taken for the route be settled by county courts; that tollgates be left open to traffic when the tollkeeper could not be on duty; that no gates be erected until a certain sum had been expended in improving the road between the gates; that no tollgate be erected on any stretch of road which had previously existed as a public highway; and that financial reports be submitted to the Superior Court at stated intervals.

The same laws allowed the corporations to select routes that would "combine shortness of distance with the most practicable ground"; established the tolls that might be collected for various kinds of traffic, based on miles traveled; forbade the collection of tolls for people going to or from religious services, funerals, mills, militia duty, or on "the common and ordinary business of family concerns within the same town"; provided that if turnpike profits exceeded a certain annual level (usually nine or twelve percent), the tolls should be lowered; and allowed the tolls to be raised if the profits fell below another level (usually six percent). Travelers were fined three times the usual tolls if caught circumventing tollgates. Finally, after a certain period of time ranging from "immediately" to forty years, the state or other public agency might pay the corporation the amount expended on the road and a percentage of profit, deducting the total of tolls collected over the life of the road, and thus make the highway a public road.

In general, New Hampshire turnpikes were model roads compared to their town-built predecessors. Not only were turnpikes more direct and usually more level, but they were constructed and maintained on sounder principles of engineering and with greater capital investment than most public roads of the era. The standards used on all turnpikes were typified by specifications given in the *New-Hampshire Gazette* when the directors of the First Turnpike advertised for bids in 1800:

> The said Road must be thrown up and raised with clear earth or gravel, thirty inches high in the centre, and rounded off in a true curve each way to the middle of the gutter or water course, on the sides of the road, twenty-six feet from centre to centre of the gutters, which must also be slop'd outwards; and have water courses across the road and from the gutters, sufficient to prevent any water's remaining thereon.

The notice specified that the water courses or channels across the road should be covered with plank, and further described the procedure when the road met bogs and streams:

> In meadow or swamp land a good foundation must be laid with wood or stone, and covered as aforesaid. . . . The bridges are to be twenty feet wide and built with piers of our common pine timber, three posts to a pier, placed on a mud sill twenty feet apart, with five sufficient strings of timber, to be covered with good three-inch pine plank . . . with stone abutments where materials can be had. And over any dead or still water, of inconsiderable depth, or flats adjoining running streams, causeways of wood or stone covered with gravel excepting courses [openings] for the water.[65]

Milestone, granite, First New Hampshire Turnpike. One of the few remaining milestones on the turnpike, this monument stands on a little-used section of the road in Epsom twelve miles east of the site of Concord's Federal Bridge.
Photographer, Bill Finney

Although the law did not require it, most turnpikes marked their routes with milestones; the First Turnpike, for example, paid $104.84 to Jonathan Eastman for "37 Mile Stones Set upon [the] Road" at seventeen shillings each.[66] A few of these markers, of Concord or Durham granite, still remain along the roadside, as do some of the milestones of coarser granite along the Londonderry Turnpike. These markers were useful to travelers, but also allowed the corporations to assign repair of maintenance crews to any point or section of the road.

Both the building and maintenance of these roads were accomplished with the simplest of tools. An inventory of the Dover Turnpike shows that the corporation owned two horses, eight oxen, four ox yokes, four horse collars, and two saddles for draft horses. Their road equipment consisted of three ox carts, two horse carts, one truck, three drays, two plows, two horse scrapers, one ox scraper, and twelve wheelbarrows. The inventory of hand tools included two saws, twenty-nine shovels and spades, twenty hoes, four crowbars, two broad axes, eight narrow or felling axes, one adze, four pickaxes, one block and tackle, chain, rope, and blasting equipment. An equally large part of the inventory was composed of bedding and cooking or eating utensils for the laborers, suggesting that road crews were housed in temporary camps along the way.[67]

The First Turnpike had two large covered wagons, probably used to haul both materials and men. These vehicles had special wide wheels which prevented rutting the highway surface even with heavy loads; the iron tires of the larger of these wagons weighed a full 677 pounds. The directors also voted to buy "a Roller made of wood of nearly one ton weight, not exceeding eight feet in length, and so constructed as to be drawn by oxen for the purpose of rolling and settling the Road when made."[68] Captain Stephen Harriman, builder of the Andover section of the Fourth Turnpike, had a still more exotic piece of road equipment:

He built a light, but strong, frame house, about thirty feet long, resting on solid wooden trucks for convenience in moving from point to point as the work progressed. Two smart, capable daughters did the cooking for a gang of more than twenty workmen, who lived in tents. Eight yoke of oxen used on the road were able to move the building along as required, and a span of horses brought up rear of the procession on "moving day," drawing a large iron-hooped brick oven built on a solid platform supported by wheels.[69]

The vast quantities of earth that had to be moved in constructing turnpikes were loosened by pick and shovel and carried in wheelbarrows. For small excavations, horses and oxen were hitched to the breaking plow and the scraper. Earth was first broken by a procedure described by a traveler in the 1830s: "A plough, drawn by four, and occasionally six oxen, with two drivers, one man holding by the stilts, and another standing on the beam, is passed along the margins of the road, turning every fifty yards."[70] Then

came the scraper, "a slightly curved, broad board, edged with iron, and a long handle attached, which upon being elevated by the person who had the guidance of the machine, penetrated the loose earth, and scooped itself full, when, again being depressed, the load was moved by a yoke of oxen to that part of the road which required repairs."[71]

When this procedure was not followed by a roller, the result was described by a traveler as "road-destroying" rather than road-mending. When a road-builder of 1832 declared, "I've been at work fixing the road till sun-down, and making it as easy for you as I could by throwing dirt on it," the beneficiary of the labor noted sourly to himself, "we could scarcely move two miles an hour through this marsh of his creation."[72]

The author of *The New-Hampshire Highway Surveyor's Account Book* noted in 1855 that the state's roads were not then macadamized or paved with sharp, broken stones and rolled. Rather, "the common gravel, with a mixture of marl [clay soil] answers probably a better purpose than anything else for a road. When once firmly pressed down and made smooth, it is unequalled in hardness and durability. It absorbs very little water from frequent rains . . . the small stones are soon crushed, and the whole mass in a short time becomes exceedingly compact and solid."[73] A hard road of this kind was its own reward, since animals could pull their loads more easily on such a surface and draft animals moving without strain did not gouge the road with their hooves.

Yet such roads required vigilance, especially in New Hampshire where frost constantly brings stones to the surface. A maintenance agreement for the Third Turnpike required that "the road be kept clear of loose stones, and large ones removed where they are obstructive to the traveller, the water kept from running in the travelled way: holes and gullies *in* and *by* the sides of the road to be filled so as that the road shall keep its present width, and travelling [made] safe for carriages by day or night."[74]

One of the great hazards to a gravel road was the rutting or slicing of the surface by narrow iron tires, especially on heavily loaded vehicles. Timothy Dwight complained in 1795, "The track or rut formed by the wheels of these heavy laden wains is very deep, and becomes not only inconvenient, but dangerous to carriages of a shorter axle. We struggled with these troublesome roads for some time before we reluctantly gave up the remainder of our proposed journey."[75] In 1803, the directors of the First Turnpike encouraged the use of wide tires when they voted to allow "all carts, waggons and other carriages of burden with eight inch wide felloes [rims] on their wheels to run toll free over the Turnpike until July 1, 1804 and at half toll for five years thereafter."[76] The advantages of proportioning felloe width to vehicle weight eventually became so well understood that it was applied to all of New Hampshire's roads. A law of 1899 required that all wagons carrying from two to four tons should have felloes at least four inches wide; from four

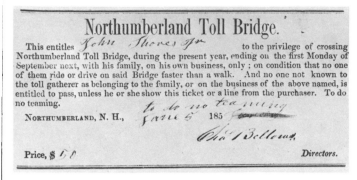

Pass, Northumberland Toll Bridge, Northumberland, N.H., circa 1855. Many turnpike and bridge corporations offered one-year passes, like this one costing $50, to those who traveled a route frequently.

NHHS Collections   Photographer, Ernest Gould

The Great Falls of the Connecticut River at Walpole, *N.H., 1791, ink on paper, by John Trumbull. Believed to be the only view of Enoch Hale's first bridge of 1785, this sketch shows the daring use of cantilevered struts to support the stringers which carried the road surface.*

Courtesy, Charles Allen Munn Collection, Fordham University Library   Photograph courtesy of the Frick Art Reference Library

to six tons, five inches wide; and more than six tons, six inches wide.[77]

Winter travel, though appreciated for ease and speed of hauling, required much labor on the part of the turnpike corporations. The Third Turnpike was typical of all companies in requiring its crews "after the falling or drifting of great snows, immediately to make a passable way through the same." The ledger of the First Turnpike has many entries for "shoveling" and "breaking the Road with two hands and Cattle." Drifts could often be "broken out" sufficient for sleighs simply by driving teams of horses or oxen through the snow. Sometimes, however, snowplows were used. Although Belknap had described such a device in 1792, the "turnpike snowplow" was reputed to be the invention of Deacon Amos Pettingill of Salisbury sometime after 1800. "There are those still living [in 1881] who can remember him with a string of 30 to 40 yoke of steers and oxen cutting a good road 15 feet wide through the snow drifts for miles."[78] Since bare ground could be as great a' barrier to winter travel as drifts, the Third Turnpike required its road surface "to be covered where the snow is blown off."

Streams were one of the great barriers to rapid turnpike travel. The Connecticut, Merrimack, and Piscataqua rivers threw formidable barriers in the way of long-distance commerce. No large-scale network of roads could be considered successful until bridges were erected. Due to the ingenuity of several New Hampshire natives, some of the great bridges of the turnpike era, remarkable engineering monuments of the early Republic, were erected across these rivers.

The first of these noteworthy spans preceded the turnpike era. In 1783, the legislature passed a law giving Enoch Hale of Rindge "the liberty and privilege of building and keeping a bridge over Connecticut River at the great falls, called Bellows Falls, in or near the town of Walpole," and giving Hale the exclusive right to collect tolls from travelers "either by themselves or with horses, Carriages, cattle

or creatures of any kind, or any other thing."[79] Opened in 1785, Hale's bridge was the first span across the Connecticut. It took advantage of a high rock outcrop near the center of the stream to provide a central pier that was safe from all but the highest floods. The bridge stood until 1797, when it was replaced by another of similar design.

The structure of Hale's bridge was remarkable for pushing a known technology beyond its accepted limits. Considered while under construction to be a foolhardy experiment, the bridge was essentially a "string bridge." As on the narrower spans traditionally built in New Hampshire, the weight of the structure and its traffic was borne by four parallel stringers extending from one point of support to another. In this case, however, the stringers are said to have been a fully ninety-eight feet long between piers, and to have been composed of timbers spliced end-to-end rather than single pieces of wood. To support the great spans, each stringer was braced from beneath by diagonals which extended upward from the bases of the abutments and the pier, thus greatly shortening the unsupported length of the floor beams of the bridge. The total length of Hale's bridge, from shore to shore, was 365 feet.[80] This bridge and its successor were of such economic importance that the Third New Hampshire Turnpike and the Green Mountain Turnpike of Vermont were directed to this critical river crossing.

New Hampshire's second long river bridge was likewise a stringer span. A law of June 1792, gave tavernkeeper Robert MacGregor of Goffstown and others (many of whom were understandably merchants from Portsmouth) the right to incorporate themselves as the "Proprietors of the Amoskeig Bridge" and to span the Merrimack below

Bridge at Bellows Falls with Mr. Tucker's House from above the Fall, *circa 1810, ink and watercolor on paper, anonymous. This sketch shows the similarity of construction between Enoch Hale's first bridge and a second built to replace it after 1797. At the left is the Walpole Bridge Hotel, built about 1799 by Frederick William Geyer, second owner of the Bellows Falls bridge, and later owned by his son-in-law Nathaniel Tucker.*

Courtesy, Special Collections, University of Vermont Library

Amoskeag Falls. An announcement of the opening of the bridge in the *New-Hampshire Gazette* in October 1792, pointed out that construction had begun on August 3, "at which time the timber was growing, and the rocks [for the piers] dispersed in the river," and that the work had been completed in the remarkably short time of fifty-seven days. The notice described a structure which differed little in engineering principles from Hale's bridge. The bridge was

> 556 feet in length, is supported by 5 piers and an abutment [*sic*] on each side—the piers are 60 feet in length and 80 in width—the outside [of the piers] made of hewn timber, and filled with rocks—a brace extends 20 feet from the upper end of the pier, making the whole length 80 feet at the bottom—the farthest distance between piers is 80 feet—the top of the bridge is 30 feet from the bottom of the river—about 2,000 tuns [*sic*] of timber were used in constructing the wood work.[81]

In the years before New Hampshire's turnpike system developed, the Amoskeag Bridge provided a strategic junction; a 1795 advertisement for MacGregor's tavern described the location as "on the intersection of two large roads; the one leading from Coos to Boston, the other from Hale's Bridge to Portsmouth, Haverhill, Andover, &c."[82]

The first New Hampshire bridge to demonstrate a more advanced technology was the "Great Arch of the Piscataqua," built in 1794. The arch was but a part of a pile bridge which extended a total length of 2,362 feet from Fox Point in Newington to Goat Island near the outlet of Great Bay, and then to Cedar Point in Durham. The arch itself was a true truss, in which the timbers are joined at their ends into triangular panels. Each timber is thus subjected to longitudinal stresses of compression or tension, rather than to the bending stresses of the beams in a common string bridge. Such a structure can span a great distance and carry great weight; in fact, the dead weight of the 244-foot arch,

View of the Bridge over the Piscataqua . . ., 1797, ink on paper, by Robert Gilmor. *The only known view of the "Great Arch of the Piscataqua," this sketch, made from the Newington shore, conveys an impression of the ponderous weight of the arch and the length of the pile sections of the bridge. The Piscataqua Bridge Tavern is seen on Goat Island, to the left of the arch.*
Courtesy, The Trustees of the Boston Public Library   Photographers, Geoffrey Stein Studio, Inc.

between Rock Island in Newington and Goat Island near the center of the channel, would have been so great as to render its live loads insignificant by comparison. It was reported that the entire bridge, including the pile sections, consumed ten million pounds of timber.[83]

The building of trusses had long been familiar to New England carpenters, who used such structures to roof large buildings such as meetinghouses. The problem of advancing this technology to solve the far greater challenge of spanning rivers occupied the minds of many practical men during the late 1700s and early 1800s. Lebbeus Gordon of Salem, New Hampshire, was among those who approached the proprietors of Piscataqua Bridge with a proposal for an arched truss. His design was described as

> a MODEL of a large Arch . . . 300 feet in Length . . . made to answer without Mortis, Trunel or Iron, and can be repaired without Shores, or hindering the passing, by taking any stick or number of sticks out from one to fifty—the whole Arch may be repaired in like manner.[84]

Gordon's model was reported to have been "well approved of by the Directors of Piscataqua Bridge," and Timothy Dwight asserted that it "was almost entirely followed in the construction."[85] But most accounts of the completed arch agree that its designer was Timothy Palmer of Newburyport. In 1792, Palmer had built a bridge with two arched-truss spans between Newbury and Salisbury, Massachusetts. Palmer designed the triple-arched bridge at Haverhill, Massachusetts, built simultaneously with the Piscataqua Bridge, and in 1797, received a United States patent for "improvements in bridge construction." Dwight recorded an experiment that proved the remarkable strength of Palmer's trusses:

> Six gentlemen placed themselves together upon an exact model of one of the arches, ten feet in length; in which the largest pieces of timber were half an inch square, and the rest smaller in proportion. Yet not the least injury was done to the model. Of this fact I was a witness; and was informed by the gentlemen present, that eleven persons, a few days before, stood together on the same model, with no other effect, than compacting it more firmly together. The eleven were supposed to weigh at least 1600 pounds.[86]

Brass seal used by the Proprietors of the Cornish Bridge, circa 1796. The design on this seal resembles a stone bridge, but may actually depict the first Cornish Bridge, built with the wooden arched truss designed by Timothy Palmer.
NHHS Collections   Photographer, Bill Finney

Palmer's designs proved to be the means of bridging the Connecticut River as well as the Piscataqua and Merrimack. In 1796, his arched truss was used in the White River Falls Bridge, between Hanover and Norwich, Vermont, and in the Cornish-Windsor Bridge. Perhaps due to inexpert workmanship, the former collapsed from its own weight without warning eight years after being opened to traffic.

New Hampshire produced many skilled bridge builders, but one, in particular, combined engineering theory with

Photograph, stone arched bridge at Fuller's Tannery on the Second New Hampshire Turnpike, Hillsborough Lower Village, N.H. More than any other region in New Hampshire, Hillsborough County is characterized by arched bridges constructed of granite blocks laid without mortar. Many of them use two arches to span the stream; this photograph, made in 1936, shows one span of such a double-arched bridge.

Courtesy, Historic American Buildings Survey, Library of Congress   Photographer, L. C. Durette

simplicity of design. In 1830, Colonel Stephen H. Long, a native of Hopkinton, a graduate of Dartmouth, and an officer in the United States Topographical Engineers, patented a truss which lent itself to mathematical analysis and thus to modern methods of bridge construction. Growing knowledge of engineering mechanics during the nineteenth century allowed trained engineers to calculate the stresses in bridge members under given loading conditions, and thus to proportion trusses to accommodate pre-established design loads. Long's all-wood bridge truss was later superseded by a comparable design by William Howe of Massachusetts, in which the truss members subjected to tension were composed of iron or steel rods rather than wood. Both of these trusses possessed straight chords (top and bottom members), and thus allowed a level roadway like that of the simple stringer bridge, instead of the arched surface of Palmer's trusses.

Yet for New Hampshire's many self-trained bridge builders who substituted practical intuition for formal training in engineering, other truss designs were preferred to Long's and Howe's. In 1817, Theodore Burr of Massachusetts patented a bridge which combined a paneled truss with an arch of hewn timber. Burr's design combined the advantages of a level roadway with the proven strength of the wooden arch. In 1820 and 1835, the architect Ithiel

Town of Connecticut patented designs for lattice trusses, in which the web of the bridge was composed of a closely-spaced diagonal grid of planks or timbers which were merely pinned together. Town's truss, in particular, became a favorite of New Hampshire bridge builders, and was often reinforced either initially or after construction with arches of laminated planks. Several New Hampshire builders used similar arch-and-truss combinations, which generally proved successful for the limited highway loads of the nineteenth century. It troubled no one at the time that these combinations of two structural systems were not susceptible to mathematical analysis by the relatively unsophisticated methods known to nineteenth-century engineers. The bridges worked and, when protected by roofs and wall sheathing to keep the trusses dry, they lasted indefinitely. Such spans soon permitted the secure bridging of streams both on the turnpike system and on town-owned local roads.

Even as New Hampshire's system of turnpikes and bridges was developing, other visionary planners were proposing an alternative method of transportation. The Piscataqua River system, although running through a limited geographical region, had proven to be a resource of incalculable value to transportation since the 1600s. Both the Merrimack and Connecticut rivers had likewise pro-

Wooden model of Colonel Stephen H. Long's bridge, circa 1840. Used to demonstrate Long's bridge patent to prospective builders, this model shows the simple yet effective design developed by the inventor and mathematician from Hopkinton, N.H.

Courtesy, New Hampshire Antiquarian Society
   Photographer, Bill Finney

Photograph, repairs to the Ledyard Bridge between Hanover, N.H., and Norwich, Vermont, 1918. Students in the carpentry course of the Dartmouth College Training Detachment gained practical experience by replanking the floor of the Ledyard Bridge, a Town lattice truss, at the end of World War I.

Courtesy, Dartmouth College Library

Lithograph (detail), City of Concord, N.H. From the High Bluff About 80 Rods North East of the Free Bridge, *circa 1855, John H. Bufford after Henry P. Moore. Concord's Free Bridge, the first to span the river at this site, was built in 1839 as an alternative to the toll bridges at the northern and southern ends of town. In 1849-50, this covered truss bridge replaced a stringer bridge at the same location. The coach approaching the bridge is thought to have been the Pittsfield stage.*

NHHS Collections   Photographer, Ernest Gould

View of Samuel Blodget house and Amoskeag Canal, 1881, watercolor on paper, by Henry Walker Herrick. Painted from sketches made by the artist when the Blodget house still stood, this view recalls the early nineteenth century when the Blodget Canal first opened the upper Merrimack River to navigation.

Courtesy, Manchester Historic Association   Photographer, Ernest Gould

vided cheap transportation of logs and mast timbers. Both rivers, however, were obstructed by long and dangerous falls or rapids which made navigation by raft or boat risky at best, and impractical for heavy or steady traffic. Beginning in the last decade of the eighteenth century, a series of laws authorized attempts to bypass the most treacherous falls on the Merrimack and Connecticut rivers by locks and canals. These schemes, in turn, gave rise to still more ambitious plans for overland canals to connect New Hampshire's largest rivers and lakes. While the great canals were never built, New Hampshire's river canals eventually exerted a strong influence on the movement of goods to and from the regions to the south.

River canals, though short, often posed engineering problems that were almost too great for the technology of the day. The difficulty of finishing the Bellows Falls Canal, at Hale's bridge on the Connecticut River, demonstrates the perils that faced those who risked their capital in the hope of collecting tolls from river traffic. This canal was chartered by Vermont in 1791 and by New Hampshire in 1792, and was said to be the first navigation canal in the United States. Work consumed four years, from 1794 to 1798, and the contractors faced floods which swept away their dams; a ledge of granite which had to be channeled by blasting and which in places was too hard to be drilled for gunpowder; quicksand; and underwater obstacles which had to be blasted (using tin tubes to keep the powder dry) or excavated.[87]

Similar difficulties beset Samuel Blodget of Derryfield when he attempted, beginning in 1794 with his own funds and then with a corporation chartered in 1798, to bypass Amoskeag Falls and thus to connect the upper Merrimack with the Middlesex Canal and Boston. In 1803, seeking an extension of the lottery that had been authorized to support the construction, the seventy-nine-year-old Blodget showed the determination that had nearly brought the project to completion but had consumed his personal fortune in the process:

It is very painful indeed to me, to reflect on ten years of ardent exertion, at this stage of life, sparing no pains in my power, with the utmost stretch of invention, to finish this Canal, the expense of sixty thousand Dollars having already been devoted to it, and the Canal not yet completed. Many are the misfortunes and embarrassments which have unavoidably fallen to my lot, in the course of this great work; but neither of these, nor the addition of old age, shall deter me from persevering in the laudable undertaking, so long as kind Providence indulges me with those powers and faculties which I am now possessed of: For although I cannot expect to reap any advantage myself by this Canal; yet I have the pleasing hope, that the great public, and my heirs, may derive important benefits from it.[88]

A report of two years later, when the canal was operable if still not complete, showed that in 1805, the canal had conveyed over a million feet of pine and oak boards and planks, 15,250 clapboards, 343,500 shingles, 152,180 staves, and many other forest products totaling nearly 4,000 tons. Urging support for completion of the locks, the report made an appeal to the livestock market in Boston. By transporting cattle by water from the "great and goodly country" above the falls, the report claimed, the creatures would arrive at market "plump and healthy, unhurt by sweating, not overheated by driving, free from a fever, and fit for slaughter at their arrival, with a saving of 91,000 dollars!"[89]

Eventually, this and other enterprises did succeed. With the bypassing of Hooksett Falls (authorized in 1794), Garvin's Falls, and Turkey River Falls (authorized in 1808), Concord was connected by water with Boston by way of the Middlesex Canal in Massachusetts. Thus, all those roads and turnpikes which converged on Concord were given a water outlet, as well as land routes, to the great Boston market. With similar improvements, the Connecticut River likewise became a navigable waterway from New Hampshire southward.

Portsmouth, meanwhile, suffered the same exclusion because of the canals that it had from most of the turnpikes. Samuel Morey and others proposed an overland canal between the Piscataqua River and Lake Winnipesaukee (with an extension to Squam Lake) in 1793. The same idea was reintroduced several times, and a route actually surveyed, with the idea that the wealth of the lakes, at least, might be channeled to New Hampshire's port instead of to Boston. But topography conspired against the seacoast, and New Hampshire's land and water routes continued to lead southward in defiance of the plans and hopes of Portsmouth interests from colonial times onward.

Copper seal used by the Proprietors of the Bow Canal Corporation, 1808. Built to bypass Garvin's Falls and Turkey River Falls, the Bow Canal opened the Merrimack River to navigation as far north as Concord. The seal shows a canal boat descending the locks at one of the most treacherous rapids on the river.

NHHS Collections   Photographer, Bill Finney

Pencil drawing, Dublin, N.H., 1846-49, by Maria E. Perry. New Hampshire's hilly terrain was evident even in town centers. This drawing shows an attempt to cut away one hillock, below the upper meetinghouse; ledges near the surface often made such excavation impossible. The view also shows the open, cultivated landscape that travelers welcomed after "anxious" hours of travel through uninhabited forests.

NHHS Collections   Photographer, Bill Finney

TRAVEL CONDITIONS

CHAPTER 4

DESPITE THE TIME, expense, and labor devoted to roadbuilding, highway conditions in early New Hampshire could vary widely. Travelers frequently noted in their diaries, letters, and travel accounts, the condition of the roads and the problems they encountered on their journeys. The hills and mountains characteristic of New Hampshire's terrain created special difficulties. In 1793, a Massachusetts resident described Governor's Hill near Rindge as "terrible to the Traveller."[1] In another part of Cheshire County, early roads forced settlers in Limerick (now Stoddard) to "ascend With panting & Descend with Trembling the Mighty Loft of Rol[l]ston[e]" Mountain, "whose Height Seemed almost to Reach the Clouds."[2] Whenever possible, visitors to New Hampshire would take alternate routes to avoid "the long hills, frequently above a mile in the ascent only."[3] Some of the difficulties caused by the mountainous terrain are vividly recalled by a wagon passenger in Vermont around 1810:

> The road ran either through swamps, or over high, stony, almost perpendicular hills, which we had to walk up in order to lighten the vehicle as much as possible, and which we preferred to walk down, because our driver, saying he wanted to "make up for los' time," whenever he gained the top of an ascent would give his horses the whip and gallop them headlong to the bottom, to the imminent peril of every neck concerned.[4]

At one location on the earliest road through Crawford Notch, the incline was "so steep that it was necessary to draw horses and wagons up with ropes."[5]

Many obstacles delayed early travelers on the road, including mud, ruts, "pitchholes," tree stumps, stones, and windfallen trees. One traveler noted that these inconveniences multiplied in relatively uninhabited areas, where the roads passed through forests rather than open fields:

> Whenever [trees] are left near the path, they cover it with a continual shade, and prevent the exhalation of the moisture. . . . The trees which have grown near the path shoot their roots into it and across it, both on the surface and beneath. . . . When [a horse] sinks into a spot of deep and stiff mire, he sometimes steps partly on the root hidden by the earth, and is in danger of falling. . . . At other times, he steps immediately by the side of the root, and when he attempts to take the next step, is exposed to falling by striking his hoof against it.[6]

Log causeways, known as "ribbed" or "corduroy" roads, often facilitated the crossing of swampy areas, but "furnish[ed] at best a very imperfect footing."[7] One traveler described his coach as passing "with rapid vaults from one [log] to another . . . the most unpleasant motion I ever felt."[8] The poor condition of New Hampshire's "causeys," moreover, resulted in their being dreaded by at least one visitor "more . . . than any other inconvenience attending our journey."[9]

Vast networks of rivers, streams, and brooks, throughout the hills and mountains that characterize much of New Hampshire's terrain, presented additional difficulties and dangers to early travelers. One group, journeying from Dover to Hanover in 1774, crossed the Contoocook River three times in an hour and later the same day crossed the Souhegan the same number of times.[10] In 1809, another visitor calculated that, in order to circle the base of the White Mountains, it would be necessary to ford eight large rivers.[11]

Until the early nineteenth century, bridges and ferries were not common, and the few that existed, more often than not, needed repair. Even when not neglected, bridges made of logs, like the causeways, sometimes presented dangerously slippery surfaces.

In the eighteenth century, the usual means of crossing all but the largest rivers was by fording. Travelers on horseback frequently described fords as "difficult" and "anxious," sometimes because of the nature of the stones that covered the bottom and, at other times, because of the swiftness of the current or the depth of the water ("so deep as nearly to reach our stirrups"). Around 1800, one rider records crossing, at different times, the Saco, the Ammonoosuc, and the Connecticut rivers "at a ford."[12] If a river, such as the "Great Ossapy" in 1784, was "not fordable," it could be crossed "by swimming [the] horses after a canoe," which carried the riders, saddles, and saddlebags.[13]

During this early period, most fording was done by horseback or on foot since very few elaborate vehicles were in use at this time on the roads of New Hampshire. It was

Engraving, Mount Washington, and the White Hills (From Near Crawford's), *published 1838, engraved by S. T. Davies after sketch by William Henry Bartlett, 1836-38. Throughout the nineteenth century, the White Mountain region remained a largely unchanged wilderness, crossed by primitive roads such as those found a century earlier in the southern parts of New Hampshire. The stringer bridge in the foreground appears to have been constructed wholly of logs from the spruce trees native to the hills.*

NHHS Collections   Photographer, Bill Finney

Fording the Saco River, Conway, N.H., *oil on canvas, by Alvan Fisher (1792-1863). Broad, shallow rivers with low banks, prone to flooding during storms and spring freshets, were difficult to bridge and had to be crossed by fording. Dating from the mid-nineteenth century, this view shows several women in the party of travelers.*

Courtesy, Indiana University Art Museum   Photographers, Michael Cavanagh and Kevin Montague

Photograph of chaise used in the Stark family of Dunbarton and Pembroke, N.H., early 19th century, with history of having carried Lafayette; photographed circa 1900; chaise now owned by the Shelburne Museum, Shelburne, Vermont. The chaise was ideal as the first passenger vehicle to appear on New Hampshire highways; its rugged construction and two high wheels were well suited for traveling early roads flawed by ruts, stones, holes, and stumps. This side view of the Stark chaise shows its cantilevered wooden frame which acted as a spring to absorb much of the shock from rough roads.

NHHS Collections

Photographers, Halliday Historic Photograph Company

not unusual for two people, or a family, to ride a single horse. The most common vehicle in the eighteenth century was the utilitarian two-wheeled cart, used primarily for agricultural purposes and for the transport of goods to and from market. Often referred to as simply "my wheels," these rudimentary vehicles were commonly shared with neighbors, who paid for their use in goods and services. Records from various communities indicate that the light four-wheeled wagon did not begin to rival the two-wheeled cart for common use until after 1800.[14]

The earliest privately owned passenger vehicle common on New Hampshire roadways was also of the two-wheeled type, known as the chair, chaise, or shay. In 1740, the famous evangelist Reverend George Whitefield drove nine miles in a chaise from Newbury to Hampton—possibly the earliest written reference to such a vehicle in New Hampshire.[15] As early as 1759, Portsmouth boasted its own chaise-maker.[16] The ownership of a chaise was such a significant event in a town that the name of the first person to purchase one was often recorded in the town's first published history. In a major inland settlement like Concord, the first chaise appeared in town during the late 1740s; yet many smaller towns have no record of the introduction of these vehicles until the first decade of the nineteenth century.[17] Even then, only a small percentage of New Hampshire's population owned a passenger vehicle. Of the 1,316 resi-

Engraved portrait of Estwick Evans, frontispiece of Evans' A Pedestrious Tour (Concord, N.H., 1819), engraved by Abel Bowen. Travel by foot was an important means of transportation, yet few were as well prepared to withstand its hardships as this pedestrian. When Portsmouth lawyer Estwick Evans left Hopkinton, N.H., on foot for the West on February 2, 1818, he outfitted himself in a protective buffalo-skin suit and deer-skin moccasins.

NHHS Collections   Photographer, Ernest Gould

dents of the flourishing town of Bath in 1810, only eleven households paid taxes for owning a chaise.[18]

Most New Hampshire residents in the late eighteenth and early nineteenth centuries relied for their transportation on a combination of public stages, borrowed vehicles, and their own two feet. Travel by foot was by no means limited to brief journeys. The notorious criminal Henry Tufts hiked at different times from his home in Lee to both Vermont and to Connecticut.[19] A young Portsmouth resident

Stipple engraving, Coaching Scene, 1820-25, by Moody Morse Peabody for Simeon Ide, Windsor, Vermont; produced from a copperplate now in the New Hampshire Historical Society collections. Engraved by a Peterborough, N.H., native, this scene shows the popular oval coach body that preceded the flat-roofed Concord coach. Lighter and smaller than the later vehicles, these early coaches were nevertheless far more comfortable than their cumbersome wagon-like predecessors.

Courtesy, Vermont Historical Society

set out in 1818 in the middle of winter on a "pedestrious tour of four thousand miles through the western states and territories."[20] One Merrimack girl never forgot two young women who passed through town in the 1830s on a long trek from Charlestown, Massachusetts, to Montreal after their convent was destroyed by fire; "there [sic] shoes and the bottom of there dresses were all wet and muddy."[21] And, in a lighter vein, as late as 1839, a pedestrian refused the offer of a ride in a New Hampshire stage, saying "he couldn't stop to ride, he was in a hurry."[22]

Travelers frequently described the stage vehicles they rode in. European visitors, in the late eighteenth and early nineteenth centuries, consistently noted the lightness and openness of the American vehicles: "the sides are not pannelled [sic], but open, and have pieces of leather, like curtains, which serve as weather-screens, and are let down and rolled up at pleasure."[23] The vehicles described were of a type that predated the more luxurious coach that spread the name of Concord, New Hampshire, around the world in the later part of the nineteenth century. The early vehicles, technically stage wagons rather than coaches, did not accommodate outside passengers, except sometimes on the driver's seat; the luggage was carried at the rear; the roof was supported by slender columns; and there were usually no side doors. One visitor recalled the stage which traveled up and down the Connecticut Valley around 1800:

Many a time have I clambered in, just back of the posteriors of the hind horses, at the no small risk of feeling the momentum of the quadrupeds' hoofs; and being well entered, my next business was to crawl back over the lumber, bags of oats, kegs, jugs, the mail, newspapers, to be distributed along the road, and whatever else the driver saw fit to transport, to a seat, if I was so lucky as to find one.

The same writer later contrasted this "clumsy, wagon-like" vehicle with the Connecticut Valley "Telegraph" stage of 1838. Probably by this time a fully developed Concord-type coach, equipped with side doors, sturdy roof, luxurious upholstery, and thoroughbrace supports, the Telegraph stage proved "exceedingly well adapted to [offer] forgetfulness to the drowsy traveller."[24]

In the past as now, speed depended on the means of transportation. Travelers often kept a log of the distances they had covered, as well as their hours of departure, arrival, and refreshment. Pedestrians averaged fourteen to eighteen miles per day.[25] This did not vary greatly whether in the cold of winter or the heat of summer. In 1785, Henry Tufts, spurred on most likely by criminal intentions, traveled "on foot" 120 miles from Lee, New Hampshire, to Rockingham, Vermont, in only four days.[26]

Despite Tuft's abilities as a pedestrian, he would frequently attempt to ease his journey by stealing a horse. A

VIEW OF WORKS.

Mail Stage Coach.
Omnibus.
Stage Coach.

Hack Wagon.
Australian Wagon.
California Wagon.

Express Wagon.
Large Express Wagon.
Plantation Wagon.

Concord Wagon.
Top Buggie Wagon.
York Wagon.

Broadside, advertising the products of Joseph Stephens & Edward A. Abbot, Concord, N.H., circa 1860, lithographed by Lodowick H. Bradford & Co. This broadside illustrates the wide range of specialized vehicles made in the latter part of the nineteenth century by one of the leading American manufacturers. At the upper right and left are two sizes of the famous Concord stagecoach, with its characteristic body suspended on leather thoroughbraces hung from steel springs.

NHHS Collections   Photographer, Bill Finney

horse could easily double the expected rate of travel. In the 1770s and 1780s, the Reverend Jeremy Belknap averaged thirty-five miles a day on two lengthy trips by horseback to the White Mountains and Hanover.[27]

As far as speed was concerned, traveling by vehicle was not necessarily an advantage. In 1761, a stagecoach took two days to travel the forty-five miles from Portsmouth to Boston.[28] And Henry Tufts seemed amazed that "two whole weeks were consumed" in a journey with his female companion by horse and cart from Stratham, New Hampshire, to Fairfield, Maine—a distance only ten miles greater than he had covered by foot in a mere four days.[29]

By 1797, the Portsmouth-to-Boston stage completed the trip without an overnight stop, requiring, however, an exhausting fifteen hours on the road.[30] The rate of travel was calculated to be just "under five miles an hour."[31] One visitor to the state in 1832 experienced a "fatiguing and rough journey of eighteen hours" in a coach from Concord to Conway, averaging four miles an hour.[32] By the early nineteenth century, a general speed of five miles an hour was the best that could be anticipated even on a good road.[33] In Portsmouth, beginning in 1771, anyone exceeding that speed was liable to a sentence of either forty-eight hours in prison or two hours in the stocks.[34]

By the 1820s and 1830s, improvements in vehicles and roads enabled travelers to proceed at what was then considered an "uncommon speed." In 1823, a New York stagecoach set what was presumably a world record of almost eleven miles an hour. During one stretch of the nine-hour trip from Utica to Albany, this coach covered sixteen miles in forty-five minutes.[35] On a routine basis, however, even the Telegraph stage running between Hartford and Bellows Falls in the late 1830s—allegedly conveyed at a "rapid" rate by "swift and sure footed horses"—still averaged less than seven miles an hour.[36]

Because of the restricted speeds of the eighteenth and early nineteenth centuries, all travelers—whether pedestrians, horseback riders, or stage passengers—found it necessary to rise extremely early in order to embark on a long day of travel. Stagecoaches set out from each terminus of their route as early as three o'clock in the morning.[37] One traveler, staying overnight at a stage inn in Concord in 1821, vividly recorded that "the driver roused us at four; the coach was tightly closed to exclude the cold air; and six of us, being shut in utter darkness, felt ourselves whirling upon the southern turnpike."[38] It was not uncommon to travel several miles before stopping at a tavern for breakfast.

The driver's goal was to reach the day's destination before "candle-light." Very little traveling took place in the evening, and the anxiety of travelers increased markedly as dusk approached.[39] There were good reasons for anxiety: poor nighttime visibility, the often sparsely settled and hilly terrain, the frequency of accidents and breakdowns, the changeable and extreme New England weather, poor road conditions, and inadequate directional markers. In 1784, a Spanish traveler, who had decided to continue his journey from Hampton Falls to Portsmouth even though it was almost dark, discovered, when the horses suddenly stopped and his "servant jumped to the ground," that their "coach was on the edge of a very deep hole and that only by the space of half a foot had the wheel not fallen in with all of us turned upside down."[40]

Early vehicles do not appear to have been routinely equipped with lamps. Even in an unusual journey undertaken "wholly in the night" from Hanover to Haverhill in 1828, a passenger described the stage as "without lanterns."[41] Ten years later, the driver of another vehicle carrying sightseers near Littleton "left the horses to find their own way, as he was unable to see a yard in any direction."[42] Lanterns, when available, required constant care. In one incident in 1832, a series of breakdowns detained the stage from Concord to Conway into the evening. While the "coachman attended to the intricate navigation, he requested [one of the passengers] to 'fix' the lamps, the oil and wick being of so bad a quality as to fully occupy [the passenger] in trimming and snuffing throughout thirteen most dreary miles."[43]

Traveling far in the evening was too hazardous to risk except for vagabonds and criminals. Henry Tufts deliberately traveled "under the shroud of darkness," "avoiding the glare of day." Nighttime travelers were regarded with suspicion. Probably more than once in Tufts' peripatetic career, local residents "hailed" him and "demanded [his] motives for traveling at that season of night."[44]

Even in the daytime, traveling could be a lonely and anxiety-filled experience. In much of the territory through which any New Hampshire vehicle passed, "the habitations of men," as one traveler commented, were "scattered among the extensive solitudes with a sparing hand."[45] Even between Newburyport and Portsmouth, along what is today one of the most highly developed routes in the state, a visitor found, as late as 1842, "very few farms, & yet fewer human beings. The country seemed a wilderness, animated only by numerous flocks of geese."[46]

This sense of solitude, together with an awareness of the "dangers and horrors of the predominating scenery," frequently left New Hampshire visitors with "anxious eyes and solicitous hearts."[47] Most early travelers looked only with dread on what they saw as the solemnity and gloominess of the forest and mountain, as well as with relief and pleasure on the cultivated field and other signs of man's activity.[48] This attitude was expressed perhaps most eloquently by Timothy Dwight in an account of his trip to the White Mountains in 1797:

In so vast an expansion the eye perceives a prevalence of forest which it regrets, and instinctively demands a wider extent of smiling scenes, and a more general establishment of the cheerful haunts of man. . . . [I am] transported in imagination to that period in which, at a little distance, the hills, and plains, and valleys around me will be stripped of the forests which now majestically and even gloomily overshadow them, and

Photograph of a blacksmith shop in North Chichester, N.H., 1895. This well-finished blacksmith shop, similar to many found at or near taverns, was a gathering place for travelers and local loungers. At left is a hand cart of the type used for the short-distance transportation of goods and craftsmen's tools. The omnibus at the right was used by the party of photographers who took the picture.

NHHS Collections   Photographer, Edward A. Richardson

be measured out into farms enlivened with all the beauties of cultivation. . . . Flocks and herds will frolic over the pasture, and fields will wave with harvests of gold.[49]

The frequency with which vehicles of the day tended to break down or become involved in accidents increased the sense of isolation travelers felt. In 1793, William Bentley's carriage broke down three times in the thirty or so miles between Rindge and Walpole: first the "stud of the right back spring" broke; then, due to a poor repair, the same stud snapped off completely; and finally, a linch-pin from one of the front wheels came out.[50] Another traveler described the repairs when a linch-pin was lost: "There was another [linch-pin] on hand, but the trouble was to raise the coach and put it in. The driver and gentleman took rails from an old fence to lift up the coach; the ladies got out [and the pin was replaced]."[51]

During the course of journeys, both vehicles and horses were dependent on the services of a blacksmith. One smith, located near the Thornton's Ferry tavern, often "would work all night shoeing horses so they would be ready for an early start the next morning."[52]

Accidents were common enough on early New Hampshire roads to warrant one traveler's recording that he had arrived at his day's destination "without any accident."[53]

Horses stumbling, becoming frightened, or falling through neglected bridges, along with poor road conditions in general, were the most common causes of accidents. Mishaps also occurred during difficult fords. When the Reverend William Patten attempted to cross the Lower Ammonoosuc in 1780, his "horse was turned upon his side, apparently by the force of the current. Thrown by surprise and with disadvantage into the water, it was some time before [he] could recover a standing."[54]

Because of the highly sensitive nature of a horse, even what was initially a small incident could develop into a catastrophe, as on the stage route from Portsmouth to Salem, Massachusetts, in 1831:

The stage had advanced a short distance towards Salem, when a dog suddenly sprang over the wall, into the road. This alarmed the horses, and the leaders wheeled round so suddenly, that the coach was instantly overset, and the upper part dashed to peices [sic]. None of the passengers were seriously injured, with the exception of an elderly lady belonging to Portsmouth, whose collar bone was fractured in two places.[55]

Road accidents could result in serious injuries. Early in the nineteenth century, one man refused to allow his daughter to return home by stage from Cambridge, Massachusetts, because "many have been the accidents, many the cripples made by accidents in those vehicles."[56] In fact, many people (including John Stavers himself, the famous Portsmouth tavernkeeper and stage owner) lost their lives when thrown from vehicles.[57]

In the case of less serious accidents and breakdowns, the "inexhaustible good-nature" of both passengers and drivers often impressed visitors. "I never saw any gentleman's temper give way under these accidents. Every one jumps out in a moment and sets to work to help the driver."[58] In 1837, after a wagon ascending a hill near Center Harbor tipped sideways, spilling its passengers on the ground, the driver found himself "sprawling on his back on a terribly sharp eminence of limestone, [yet still] tugged manfully at the reins, and shouted, 'Whoi-ee' as cheerfully as if he had been sitting on a cushion, in his proper place."[59]

In earlier times as now, seasonal conditions frequently caused accidents and aggravated travel difficulties. In the heat of the summer, the main complaint of the traveler, whether passenger or pedestrian, was the dust "most of the way deep and covering us in clouds."[60] Probably because of the openness of early vehicles, rain in any season was a major deterrent to travel. New Hampshire travelers frequently mentioned either that the rain delayed their journey or that it forced them to stay overnight unexpectedly at a tavern.[61] Of course, a change in the weather sometimes overtook travelers who were already underway, far from any hostelry. A traveler in Franconia Notch wrote in 1838, the weather grew "worse every moment; the driver could not keep the seats of the wagon dry any longer . . . and [the sightseers] returned without delay."[62]

In the spring, rain and melting snow caused additional problems for the traveler. It was often impossible to cross swollen rivers at the usual fords.[63] And, pools of mud, such as one in Epping known locally as the "soap mine" in which the wheels of a coach could become mired to the hubs, were springtime hazards.[64]

Surprisingly, although travel could be extremely difficult during the winter months, the weather conditions of that season did not hinder travel as much as mud in the spring or rain in the summer. Winter was, in fact, the season many travelers chose to venture through the remote notches of the White Mountains. As one English visitor described it in 1838: "During the long dreary season of thaw no one comes in sight [but when] the snow is frozen hard . . . trains of loaded sleighs appear in the passes. Traders from many distant points come down with their goods, while the roads are in a state which enables one horse to draw the load of five."[65] Indeed, the ill-fated Willey House was "sometimes . . . uninhabited during the summer season [but] in the winter a family occupied it to keep a fire, lodgings, and a little food, for travelers and wagoners, who might otherwise perish."[66]

Although rain often necessitated delays in travel plans, a certain amount of snow was considered to improve the road surface. As the daughter of a Nashua tavernkeeper

Silhouette of Samuel Ayer Bradley of Fryeburg, Maine, circa 1825, attributed to William James Hubard. The victim of a chaise accident caused by a frightened horse, fifty-year-old Bradley wrote to Concord, N.H., relatives in 1824 that his knee had been dislocated "in a most frightful manner." With the help of five men under his direction, the injured Bradley was able "with [his] own hands, [to] press the knee joint into place." This silhouette illustrates his dependency upon two canes for an unknown length of time after the accident.

NHHS Collections   Photographer, Bill Finney

ON THE ROAD NORTH OF BOSTON

recalled: "Let there be a light snow and every trader hoped and tried to be first in harnessing and breakfasting; so heavy was the travel by wagons that the snow would soon be worn off."[67] About 1808, a Newburyport girl who had been visiting an uncle in Maine for a little over a year, deliberately chose a winter month for her return journey, "taking advantage of good sleighing."[68]

Even a heavy snowstorm did not immobilize travelers completely. Around 1820, one English visitor recorded a winter journey in which a pair of sleighs carried his party from Portland to Portsmouth. "Sometimes the bells of our companion suddenly ceased, or literally 'dropt;' for, on looking behind, we [would] find that their horse had partially disappeared,—his chin resting on a snow drift, and his countenance exhibiting a most piteous expression of helplessness." At one point, before reaching Portsmouth, the two sleighs "were obliged . . . to have more than twenty men and several oxen to clear [the] way, the drifts on the road being from six to twelve feet deep."[69]

Occasionally, eighteenth-century newspapers noted that travel north beyond a certain point was possible only with snowshoes.[70] But, even at this early period, such a lack of mobility was rare enough to have been newsworthy.

Winter travel, however feasible and necessary, must have been extremely unpleasant at times. In 1828, a woman traveling in New Hampshire's Connecticut Valley, recorded "a bitter cold day, it snowed, it blowed, it rained, and I suffered prodigiously from an abominably open coach."[71] Another traveler criticized the leather curtains found on New England coaches as allowing "the wind [to] penetrate through a hundred small crevices, and with the thermometer below zero, this freedom of circulation is not found to add materially to the pleasures of a journey."[72] It is not surprising that winter travel involved frequent stops at taverns—in the words of one passenger: "to warm us."[73]

Even without the heavy snows of winter, finding one's way about early New Hampshire could prove a definite challenge. Travelers frequently reported having lost their way and having been forced to cover a greater distance as a result. Detailed road maps were unknown. At a tavern in New York State during the American Revolution, some New Hampshire farmers, who were driving cattle to the Continental Army, noticed a French officer examining a map. According to the officer:

They came into my room. I was then busy tracing my route on the map of the country; this map excited their curiosity. They saw there with surprise and satisfaction the places they had passed through. They asked me if they were known in Europe, and if it was there I had bought my maps. On my assuring them that we knew America as well as the countries closer to us, they seemed much pleased; but their joy knew no bounds when they recognized New Hampshire, their country, on my map. They immediately called their companions who were in the next room; and mine was soon filled with the strongest and most robust men I had yet seen in America.[74]

In the eighteenth century, the few available maps were so highly valued, particularly for military purposes, that professional and amateur engravers often copied them in more permanent form onto the powder horns that men carried about the countryside.

Nor were guidebooks common in this country until the early nineteenth century even though as early as 1712, *The Traveller's Guide* to England had listed not only every road in that country, but also all the "backward" and "forward" turnings" to be avoided along each route.[75] Because of the size of the United States, however, early guidebooks, such as those published by John Melish in 1814 and 1816, merely listed the roads between major cities throughout the new nation.[76] Theodore Dwight's *Northern Traveller*, first published in 1825, seems to have been one of the earliest guides to include specific directions for traveling through little-known New Hampshire areas.[77]

Although state law required ten-foot signposts at every public intersection after 1792, they were not always easy to find or interpret.[78] Known as "finger-posts," because of the "hand & finger" engraved or painted on them to indicate directions, they are more colorfully referred to in the records of at least one New Hampshire town as "parsons," because they "always pointed the way and never seemed to go."[79]

Despite the law, signposts often did not properly indicate directions and were not always kept in repair by the towns. One traveler, passing through Plaistow in 1801, "was puzzled by the guide posts directing to the left to Sweat's ferry, without any notice of the great road."[80] Another visitor to New Hampshire and Vermont, described in some detail a series of baffling signs which had twisted or blown in the wind so that they pointed toward either "some subterranean settlement in a coal-pit" or else "from the sublime direction of the letters [to] somewhere in the celestial regions." The same traveler also expressed his disappointment at finding a signpost bearing the name of a town with its distance given, but, "though commonly called a finger-post, [without] either hand or finger pointing one way or the other."[81]

On major highways, regularly spaced milestones were intended to keep the traveler on the main road. Such milestones, appearing sometimes as frequently as every quarter of a mile, marked off the distance to major points along a particular highway. The carved lettering on these stones often referred cryptically to towns by first initial only. Milestones could be both difficult to read and inaccurate. One traveler in Vermont or a nearby section of New Hampshire, after having been obliged to descend from his carriage to interpret a worn milestone, was pleased to find his opinion of these markers confirmed by an earlier visitor who had inscribed the following near where the mileage should have been: "Notice to travellers! No reliance to be placed on the milestones all the way to Burlington, for they *lie*, every one of them!"[82]

In the absence of legible road signs (a frequent occurrence

Stereograph, Henniker, N.H., circa 1875. This view of Proctor Square in Henniker, where four main roads intersect, shows one of the many guideposts erected around 1808 in response to a state law of 1792. The three-story brick house in the background was opened as a summer hotel in the late 1800s under the proprietorship of W. D. Davis, having been transformed by the addition of porches and a cupola.
NHHS Collections

despite the 1792 law), the only time-consuming recourse was to ask directions. A New Hampshire boy, helping his grandfather drive cattle from Francestown to the Merrimack Valley in the 1840s, inquired how he was to know which road to follow. His grandfather's advice, based on years of experience, was: "You have a tongue in your head, keep to the main traveled road."[83]

Travelers, however, quickly learned the wisdom of obtaining directions "before . . . quit[ting] the tavern" in the morning.[84] Directions offered by local residents typically referred to such unique landmarks as "the stone under the apple-tree" and the "house with green blinds."[85] Moreover, the noted combination of humor and taciturnity associated with the Yankee character had developed surprisingly early. In 1808, one traveler was informed: "Yes . . . you are on the right road [to Walpole]; but I reckon you must turn your horse's head or you'll never get there!" Another was advised that he could guess his way to Chesterfield just as he had guessed his informant's name was "Jack."[86]

Guides, often called "pilots," were essential for early

travelers in the White Mountains. More than one tavern-keeper in that area doubled as a tourguide.[87] To prevent catastrophes, piles of stones served as substitutes for more elaborate markers, and the Crawfords at the Notch House frequently sounded a horn to "call the lost ones from the Mountain."[88]

The possibility of getting lost, combined with the potential for accidents, breakdowns, and abrupt weather changes, caused an anxiety in most early New Hampshire travelers that did not subside until the forest had been left behind and evidences of civilization once again sighted. As stated by one visitor, however, the companionship of fellow travelers more than "compensated for the difficulties through which we passed."[89] Travelers by foot and horseback often "fell in company" with others heading the same direction.[90]

Since the number of passengers a stage could carry was flexible, however, companionship could sometimes become a liability rather than a benefit. In 1808, a traveler through New Hampshire in the Boston-to-Burlington stage complained that "upwards of sixteen persons [were] jammed

Guidepost, granite, Wilton, N.H., mid-19th century. Although most towns used wood for their "finger posts" or directional signs, some, like Wilton, chose to use stone. The state law of 1792 required that the mileage shown should indicate the distance "to the most public Place of Resort" in the adjoining town.

Photographer, Bill Finney

Milestone, granite, Pembroke, N.H., 1793. This milestone was erected on Pembroke Street by tavernkeeper David Kimball in the same year as the opening of stage service between Concord, N.H., and Haverhill, Massachusetts; eventually, it served as a marker on the Chester Turnpike when that highway was connected with the old town road. The distances indicated are 19 miles to the Chester meetinghouse, 35 miles to Haverhill, and 6 miles to Concord.

Photographer, Bill Finney

together in the most uncomfortable manner" in a coach that "at the utmost . . . should hold no more than twelve persons."[91] A passenger in the Concord-to-Conway coach some years later chose to sit with the driver "preferring exposure to the rain to being crushed to a mummy."[92]

The sounds of a crowded stagecoach are not difficult to imagine: "fifteen tongues going, at the rate of ten words a second, upon politics, commerce and agriculture."[93] Conversation ranged widely from first-hand accounts of War of 1812 battles to details of British literature.[94] Many of the most memorable discussions centered around politics: in 1808, a Newburyport girl, traveling by stage in New Hampshire, listened with rapt attention as "the conversation turned upon politics," noting that "on the federal side passion seemed to predominate over reason."[95] Although conversation was the primary pastime of the passengers, they also sang "jovial songs," shared jokes, recited poetry, and even, in one instance, pelted pigs with green apples.[96]

Travel companions also shared life stories. As a passenger in the coach from Portsmouth to Portland claimed: "When travelling in a stage coach, nothing is more common than for one traveller to ask another the history of his life, and it is hardly possible to evade answering without incur

ring the displeasure of the whole company. . . . Before we had proceeded one-eighth part of the journey, we knew each other as well as if we had been educated in the same college."[97]

Travelers praised fellow passengers as genteel, intelligent, agreeable, and accomplished.[98] Only rarely were other travelers "unsociable." It was an unusual occasion when a woman traveling from Hanover to Haverhill encountered "a stage full of the most blackguard boatmen that ever handled an oar."[99]

Because highwaymen were not a menace in early New England, it was not necessary to protect the luggage with a special guard.[100] Even though baggage was relatively safe from theft in New Hampshire, stage proprietors still disclaimed any accountability for baggage loss in their advertisements.[101] When Sarah Josepha Hale's luggage was not transferred correctly on her journey from Newport, New Hampshire, to Boston and did not arrive for three days, she published the following advice in her national women's magazine: "The lady who travels in a stage-coach unat-

Photograph of the Cogswell tavern, Hampstead, N.H., 1905. A pump and watering trough stand invitingly at the entrace to this brick tavern's yard. Taverns often provided a convenient water supply to encourage travelers to stop even though towns and country villages maintained some public wells and pumps on or near their roads.

NHHS Collections   Photographers, Halliday Historic Photograph Company

tended should always get out when the stage stops and look after her trunk."[102] It was not until 1869 that a state law levied a fine on any stage driver who recklessly injured a piece of baggage in handling it.[103]

Stage companies generally allowed a certain amount of baggage—approximately fourteen pounds—to be carried on a coach without extra charge.[104] Until the 1820s or 1830s, it was not customary to carry luggage on the top of a vehicle. Instead it was "put below the seats, or tied on behind the stage."[105] Women sometimes held one or more bandboxes, so popular at that time, on their laps.[106] The *Concord Gazette* recorded in 1829 that an exasperated stage driver had just laid down an informal rule: "No lady is allowed to carry more than *seven bandboxes*,—any one having more *can't* go!"[107] When bandboxes were carried on top of the coach, they were in imminent danger of being "smashed" in any accident that occurred.[108]

Travelers on horseback carried their clothing, liquor, and other provisions compactly in leather saddlebags. Newspaper advertisements sometimes described the contents of lost or stolen saddlebags.[109]

Although travelers often carried food with them on a journey, stagecoaches nevertheless made frequent stops to refresh the passengers. One visitor in the mid-1830s claimed to have "stopped at three or four different [taverns] in the course of each day," even in New Hampshire's "most unsettled country."[110] Besides stopping for meals, stagecoaches regularly patronized taverns to warm the passengers in the winter and to cool them during midday in the summer.[111] They also stopped to deliver, pick up, and sort mail.[112] But, it was the needs of the horses that most often dictated the frequency and duration of stops. As one Spanish traveler explained in 1784, after he and his horse simultaneously enjoyed a "very good breakfast" in Greenland: "The latter needed it more than I did."[113]

Before 1858, when the state began to encourage the construction of watering troughs near the highways, travelers often paused at taverns to water, as well as to feed, their horses.[114] While a relay system ensured that stage teams were changed regularly, individual horses were replaced when they tired. In the mid-1830s, when one visitor's "poor steed, Hornet, evinced considerable signs of having been overdriven in the hot weather," his rider did not hesitate to exchange him in Amoskeag for "a short, stout, active galloway, more suited for daily drudgery."[115]

A tall signpost and gaily painted signboard generally

Photograph of original drawing (now lost) showing the main street of Charlestown, N.H., circa 1815. Tavern signs like the one hanging from the tall post in front of Isaac Ely's tavern (later known as the Darrah tavern) were eagerly watched for by travelers hoping for refreshment or accommodation. Several of the dwellings near Charlestown's meetinghouse served as public houses at various times.

Courtesy, South Parish Unitarian Church, Charlestown   Photographer, David S. Putnam

Photograph, ''At Canterbury Shakers,'' Canterbury, N.H., 1895. The use of a coach horn is demonstrated by an excursionist seated on the roof of an omnibus at the Shaker village in Canterbury.

NHHS Collections

helped travelers to identify the tavern from a distance. As soon as the tavern was in view, the stage driver announced the approach of his vehicle by a flourish of sound from the long tin horn he carried. On the state's major rivers, operators of boats and rafts employed a similar horn to announce their approach to the riverfront taverns. In both cases, the voyagers would "blow one blast to let the Landlady [or landlord] know they were coming and one blast for every Man on board, so she [or he] would know how many to cook supper or dinner for."[116]

The New Hampshire tavernkeeper, unlike some described by foreign travelers in America, usually provided an exceptionally warm reception for his guests.[117] A traveler in the White Mountains in 1842 seemed to express some surprise when he recorded that "the landlord always comes down in person to scrape acquaintance."[118] That this instance of a personal welcome was not unique within New Hampshire is confirmed by a traveler's description of a Wakefield innkeeper "whom [the visitors] found at the door of his house, ready, in a polite and gentlemanly manner, to welcome us to his hospitality." The author of these words, a tavernkeeper herself, went on to generalize: "It is pleasant and cheering to find a *home* when the traveler is weary, hungry and thirsty."[119]

Most visitors to New Hampshire were satisfied with the quality of accommodations awaiting them at the local tavern. In 1788, when a French visitor stayed at John Greenleaf's inn in Portsmouth, he "found a neatness and cleanliness rarely met with in France—good beds, pretty wallpaper, substantial and inexpensive food."[120] In 1842, a traveler on a journey to the White Mountains wrote: "This I will say for [the] inns [of New Hampshire], for we have tried [them] in all their degrees, from the village hotel with its tall signpost & its full barroom, to the backwoods stage stopping place with its old barns and narrow rooms, and lonely situations—they are always respectable and neat, and abound in good substantial fare."[121]

Naturally, some taverns developed a better reputation than others. In mid-eighteenth century Portsmouth, word apparently spread among travelers that the Widow Ann Slayton was the landlady who kept "the best tavern for Strangers in town."[122] And, in the upper Connecticut Valley shortly after 1800, an inn, extolled as "better than most of those of which the large towns on the shore can boast," flourished in the beautiful village of Bath.[123]

Nevertheless, visitors did not hesitate to register complaints about what they commonly referred to as "the most inferior sort of tavern." "Mother Morse's" in Dublin was criticized as "a filthy house"; and a stage inn in Portsmouth was called a "dirty scrambling tavern."[124] Crowded quarters and lack of cleanliness were the focus of complaints, although especially in the early days, tavern guests could not afford to be overly critical. Even the wife of Governor John Wentworth, in asking a friend to make arrangements for the couple's lodging during their return from Wolfeboro to Portsmouth in 1770, "desire[d] things only a little

clean—for elegance is not to be found in the Country."[125] European travelers sometimes found it necessary to accept accommodations that did not meet their usual standards. In the resigned view of one such visitor, John Stavers' tavern in Portsmouth was "not the best possible, but there is nothing better in the town."[126]

For those not traveling by coach between regular stage houses, securing overnight accommodations could present a problem. Obtaining lodgings proved especially difficult during court sessions and town meetings.[127] When in Hanover in 1793 to attend the Dartmouth commencement, the Reverend William Bentley of Salem, Massachusetts, recorded that his party "continued our way from House to House, but could not obtain any lodgings till we were below the ferry on the east side of the river in Plainfield, ten miles below the Colleges."[128] In Crawford Notch, even in the middle of winter, lodging could be a problem: during three nights in January 1831, "80 two horse teams passed on, which could not be accommodated" at Crawford's inn.[129]

When a town lacked a licensed tavern, such as Littleton in 1809, travelers were "obliged to seek lodgings at a private house" or else to continue on their journey.[130] Potential tavernkeepers, petitioning for licenses in small New Hampshire towns, sometimes expressed concern that "some travelers have been like to perish in storms the Last winter past" because no tavern existed in a particular location.[131]

The overnight accommodations found at these early taverns lacked the privacy and comfort taken for granted today. Frequently, guests were not only expected to share a room with one or more fellow travelers, but, especially in rural taverns, to share a bed with a stranger. Even in Concord, the seat of state government, a visitor at a stage inn in 1821 described "the necessity of agreeing amongst ourselves for bed-fellows."[132] While guests of distinction might sometimes be assigned a private chamber, the majority of travelers, even if they did have a bed to themselves, were compelled to "submit to be crammed into rooms where there is scarcely sufficient space to walk between the beds."[133]

Generally, the men and women guests slept separately, sometimes in dormitory-like rooms as in one early Merrimack tavern: "There were two large rooms up stairs. One was finished off nicily [sic] where the Lady travelers slept, and the other was unfinished for the men when they put up for the night."[134] Lucy Crawford recalled a variation on this sleeping arrangement in her family's crowded hostelry, where, in the 1820s, men guests "were obliged to stow closely at night, and near the roof, as we had but two small sleeping rooms down stairs, and these were generally occupied by ladies; the gentlemen [went] up stairs, [where they] lay so near each other, that their beds nearly touched."[135]

During the eighteenth and early nineteenth centuries, foreign travelers, unfamiliar with the ancient custom of bundling even though it had originated in Europe, gener-

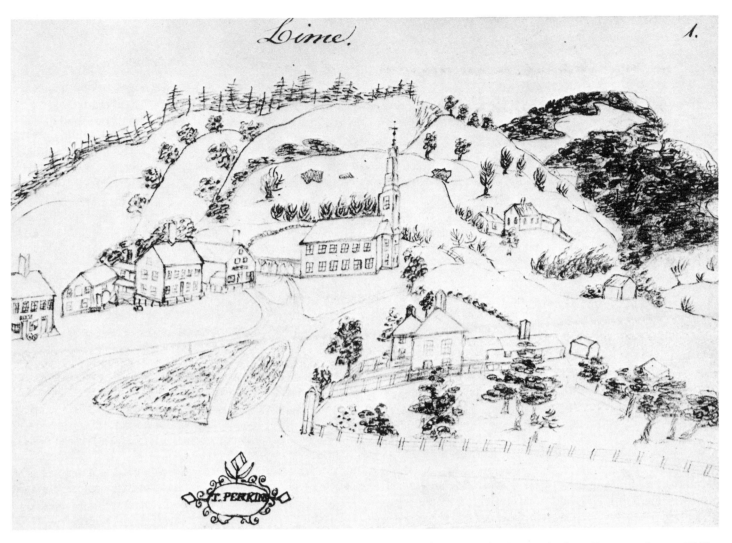

Ink drawing of Lyme, N.H., 1836, by Caroline M. Fitch. Accompanying her father on a business trip from Boston to Lyme, N.H., in 1836, Caroline Fitch sketched her destination at the front of the diary in which she chronicled the adventure. The prominence of the Perkins tavern sign as she drew it in the foreground suggests the importance of taverns to travelers on long, tedious journeys. Thomas Perkins' tavern with its attached stable can be seen at the left.

Courtesy, Old Sturbridge Village   Photographer, Henry E. Peach

ally considered it a curious American practice in which "a man and woman [slept] in the same bed, he with his [knee breeches], and she with her petticoats on; an expedient practised in America on a scarcity of beds, where, on such an occasion, husbands and parents frequently permitted travellers to bundle with their wives and daughters."[136] A courtship ritual as well as a travel expedient, this custom survived in America to a later date than in most parts of Europe. Yet no instance of bundling in a New Hampshire tavern appears to have been recorded. In neighboring Vermont, however, a British soldier during the Revolution was invited to share a bed with the host's sixteen-year-old daughter. After politely refusing to be the first "Britainer" Jemima had "bundled with," the soldier went on to comment that this "custom, along the sea coast, by a continual intercourse among Europeans . . . is in some measure abolished."[137]

As the nineteenth century progressed, the availability of private rooms appeared more frequently in advertisements. Even so, their wording suggests that such accommodations were reserved for the wealthier guests. In 1824, Joseph M. Salter, tavernkeeper at the "sign of General La Fayette" in Wakefield, specified that "Gentlemen and Ladies travelling, may be accommodated with private rooms."[138]

According to reminiscences published in numerous town histories, servants, teamsters, and other less-wealthy travelers were fortunate if they found a bed at all. In the crowded public houses of the time, men, particularly of the lower classes, often expected no better accommodation than to sleep by the fire on the taproom or kitchen floor, wrapped in their coat or in a blanket or buffalo robe brought with them for this purpose. A group of New Hampshire drovers, staying overnight at the same New York tavern as a French army officer during the Revolution, cheerfully gave up their beds to him and his aides, saying that they "would rather sleep on the floor than permit [him to want a bed and] that they were accustomed to it and it would be attended with no inconvenience."[139] Such differences in the quality of accommodations by class or station were, of course, reflected in the prices charged.

Even in the relative comfort of a private chamber, the conveniences provided at an early tavern were few. If the landlord did not offer to "light . . . his guests up-stairs," the latter was expected to "walk to the bar, and solicit the favor of being supplied with a candle."[140] Once in the dimly lit bedchamber, there was little alternative but to retire early, as seems to have been the custom among travelers.[141] The rooms were not only dark but also could be cold. John Parker's tavern in Nashua was typical in that "the bed rooms were not large [and] no fire was furnished even in winter unless ordered."[142]

Other inconveniences also disturbed the comfort and repose of even the most wealthy tavern guests. Daytime disturbances mentioned by travelers included "pigs and fowls [that] enjoyed the freedom of the bar-room" in a Franconia Notch inn; and the tavernkeeper's children, in one case Salisbury's Daniel and Ezekiel Webster, "little boys with dirty faces and snarly hair [who] came to the table and asked me for bread and butter."[143] But, then as now, the most annoying disruptions seemed to occur during the night. The "noise and bustle" for which a public house was noted continued well into the evening. "A numerous company . . . reading the news" disturbed the repose of one Portsmouth visitor to Ann Slayton's tavern in 1744: "Their chit-chat and noise kept me awake 3 hours after I went to bed."[144] Over three-quarters of a century later, a guest at an inn in Concord was similarly annoyed that the "scene of bustle, unprecedented by any thing I had ever met before in a common country town, presented itself till midnight."[145]

More than one weary New Hampshire traveler found his long-anticipated rest interrupted by insects. In 1773, a lodger at a Deerfield tavern recorded in his diary that "being unable to sleep, on account of myriads of fleas, we retired, about midnight, to the barn, and slept unmolested in a bin of clean straw."[146] About the same time, a visitor to Boscawen "lodged at Capt. Gerrish's but slept not, the bed being preoccupied by innumerable vermin."[147] This nuisance was by no means confined to New Hampshire. A French visitor to Philadelphia claimed that "bedbugs harass the entire continent in hot weather."[148]

The need to share beds also hindered the chances of peaceful slumber in an early tavern. According to one foreign visitor: "even while one traveler is asleep, another often enters to share his bed."[149] Around 1780, the infamous ruffian Henry Tufts wrote that even though he was privileged to obtain a "chamber" (or private room) in a tavern near Chester, he was "in the dead of night . . . not a little astonished at feeling by [his] side, unstripped of his garniture, a rough bedfellow."[150]

Prices varied over time and with the type of accommodation provided. Travelers occasionally expressed pleasure at the reasonableness of tavern charges. "When we were at [Sandown], we had a lunch of chicken, grilled lamb, beer, and a glass of cherry wine, and the horse had his oats, and all this cost only three shillings, or eight sous."[151] In the seventeenth century and during the financial difficulties of the Revolutionary era, maximum prices charged for food and shelter for both man and beast were legally established in shillings and pence.[152] In the early nineteenth century, the price for a day's board and lodging in the city averaged from one dollar to two dollars and fifty cents. In rural areas, fifty cents per day was the norm.[153] Around 1830, the minimum charge for boarding a horse was about twenty-five cents; Nathaniel W. Ela, who owned a tavern at Dover Landing, promised "the best of Hay and Provender," advertising in that year that "if any Tavern in this Village keep [horses] cheaper [than twenty-five cents], I shall."[154]

Tavernkeepers kept handwritten accounts of what was owed to them by each of their regular customers. The goods and services supplied to the tavernkeeper by these same customers through years of business appear on the opposite side of the ledger page. Often no one attempted to balance these accounts until one party died and his estate was being settled.

Even strangers sometimes paid with goods and services rather than cash. In 1810, a boy passing through Concord later recalled paying for his lodging and breakfast at William Stickney's tavern by sawing wood.[155] Some of the visitors to New Hampshire were itinerants by profession who used their skills in such areas as medicine or theatrical performance to defray their travel expenses.[156] Almost a century before the state officially authorized boardinghouse owners to place liens upon the baggage of guests who had not paid, a lodger at a tavern in Gilmanton, who found himself suddenly penniless, "was obliged to leave in pawn, his saddle, and ride home without that conveniency."[157]

The overall cost of travel varied greatly depending on the means of transportation. In the 1830s, a journey from Boston to Exeter by rented gig was said to cost three times more than by public stage.[158] Throughout most of the nineteenth century, five to ten cents per mile was the average reimbursement allowed by the state for official travel expenses.[159] Especially at the beginning of this period, when the average daily wage was just one dollar, travel was disproportionately expensive. Also contributing, but in less tangible ways, to the overall costs of travel in early New Hampshire was the wear-and-tear on vehicles and teams passing over rough highways, as well as comparable strains imposed on the traveler's own time, energy, comfort, privacy, and peace of mind by the rigors of the highway life.

TRAFFIC AND COMMERCE

CHAPTER 5

THE MERRIMACK, CONNECTICUT, and Saco river valleys, which had enticed settlers into the wilderness, formed a stronger link between inland towns and the seaports of Massachusetts, Connecticut, and Maine than with coastal New Hampshire. Reflecting these historic connections, networks of coaching, freighting, droving, peddling, and postal routes developed with little regard to state boundaries. Also gradually extending throughout the New England countryside, regular circuits established by itinerant doctors, ministers, teachers, artists, and performers provided professional services not always available locally, and introduced changing urban styles, attitudes, and mores into the traditional agrarian culture.

Public passenger service in New Hampshire was surprisingly late in developing, the first regular stage route not being established until 1761. In inland areas, even the largest communities lacked regular stage service until around 1800. Throughout the seventeenth and eighteenth centuries, most travel proceeded either by foot, by horseback, or by privately owned or rented vehicle. In 1761, the Portsmouth advertisement proclaiming the news that a two-horse, four-passenger stage would be running to Boston and back once a week held out a welcome promise to those "Gentlemen and Ladies [who] are often at a Loss for Good Accommodations for Travelling from hence" that from now on they "will be wholly freed from the Care and Charge of keeping Chairs [or chaises] and Horses, or returning them before they have finished their Business."[1]

Daniel Webster later recalled that, during the first years of the nineteenth century, "stage coaches no more ran into the center of New Hampshire than they ran to Baffins [sic] Bay" in the Arctic.[2] Before this time, a stagecoach was such an unusual sight that children rarely forgot their first glimpse of one. A Massachusetts woman who lived into her nineties always remembered her "delight" upon examining her first stagecoach during the 1790s—a "huge leathern conveyance, with its gaudily emblazoned yellow body and the four prancing white steeds."[3]

The expansion of stage service during the first few decades of the nineteenth century was dramatic. Since a stage line was a "speculation by which as much money is to be made as possible by the proprietors," the success of one such venture naturally inspired others.[4] By 1821, twenty-six passenger stages were passing weekly through Portsmouth alone.[5] In the same year, a Massachusetts gentleman, who claimed to have owned the country's first public stage, expressed his astonishment at the "augmented numbers [of stages] . . . which are now moving in every direction, and all over the republican empire." The same man enthusiastically continued: "I have no doubt but that there are twenty stages, leave Boston daily; and it is magical to view them, (from the state-house dome,) darting out like radii, [to] various points of the compass."[6] As maps of the period illustrate, many of the stage routes converging on Boston originated in or beyond New Hampshire.[7]

By 1840, six regular stages crossed the bridge between Portsmouth and Maine every day except Sunday on the

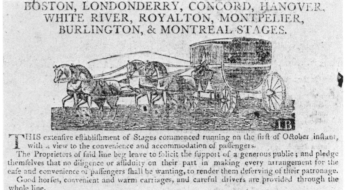

Engraving of coach by Jedidiah Baldwin, from newspaper advertisement for stage line, Dartmouth Gazette (Hanover), *1807. Although many New Hampshire towns lacked stage service in the early nineteenth century, those located along turnpikes enjoyed relatively frequent and rapid transportation. The advertisement following this engraved heading describes the network of good roads and taverns, as well as the reliable vehicles and drivers used by this stage line to ensure swift and safe travel.*

NHHS Collections   Photographer, Ernest Gould

important coastal route.[8] At the same time, no fewer than eighty-four coaches departed weekly from Concord bound for various points.[9] Because of its central location and political significance, the capital city soon became the busiest of several coaching junctions that eventually developed within New Hampshire. Stage proprietors, whether individuals or corporations, meticulously described in their local advertisements the connections possible at such staging intersections. As its proprietors claimed in 1801, the "Exeter Stage," for example, arrived in Portsmouth "early enough for passengers to take passage in the Eastern Stage" along the Maine coast."[10]

Attempting to appeal to potential customers in an increasingly competitive field, stage proprietors emphasized the reliability of their drivers, the comfort of their vehicles, and the care given their horses. In 1774, New Hampshire's first stage line was able to boast that its trusty vehicle had "for twelve Years . . . never been overset, nor any Passengers met with any Hurt."[11]

Advertisements often highlighted the "excellent public houses" at stage stops along a particular route. At a time when a trip from Boston to Burlington, Vermont, could take from Monday morning to Thursday afternoon, tavern quality was a very important feature of stage travel.[12] In 1782, John Greenleaf advertised that, on his Portsmouth to Boston coach route, he "has taken care that at every Inn [where] he stops, proper Refreshments shall be prepared by the Keepers thereof."[13] Advertisements were sometimes quite specific concerning the taverns which a stage line patronized. In 1805, for instance, a new stage running twice weekly along the Merrimack Valley from Boscawen to Nashua enticed passengers with promises to "stop and breakfast at Mr. *Gale's* tavern, in Concord . . . dine and exchange horses at Mr. *Gillis's* tavern, in Bedford, at noon, and arrive at esq'r *Taylor's* tavern, Nashua Village, the same evening."[14]

The vehicle used in the earliest days of public transportation was not the coach later typically identified with stag-

View Along the Connecticut River, Showing Windsor, Vermont, and Mt. Ascutney, *gouache on paper, 1850, by Nicolino Calyo. This view of the Connecticut River valley illustrates the world of nineteenth-century transportation. The river teeming with traffic, the road in the foreground, and the Cornish-Windsor bridge at the left remain unchanged from the late 1700s; however, the railroad points to the coming revolution in transportation.*

Courtesy, Shelburne Museum, Shelburne, Vermont
  Photographers, Helga Photo Studio; photograph courtesy of Hirshl & Adler Galleries, Inc.

ON THE ROAD NORTH OF BOSTON

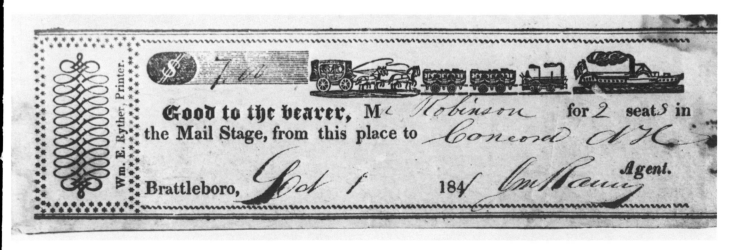

Stage waybill for Keene, Brattleboro and Boston Citizens' Union Line, (detail), 1831. Surviving waybills show the care with which every element of stage transportation was itemized and priced.
NHHS Collections   Photographer, Ernest Gould

ing. In 1761, a simple four-passenger "chair" or chaise initiated New Hampshire's stage service. A coach, billed as the "Portsmouth Flying Stagecoach," soon alternated with the "Stage Chair" or "Post-Chaise," depending apparently on the number of passengers. Although Portsmouth craftsmen were skilled in chaisemaking, the first coaches used in New Hampshire are believed to have been made in Boston.[15] It was only after 1826 that Concord's Lewis Downing with his partner, J. Stephens Abbot from Salem, Massachusetts, undertook the local manufacture of stagecoaches. Until the formation of this partnership, even Downing's Concord shop appears to have concentrated on the production of wagons, heavy freight vehicles, and two-wheeled chaises. Abbot and Downing's well-built "Concord Coach" with its improved suspension system, relying on leather thoroughbraces rather than wooden or metal springs, eventually commanded a worldwide market. The popularity of this locally produced vehicle was a

phenomenon, however, of the mid-to-late nineteenth century.[16] Even in the 1830s, "stage wagons" and other vehicles only "by courtesy called Stage" continued to operate on the more rugged routes through the state's mountain notches.[17]

Stage vehicles often carried packages, mail, and newspapers, along with their passengers. Mail service, however, at least along the coast, long pre-dated the era of stages. From the late seventeenth century, mail carriers rode "single Horse Post" along the "eastern" route from Boston to Portsmouth, later continuing along the Maine coast.[18] When the first post office was established in Portsmouth in 1693, its location may have been a tavern, the legislation specifying that the "officer of the Post house, haveing Licens granted to Retaile Beer, Sider & Ale, w'thin Doores according to Law, Shall have his Excise ffree," in partial recompense for his postal services.[19]

A professional traveler like a post rider, especially in the

Ticket for the mail stage between Brattleboro, Vermont, and Concord, N.H., 1841, printed by William E. Ryther.
NHHS Collections   Photographer, Ernest Gould

Ambrotype showing stagecoach at Henry L. Thayer's hotel, Littleton, N.H., circa 1865. This early photograph captures the arrival of a Concord coach at one of New Hampshire's most popular hotels. The passengers have mounted to the top of the stage to pose with the dashing driver, but the muddy road and warm clothing suggest that most would have completed their journey inside.
NHHS Collections

seventeenth century, needed every aid that a sparsely settled country could provide. By law, "all Inn Keepers and fferrymen [were] Ordered to further [the post rider] in his Journying, with Necessary Provision for Himself, and Horse and, with Speedy Transportation."[20] Even in the late eighteenth century, however, both Newbury and Portsmouth ferries tended to delay the rider on the "Continental Post Road," requiring, even under the best circumstances, at least "one hour for crossing Portsmouth ferry."[21] Severe weather conditions sometimes reduced the speed of early mail service to pedestrian level. In 1705, the Boston newspaper reported: "The East post came in Saturday, who says there is no Travailing [*sic*] with horses, especially, beyond Newbury, but with snowshoes."[22]

The 1759 newspaper advertisement of Thomas Welch of Kingston, who was "determined to Ride as a Carrier from the Town of Portsmouth to Albany, during the Summer Season," provides the first evidence of mail service in inland New Hampshire. Welch's advertisement concludes with a list of taverns along his route at which letters and other business could be left for him.[23] In the early 1770s,

a Mr. Porter of Lebanon claimed to ride post from Portsmouth to Dartmouth College "every three Weeks in all sorts of Weather."[24] Welch and Porter, however, may have been among the "private overland carriers" who were widely blamed for depriving the government post office of revenue.[25]

Mail service, in these early days, was neither reliable nor prompt. In 1776, Matthew Patten recorded having spent two consecutive days at Robert MacGregor's tavern in Goffstown, waiting "to meet the Post," which finally appeared on the third day.[26] Two years later, according to the calculations of Josiah Bartlett of Kingston, writing home to his wife from Philadelphia, "I find my letters to you by the post are near a month old When you Receive them."[27] Because of these difficulties, much mail prior to the establishment of state postal routes in the 1780s and 1790s was entrusted either to traveling acquaintances or, along the coast, to reliable sea captains. Any single letter, moreover, was likely to contain several others for forwarding.[28]

Mail stages eventually took over much, but not all, of New Hampshire's postal delivery. In the early 1770s,

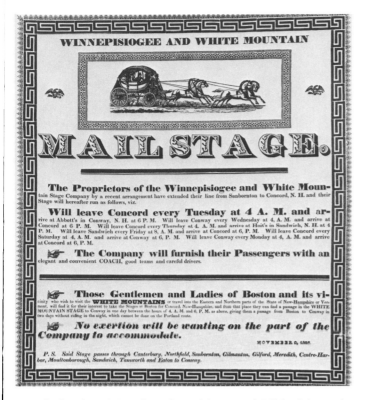

WINNEPISIOGEE AND WHITE MOUNTAIN

MAIL STAGE.

The Proprietors of the Winnepisiogee and White Mountain Stage Company by a recent arrangement have extended their line from Sanbornton to Concord, N. H. and their Stage will hereafter run as follows, viz.

Will leave Concord every Tuesday at 4 A. M. and ar-rive at Abbott's in Conway, N. H. at 6 P. M. Will leave Conway every Wednesday at 4, A. M. and arrive at Concord at 6 P. M. Will leave Concord every Thursday at 4, A. M. and arrive at Hoit's in Sandwich, N. H. at 4 P. M. Will leave Sandwich every Friday at 8, A. M. and arrive at Concord at 6 P. M. Will leave Concord every Saturday at 4, A. M. and arrive at Conway at 6, P. M. Will leave Conway every Monday at 4, A. M. and arrive at Concord at 6, P. M.

☞ **The Company will furnish their Passengers with an** elegant and convenient COACH, good teams and careful drivers.

☞ **Those Gentlemen and Ladies of Boston and its vi-**cinity who wish to visit the WHITE MOUNTAINS or travel into the Eastern and Northern parts of the State of New-Hampshire or Vermont, will find it for their interest to take the Stages at Boston for Concord, New-Hampshire, and from that place they can find a passage in the WHITE MOUNTAIN STAGE to Conway in one day between the hours of 4 A. M. and 6, P. M. as above, giving them a passage from Boston to Conway in two days without riding in the night, which cannot be done on the Portland route.

No exertion will be wanting on the part of the Company to accommodate.

NOVEMBER 6, 1826.

P. S. Said Stage passes through Canterbury, Northfield, Sanbornton, Gilmanton, Gilford, Meredith, Centre-Harbor, Moultonborough, Sandwich, Tamworth and Eaton to Conway.

Broadside advertising the Winnepisiogee and White Mountain Mailstage, 1826; including woodcut of coach copied after Moody Morse Peabody's earlier stipple engraving. This broadside hints at the extensive and reliable network of mail stages that crossed central New Hampshire, and reflects the new demand for transportation of tourists into the White Mountains.

NHHS Collections   Photographer, Bill Finney

coaches running between Portsmouth and Boston provided this service illegally at first, carrying mail without proper authorization.[29] By the time mail stages had become more established, certain travelers, sharing their coach with the mails, noted delays while the letters were being sorted.[30] According to an 1852 New Ipswich reminiscence, the stage driver watered his horses and shared jokes while "the mail bag [was] being examined."[31] As one visitor to upstate New York explained:

> The letters in America, instead of being put into separate bags for each town as in England, are carried in one huge leather case, which the postmaster is allowed to detain ten minutes, so that he may pick his letters out of the general mass. The coachman . . . drives up to the office, sometimes a small tavern, and throws the bag, about the size of a flour sack, upon the hard pavement, or muddy road as most convenient; it is then trailed along into the house, and, being unlocked, the lower end is elevated, and out tumble all the letters, newspapers, and pamphlets, in a heap on the floor. At [one] little village . . . I had the curiosity to look into the bar for the purpose of seeing the mode of sorting letters, and witnessed a scene which could never answer in any other country. The sorters consisted of an old grey-headed man, at least seventy-five years of age, an

old woman, "with spectacles on nose," the old gentleman's equal in point of years, and a great, fat, ruddy-faced damsel of twenty-five, backed by half a dozen dirty little barefooted urchins, who were all down upon their knees on the floor, overhauling the huge pile before them, flinging those letters which were for their office into a distant corner of the room, amongst sundry wet mops, brushes, molasses barrels, &c.; and those which were for other towns on our route were again bagged in the same gentle style, part having to undergo the same process every fifth mile of our day's journey.[32]

The vehicles employed for mail service varied as widely as those used for passenger service. Particularly in the mountains, a one-horse wagon or cart often sufficed, even into the 1830s.[33] As late as 1840, mounted post riders were still being commissioned.[34] A visitor to the White Mountains in 1842 left us a vivid caricature of this rapidly fading occupation:

> One fellow we passed, on horseback, was quite a ludicrous figure. He carried the mail. His legs stuck out like compasses, his arms bobbed up & down in good time with the mailbags, which rested behind on the horse's flanks. He wore an old broad hat, carried an apple in one hand, and a stick up in the other.[35]

At least in an earlier era, a "post-horn" to announce the arrival of the mail was among the mounted carrier's standard equipment.[36]

In 1809, Francis Bowman, on resigning his position as post rider from Amherst through the northern part of Hillsborough County, described himself as having "long and faithfully served as 'the herald of a noisy world,' with news from all nations 'lumbering at his back.' "[37] Indeed, the post, whether conveyed by horse or stage, almost always circulated newspapers as well as mail. In 1779, Matthew Patten entrusted a nearby tavernkeeper with payment "to give the post for the next three months of the Worcester news paper."[38]

The desire for news was insatiable in rural areas. Complaints to printers suggest that newspapers left in bundles at local taverns were often appropriated by those who, though not willing to purchase a newspaper themselves, were "for engrossing and coveting their Neighbours'."[39] A traveler passing through Walpole in 1808 found it "entertaining to see the eagerness of the people on our arrival, to get a sight of the last newspaper from Boston. They flocked to the post-office and the inn, and formed a variety of groups round those who were fortunate enough to possess themselves of a paper."[40] One such group of local news-seekers near Alton Bay actually wrote to Portsmouth's *Gazette* editor in 1770, claiming that they had "happen'd to meet at the Tavern to'ther [*sic*] Night, read over . . . last Week's Paper, and were greatly delighted with all the News. . . ."[41]

Both the number of newspapers and of official post offices within the state grew rapidly in the early nineteenth

Sign from Benjamin Swan's Union-House, Haverhill, N.H., 1836. Few records remain of the heavy, wide-wheeled freight wagons of early nineteenth-century New Hampshire. This tavern sign signaled hospitality to freight drivers by depicting one of their six-horse teams and canvas-covered wagons.

Photograph courtesy of Katharine Blaisdell

century. The development of mail service, moreover, echoed the growing complexity of the staging network. But the transport of passengers and news, whether in the form of private mail or printed publications, long remained secondary to the freighting of goods and products essential to the region's economy. By the early nineteenth century, great caravans of ox and horse teams were constantly engaged in carrying farm produce either in canvas-covered wagons or sleighs across New Hampshire toward distant markets. Even as early as 1769, a Piscataqua resident described ox teams going 80 to 100 miles to the Boston market.[42] By 1831, nearly one hundred horse teams passed daily through Crawford Notch during the month of January; a few years later, a Keene resident counted between sixty and seventy sleighs passing through town on a single day with country produce headed for Boston.[43]

Much of this traffic, described as coming "from the depths of the country," originated in Vermont, Canada, and Maine.[44] In 1825, parts of Vermont, even though two hundred miles northwest of Boston, had a "decided preference . . . for the Boston Market, [over] that of Montreal or New York."[45] The heavy freight traffic through Crawford Notch to the northern seaport of Portland, Maine, carried products from the rich agricultural regions in Vermont, as well as Canada's English-speaking settlements and New Hampshire's Upper Coos region.

The usual destination of New Hampshire's own products was Boston, especially from the southwestern quarter of

The Pemigewasset Coach, *circa 1899, oil on canvas, by Enoch Wood Perry, Jr. This nostalgic painting looks back to a form of transportation that was rapidly disappearing by the end of the nineteenth century. Those who wished to catch a final glimpse of the stagecoach frequently traveled to the White Mountains, where the reliable old vehicles still served grand hotels and communities distant from the railroad. In some areas, Concord coaches continued to run after the turn of the century.*

Courtesy, Shelburne Museum, Shelburne, Vermont

Wall painting (detail) from ballroom, Coburn Tavern, East Pepperell, Mass., circa 1825, attributed to Rufus Porter. A militiaman himself, Porter depicted military drills in several of his wall murals. This detail, although an idealized representation, shows the traditional link between the tavern and the militia.

Courtesy, George G. Hayes   Photographer, Bill Finney

Sign from the tavern of John George, Concord, N.H., circa 1815. One of Concord's popular taverns, the Eagle Hotel opened under John George at the end of the War of 1812. To appeal to the patriotic fervor of the era, the tavern sign featured the Federal eagle, a widespread symbol of the American republic.

NHHS Collections   Photographer, Bill Finney

View of Lebanon, N.H., circa 1825, oil on canvas, by Almira Simons. This painting by a local woman shows two taverns near the meetinghouse at the intersection of the Fourth New Hampshire Turnpike and the Croydon Turnpike. Doctor Phinehas Parkhurst, pictured here in his riding chair or chaise, kept tavern for a while in the house to the left of the meetinghouse. The mules visible in the left foreground were raised by Dr. Parkhurst and then driven south to distant markets.

Courtesy, Lebanon Public Library   Photographer, Bill Finney

Portrait of James Fogg Langdon, circa 1830, oil on wood panel. For thirty years, Langdon, long a resident of Plymouth, N.H., was not only the proprietor of stage lines running south to Concord, east to Dover, west to Haverhill, and north to Stanstead, Quebec, but also a stage driver. His passengers recalled his "honesty, cheerfulness, and obliging nature." When railroads superseded stage service, Langdon, like many other coachmen, founded his own express service, which, after a number of mergers, formed part of American Express.

NHHS Collections   Photographer, Bill Finney

Cornish Bridge, Connecticut River, 1848, watercolor on paper, by Edward Seager. Built in 1825 to replace the original bridge of 1796, destroyed by a flood the year before, this span survived until it was washed away by another flood in 1849. Unlike the original arched truss, which had been left exposed to the elements, this second bridge had its trusses encased in sheathing for protection against damaging moisture. The trusses were braced against the wind by a series of rectangular frames which locked the two sides of the bridge firmly together.

Courtesy, Eugene B. Sydnor   Photograph courtesy, Hirschl & Adler Galleries, Inc.

Engraving, Mill View at Great Falls, N.H., *(now Somersworth, N.H.), circa 1835. This view of a mill village shows covered freight vehicles of both the two-wheel and four-wheel types. In nearby New Market during the same period, wagons were used to transport raw cotton and finished cloth to Portsmouth after the river froze in winter.*

NHHS Collections   Photographer, Bill Finney

the state.[46] Teams forming lengthy caravans, however, also could be found headed toward each of the major coastal settlements between Boston and Portland. Along the Merrimack River in New Hampshire, many of the settlers had migrated from Essex County, Massachusetts, and that region's leading seaports—Salem and Newburyport—were favored market towns into the nineteenth century.[47] At the

same time, the ports of the Piscataqua River basin, although losing a large portion of the produce from New Hampshire's vast hinterland to the Portland and Boston markets, managed to retain a considerable share of team traffic, both from southern Maine and southeastern New Hampshire.[48] Mile-long caravans passing regularly from Concord to Durham and Portsmouth long survived in local memory.[49]

Regardless of their origin or destination, the wagons and sleighs traversing New Hampshire carried agricultural and forest products, along with local wares, to exchange for difficult-to-obtain imports from Europe or the West Indies. Loads bound for market typically contained meat, butter, cheese, poultry, grain, cider, dried apples, peas, beans, hides, wool, furs, venison, and locally caught fish. By the 1820s, large quantities of salted lake trout from the Winnipesaukee region also were being sent to the Boston market.[50]

Foremost among New Hampshire's manufactured items were the timber products on which the provincial economy was so firmly based. Between 1770 and 1775, the port of Piscataqua alone exported nearly 74 million board feet of pine planks and boards, over 6 million barrel staves and heads, 1.7 million barrel hoops, almost 42 million wooden shingles, and 98,000 clapboards.[51] Merchants in Dover, where, in 1795, commerce "consist[ed] chiefly in lumber," were probably following tradition when contracting with professional teamsters during the 1830s to haul overland

Photograph showing oxen in Meredith, N.H., in the 1880s. Great caravans of ox teams were sometimes assembled for special purposes, most commonly for transporting huge loads of firewood into town over snow-covered roads. Although a slow traveler, the ox was prized for his steady nature and great strength.

NHHS Collections   Photographers, F. B. Wilson & Co.

Photograph of an ox team, Chichester, N.H., or vicinity, circa 1900. Dressed in heavy winter clothing, this driver of a freight wagon has hitched his ox team with horse harness and is driving them with reins rather than leading them on foot in the usual way.

NHHS Collections   Photographer, Charles D. Towle

large quantities of boards from inland locations such as Alton Bay.[52] In the early to mid-nineteenth century, southwestern New Hampshire gained prominence for the manufacturing of barrels which were shipped to the Boston market in wagons fitted with special racks to expand their capacity.[53] The transportation of firewood into the larger towns was also an undertaking of such scale that travel on certain roads often proved "annoying . . . because you met so many . . . ox teams drawing wood."[54]

On the trip home, the wagons and sleighs were laden with dried codfish, salt, spices, molasses, flour, rum, tea, dry goods, hardware, and a variety of articles either imported or produced in the coastal towns. As late as 1825, communities as far away as northern Vermont continued to "depend on the Boston market for all kinds of nails, spikes, and glass, and drugs and medicines."[55]

Although in the eighteenth century, "teams of great overgrown oxen" were the norm, by the early nineteenth century, it was no longer rare "to meet a Team with a horse in it."[56] Depending on size and load, wagons were pulled by teams of from four to ten horses. Some of the drivers were professional teamsters working for local farmers and merchants; others were farmers themselves who periodically joined their neighbors in a caravan to the coast. Compared by one early historian to the great caravans of Asia, trains of covered wagons and sleighs were remembered as "almost fill[ing] the roads from Montpelier to Boston, when the traveling was good."[57]

The road speed of oxen was only about one-and-a-half miles per hour, and a freight trip between northern New Hampshire and Boston could take a full two weeks on the road.[58] Public accommodations along the route, therefore, were of prime importance to all teamsters. From the viewpoint of an individual journeying from Salem, Massachu-

ELA'S TAVERN,
ON DOVER LANDING.

THE subscriber would inform his friends and the publick in general, that he continues to keep TAVERN at the OLD STAND, where he would be happy to wait on his old customers and the publick, who travel thro' Dover. Those that call, will find a large and as convenient STABLE as there is on the road they travel. Those gentlemen that come with Loaded Sleighs can drive in, where the Traders will come and buy their Loads. My old customers shall not leave me on account of Prices—my price for Keeping HORSES is twenty-five cents, and if any Tavern in this Village keep cheaper, I shall.

All the STAGES that leave Dover, call at my House every morning for Passengers.

My House is large and convenient, and well furnished with PROVISIONS and LIQUORS, and hands to wait and tend.

My STABLE is furnished with the best of HAY and PROVENDER, and a good Ostler.

NATHANIEL W. ELA.

Newspaper advertisement for Nathaniel W. Ela's tavern at Dover Landing, Dover Gazette & Strafford Advertiser, 1830. This advertisement was written to attract the business of teamsters journeying to Dover, an important center for the exchange of country produce and coastal merchandise. In the winter of 1831, a local diarist noted: "Sometimes the teams would reach from Garrison Hill to the Landing. They had to wait for the team ahead to unload and load up again and start for home."

NHHS Collections   Photographer, Ernest Gould

setts, to Manchester, New Hampshire, in 1810, "the Inns of our Interiour accommodate to the demands of the Teams & not to the few travellers who have not the business of the Roads as their object."[59] Teamsters, however, though "add[ing] much to the appearance of business [at the local tavern] left a very small profit to the landlord," typically carrying with them provision both for themselves and their animals.[60] Around 1811, one innkeeper in New Hampshire or nearby Maine, answering the knocks of a late-night guest rather reluctantly, claimed to have been much "troubled with teamsters from the back settlements, who only came in to warm themselves and get a drink."[61]

While professional teamsters were on the highway year-round, caravans of farmers most commonly appeared in the mountain notches when road surfaces were ideal for sleighing. As late as 1908, farmers and woodsmen were described on one occasion as "taking liberal advantage of the recent storms to draw all sorts of merchandise to market & the

Photograph, Phoenix Stable sleigh, Concord, N.H., circa 1880. During the late nineteenth century, this large open sleigh provided reliable winter transportation to and from Concord's Phoenix Hotel (known by this date as the Phenix). Like all winter travelers of the era, the passengers are garbed in heavy bearskin or buffalo coats and fur caps.
NHHS Collections   Photographer, W. G. C. Kimball

number of ox teams & horse sleds we passed surprised me. Even in Henniker village the procession was endless."[62] Merchants in the larger towns, hoping to benefit from the sudden increase in activity, placed timely advertisements in local newspapers, as did one of the capital's dry-goods shops in January 1832: "Good Sleighing to Concord, N.H.!"[63] Urban taverns, such as Nathaniel Ela's at Dover Landing, offered special services for those marketing goods in the winter: "Those that call, will find a large and as convenient STABLE as there is on the road they travel. Those gentlemen that come with Loaded Sleighs can drive in, where the Traders will come and buy their Loads."[64] When unexpected thaws suddenly destroyed the road surface that had enticed the farmers from home, they became more dependent than ever on public hospitality.[65]

The winter season was, in fact, one of the busiest for all types of highway traffic. According to a Nashua newspaper of December 1843, "Snow is the life of business at this season, and never fails to impart to our village a life and activity not seen at any other time of year. Our streets are filled with sleighs of every description passing to and fro."[66]

From the eighteenth century, sleighing purely for pleasure added much to winter's already-heightened highway traffic. In February 1774, one Portsmouth couple traveled three hundred miles in three weeks with a "Sley and Pair," vis-

iting every section of New Hampshire from the Coos to the "Monadnocks."[67] And, two decades later, sleighing parties traveled to Byfield, Massachusetts, from as far away as Hampstead and Derry to see the area's first woolen mill, which had "created a great sensation throughout the whole region."[68] Formal sleighing parties were also immensely popular. A Merrimack girl later recalled: "After the sleigh ride, they would go to some tavern for supper and in the evening have a dance in the hall."[69] As early as 1777, a visitor to neighboring Massachusetts found it not unusual "to be awaked with the singing and noise [these winter revelers] make, and by the number of bells affixed to the horses, on the return of some of these parties."[70]

Public transportation also proceeded apace despite winter's difficulties. At least in the early nineteenth century, "stage bodies [were often] taken from the wheels and put on runners."[71] In 1808, the motion of such a stage "placed on runners" left at least one New Hampshire traveler extremely nauseated.[72] In other cases, stage proprietors substituted open sleighs during the winter season for the usual wheeled vehicles.[73] In April 1862, when the stage arrived "on wheels" instead of runners, one Sandwich schoolgirl considered it worthy of note in her diary apparently as a sign of spring.[74]

One major product of New Hampshire's agrarian society required neither wheels nor runners for its transport to

Wood engraving, Market Square, Portsmouth, N.H., *from* Gleason's Pictorial Drawing-Room Companion, *1853. The rural world reached even to the heart of the nineteenth-century city. This view of the center of Portsmouth shows traffic largely from the country, including wagons of hay, a cart of cordwood, and a drove of cattle.*

NHHS Collections   Photographer, Bill Finney

market. Cattle, sheep, pigs, horses, mules, turkeys, and geese were driven to market, most often Boston, although occasionally other major towns between Boston and Portland. Tollgate records show that in the year 1837 alone, 13,233 sheep and 2,420 cattle crossed the Connecticut River over the Cornish bridge, headed toward Boston from Vermont farms.[75] A Wentworth resident later recalled as many as two thousand sheep in a single drove.[76] October and November were the heaviest months both for droving and slaughtering livestock.[77]

New Hampshire was long famous for its "great multitude" of beef cattle, some of the largest in New England.[78] As early as the mid-seventeenth century, offspring of the Danish cattle imported for hauling lumber in the earliest years of settlement were being driven to Boston—already considered the most profitable market.[79] The late eighteenth century witnessed "from the upper parts of New-Hampshire, great herds of fat cattle [being] driven to the Boston market; whence the beef [was] exported fresh to Nova-Scotia, and salted to the West and East-Indies."[80]

The small town of Brighton, Massachusetts, gradually developed into the leading cattle market serving Boston. Herds from Vermont, Maine, and even Canada passed through New Hampshire on their way to Brighton market.[81] New Hampshire newspapers reported daily sale

prices at Brighton, as well as annual sales totals. In 1831, Brighton market handled the sale of 33,922 beef cattle, 84,453 sheep, and 26,871 swine.[82]

Sometimes drovers headed for markets other than the coastal ones that typically attracted them. During the American Revolution, a visitor to New York State encountered "thirteen farmers and two hundred and fifty cattle coming from New Hampshire" to help supply the army.[83] And, by the early nineteenth century, the northern part of the state had begun to send many of its cattle to Quebec.[84]

Farmers also drove their cattle long distances for summer pasturage—from Newbury, Massachusetts, to Boscawen, New Hampshire; from Concord, Massachusetts, to New Ipswich; and from Seabrook to Sanbornton.[85] The direction of these annual drives often reflected the migration patterns of early settlers.

Frequently, large herds from a number of farms were laboriously gathered together and driven to market or summer pasturage.[86] Although by the late nineteenth and early twentieth centuries much of the beef cattle industry had moved west, herds of dairy cattle still traversed the state, even utilizing industrial Nashua's main street.[87] Cattle herds attracted local attention whenever they passed, especially from children, "waving, one bunch every mile, to the drove pounding by."[88]

Wood engraving, View of the Celebrated Cattle Market at Brighton, Mass., *from Gleason's Pictorial Drawing-Room Companion, 1852, probably by Asa Coolidge Warren. The extensive stockyards at Brighton, Massachusetts, long served the Boston market and were the destination of many of the cattle raised or fattened in or beyond New Hampshire.*
Courtesy of the Trustees of the Boston Public Library   Photographers, Geoffrey Stein Studio, Inc.

Photograph, ''Town Square, South Berwick, Maine,'' circa 1890. Droves of cattle were frequently moved through the countryside of northern New England, often on their way to summer pastures or, especially in October and November, to market. This small herd is vainly seeking forage during a brief stop in the center of South Berwick, Maine, during an autumn drive.
Courtesy, Old South Berwick Historical Society
   Photograph courtesy of John P. Adams, reproduced by permission of University Press of New England

RATE OF TOLL.

	Cts
E[ach] foot pafsenger	3
H[orfe] rider	8
T[wo wh]eeled Pleasure carriage	20
F[our wh]eeled do. do.	50
C[urri]cle	30
Cart or waggon by one beast	10
Drawn by two beasts	15
Loaded do.	25
By three do. empty	20
Loaded do.	30
By four do. empty	25
Loaded do.	37½
Each additional beast	5
Sleigh drawn by one beast	10
By two do.	15
Sled by one do.	6½
By two do.	12½
By four do.	25
Each additional beast	5
Horfe jack or mule	4
Neat cattle	3
Sheep & swine each	1

Toll sign from Cornish Bridge, circa 1796. There was a charge for virtually everything, even sheep and hogs, that crossed a toll bridge. The toll books for the Cornish-Windsor Bridge show that on a single day in September 1833, 1,000 sheep crossed the bridge.
NHHS Collections   Photographer, Bill Finney

Since New Englanders exported horses to the West Indies for use in the sugar mills, droves of horses were herded to the seaports.[89] Although coastal New Hampshire merchants occasionally advertised their desire to purchase horses for shipment, the ports with the largest horse markets were typically those in Connecticut.[90] Approximately three times a year, one trader herded droves of horses from Charlestown, New Hampshire to Middletown, Connecticut. The horses were bridled and tethered to a guide rope, which in turn could be fastened to a wagon at each end, usually requiring one drover for every twelve horses.[91] In 1806, upon the arrival in Middletown of a drove of twenty-nine horses from New Hampshire's Connecticut Valley, eighteen were shipped immediately "on Board of the schooner Friendship."

Flocks of turkeys also paraded unwittingly toward their own fate. Around the turn of this century, an elderly man recalled one "gobbler of especial dignity" who had helped him lead five hundred others from St. Johnsbury, Vermont, to Lowell, Massachusetts. Though he recalled having stopped during this particular trip at a tavern in Warren, New Hampshire, the turkeys themselves needed no special enclosure.[92] As a local historian recalled, "When the shades of evening had reached a certain degree of density, suddenly the whole drove with one accord rose from the road and sought a perch in the neighboring trees. The drover was prepared for such a halt, and [often] drew up his covered wagon beside the road, where he passed the night." Turkeys could create accounting problems: "It was not unusual for a small flock of them to join a drove as it was passing through. On the other hand, stragglers from the drove frequently found agreeable companions in local flocks and tarried instead of pursuing their course."[93]

Since cattle and sheep were more valuable individually yet also tended to stray, they were enclosed overnight in the tavern yard or nearby field.[94] In the evening, following an average drive of twenty miles, "the large yards near the tavern would be filled with a bleating, bawling assortment of creatures tired by the travel and excited by the new surroundings."[95] Brands and metal ear tags helped drovers identify their own animals, minimizing confusion between droves and local herds.

The same agricultural, forest, and industrial products that were carried overland by wagon were also shipped by river whenever possible. Even herds of sheep were sometimes transported this way. Though by no means an improvement as far as speed was concerned, water travel was both less costly and more efficient, requiring less human and animal energy to move the same or a larger quantity of goods.

From the days of earliest settlement, the three major river systems—the Connecticut, the Merrimack, and the Piscataqua—carried cargoes to and from tidewater markets in Connecticut and Massachusetts, as well as in New Hampshire. In 1858, a trip through New Hampshire's Merrimack Valley inspired Henry David Thoreau to exclaim: "A river touching the back of a town is like a wing, it may be unused as yet, but ready to waft it over the world"[96] Local taverns served both the river and the highway traffic.

Before the canal era, the navigability of New Hampshire's major rivers was hindered by waterfalls, rapids, and sandbars. A series of relays sometimes became necessary around major obstacles, requiring horse and ox teams to carry the freight from one vessel to another.[97] Ascent of some of the less treacherous rapids, often extending for miles, was possible only with guidance from local pilots. At certain points along the route, so-called "swift-water men" boarded each upward-bound vessel "armed with poles 16 to 23 feet long, tipped at one end with a spike, a foot long." According to the reminiscences of one of these men stationed at Hinsdale on the Connecticut River, they "would post themselves on either side of the boat and each of the crew in turn would walk from the bow to the mast-board, usually about one-third the length of the boat, with the spike planted on the bottom, the other end of the pole pressed against his shoulder." According to the same recol-

Engraving, The New Hampshire Granite Ledge, *from a share certificate for the Concord Granite & Railway Company, 1837-38, engraved by Caleb Deeley. This view of the granite quarries in the ledges of Rattlesnake Hill in Concord, N.H., shows some of the traffic that made the Merrimack River an important transportation artery. The flatboat under the overhang of the shed is being loaded with granite drawn there by horse railroad; the boat in midstream has hoisted a sail to speed its downriver journey.*

NHHS Collections   Photographer, Bill Finney

lection: "Often this crew was reinforced by one or two pair of oxen, which were hitched to a tow line of some 400 feet in length" or else to a capstan around which the rope was wound.[98]

Most of the cargo-bearing vessels on New Hampshire's rivers were simple flatboats and rafts or the more sophisticated gundalows associated with the Piscataqua basin. Characteristic of the Piscataqua gundalow was its rounded spoon-shaped bow; its lateen sail, which could be lowered to permit passage under bridges; and its leeboard, which could be lifted to allow sailing in shallow water. Schooners of from sixty to eighty tons burden also ascended the Piscataqua, at least as far as Dover.[99] The cargo of all these vessels was basically the same as that transported by wagon between inland communities and their respective seaports.[100] Vessels on both the Piscataqua and Merrimack also eventually served the growing industrial communities along their banks by transporting cotton, coal, and other raw materials; brick, stone, and wood for industrial and urban construction; and finished factory products.[101] Tents, probably of canvas, protected the more fragile varieties of merchandise, including dry goods.[102]

Both the flatboats and gundalows were equipped with sails, but relied on the natural river flow whenever possible. The current of the Connecticut River carried boats down at three to four miles per hour. A voyage back and forth between Haverhill, New Hampshire, and Hartford, Connecticut, averaged twenty-five days. The return trip proved the more time-consuming, boatmen having to "avail themselves of the eddies, or back currents, which are often found on the borders of the river."[103]

In 1838, in comparing the pace of travel on the Connecticut River with that in parts of the country where steamboats were already popular, one European visitor described New Hampshire's "flat-bottom boats moving with snail-like slowness up the stream, by the force of the boatman's oars and poles . . . as they did twenty-five years ago on the Ohio and the Mississippi."[104] It is ironic that, although inventors John Fitch of Windsor, Connecticut, and Samuel Morey of Orford, New Hampshire, had, as early as the

Lithograph, Concord, New Hampshire, 1853, *printed by M. & N. Hanhart, London, after painting by George Harvey, 1852. Logs and masts long remained a major commodity transported down the Merrimack and Connecticut rivers. This view of two connected log rafts shows the oarsmen steering the rafts by means of long sweeps or rough oars.*

NHHS Collections   Photographer, Bill Finney

1780s and 1790s, put the Connecticut Valley in the forefront of steam navigation, this means of transportation, for a variety of reasons, never became economically practical on New Hampshire's rivers.[105]

Until new legislation in the early nineteenth century required lumber on the Connecticut River to be "rafted," tremendous quantities of masts, spars, and logs "floated at random" downstream to market.[106] Farmers along each of the rivers frequently complained of damage which the lumber caused to their property, but it was only after the increased construction of bridges, milldams, and canal locks around 1800 that an alternative method of timber shipment became mandatory.[107]

Logs were temporarily assembled into rafts to be sold for lumber following a single cargo-carrying voyage down river. "It took two men to navigate each raft with rough oars at opposite corners." The crew returned upriver by other means of transportation, carrying their oars over their shoulders. The rafts were constructed in such a manner that they could be broken up easily into sections known as "boxes," to allow passage through canals. "Swift-water" men boarded the rafts at certain points to help guide them

through rapids and other difficulties. The pilots "knew the rocks perfectly and they took the head of the first raft, guiding that, the rest following in exactly the same course." One fleet of such rafts on the Connecticut River reportedly spent twenty-five days navigating the distance between White River Junction, Vermont, and Holyoke, Massachusetts.[108]

At each landing, one or more public houses—known as river taverns—served the needs of the hardy boatmen. Riverboats during this era did not travel at night. The crew either slept and ate on board at a mooring, or at the local inn.[109] In Concord, near the famous "Great Bend" in the Merrimack, it was customary at Nathaniel Garvin's tavern "to blow mighty blasts on a big horn to warn the [hostess] to have dinner ready by the time the men had docked."[110] In Hinsdale on the Connecticut, even the sheep are said to have disembarked to spend the night in the barn of an inn later called the Sheepskin Tavern.[111]

Both the boatmen and lumbermen had a reputation for "merrymaking, drinking and fighting."[112] Reverend Jeremy Belknap noted this tendency as early as 1792: "The free indulgence of spiritous liquors, has been, and is now,

Photograph of Herbert Benton Swett, tin peddler from New London, N.H., circa 1900. Although Swett was considered "the last of the old-time Yankee tin peddlers in New England," wagons and products like his would have been common sights on New Hampshire roads during the nineteenth century. Swett often exchanged his tinware for rags, which he later sold in Boston.
NHHS Collections   Photographer, D. J. Lindsay & Co.

ON THE ROAD NORTH OF BOSTON

one of the greatest faults of many of the people of New-Hampshire; especially in the neighbourhood of the river Pascataqua [*sic*], and its branches, and wherever the business of getting lumber forms the principal employment of the people."[113]

Goods were transported in and out of New Hampshire not only by fleets of rafts and caravans of teamsters, but also by individual peddlers. "Hawkers [and] Pedlars . . . passing to and fro' through the Countrey to Vend Goods, Wares and merchandi[se]," had been common since the seventeenth century.[114] By the nineteenth century, some carried a general assortment of "Yankee notions," while others specialized in a particular product. Local craftsmen, including potters, tinsmiths, and woodenware manufacturers, often peddled their own wares through the surrounding countryside.[115]

Although many later-prominent New Hampshire merchants began their sales careers from a peddler's backpack, display trunk, or wagon, little is known about their early peripatetic careers.[116] One peddler, Ebenezer Graves of Ashfield, Massachusetts, however, did keep a diary during one of his trips in 1853 through parts of New Hampshire and Maine.[117] He specialized in silk, buying and peddling it along the way, somewhat akin to the New England peddler about whom one European traveler wrote: "To buy cheap and sell high comprehends for him the whole cycle of human knowledge."[118] Graves, the silk peddler, traveled partly by foot, partly by stage, and partly by railroad, noting at one point: "It is . . . much more comfortable riding than footing, [even] if it does take off the profits some." He peddled not only in rural areas, but also up and down Concord's city streets.

Many other itinerants besides traveling merchants earned their living by providing goods and services, sometimes seasonally, to a scattered population. Such itinerants did not always travel from house to house, but often advertised their presence at one of the local taverns. Traveling professionals, for instance, were often the main source of medical and dental services. In 1770, Doctors McLain and White from New York were available "to be spoke with at Capt. Zechariah Foss's, Inholder in Portsmouth," offering "with God's Assistance [to] cure the Gravel, Hystericks, Old Sores and Humours in the Blood . . . without asking Questions."[119] Similarly, traveling dentist S. Wood advertised in 1829 that he had "taken rooms for a few days at the EAGLE HOTEL, where he will wait upon the Ladies and Gentlemen of NEWPORT and the adjoining villages, in performing any operation that may be necessary for the preservation & beauty of their TEETH."[120] Often such services could be performed either at the tavern or at the patient's home, after arrangements had been made at the tavern. Other itinerants specialized in animal health. During a distemper epidemic in 1768, Lebbeus Burton, claiming to have gained his experience in England, offered to "undertake to cure this Disease for one Guinea each Horse" for anyone contacting him at Stavers' tavern.[121]

Saddlebags of Doctor Elias Frost of Meriden, N.H., early 19th century. Physicians frequently traveled on horseback and, whether their professional circuits covered one or several communities, they often carried their medical supplies compactly in a pair of leather bags hung from a single strap over the horse's back. Dr. Frost's saddlebags are subdivided with a multitude of small compartments for vials and paper packets of medicine.
NHHS Collections   Photographer, Bill Finney

Traveling preachers were also among those whose dedication to their calling was tested by the difficulties of a wandering life. As early as 1702, a missionary attempting to convert dissenters back to the Church of England made an extensive journey throughout the settled parts of North America. After speaking in Dover at a Quaker meeting, he immediately boarded a waiting vessel, going "down the River that Night to the Town called *Strawberry-bank*, and lodged there at an Inn, or Publick House of Entertainment."[122] Especially in eras of heightened religious activity, such as around the turn of the nineteenth century when at least two new Christian sects were formed in New Hampshire, traveling ministers sometimes preached in local tavern halls.[123] Individuals active with both of these new sects—the Free-Will Baptists and the other simply called the "Christ-ians"—wrote detailed memoirs of their constant journeying.[124] In the winter of 1822, a Free-Will Baptist minister, David Marks, traveling through the state mostly by foot despite the season, claimed to have "a chain of appointments four hundred and fifty miles in length." During a six-day period the following year, he preached in eight towns between Bradford and Enfield. It is not surprising, therefore, that while staying overnight at an inn in Stoddard, he later remembered being comforted by the thought that "my blessed Master had prepared for me a home, where through grace I hoped soon to rest forever from the arduous toils of a travelling life."[125]

Other professional itinerants brought culture in various

forms to New Hampshire towns, large and small. Often teachers of dancing, instrumental music, and singing had come originally from France or England. Their teaching schedules displayed a variety of patterns. Some taught classes in several locations, moving on different weekdays from town to town or from tavern to tavern, while others settled briefly in one location only to move on to another after a few months or seasons.[126] When, in 1819, Mr. Bossieux, a "professor of dancing" from France, advertised that he would "tarry" in Portsmouth three months to teach dancing, he claimed to have already "exercised this art . . . in several places of this Country through which he has passed since the two years he has been in America." Anyone wishing private instruction at home was requested to call on him at Davenport's Hotel.[127] At the opposite side of the state, Abram Pushee taught dancing at Darrah's hall in Charlestown, the hall of the Eagle Hotel in Newport, and at the Lafayette Hotel in Lebanon, probably on different days of the week. As a Lebanon student recalled, "the rules of politeness" were taught along with the "science of dancing."[128]

Depending on which "master" was in residence at the moment, eighteenth-century Portsmouth citizens could learn to play the violin, bass viol, cello, guitar, flute, clarinet, oboe, harpsichord, organ, or pianoforte.[129] Ichabod Johnson taught both vocal and instrumental music in many New England towns, including New Ipswich and Portsmouth, where he lodged at the Ark Tavern in 1796.[130] Captain Matthew Buell of Newport was long remembered as having taught a singing school in Sutton three days a week and at as many different taverns.[131] And, the well-known Massachusetts composer Samuel Holyoke was staying, at the time of his death in 1820, at Meshach Lang's tavern in East Concord, while teaching music locally during the winter season.[132]

Drawing was also taught by some of the itinerant portrait and decorative painters whose travels brought to the New Hampshire home not only art and decoration but also a greater sense of family identity.[133] Artists frequently advertised, as did Mr. and Mrs. Shute at Nettleton's Hotel in Newport in 1833, that if an accurate likeness of the sitter failed to be transferred to the canvas, "the work may remain on our hands."[134] According to an artist visiting Portsmouth in 1801, the "price of Likenesses either in portrait or Miniature is frequently so high, as to deter numbers of persons from possessing the resemblance of their relatives or friends."[135] As a result, numerous artists who cut paper profiles or silhouettes traveled around the countryside. William King, intending to work one week only at the Hanover tavern of James Wheelock, advertised in 1806 that he had cut more than "twenty thousand [silhouettes] in *Salem, Newburyport, Portsmouth, Portland*, and their adjoining towns."[136] Such paper profiles were available at only a fraction of the cost of a painted oil portrait.

Itinerant artists often took rooms at local taverns where potential clients could examine samples of their work and

Portrait, Landscape & Fancy
PAINTING.

BLUNT and CODMAN having taken a room for a few weeks, at Mr. William Stickney's tavern, offer their services to the Ladies and gentlemen of Concord and its vicinity, in the above lines of their profession.
Persons wishing portraits, can (if preferred) be waited on at their houses.
Concord, Oct. 4, 1819.   37

Portrait of General Henry Sweetser, oil on canvas, 1819, by William P. Codman; newspaper advertisement of Codman and partner John S. Blunt, New-Hampshire Patriot & State Gazette (Concord), 1819. This signed and dated portrait was commissioned in response to the artist's Concord advertisement. The subject, a Chester tavernkeeper, was the husband of Susannah West; her family lived in Concord a few doors from Stickney's tavern, where the portrait was most likely painted.

NHHS Collections   Photographer, Bill Finney

make appointments for sittings. The portrait painting and profile cutting took place either at the tavern, or, "if preferred," at the subject's home. In 1801, a Massachusetts visitor in Exeter expressed his pleasure in finding "at the public house Mr. Hancock of Boston who had come to [New Hampshire] as a Miniature painter."[137] One Vermont-born artist noted, in recording the humble begin-

WM. KING,
TAKER OF PROFILE LIKENESSES,

RESPECTFULLY informs the Ladies and Gentlemen of Hanover and its vicinity, that he has taken a Room at Mr. *James Wheelock's*, where he intends to ftay one week to take

Profile Likeneffes,

with his Patent Delineating Pencil.

He takes the Profiles in fix minutes, on a beautiful *wove paper*, with the greateft poffible correctnefs, which is well known, he having taken above twenty thoufand in *Salem, Newburyport, Portfmouth, Portland,* and their adjoining towns ; and from them he has felected a few as fpecimens, which may be viewed at his Room.

His price for two Profiles of one perfon is *Twenty-five Cents*—and frames them in a handfome manner, with black glafs, in elegant oval, round or fquare Frames, gilt or black—Price from *Fifty Cents* to *Two Dollars* each.

Mr. KING refpectfully folicits the early attendance of thofe Ladies and Gentlemen, who intend to have their Profiles taken, as he muft leave town at the above named time.—Conftant attendance from 8 in the morning till 10 in the evening.

March 24, 1806.

N. B. Thofe who are not fatisfied with their Profiles previous to their leaving his Room, may have their money returned.

JOHN PUTNAM,
PHYSIOGNOTRACE,

Respectfully informs the Ladies and Gentlemen of Amherft and its vicinity, that he has taken a room at Capt. *T. Page's* tavern, where he intends ftaying four days from the date, to take PROFILE LIKENESSES, with his new invented delineating pencil, which, for accuracy, excels any machine, before invented for that purpofe. He reduces to any fize from the fhadow ; therefore the perfon is not incommoded with any thing paffing over the face, nor detained over three minutes at the machine.

Auguft 13, 1805.

e

Newspaper advertisements for silhouettists William King and John Putnam, Dartmouth Gazette *(Hanover), 1806, and* Farmer's Cabinet *(Amherst), 1805. Until the age of photography, the silhouette or profile was the only form of portrait most people could afford. Itinerant profile cutters, sometimes giving themselves impressive titles, advertised their skills and newly invented instruments in local newspapers as they moved from tavern to tavern.*

Courtesy, Dartmouth College Library and NHHS Collections

nings of his own painting career: "I put up at a tavern and told a Young Lady if she would wash my shirt, I would draw her likeness."[138] After staying in town for a few weeks, the typical artist put an advertisement in the local newspaper advising "those who may wish their PORTRAITS Painted by him, that they must apply soon, as he contemplates leaving this place in a short time."[139]

Performers constituted another category of artists whose work kept them constantly on the road. In addition to actors, musicians, ventriloquists, magicians, puppeteers, and acrobats, whose counterparts are still active today, there were other types of traveling performances and exhibitions whose popularity has faded with time. Before the motion-picture era, optical shows caused a sensation wherever seen. Visitors to Joseph Bellows' tavern in Walpole in 1797 could see an astonishing display of wax figures, "large as life," including one showing the "Guillotine, with an exact representation of the King of France, at the eventful moment when he suffered."[140] This exhibition of waxwork, accompanied by music on the hand organ, moved on the next week to neighboring Charlestown. Half a century later, a "Grand moving Diorama" was the feature certain to draw a large crowd. At Franklin Hall in Portsmouth in 1840, one program included both "a Thunder-Storm on the Mississippi River, being upwards of 200 feet in length" and the "Magnificent Spectacle of the CONFLAGRATION OF MOSCOW."[141]

From the eighteenth century, simpler versions of these spectacles, known as "peep shows," were carried around the countryside by rootless wanderers like Henry Tufts. The major tool of his trade at one period of his life was "a

Ticket for performance by New Hampshire magician and ventriloquist Richard Potter, circa 1830. One of New England's most famous magicians, Potter was a resident of Andover, N.H., from around 1814 until his death in 1835. "Hocus-Pocus Potter" performed at taverns throughout New Hampshire, including Benjamin Thompson's in Andover, Joseph Darrah's in Charlestown, and the Lafayette Hotel in Lebanon.
NHHS Collections   Photographer, Ernest Gould

set of pictures [probably hand-colored engravings] called *shows*, which were viewed by looking through magnifying glasses, artificially disposed for the purpose." Tufts claims to have carried these "shows" about for one winter, exhibiting them "with great ostentation, at about a groat a sight."[142]

Also paraded for display purposes at taverns throughout the state were a variety of both natural and contrived wonders and curiosities. Egyptian mummies were on display in Warner in 1828, American Indians in Northwood in 1828, a lamb born sporting a fashionable woman's hairdo in Portsmouth in 1774, and a well-preserved twenty-eight-foot-long sea monster in Dover in 1828.[143] Other unusual attractions included a "White [or albino] Negro boy" in Portsmouth in 1764; Siamese twins in Dover in 1831; a child giant in Portsmouth in 1819; and an armless boy, who could perform amazing feats with his toes, in Claremont in 1834. "Gentlemen or Ladies" in Portsmouth could even request that the Virginia-born albino, whose mother and father were "both Black," be transported to their homes for convenient examination, simply "by applying to the Owner at the Sign of the Earl of Halifax."[144]

Before traveling circuses or menageries became common in the second quarter of the nineteenth century, even a single exotic animal—a lion, tiger, elephant, or camel—on display at the local tavern was an outstanding community event. Although two camels imported from Arabia were exhibited at Stavers' tavern in Portsmouth as early as 1789, most of the first exotic animal visits to smaller towns were in the 1810s and 1820s.[145] The earliest showing of an elephant at Lebanon about 1812 is said to have "brought together more people than had ever collected at any time before on any occasion, estimated at 5000 [and] they came from all [the] adjoining towns"; the elephant, whose name was Betts, was exhibited in the tavern barn.[146]

In 1811, a circus of an early variety visited Portsmouth.[147] Although tickets could be purchased "at Mr. Davenport's bar room at any time," the performance was probably held, as in Newburyport a month earlier, in a specially erected "pavilion" in an "unoccupied lot," in this case near Jefferson Street. The acts consisted primarily of feats of horsemanship and acrobatics, together with a hornpipe dancer and clown.[148] Separate acrobatic shows, equestrian demonstrations, and traveling menageries gained popularity throughout the state in the 1820s and 1830s. The traveling performers set up headquarters at the local tavern, often—as was the case in Farmington—in the innkeeper's field "that lay back of the tavern." Occasionally, a "side show" of wax figures would simultaneously enliven the tavern's hall.[149]

A menagerie, sometimes billed as a "Grand Caravan of Living Animals," must have been a sight to behold as it traveled New Hampshire highways. Perhaps in a deliberate attempt to preserve the effectiveness of the paid performance, circuses traveled primarily at night. One Merrimack girl recalled a dimly lit caravan: "Sometimes a

RARE
Curiosities.

To be seen at *Mr. Pattee's Hall in Warner on Tuesday the 2nd January, for one day & Evening only.*

TWO

Mummies,

FROM

Egypt.

The public is respectfully in-formed that the proprietor has at great expense procured these wonderful preservations of the human body, as specimens of the ancient and now lost art of embalming. He hopes that the learned and curious will be gratified in viewing them.

They were taken from the Catacombs at the ancient city of Thebes, by the permission of the Pacha of Egypt, by an American gentleman and brought by him to Boston.

Broadside advertising an exhibition of Egyptian mummies at Richard Pattee's tavern in Warner, N.H., (detail), 1828. Among the wonders and curiosities exhibited at local taverns was a pair of mummies (male and female) owned by Massachusetts artist Ethan Allen Greenwood. The printed broadside would have been posted at the tavern to announce the coming attraction.
NHHS Collections   Photographer, Ernest Gould

FEMALE ELEPHANT.

THE only Elephant, now in America, is in this town, and may be seen at Mrs. HODGDON's tavern to-day, and Monday next.

Admittance 25 cents, for all over twelve years old—from that to five, 12½ cents.

Dover, Oct. 7, 1815.

TO THE CURIOUS!

To be seen at Mr. STAVERS' Tavern, (PORTSMOUTH)

TWO CAMELS,

MALE and FEMALE, imported from ARABIA.

AFRICAN LION.

For one week only.

JUST arrived, a LIVING AFRICAN LION, to be seen at the Bell Tavern, Congress-street, from 9 o'clock in the morning until 9 o'-clock in the evening. The form of the Lion is strikingly majestic, his figure is respectable, his looks are determined, his gait is stately, and his voice tremendous.

In a word, the body of the Lion is the best model of strength, joined to agility. Yet powerful and terrible as this animal is, its anger is noble, its courage magnanimous, and its temper susceptible of magnanimous impressions. It has often been known to despise weak and defenceless animals, thrown to be devoured by it; to live in habits of cordiality with it; to share its subsistence, and even to give it a preference when its portion of food was scanty.

This Lion is the surviving one of a pair which were on board the brig William, from the river Senegal bound to Liverpool, and was intended as a present to the Prince Regent of Great-Britain. He is perfectly docile and obedient to his keeper; will lick his hand and permit him to handle his paws, to play with him, and often manifests a great fondness and affection for him.

☞ Price of Admittance 25 cents.—Children half price.   april 30.

Three newspaper advertisements announcing the display of exotic animals at taverns: the elephant was advertised in the Dover Sun, *1815; the lion,* New-Hampshire Gazette (Portsmouth), *1816; and the camels,* New-Hampshire Spy (Portsmouth), *1789. Until menageries and circuses became popular, exotic animals, exhibited alone or in pairs, created a sensation at tavern after tavern. The elephant, exhibited in Dover in October 1815, had appeared for three days at the tavern of Captain Horace Wells in Keene two months earlier.*

NHHS Collections   Photographer, Ernest Gould

Broadside advertising acrobatic performance of Mr. Vilallave and his company, (detail), Portsmouth, N.H., 1827. Acrobats were among the diverse itinerant performers whose lives and work revolved around the local tavern. The "exhibition" of Mr. Vilallave's company included "bending feats" and tightrope dancing. Although this particular performance took place at Jefferson Hall, tickets were available at the "Bar of Mr. Robinson's Hotel."
NHHS Collections   Photographer, Ernest Gould

Circus would pass in the night with a Carivan of Animils" and, by lighting a fire, those along the route "would get a free sight. . . . One night when the Boys heard they were coming, they colected all the Shaveings they could find and strewed them all along beside the road. And when the Elephants and Camels went by, they for once had a free show." The next stop for the circus was at the local tavern, where many would pay for a show less exciting than the fire-lit glimpse.[150]

Itinerants of all types encountered some degree of distrust on the part of the native population. Although the vast majority carried out their business in a professional manner, a few miscreants sullied the reputation of the entire class. Because of the general fear that a peddler's wares might prove to be stolen property, it was actually illegal until the nineteenth century for anyone to peddle in New Hampshire except in his own town.[151] Dishonest but versatile individuals like Henry Tufts traveled the countryside, moreover, practicing trades and professions for which they had little actual training. At various times Tufts preached, told fortunes, and defrayed his "itinerary expenses" by "doctoring," employing cures he had learned from the Indians.[152] In 1773, one presumably respectable Portsmouth music teacher absconded, without paying his debts, and, in 1832, a portrait painter similarly neglected to pay his bill at the Eagle Coffee House in Concord.[153]

Apparently, there were enough instances from earliest times of illegal activity on the part of itinerants that, as of 1718, any of the following were considered "vagabonds" and could be sent to the "house of Correction," without having committed any offense beyond the simple fact of their occupation: "Persons using any subtle Craft, Jugling,

or unlawful Games, or Plays, or feigning themselves to have knowledge in Physiognomy, Palmestry; or pretending that they can tell Destinies, Fortunes, or discover where lost or stolen Goods may be found, Common Pipers, [or] Fidlers."[154] By the nineteenth century, however, a system had been established in which licenses were required from the individual towns by all "showmen, tumblers, rope dancers, ventriloquists, or other persons, who shall for pay, exhibit any animals, wax figures, puppets, or any extraordinary feats of agility of body or slight of hand, rope-dancing, or performing feats with cards, within any town within this State."[155]

Some of the traffic passing through New Hampshire was clearly illegal. In the early nineteenth century, embargoes against foreign commerce, inspired by the controversy with Britain, brought about a brisk smuggling trade back and forth across the Canadian border. By 1811, Sarah Emery of Newburyport was aware that Boscawen farmers were supplying her seaport with fashionable dry goods, clandestinely conveyed from Canada by sleigh.[156] Around 1808, a European traveler noted the "variety of curious expedients . . . resorted to by the Americans in smuggling their produce over the line; buildings were erected exactly upon the boundary line, one half in Canada, the other half in the States; the goods were put in at night, and before morning were safe in Canada."[157]

According to tradition, the Dodge tavern at Walpole was one place smugglers often sought refuge.[158] Customs officers kept a careful watch on taverns in their attempt to control illegal commerce.[159] In 1831, however, when smuggling was discovered in Crawford Notch on an even larger scale "than during the War," Abel Crawford, the leading tavern-keeper in that part of the country, was counted upon as a "suitable man" to help stop this activity. A letter recommending him as an "inspector" pointed out that his location was exceptionally convenient for such a task, because "every one must stop at his house to pay toll over the Jefferson Turnpike.[160]

Clandestine activity along New Hampshire highways also included the fugitive slave traffic. In the early nineteenth century, large numbers of slaves escaped from the South as stowaways aboard vessels bound for New England ports. Particularly after the Fugitive Slave Act of 1850, an informal network developed, headed by the Vigilance Committee of Boston, and extending into New Hampshire, with the sole mission of assisting runaway slaves to safety in Canada. Three of the main routes from Boston and Salem on the so-called "underground railroad" passed through New Hampshire; other routes originated at southern New England ports and followed New Hampshire's Connecticut Valley northward. Often the fugitives were transported by night in teamsters' wagons, concealed among the freight.[161] The tavern sometimes provided temporary refuge for those fleeing bondage. A number of New Hampshire taverns are reputed to have served as way stations on the underground railroad. The town of Lyme, for

Sheet music cover, "Greys' Quick Step," (detail), 1839, scene captioned: "On their tour of Camp Duty from Portsmouth to Haverhill," lithographed by Thomas Moore after William Lydston, Jr. This lithograph portrays the march of the Columbian Greys to Haverhill, Massachusetts, following an encampment in Portsmouth, N.H., in July 1839. The "Greys' Quick Step" was composed for the Boston militia company by B. A. Burditt and first played during the Portsmouth encampment by the Boston Brigade Band.

NHHS Collections   Photographer, Ernest Gould

example, is said to have been active in speeding escaped slaves northward, and Beal Tavern on the road to Dorchester is identified as one of the buildings where slaves were hidden on their way to Canada.[162]

Many other strange and thrilling sights have passed along New Hampshire highways in turn. More than one team of White Mountain explorers attracted local attention because of the barometers and the sextant they carried in order to determine the height and location of mountains.[163] Military expeditions, both as peacetime exercises and during wartime crisis, produced an indelible impression on those who witnessed them. According to a Lebanon resident:

During the war of 1812 to '15, business was brisk and lively, and the whole country was animated and excited. United States soldiers were occasionally passing through on this route from Boston to Burlington . . . often staying over night, occupying the house and barns [of the Benton tavern]. The boys would learn

from the stage driver when soldiers were coming, and often met them near Elder Scott's where they always formed into companies and marched through the village, to the music of the fife and drum. . . . It seemed like a holiday. The passing of troops and the government wagons with stores for the army, were events which made a deep impression upon our young minds.[164]

Later in the nineteenth century, military companies from out-of-state sometimes held encampments in New Hampshire or made ceremonial tours accompanied by one of the newly popular brass bands.[165]

Another phenomenon of the highway, often forgotten today though never far from the consciousness of those who observed it, was the almost epic-scale overland trek of Irish immigrants from Quebec, where their vessels docked, to Lowell, where canal construction and textile work awaited them. As later recalled by one eyewitness in Merrimack: "They traveled down through the Country in great droves of Men, women, and children with great packs on there [*sic*] backs.''[166] And in 1834 in the midst of this migration, a New London resident wrote to her daughter:

You don't know how many Irish people there are travelling down this way every day. . . . I guess that there was 20-30 stopped to Uncle Herrick's [tavern] the other night. There was about 40 stayed there over night. . . . they slept in the stable upon some straw [—] men, women, and children all together. They looked like human misery indeed.[167]

By the early nineteenth century, highly diverse traffic, including immigrants, military troops, scientific expeditions, fugitive slaves, smugglers, itinerants of all kinds, droves of animals, caravans of wagons, post riders and mail stages, could be found crossing New Hampshire. The steady flow of traffic formed a strong link between the state's rural communities and the outside world.

Daguerreotype, the Manchester (N.H.) to Haverhill (Mass.) stage at Abel G. Quigg's Central House in Chester, N.H., 1848-55. This photograph provides the earliest known image of a once common scene: a coach with passengers at a New Hampshire stage stop. Remaining motionless because of the long exposure required for a daguerreotype, the stage driver poses in the act of handing a bundle of newspapers to the tavernkeeper or a member of his staff. A ''Post Office'' sign over the far door hints at the innkeeper's many roles.
Courtesy, Private Collection

PEOPLE OF THE ROAD

CHAPTER 6

AN INDEFINABLE MYSTIQUE surrounds many of the early New Hampshire men and women whose lives and work centered on the highway. Mention today of the stage driver, ferryman, tavernkeeper, highwayman, and horsethief conjures up a series of images which may or may not reflect the realities of former times in New Hampshire. Although published recollections and anecdotes are invaluable as recorded oral history, later writers have repeated and embellished this evidence to the point that fact and fiction are often indistinguishable. Only by returning to the actual words of travelers and natives alive during the height of the tavern and turnpike era can we hope to understand the people whose daily work so directly affected travel in early New Hampshire.

Of all the "people of the road," stage drivers seem to have inspired the most vivid recollections. The reason seems to be the impression these capable "knights of the whip" made on the younger generation: "The little boys remember it a month, if the stage-driver speaks to them."[1] A Newburyport student, who entered Phillips Exeter Academy in 1817, recalled his trips home at the end of a term:

> Quite a number of stage coaches were always sent on to take us. When they arrived what a scramble ensued to see who should ride with Pike, who with Annable, or Knight, or Forbes, or some other good-natured driver—experienced in stages and careful of their young charges, as if they were all destined to be governors, or judges, or presidents. We used to consider it the seat of honor on the outside with the driver, there to listen to his stories and to enjoy his company.[2]

Published town histories have immortalized hundreds of individual stage drivers by recording not only their names and nicknames, but also anecdotes demonstrating their diverse skills and idiosyncratic behavior. Described more recently as "a class by themselves," stage drivers seem to have performed even the most routine task with unforgettable flair. "How majestically he rounds to at the door of the tavern! . . . How he flings the reins and the tired horses to the stable-boy, who presently returns with a splendid relay! How he accepts these from the boy, with that sort of air with which a king might be supposed to take his crown from the hands of a valet!"[3]

The stage driver was indeed a man respected in his community. According to an English traveler around 1800, the New England stage driver "was frequently the owner of a farm or inn, and of a share in his conveyance."[4] A visitor in 1842 rode in the Conway stage "with a good gentlemanly driver, who owns the whole establishment, and drives on his own hook."[5] In the early nineteenth century, drivers so often held prominent rank in the militia that "captain" became an acceptable form of address for stage drivers.[6] English visitors, accustomed to the military as a "highly respectable separate profession," were apparently amused that one person could be both stage driver and militia captain.[7] However, at least one English tourist, passing through New Hampshire in the 1830s, recognized that the two positions were not incompatible: "I did not inquire if our driver was actually a military captain, but so far as appearance entitles a man to rank, he might have been a field-marshal."[8]

According to one claim, the driver wielded a certain amount of political influence as well. The sight of a printing office at Walpole in 1808 inspired an English visitor to generalize that "those who are remotely situated from a town where [newspapers] are published, must depend upon the *politics of the coachman*, for such a paper as he chooses to bring them."[9] The fact that the driver was often trusted to make deliveries, transact business, and settle accounts on behalf of parties in different locations also suggests the responsible nature of his position and the respect in which he was held.

Remarks made by some travelers, however, suggest that passengers, especially foreigners, did not always consider their driver—however admirable—as an equal. One English visitor commented: "At New Ipswich, the driver of the stage seated himself at table with the passengers, which was the only instance of the kind that came under my observation. Some of the passengers were of the most genteel description, and the driver conducted himself with propriety."[10] Another English traveler at an inn in Conway, after noting that "the driver of the stage was one of the breakfast party, and appeared to be the principal personage at the table," concluded rather disdainfully: "I see no rational objection to this, if they are clean and well-behaved."[11]

Unlike Europeans, most American passengers did not

treat stage drivers as servants. An English traveler, who had just helped a "slight" coachman by lifting four heavy trunks on to the vehicle, found it necessary to explain that "the Americans never refuse to assist each other in such difficulties as this."[12] Also, in the new democracy passengers did not observe the European practice of tipping. A local resident later recalled, however, that, on at least one stage route from Rutland, Vermont, to Boston, the driver was not above "expect[ing that] the cigars and drinks would be free at all the points where horses were exchanged."[13]

Stage drivers were often entrusted to make purchases or deliveries for rural residents. Certainly the most outlandish is the tale of a driver on the Hanover to Chelsea, Vermont, stage, who claimed to have been given at one stop a couple of chickens to take to the tavern in Chelsea and, at the next stop, the body of a child to place in a tomb. The conclusion of the story is not difficult to imagine: "In his hurry he placed the chickens in the tomb and handed the child to the tavernkeeper."[14] Whether or not this story derived from a specific incident, it reflects the reliance of local residents on the stage driver for deliveries and business transactions of all sorts. Theodore Davis, who had just established a stage between Portsmouth and Boston in 1772, advertised that "the utmost Fidelity may be depended on, in any Affairs, which he may be intrusted with."[15] At least one New Hampshire stage driver, whose reputation was earned by his successful transport of large sums of money to and from Boston banks, eventually set up his own express company—one of the progenitors of American Express.[16]

Numerous other tasks associated with the stage driver's job would have been forgotten over the years if they were not recorded in various travel accounts. Certain drivers were known to bring trinkets from the city to invalids along the route, to help search for articles lost on the road by clients, and, in other similar ways, to show a deep personal concern for the welfare of passengers, particularly the younger ones.[17] A woman later recalled a childhood journey through Portsmouth and Newburyport: "How well I remember the kind, smiling face of Robinson, as next morning, whip in hand, he appeared at the parlor door and inquired for the 'little girl' who was to go with him! His hearty 'good morning' and 'all ready, miss,' as I presented myself, are still sounding in my ears."[18]

Patience and flexibility must have been chief among the personality traits of an early New Hampshire stage driver, dealing with such a diverse clientele. Individual drivers tried to accommodate passengers' needs. In one remarkable instance, on the stage from Keene to Fitzwilliam in 1836, the coachman allowed a woman to finish "sudsing" her son's pantaloons before boarding and hanging her wash out the coach window to dry.[19]

Although most drivers no doubt confirmed this legendary reputation for good humor, instances of "unsociable," "insolent," "surly," and "ill-tempered" drivers were not

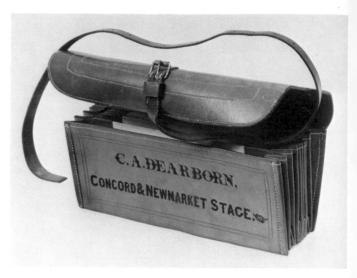

Leather dispatch case used by stage driver Charles A. Dearborn on the Concord & New Market Stage; made by Josiah Cummings, Springfield, Mass., circa 1865. Local residents often entrusted important papers as well as large sums of money to the stage driver. The leather case which one New Hampshire driver acquired to protect such dispatches survives practically unused, probably because his coach line was discontinued with the ascendancy of the railroad.

NHHS Collections   Photographer, Bill Finney

unknown.[20] While one traveler in the White Mountains was speaking to another passenger about the route to Littleton, his driver is reported to have interrupted, exclaiming: "I should think I ought to know the route. Nobody knows the route better than them thats driven on it, Sir." As the narrator next confessed, "We heartily resolved to blow him up, the first opportunity."[21]

Despite their proverbial patience, drivers occasionally seemed to be "in hot haste," "in a fever of impatience," and "flying in and out of the vehicle with the crack of a harlequin."[22] The town history of Hampton Falls records the time-honored custom of yielding way on the highway to a stagecoach, so that it could keep on schedule. "Those who did not do this received a salutation from the driver which was more forcible than elegant. The driver would then rein his team as near to the offending individual as possible, to give him the benefit of the long stage whiffle-trees, which would not lightly brush against the private team."[23] Variations in the behavior of stage drivers are perhaps explained by one observant traveler who noted "a great difference in the behavior of the drivers of the mails, and coaches which are *timed* by the post-office, and others which are not."[24]

Most travelers enthusiastically praised the driver's skill and dexterity in managing the reins for six or eight horses, while "steering between dangers." One of the more graphic descriptions was written by an English traveler who visited New Hampshire in 1832:

ON THE ROAD NORTH OF BOSTON

We had six-in-hand throughout our journey . . . and I never saw men more expert at their business than coachmen on the 260 miles road between Boston and Burlington. It was rather amusing to witness the manner in which they restrained the horses when descending a steep hill, wrapping the reins of the leaders round their arms up to the elbows, using their feet to those of the wheelers, and then, leaning back on their seat, with the whip thrown upon the roof of the coach, they tugged away with both hand and foot.[25]

Not every driver, apparently, was as skilled—a Frenchman, who barely avoided a serious accident while traveling from Hampton Falls to Portsmouth in 1784, termed his coachman "an ignoramus."[26]

Surprisingly, music was another frequently mentioned talent. Most coachmen employed a long tin horn to announce their arrival at a stage stop. Some, like Colonel Silas May on the Concord to Haverhill, New Hampshire, stage, played the bugle instead. Residents along his route recalled that he "not infrequently drove six horses with one hand, while with the other he held his bugle and played those beautiful tunes, the gladdening echoes of which floated over forest and dell."[27] Although none of the flourishes played by New Hampshire drivers appear to have been transcribed, some tunes popular among their English counterparts have survived in printed form.[28]

Many stage drivers developed a flair for words, entertaining their passengers with stories, jokes, and miscellaneous information. An English actor, performing in New Hampshire in 1808, succeeded, perhaps because of shared theatrical tendencies, in capturing the essence of the New England coachman:

He was a general book of reference, almanac, market list, and farmers' journal; a daily paper published every morning, a focus which, by some peculiar centripetality, drew all things towards it. . . . Very often the driver was a wag, who had a joke for his passengers, perhaps as old as his stage, and as little likely to stop running. . . . The reserve of an English conveyance is proverbial, the animation of the one in which we found ourselves offered the greatest possible contrast.[29]

An example of the stage driver's sense of humor appeared in an Amherst newspaper in the early nineteenth century. Joseph Wheat was a driver noted both for his skill at versification and his exceptionally long nose. When the citizens of Amherst complained that he did not sound the usual horn to announce his approach, he suggested that "whenever they should see *the nose*, they might expect *the stage* in about ten minutes."[30]

Alice Morse Earle, author of *Stage-Coach and Tavern Days*, one of the earliest books on the subject (published in 1901), recollected being keenly disappointed at her first sight, which happened to be in Charlestown, New Hampshire, of an actual coachman: "a man, even on a day of Indian Summer, all in hide and fur: moth-eaten fur gloves, worn fur cap with vast ear-flaps and visor, and half-bare

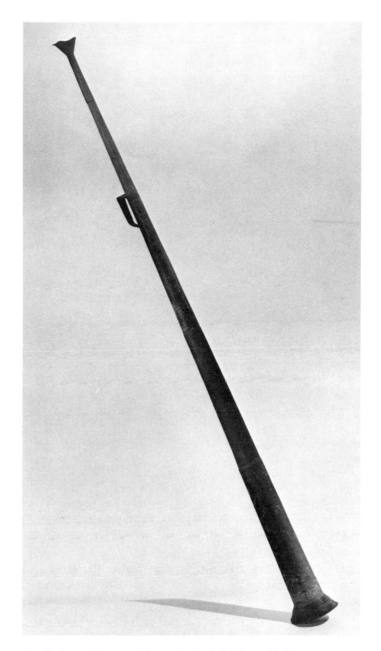

Coach horn, japanned iron, Philadelphia, mid-19th century. Coachmen sounded rhythmic blasts on long, slender horns, both to signal other drivers and to entertain passengers. The coach horn, sometimes referred to as a "yard-of-tin," could reach almost five feet in length. Horn signals were depended on in mountainous territory to warn descending vehicles to yield the right-of-way to those ascending the hill.

Courtesy, The Metropolitan Museum of Art, The Crosby Brown Collection of Musical Instruments

buffalo-hide coat, and out of all these ancient skins but one visible feature, a great, shining, bulbous nose."[31] (Could she have seen the legendary Joseph Wheat?)

The clothing worn by stage drivers was diverse, determined by personal preference and individual level of physical endurance. In the exceptionally rainy May of 1831, as

Printed invitation to the Annual Stageman's Ball, (detail), Concord, N.H., 1839, printed by William White. Once a year, as many as one hundred and fifty stage drivers from New Hampshire and neighboring states gathered with their dancing partners in the coaching capital of New Hampshire for a festive evening. Following this event in 1840, the newspaper reported: "Every thing was done up in the neat and elegant style, peculiar to the gentlemen of the whip on such occasions."

NHHS Collections   Photographer, Ernest Gould

on that Indian summer day in Charlestown, a Newport newspaper found it worthy of note that "the Stage drivers come in wrapped in their shag fear noughts [heavy coats of shaggy woolen cloth] and mittens as though it was midwinter."[32] Another contemporary noted that a stage driver would "no sooner touch anything without gloves" than would a "fine lady."[33] Simultaneously, however, another observer recorded about New England drivers in general that "no one more abhorred a superfluity of clothes. A straw hat was his creed, and he would often wear nankeens [heavy cotton trousers] and shoes in frosty weather."[34] Confirming this preference, a White Mountain traveler, during a snowstorm in the winter of 1828, marveled at her "hardy stage driver [who] came through the Notch in the hardest of it, blithe and gay, even without socks or overshoes; [moreover] he entered the house and never came near the fire!"[35]

In the mid-nineteenth century, the height of the coachman's year was the annual stage-driver's ball. Such events are known to have taken place at the Eagle Coffee House in Concord and the Exchange Hotel in Haverhill. In 1837, a newspaper in the capital city described the local ball: "It was numerously attended, and embraced as many elegantly dressed and beautiful ladies, and hale goodlooking gentlemen as we have seldom seen collected on a similar occasion. The Governor was present and participated in the festivities of the occasion."[36] Such "splendid" balls were eloquent testimony both to the social respectability and the camaraderie of New Hampshire's "knights of the whip."

The ferryman was less idealized than the stage driver but also an important individual in early New Englanders' travels. Legal records from the seventeenth through the nineteenth centuries offer us a realistic picture of the ferrykeeper as an essential public servant. In return for the exclusive privilege of keeping a ferry at a certain location, the ferryman typically expended "great Sums of Money, Time, & Labor," as well as "Trouble," in constructing and keeping in repair not only boats, capable of transporting horse teams, but also the roads through his own property to the ferry landing. For as long as the ferryman was in constant attendance and his boats were maintained in good condition, the right granted by the legislature to keep a ferry was held legally not only by the ferryman himself but also by his heirs, so that often several generations of a single family operated a particular ferry.[37]

Rivals for the privilege of keeping a ferry at a certain location sometimes petitioned the legislature: "said Ferry has not been properly provided with Boats, to carry over loaded Teams by which means men's lives and properties, have been much exposed, and some have sustained, great damage and loss." In at least one instance, the competition between neighbors owning riverfront property was so intense that one party attempted to multiply the signatures on its petition by distributing "cherry Rum" and grog during town meeting. According to further testimony concerning this 1786 Hinsdale incident, a third party, on behalf of one of the applicants, allegedly threatened a fellow townsman, who was not inclined to sign the petition in question. "Said he you will want to cross offen and you hant always money Implying as I understood that If I would

Photograph, Ashley Ferry, Claremont, N.H., 1896. Ferrykeeping was an occupation often shared by an entire family, and the right granted by the legislature to keep a ferry was often passed on from generation to generation. At this ferry site in 1831, sixty-five years before the photograph was taken, an eleven-year-old boy fell overboard and drowned while helping his father carry passengers across the Connecticut River.

NHHS Collections   Photographer, William A. Wright

not sign said Paper I should not be carried across s^d farry [*sic*] without the money in hand.''[38]

In addition to granting exclusive and inheritable privileges to encourage the operation of ferries on rivers around the state, the New Hampshire legislature waived town and state taxes for all ferrymen who allowed magistrates, jurymen, military troops, and others on public missions to cross with little or no charge. Ferrymen were also personally exempt by New Hampshire law from militia duty.[39]

Since the earliest ferry grants also specified that the ferrykeeper ''shall have liberty of Selling beer and Cyder free from Excise,'' the ferryman often kept a tavern as well.[40] When Christopher Frederick of New Castle was accused of selling ale without license in 1723, he argued successfully that all ferrymen were allowed to sell strong drink.[41]

One surprising aspect of ferrykeeping was the use of child labor in boat operation, at least during the early nineteenth century. One traveler, who crossed the Connecticut River at Orford in 1803, wrote that ''the boat was managed by two children, smaller than I had ever seen trusted with such an employment. But the expedition and safety with which we crossed the river proved their perfect competency for the business, and convinced me that we generally estimate the capacity of children beneath the

truth.''[42] The drowning of an eleven-year-old boy, however, at Ashley's Ferry in Claremont in 1831, tragically demonstrated the dangers when such work was imposed on a child. At 8:30 in the evening, ferrykeeper Abram Jones had ''called on his little son, who was then abed, to arise and accompany him for the purpose of steering the boat. . . . The cause of the accident is unknown, but it is probable he had again fallen asleep; as he was in the constant practice of steering the boat, as well as occasionally rowing across alone.''[43]

As the decades passed, the ferryman's grant of privileges from the government was jeopardized by the right reserved to the legislature ''to build a Bridge [in the same location] whenever the public good may require.''[44] In 1820, a Claremont ferrykeeper questioned the state legislature's ''constitutional right to grant to any individual the privilege of erecting a toll bridge within the limits of said grant of ferry without the express consent of the owners of said right of ferry.''[45] Eventually, improved bridge technology compelled many ferrykeepers to rely more heavily for their livelihood on their often extensive landholdings; fortunately, the riverfront property which had qualified them to keep a ferry, was usually fertile enough to be cultivated successfully. Those ferrymen who also served as tavernkeepers often continued to accommodate travelers.

Portrait of Levi Jones, Milton, N.H., circa 1825, watercolor on paper, possibly by the obscure itinerant artist known only as Mr. Wilson. Jones kept a tavern at Plummer's Ridge on the important early route from Portsmouth to Wolfeboro; he was also a prosperous farmer, landowner, and businessman. He held office in the statewide Masonic Grand Lodge as well as serving at various times as town clerk of Milton and as state representative.

Courtesy, The Currier Gallery of Art
  Photographer, Bill Finney

Portrait, General Jonathan Chase, Cornish, N.H., circa 1790, oil on canvas, attributed to Joseph Steward. Dressed here in his military uniform, Cornish's first tavernkeeper was an influential landowner, farmer, and surveyor, who served his community as selectman, town treasurer, and eventually, state representative. Like many innkeepers, Chase was also a military leader and, after distinguished service during the Revolution, he was named brigadier general in the state militia.

NHHS Collections   Photographer, Bill Finney

The early New Hampshire tavernkeeper was one of the most prominent individuals encountered by travelers. Contrary to present-day assumptions, innkeepers formed, in words used by one New Hampshire guest, "the natural aristocracy of America."[46] As a Massachusetts visitor to New Hampshire around 1795 explained, the eminent social position of the New England tavernkeeper did not derive from English precedent:

> Your countrymen so often laugh at the fact that inns in New England are kept by persons whose titles indicate them to be men of some consequence. . . . Our ancestors considered an inn as a place where corruption would naturally arise and might easily spread; as a place where travelers must trust themselves, their horses, baggage, and money; where women as well as men must at times lodge, might need humane and delicate offices, and might be subjected to disagreeable exposures. To provide for safety and comfort, and against danger and mischief in all these cases, they took particular pains in their laws and administrations to prevent inns from being kept by vicious, unprinci-

pled, worthless men. . . . In consequence of this system, men of no small personal respectability have ever kept inns in this country.[47]

In 1824, an American author stated of the New England tavernkeeper: he "is often a magistrate, the chief of a battalion of militia, or even a member of a state legislature. He is almost always a man of character; for it is difficult for any other to obtain a license to exercise the calling."[48] Those wishing to open a "house of public entertainment" petitioned the county court for a license. As of 1687, New Hampshire law specified that such license be granted "to such onely as are persons of good repute and have convenient Houses and att least Two Bedds to entertaine Straingers and Travellors."[49] Since New Hampshire law limited the number of taverns which could operate in a given town, the competition among prospective innkeepers was keen. Surviving petitions demonstrate that each applicant not only had to prove that his house was located either on a major thoroughfare or at a local center of activity, but also that he himself was a man "of sober conversation."[50]

Because of such strict licensing procedures and the ensuing competition, successful tavernkeepers were often prominent figures in society. John Folsom, who operated a well-known hostelry on the Londonderry turnpike at Lake Massabesic, was a judge, a deacon, and a state representative.[51] In 1751, tavernkeeper John Hall of nearby Derryfield (now Manchester) became the agent for obtaining his town's charter, as well as the first town clerk; he also served as clerk in the Crown Point expedition of 1755 and later as a member of the Revolutionary Committee of Safety.[52] Other tavernkeepers were frequently prominent in the militia. Both Benjamin Pierce of Hillsborough and Jonathan Chase of Cornish attained the rank of brigadier general in the New Hampshire militia.[53] Captain Hezekiah Hutchins, a Hampstead innkeeper, pursued an exceptionally impressive military career, of which he said, in offering his services during the Revolutionary War, that he had "bin in all the wars In this Cuntry sense the taking of Luesburg the first time."[54] In 1820, Exeter's James Burley, tavernkeeper and major of the state militia's first brigade, published a book on military discipline.[55]

More than one traveler remarked upon the connection of innkeepers with the militia. A wayfarer arriving at Bellows Falls from New Ipswich in the mid-1830s commented that "the hotel-keepers of the country are the noblesse of the district, and are generally chosen, by the people, officers of the militia."[56] Once again English citizens were "apt to make themselves merry" with the fact that American defense was "without the agency of any better colonels, than such as sometimes act as inn-keepers."[57]

The operation of a public house was often not the sole occupation of its owner. Many who became licensed as tavernkeepers continued to work at their former trades or professions. Besides keeping a tavern, Thomas Packer of Portsmouth and William Hardy of Poplin (now Fremont) served their communities as physicians; John Davenport of Portsmouth as goldsmith; James Chase of Gilmanton as cabinetmaker; and Stephen C. Webster of Salisbury as a skilled woodworker or joiner.[58] Many innkeepers in rural areas were also farmers or shopkeepers: Abel Crawford cleared a hundred-acre farm near Crawford Notch and cultivated an orchard of seven hundred apple trees; Colonel Andrew McMillan of nearby Conway worked as a local merchant.[59] A visitor to Lancaster in 1828 described her landlord as "a plain farmer of considerable property; keeps a great dairy; a great many cows, calves, pigs, sheep."[60]

Tavernkeepers' supplementary trades often were based on the needs of travelers. It is probably more than coincidence that, in the mid-eighteenth century, several owners of inns and coffeehouses in the Portsmouth area also advertised as hairdressers.[61] In an era when New Hampshire gentlemen wore "Tye, Full-bottom'd, Brigadeer, and Bob-Wiggs" and women supplemented their natural hair with curls, "toupees," and "rolls," travelers in fashionable urban areas could not afford to be without a handy "peruke maker and hair-dresser."[62] If the innkeeper himself was

Daguerreotype of Abel Crawford, after portrait by Chester Harding, 1846. A farmer and state legislator, Abel Crawford was the patriarch of a family noted for tavernkeeping in a remote area of the White Mountains. Abel's tavern was referred to by travelers as "Old Crawford's"; eventually, two of Crawford's sons, Ethan Allen and Thomas J., built inns in the same vicinity.

NHHS Collections

not a skilled hairdresser or wigmaker, one would often open shop "opposite" the tavern.[63]

Tavernkeepers served another important need of the traveler, as well as of the local population, by boarding animals and keeping horses and vehicles for rental purposes.[64] This practice often led to horsebreeding, horseracing, veterinary medicine, and blacksmithing. John Stavers sometimes advertised his own or other stallions by name ("Raven," etc.) as available at the "Earl of Halifax Tavern" to "cover mares."[65] The obituary of John Nealey, a longtime landlord of the Northwood Hotel, stated that "so good was his judgment in the treatment of diseased animals that he was frequently consulted by farmers and others whose horses and cattle had been attacked by illness, or made lame from accident."[66] And surviving financial records show that Jeremiah Fellows of Kensington and David McCrillis of Canterbury shrewdly combined innkeeping with blacksmithing skills.[67]

In providing daily tavern fare, most innkeepers acquired exceptional culinary skills. Any occasion calling for refreshments, whether a special celebration held at the tavern or a catered event elsewhere in town, was an oppor-

THE HORSE
SUPERIOR,
RAISED IN NEW-YORK.

That excellent half-blood English Horse, **THE SUPERIOR**, will stand the ensuing season, commencing May 9th, for the use of Mares, at the following places, viz.—On every other *Monday*, at Perkins' in Hopkinton ; on every other *Tuesday*, at George's, in Concord ; on *Wednesdays*, at the stable of the subscriber, in Hopkinton ; on every other *Thursday*, at S. B. Gerrish's, Boscawen ; on *Fridays*, at D. Corser's, (near Fellowes' store,) Boscawen ; and on *Saturdays*, at Warner Upper Village.

Said Horse is of a beautiful dark chestnut color, is fifteen hands high, and of elegant symmetry and proportion. His gait is majestic, and in strength and speed he is surpassed by no horse in the country. His stock is every where approved ; and gentlemen desirous of improving in their breed of horses, need only to examine his colts to be satisfied of this fact.

TERMS.—$1 50 the leap ; $3 the season ; $4 to insure a foal. All mares warranted, and disposed of within a year, to be considered with foal.

CARTER BUSWELL.

Hopkinton, May 9, 1825.

J. B. Moore, Printer, Concord, N. H.—where all kinds of ncy Job-Printing is executed with accuracy, neatness and despatch.

Broadside advertising a stallion named ''Superior,'' Hopkinton, N.H., 1825, printed by Jacob Bailey Moore. Until the era of specialized livery stables, the tavernkeeper played an important role in all aspects of animal husbandry. Advertisements often featured his own or other horses available for breeding purposes at the tavern. During the spring of 1825, the stallion ''Superior'' traveled from tavern to tavern, following a schedule repeated weekly.

NHHS Collections   Photographer, Ernest Gould

tunity for the tavernkeeper to demonstrate his skill as professional cook. In 1810, the Associated Mechanics and Manufacturers of the State of New-Hampshire "partook of an elegant entertainment [or meal]" at their own hall provided by Portsmouth tavernkeeper John Davenport.[68] More than half a century earlier, Royal Governor Benning Wentworth regularly summoned tavernkeeper John King to his home at Little Harbor to help him shave and dress his hair as well as to cook special meals for his guests. A servant in the Wentworth household later recalled that, during the time she was employed there, "John King often came to the Governor's to Cook, and dressed several Turtles."[69] And, during an excursion into New Hampshire in 1822 by the Norwich, Vermont, military academy, a tavernkeeper in each major village along the route prepared a banquet to be served outdoors to reinvigorate the cadets as they marched into town.[70]

Although many men supplemented innkeeping with other means of livelihood, the disabled or infirm often found keeping a public house one of their few options for employment. In numerous petitions surviving from the colonial period, handicapped New Hampshire citizens seeking tavern licenses claimed that they could no longer earn their living by their usual occupation because of either visual or physical disabilities, sometimes combined with advanced age.[71] In 1698, for instance, Sarah Robey of Hampton pleaded "that your petitioner being a pore widow of about sixtie years of Age hath for this ffower or five years lost the use of my limbs and hath not bin able for the above sayd time to stand on my ffeet nor to dress or undress my self no more than a child And have no way to maintain my self but by keeping a public House of Entertainment."[72] About a century later, "the sight of [a Jefferson, New Hampshire] innkeeper walking around the room in a singular kind of fit, perfectly possessed of his senses, but unable to speak, and exhibiting a countenance constricted and ghastly," is known to have interrupted the meal of at least one group of visitors.[73]

Despite the rigorous licensing procedures, not all tavernkeepers were models of virtue. In 1828, a Portsmouth visitor described her landlord as "a very insolent, undeserving man . . . the third mean tavernkeeper I met with in New-England."[74] In 1805, three patrons of Henry Clough's tavern in Enfield claimed to have been treated in such "an unbecoming manner" that they decided to put an advertisement in the nearest newspaper to "warn and advise all those, who may have occasion to journey by or near said inn, to regard it as the residence of beings, who merit the derision of mankind."[75] Even innkeepers accused of murder, or attempted murder, were not unknown in early New Hampshire.[76] With some exceptions, however, the system generally ensured tavernkeepers of the highest calibre. In response to European visitors' frequent criticism of the American tavernkeeper's independent attitude and lack of servility, one New Englander, who often traveled in New Hampshire, argued that he had "found innkeepers

in various instances poor, ill furnished, and unpolished, but cannot recall more than two or three instances in which they have been disobliging."[77]

Tavernkeepers often far exceeded minimum standards of hospitality, however; many were noted for their sociability, eloquence, and refinement. As early as 1744, a guest characterized a Hampton innkeeper as "very fond of speculative points of religion and . . . for spiritualizing of everything."[78] More than a century later, an innkeeper at Jefferson described an echo in such unconventional terms that his English visitor exclaimed: "Had destiny not called on Mr. Plaistead to keep an American hotel, he might have been a poet."[79] The Crawfords, owners of several popular White Mountain inns, were noted in particular for their eloquent storytelling, primarily about events supposedly occurring in the mountains.[80] At least one guest expressed some skepticism: "How much of all of this is true, I know not—Crawford draws largely on his imagination for facts."[81]

A tavernkeeper did not expect to operate even the smallest public house without the assistance of family members, servants, and, in some cases, slaves to carry on the repetitive daily chores. One tavern in nearby Berwick, Maine, was probably typical in that each of the "numerous servants" was "employed both upon the extensive farm and the business of the inn."[82] Reliance on "trusty servants" also explains the ability of severely handicapped innkeepers to conduct their businesses effectively.[83] In 1838, one Conway inn boasted among its male staff, in addition to the landlord himself, a "waiter, ostler, groom, driver, porter, and stable-boy."[84] Young women, either family members or "country girls," often served as tavern waitresses and cooks.[85] As late as the 1830s, however, a traveler bemoaned the lack of chambermaids to wait on guests in their rooms in American inns.[86]

In 1838, at a lonely house in Franconia Notch called the Lafayette Hotel, "the host, two boys, and a nice-looking, obliging girl, wearing a string of gold beads, did their best to make [one visiting Englishwoman and her party] comfortable."[87] The family and staff of the average innkeeper were "well drest" and emitted "an air of decency and civility."[88] At Gibbs' in Littleton, a young lady of the family was so well versed in etiquette that she astonished her guests by correcting their table manners.[89]

It was not uncommon for the wealthier eighteenth-century New Hampshire tavernkeepers to own slaves. In 1723, Susanna Small of Portsmouth inherited from her father, Thomas Packer, not only his tavern license but also his "Negro Garle named Venus."[90] Almost half a century later, David Webster, the first tavernkeeper in the new settlement at Plymouth, purchased from Methuen, Massachusetts, "one negro-man, named 'Ciscow,' and one negro-woman, named 'Dinah,' wife of said 'Ciscow,' both being servants for life."[91] These slaves assisted in the daily operation of their owners' taverns.

With the exception of slaves, most hired help in Amer-

A likely, fmart young WOMAN is wanted as an Affiftant in a Tavern; one who is known by her good behaviour. Inquire at the Dunftable Hotel.   I. M.
Oct. 6.   3e52.

Newspaper advertisement (detail) for Isaac Marsh's Coachman and Farmer's Tavern, Dunstable Harbor (Nashua), Farmer's Cabinet (Amherst), 1805. Innkeepers employed local residents, frequently young men and women, to serve as waiters and waitresses, hostlers, grooms, stableboys, porters, and general assistants. Tavernkeepers had difficulty retaining a trained staff, however, because employees were often enticed away by the plentiful opportunities typical of a growing nation.

NHHS Collections   Photographer, Ernest Gould

ica, unlike in Europe, "only remain[ed] in service until they [could] save a little money, when they constantly quit their masters."[92] The difficulty of retaining domestic servants in colonial America plagued even New Hampshire's Royal Governor Benning Wentworth.[93] (According to a legend popularized by a Longfellow poem, Wentworth himself married one of his own servants, Martha Hilton.[94])

It is not surprising that with the potential for upward social mobility in America, a European traveler could note as early as 1807: "Liberty and equality level all ranks upon the road, from the host to the hostler."[95] More than one traveler, including an Englishman staying at the White Mountain House in 1838, expressed horror that the servants waiting on table sat down and joined the guests.[96] Whether justifiably or not, travelers often lamented the "negligence and inattention of innkeepers' servants." As some visitors were preparing to leave their otherwise satisfactory inn at Bartlett, New Hampshire, in 1797, they discovered to their dismay that "the servant who should have bridled [their] horses was missing"; they regretfully concluded: "We were obliged to perform that office for ourselves."[97]

Others were quick to point out that whenever European travelers managed to modify their habits and treat American tavern workers as equals, there were suddenly no limits to the services offered. According to an imaginary traveler, devised by James Fenimore Cooper to explain American ways to European critics, "It is not thought in reason, in New-England especially, that one man should assume a tone of confirmed superiority over the rest of mankind, merely because he wears a better coat, or has more money in his purse."[98] One foreign visitor recommended to another that, in order to obtain better service in America, he should "ask as a favour, what he had a right

to command as a duty—[and] treat the heads of the public houses with marked respect, and their sons and daughters, who might be in attendance, and even the servants, with kindness and courtesy, avoiding the use of terms and epithets which might imply inferiority and servitude."[99]

Much was also said about the fact that, except in the largest cities, tipping servants or calling them by the sound of a bell was not appropriate behavior in the American tavern.[100] As Cooper again explained: "Servility forms no part of the civilization of New-England, though civility be its essence."[101] This aspect of the New England temperament was not without advantages to the European tourist, one of whom commented: "From the servants one meets with great attention, not combined with deference of manner, still less with that obsequiousness which informs you by a suggestive bow, at the end of your visit, that it has been meted out with reference to the probable amount of half-sovereigns, shillings, and sixpences at your disposal."[102]

Ranging from teamsters to itinerant artists, from local farmers to European travelers, inn patrons generally shared little in common besides their reliance on the local tavern for refreshment, shelter, and sociability. Even in the most remote territory, an unpredictable clientele of diverse backgrounds converged on the tavern each evening. Henry David Thoreau, staying at James Tilton's inn in West Thornton on his 1839 hike into the White Mountains, best captured the tavern's almost magnetic attraction for a wide variety of people: "Sometimes we lodged at an inn in the woods, where trout-fishers from distant cities had arrived before us, and where, to our astonishment, the settlers dropped in at night-fall to have a chat and hear the news, though there was but one road, and no other house was visible—as if they had come out of the earth."[103]

Stereograph, "Interior of Tip-Top House, Mt. Wash[ingto]n N.H.," circa 1860. This earliest photographic image of a tavern-like interior shows guests enjoying the hospitality of the taproom, presided over by the man one visitor called the "affable bartender." The central position of the stove, the simple Windsor furniture, the hooks for outer garments, and the broadsides posted on the wall are all reminiscent of the mountaintop tavern's more commonplace predecessors.

Courtesy, Douglas A. Philbrook   Photographer, S. F. Adams; photograph courtesy of Mount Washington Observatory

In specific locales, certain groups of people, like the trout fishermen on the Pemigewasset, were more in evidence than elsewhere. Such was the case in the early nineteenth century in Hanover, where students at Dartmouth College "principally board[ed] in the public houses."[104] And, in Loudon, a "house of entertainment" kept by Revolutionary pensioner Lieutenant Samuel Piper attracted other veterans: "Revolutionary soldiers were entertained by him, free of any expense," and one of his local customers claimed to have "often met many of them at his house."[105]

Unfortunately, innkeepers do not seem to have kept guestbooks or "albums" until the early nineteenth century, and even then, such books appeared only in areas of the state where tourists were an important component of tavern clientele.

Interactions among tavern guests generally took place either around the table or by the fireside. Speaking of New England in general, one traveler remarked in 1794: "There is no shyness in conversation, as at an English table. People of different countries and languages mix together, and converse as familiarly as old acquaintances."[106] Later in the evening, except in the summertime, the center for conversation moved to the fireside. In 1842, one visitor, stopping for a meal at an inn in Bartlett, noted that a fire was kept in the "barroom" stove as early as September. Lodging at Crawford's Notch House that night, the same visitor colorfully observed: "In the evening, we sat down by the kitchen fire & . . . had a shifting scene before us, which Hogarth might have envied. Every now & then a tired walker would stagger in from the Mountain [bringing with him] a vast fund of shrewdness."[107] One English traveler, who visited both New Hampshire and Vermont around 1810, expressed amazement at the range of tavern conversation, both in subject matter and quality: "Throughout the evenings the public room was filled with guests, and a great deal of political, agricultural, and commercial, besides barometrical and thermometrical conversation was carried on, usually either too profound to be understood or too shallow to be worth attending to."[108]

Travelers seemed to find their fellow tavern guests talkative and curious despite their initial reserve. A visitor to Littleton in 1838 described the "talkative father" of one family as "delighted to get hold of some new listeners. He sat down upon the side of the bed, as if in preparation for a long chat, and entered at large into the history of his affairs."[109] Speaking of an elderly woman famous for entertaining sightseers on Red Hill near Center Harbor, the same traveler facetiously claimed: "The exercise she takes in speaking must be one cause of her buxom health."[110]

Although naturally talkative, local residents, when first approached by a stranger, often appeared taciturn. As one Englishman noted, shortly after debarking from his ship at Portsmouth in 1807: "If . . . a question is asked . . . by a person apparently a foreigner, [Americans] hesitate, and avoid giving a reply by demanding [the visitor's] business, leaving the stranger under that most unpleasant sensation which is produced by a doubtful and ambiguous reception."[111]

This characteristic aloofness frequently veiled an insatiable curiosity which, from all accounts, was the local tavern habitué's general reaction to visitors from afar. Inevitably, a "string of questions"—issuing "as it were, in one breath"—replaced the native's initial silence.[112] Many foreign guests expressed annoyance at this general inquisitiveness: "A stranger may travel in New England many a day without being once asked to eat or drink; but he cannot call at any house whatever without being required to give an account of himself by every person therein."[113] A visitor did not have to be from a very distant point to elicit the curiosity of local residents. A young woman from Newburyport, stopping at Stickney's tavern in Concord around 1815, found a group of women gathering about her in the tavern sitting room.

"You are from below?" questioned my interlocutor. "Yes," I returned, naming my place of residence. As I ceased speaking the group thronged about me. "Would I please excuse, but was this the newest style for riding dress?" Having examined my habit and bonnet minutely, and farther inquired respecting Boston fashion, the conversation was abruptly ended by the entrance of [my husband] accompanied by [theirs.][114]

Conversations among tavern guests were not always lighthearted. Disputes occasionally flared up, most commonly over local matters, but sometimes as a result of misunderstandings between residents and visitors. The ready availability of alcohol increased the likelihood of tavern conflict.

As early as 1744, one of the first foreign travelers to record his New Hampshire adventures vividly described how he managed to avoid a tavern brawl instigated by a local resident: "Having now entered New Hampshire Goverment [sic], I stopped att a house within 5 miles of Portsmouth to bait my horses, where I had some billingsgate [a slang term for 'foul language'] with a sawcy fellow that made free in handling my pistols. I found a sett of low, rascally company in the house and, for that reason, took no notice of what the fellow said to me, not being over fond of quarreling with such trash. I therefor mounted horse again. . . ."[115] In a similar situation at a tavern near Chester about 1780, Henry Tufts was not as successful in escaping the threats of a local "bully."

Wishing to prevent consequences, I desired the interposition of the landlord, who was a great, black, thickset Irishman, to no purpose; he only inquired, in round Irish, if I feared the fellow; I replied in the negative; but that being a stranger, it was my wish to avoid contention. . . . My antagonist was inflexible in urging on the dispute. He now made at me with fire and fury in his aspect. We exchanged a number of blows; I had, however, the good fortune to bring him by the board; while, in falling, he upset a table, that stood in the floor completely furnished for breakfast. Still the combat held with redoubled ardor, and ended only from the intervention of the company; whose opinion was, that ample harm had been done already. My opponent had been so roughly handled, in this squabble, that he mentioned not a syllable more of renewing the contest.[116]

Early court testimony offers a startlingly vivid picture of conflicts among tavern guests. On November 14, 1777, for instance, the skilled Portsmouth woodcarver Ebenezer Dearing was cruelly assaulted at the house of John Folsom, innholder in Greenland, by a man who somewhat earlier in the evening had boasted to one of the eventual deponents, then sitting by the tavern fire: "Here is Dearing and I mean to give him a licking before he goes away if you wont concern your Self in it." As Dearing left the tavern and entered the "west" shed to get his horse, the defendant "then & there with his Fists did Strike the Plaintiff in various Parts of his Body, and threw him on the Ground, and while the Plaintiff was lying on the Ground the [defendant] did then & there kick the Plaintiff, with his Feet, on the Hip and other Parts of his Body so that his Life was even dispaired of. . . ." According to further testimony, the tavernkeeper reproached the assailant: "How can you Hurt my House so." The doctor who examined Dearing testified that, over two months later, his bruised "parts . . . had not reasumed [sic] their natural color."[117]

Occasionally, a quarrel between tavern guests ended in manslaughter. As the result of what seems to have been an evening of heavy drinking at Randall's tavern in New Durham, Elisha Thomas was hanged in Dover in 1788 for the murder of his close friend Captain Peter Drowne. In the speech he made just before his execution, Thomas lamented: "Alas! I am now called off the stage of existence, at the age of forty-two for a crime that I should as soon

Life and Dying SPEECH

Of ELISHA THOMAS, who Suffered at Dover, June 3, 1788—for the MURDER of Capt. PETER DROWNE.

Broadside (detail) reproducing the final statement of Elisha Thomas of New Durham, N.H., condemned to hang for the murder of Captain Peter Drowne; statement written in Dover Prison, 1788. Occasionally, violence erupted in taverns, undoubtedly fueled by readily available alcohol, as in the case of Elisha Thomas, accused of murdering a close friend after an evening of fellowship at Randall's tavern in New Durham. On June 3, 1788, Thomas' execution by hanging drew crowds to Dover from neighboring towns.

NHHS Collections   Photographer, Bill Finney

thought of perpetrating on my wife and children, as on Capt. *Drowne*."[118] The accused may have been innocent of the crime, but his hazy memory of the circumstances did not favor his defense.

Strict governmental regulation of taverns throughout the seventeenth and eighteenth centuries did much to discourage conflicts among tavern guests. In 1663, shortly after "James Keat acknowledge[d] his excessive drincking [that] night hee brake Rachel Websters signe & doore," the tavernkeeper was fined for "keeping bad ordr in her house."[119] Exactly a century later, a Piermont resident, charged with "prophane cursing at the house of Aaron Storrs Innholder in Hanover . . . saying that he wished said Storrs *damned*," paid a fine for his misdemeanor to the poor of the "College District."[120]

Although innumerable, highly diverse individuals patronized New Hampshire taverns in the early days of travel, only a few visitors were famous enough to be written about extensively in the newspapers of the time and recorded in town histories. In 1789, during his grand tour through New England, George Washington ate and slept at several New Hampshire taverns along his route. And, in 1824 and 1825, the beloved American Revolutionary hero from France, the Marquis de Lafayette, passed through New Hampshire twice during his celebrated return to America. These official tours, as well as those of less-illustrious figures, were characterized by elaborate processions, accompanied by cannonfire and bells, by frequent stops at local taverns for refreshment, by speeches delivered from tavern porches or balconies, by public banquets served either in the tavern hall or catered by local innkeepers, and finally by an endless series of toasts and festive balls. Although Washington and Lafayette were hardly ordinary guests, their brief visits will remain forever the highlight in the history of each of the taverns that welcomed them.[121]

A large proportion of the tavern's typical clientele was female. Women were highly visible among the "people of the road"—but not only as travelers and tavern guests. They also kept taverns, ferries, and tollgates.[122] Generally, women obtained such positions only when it became necessary to support themselves, often after the death of their husbands. In a typical case, Lucy Read of Litchfield, whose husband had kept a ferry on the Merrimack for twenty-five years, petitioned the governor and Council in 1772 to confirm her right to "improve" the "accustomed Ferry." Factors favoring her application included her six children "all now under age," as well as her "Consider-

Painting probably representing Lafayette at the Leavitt tavern, Chichester, N.H., 1825, watercolor on paper, by Joseph Warren Leavitt. The most memorable tavern guests, in New Hampshire as elsewhere, were the nationally famous political and military heroes who occasionally made ceremonial tours through the countryside. On his return to New Hampshire in 1825, the Marquis de Lafayette is said to have stopped at Leavitt's tavern in Chichester. This painting by the tavernkeeper's son is believed to represent that visit.
Courtesy, Private Collection

able Expence" for ferry maintenance since her husband's death.[123]

By the late seventeenth century, tavernkeeping was considered an especially suitable occupation for single women and widows. In fact, more than one-third of the innkeepers licensed in the late 1690s, under new provincial legislation, were women.[124] Only in the unusual case of a tavern known to attract unruly guests was renewal of a hostess's license dependent on her "gett[ing] an honest man into her house to govern the same."[125] Like their male counterparts, however, women tavernkeepers relied heavily on family members and domestic servants to help with tavern operation. Typically, even when the husband held the tavern license, the "women of the family [were fully occupied] cooking and waiting from sunrise till midnight."[126] Guests frequently had words of praise for the innkeeper's wife, whose diligence and hospitality merited her the usual title of "landlady."[127]

The freedom of women to travel and patronize taverns in the eighteenth and nineteenth centuries has been greatly underestimated, perhaps because of the stricter Victorian mores intervening between then and the present day. Susanna Johnson Hastings of Charlestown, in settling the estate of her first husband who was killed by Indians in 1759, claimed to have made "three journeys to Portsmouth, fourteen to Boston, and three to Springfield." Several decades later, Mrs. Hastings was still an active horsewoman in her early seventies. In 1801, when she was returning from a visit to Rockingham, Vermont, accompanied only by another woman, the horse on which they were both mounted was startled by a boy "wheeling a load of flax"; Mrs. Hastings was thrown violently to the ground. Eight years later, the same woman, dauntless still at the age of eighty, managed to survive a serious wagon accident.[128]

Women routinely set forth alone on lengthy stage journeys. In 1828, despite all recommendations to the contrary,

ON THE ROAD NORTH OF BOSTON

Portrait of Susanna (Willard) Johnson Hastings, Charlestown, N.H., 1800-1805, oil on canvas, attributed to William Jennys. Hastings was a New Hampshire woman who, like many others, chose to open her home as a tavern when required to support herself after the death of her husband in 1759. Little is known of her tavernkeeping career, which continued until her second marriage in 1762. Most often remembered today because of the three years (1754-57) she spent as a captive of the Indians and French in Canada, Hastings was admired in her community for her remarkable "fortitude," "veracity," and "character."

Courtesy, Mrs. Reginald Rowland
  Photograph courtesy of Billings Farm & Museum

the intrepid widow Anne Newport Royall, a Maryland native, ventured by herself into the northern parts of New Hampshire in the depth of mid-winter.[129] Sarah Connell, a young woman living in Bow around 1810, recorded in her diary the details of numerous trips she made to visit friends and relatives living as far away as Newburyport, Massachusetts, and Portland, Maine. She meticulously noted the presence or absence of other women in the coach: sometimes "there was no other female in the stage beside myself till I got home." Although she often described the "gentlemen" as "polite and attentive," the presence of another woman in the stage generally "rendered the ride much

Sarah Purcell

H AS removed to that commodious houſe in Congreſs-ſtreet, lately occupied by Colonel William Brewſter; where ſhe has opened a TAVERN, and aſſures her friends and the public, that thoſe who may favor her with their cuſtom, ſhall be entertained as genteely, and on as reaſonable terms as at any tavern in America, and every favor gratefully acknowledged.

Newspaper advertisement for the tavern of Sarah Purcell, Portsmouth, New-Hampshire Mercury (Portsmouth), 1786. The widow Sarah Purcell is remembered locally as the landlady who entertained naval hero John Paul Jones during his 1781 stay in Portsmouth while he supervised the construction of the ship America. After her husband's death in 1776, Purcell kept taverns or boarding houses at various times not only in the building known today as the John Paul Jones House, but also in the Packer Tavern on Pleasant Street and the Bell Tavern on Congress Street.

NHHS Collections   Photographer, Ernest Gould

pleasanter." Frequently, she was already acquainted with one or another of her fellow passengers, but sometimes observed: "my companions were all strangers to me."[130]

It is not surprising to today's travel-oriented population that the same Miss Connell would have "dine'd in Portsmouth at Davenport's tavern," while on her way in 1807 from Portland to Newburyport in the stage. But, the fact that two unaccompanied girls might visit a tavern in a neighboring town for refreshment does not agree with present-day assumptions about earlier customs. In June 1809, however, Sarah Connell, then eighteen, wrote in her diary: "In the afternoon Susan Ayer and myself rode to Hopkinton, a pleasant little Town 7 miles from Concord. We stop'd at Bailey's tavern, took a little refreshment, then walked out. We were in high spirits, and enjoyed our frolic highly. We left there at six o'clock. We had a very pleasant ride home."[131]

Even illness, pregnancy, or old age did not prevent women from undertaking lengthy journeys. On a trip from Newburyport to Bow in 1817, Sarah Connell, by then the

Lithographed portrait of Sophia (Cushing) Hayes Wyatt of Dover, N.H., frontispiece of The Autobiography of a Landlady of the Old School, 1854. *Former schoolteacher Sophia Wyatt, with her second husband, kept Gage's Inn beginning in 1816, gradually transforming it into the Dover Hotel. Although the Wyatts adjusted well to the changes of the mid-nineteenth century, operating Dover's New-Hampshire Hotel as one of the earliest temperance houses in the state, Wyatt described herself during this era of transition as a "landlady of the old school."*
NHHS Collections   Photographer, Ernest Gould

wife of Doctor Samuel Ayer, described herself as "very unwell, and suffer[ing] much from fatigue of body, and anxiety of mind."[132] In 1846, the passengers of a single coach included both "a young mother, with her sick infant of ten weeks" and "an aged woman" with her grandson.[133] And in 1813, a pregnant mother of five, deserted in northern Vermont by her husband, set out in a cart with her children on a journey of two hundred miles to return to her family home just south of Nashua.[134] Sometimes illness overtook a woman or her family along the route. Sarah Connell recorded one such instance in 1809, when she and her mother

> walked up to Stickney's tavern, to see one Mrs. Emery, who came from Haverhill in the stage in company with Mama. She brought her little infant, not quite seven months old with her. The child was taken dangerously ill on the road, so that she was obliged to tarry in Concord. . . . We called to give her an invertation [sic] to keep with us, till her child was well enough, for her to continue her journey. . . . She was a stranger to us, but

her situation in a public house with her sick infant would have been very unpleasant.[135]

By the mid-nineteenth century, foreign travelers were commenting on the relative independence and mobility of American women. In 1857, a Russian visiting Boston exclaimed: "The young girls were walking alone, without any escorts, mothers, brothers, or fathers."[136] In the same decade, an English woman found it surprising though true that "a lady, no matter what her youth or attractions might be, could travel alone through every State in the Union, and never meet with anything but attention and respect."[137]

One early restriction on female travel—soon overcome, however—was against sitting outside the coach with the driver, a position described in the early 1830s as "so seldom occupied by women, that no respectable female would venture to sit there, at the risk of being laughed at or insulted."[138] By the late 1830s, however, sitting on the stage roof itself was a novelty which both men and women were eager to experience. Having seen several other women take seats on top of the stage, one woman from the South, traveling through New Hampshire in 1836, decided "to try it from Keene to Fitzwilliam, before breakfast" and discovered the thrill of seeing "the driver snapping his long whip beneath, and the landscape stretched around." She concluded: "I felt the same excitement as if riding on horseback."[139]

As early as the 1820s, women were included in the parties who were beginning to tour the White Mountains for purposes of "health and amusement." And, in 1821, long before the days of the cog railway or carriage road, three Austin sisters from Portsmouth were the first women to attain the summit of Mount Washington on foot.[140]

Not everyone experienced the same degree of freedom that enabled women to travel, to frequent taverns, and to work in related occupations. In the early 1830s, a young black schoolmistress on her way from Boston to Exeter, New Hampshire, to visit some friends was "unable to procure a seat in the stage, as the driver, though her place had been [reserved] the night before, refused to carry her, except on the outside. . . . She declined . . . to subject herself to such humiliation, and proceeded to Exeter with her brother, in a gig." The total cost of her transportation, including rental of a vehicle and loss of two days' work on the part of her brother, was six times what her coach fare would have been.[141]

The sympathetic English visitor who recorded this incident, noted, while still speaking of free blacks in Boston, that "even a license for keeping a house of refreshment is [often] refused, under some frivolous or vexatious pretence; though the same can easily be procured by a white man of an inferior condition and with less wealth."[142] Probably because of similar discrimination in licensing, no early New Hampshire tavernkeeper is known to have been black; however, neither urban nor rural innkeepers in eighteenth-century New Hampshire hesitated to rely on the assistance of black slaves for their daily tavern opera-

Mount Jefferson from Mount Washington, *oil on canvas, attributed to Hippolyte-Louis Garnier, circa 1845, after engraving published 1839, based upon drawing by William Henry Bartlett, 1836-38. Even before a bridle path was cleared to the top of Mount Washington in the mid 1830s, women were among those who ventured up the mountain on foot. By 1833, Ethan A. Crawford claimed to have "repaired the foot path 'so well and so wide' that gentlemen and ladies can walk up the mountain 'hand in hand.' "*
NHHS Collections   Photographer, Bill Finney

tion. Another position of responsibility denied early American blacks was that of driving a mail stage; as recorded in the first decade of the nineteenth century, "the driver, by the post-office regulations, must be a white man."[143]

For certain groups in colonial times, even the simple act of visiting a tavern—the recognized social center of the community—was not a right taken for granted. A provincial law passed in 1716 levied a fine on any tavernkeeper who "shall suffer any Apprentice, Servant or Negro, to sit drinking in his or her House, or to have any manner of Drink there, without special Order or Allowance of their respective Master."[144] In the seventeenth century, heavier fines and stricter regulations forced all citizens to obtain "express License from Some of his Ma[jes]ty's Councill, or any two Justices of the Peace" before either selling or giving liquor "to any Indian or Nigroe."[145]

While apprentices, servants, and slaves were expected to submit to authority, one group within New England society defied the strong social constraints of the period.

A criminal underworld originating in the slums of London had its counterpart even on the highways of rural New Hampshire. Fortunately for historians, at least three early New Hampshire criminals spent their later years recording their scandalous careers. Stephen Burroughs of Hanover, Henry Tufts of Lee, and Seth Wyman of Goffstown, all led shiftless lives, supporting themselves by stealing and passing counterfeit money. Although certain details of their memoirs may be fictitious, the basic elements of the world they depict are confirmed in contemporary legal documents.

Tufts, a rural New Hampshire resident, was part of an extensive criminal network, which he described, around 1780, as a series of "confidential friends, of whom I now had a connected string, reaching from New York, to the District of Maine; and from thence through Vermont to Canada line." With these allies, Tufts conversed in the "flash lingo"—a slang jargon developed by the English underworld.[146]

A NARRATIVE

OF THE

LIFE, ADVENTURES, TRAVELS AND

SUFFERINGS

OF

HENRY TUFTS,

NOW RESIDING AT

LEMINGTON,

IN THE DISTRICT OF MAINE.

IN SUBSTANCE, AS COMPILED FROM HIS OWN MOUTH.

Ab ovo usque ad mala.
OVID.

Meliora video, proboque, deteriora sequor.
IDEM.

ENTERED AS THE ACT DIRECTS.

DOVER, N. H.
PRINTED BY SAMUEL BRAGG, JUN.
1807.

Title page of Henry Tuft's autobiography, first edition, Dover, N.H., 1807. Born in New Market but long a resident of nearby Lee, Tufts described his criminal activities, frequently revolving around early New Hampshire taverns and highways, in his memoirs.

NHHS Collections   Photographer, Ernest Gould

Each of the three criminals-turned-author seems to have been even from his youth totally incapable of resisting the temptation to steal. Burroughs and Tufts both admitted robbing local farmers of their beehives for the honey, the former having done so by sleigh in the middle of winter.[147] About 1797, at the age of thirteen, Seth Wyman, who had first demonstrated his pilfering skills as a toddler, decided to try his hand during the Goffstown militia training: in the evening, while "the officers and soldiers had a supper in the tavern . . . I took the opportunity to take a look into every corner, when locks did not hinder me, looking as usual for something worth pilfering." Wyman's later misadventures

frequently revolved around the roadside tavern. In 1805, on a long trek to Goffstown after a sojourn in Maine, he ransacked two loaded sleighs standing in front of a tavern.[148]

Tavernkeepers and their guests often became the victims of roving criminals and misfits. A considerable amount of cash, along with numerous items of clothing, was stolen in 1771 from a tavern in Chester by a man who "some Times calls himself a Shoe-Maker, some Times a Goldsmith" and who had shortly before broken into a shop in Haverhill, Massachusetts.[149] In the early 1830s, after stealing a silver watch and snuff box from a tavern in Merrimack, one vagabond—allegedly insane—secreted his loot inside a feather bed or straw mattress at the Eagle Coffee House in Concord.[150]

Although saddlebags and wagons, as well as other items of value to travelers, were often stolen from tavern yards, there was little or no actual highway robbery in early New England.[151] Armed highwaymen, who waylaid stagecoaches in both England and the American West, were not a significant threat to New Hampshire travelers. One case is recorded, however, of a horseman who followed a stage through Weare in order to cut the strap which secured a valuable trunk to the back of the coach.[152]

One of the most common forms of crime to affect travel on New Hampshire's early highways was horsetheft. Advertisements offering rewards for the return of stolen horses were common in practically every newspaper throughout the eighteenth and nineteenth centuries. The anxious owners described—sometimes in great detail— their animal's markings, defects, and preferred gaits, as well as any harness or saddle taken. As Henry Tufts informs us, however, experienced horsethieves, including himself, "kept on hand, or in suitable places of deposit, a variety of paints of different colors; by means of which, [they] could so alter the looks of any horse, that the owner must be puzzled to know him again while the disguise lasted, which was usually a week or more."[153]

Tufts, probably typical of New Hampshire horsethieves, would ride his stolen property as quickly as possible across the state line to sell in either Vermont or Massachusetts. At the same time, local inhabitants made every effort to follow the thief's trail while still fresh. In 1804, the town of Salem paid a local tavernkeeper four dollars "for Rideing three Days after the thief that Stole Joseph Thom's horse."[154]

In the early nineteenth century, the inhabitants of several New Hampshire towns were so concerned with the increase in stolen horses, that they formed local organizations to deter thieves. The town of Henniker, in 1815, expressed its concern in the form of an official resolution.[155] The following year, at Asher Southworth's Walpole tavern, a group of local citizens organized the "Walpole Detecting Society," which a few years later evolved into the "Walpole Society for Detecting and Punishing Horse Thieves and Pilferers and Plunderers of Gardens and Fruit Orchards."[156]

New England's developing road network facilitated the

$100 REWARD!

Stolen from the pastures of the

subscribers in Barrington, Tuesday night, August 4th, by WILL-
IAM HODGE, alias BILL HODGE, alias LITTLE HODGE
of Barnstead

TWO MARES,

one of them was a very large sorrel saddle back, both hind and one
fore foot white, long tail, star in her forehead, **4** years old, never been
used. The other a dark chesnut, with white hind feet, long tail,
white stripe in her face, **7** years old, steps remarkably quick, been
used but very little. Hodge is a talking, bragging fellow, **25** years
old, **5ft. 4in.** high, straight black hair, walks very erect, has a sharp
black snakish eye, & take him altogether looks like what he really is,
a Thief. He carried these Horses the same night they were stolen
without any Saddle and with a wire Bridle on the one he rode and
an old leather one on the other to Parsonsfield, Maine, where he
arrived before sunrise. Notwithstanding the very suspicious appearance of the man and his horses (the Colt having but one shoe
on) he put up at the house of IRA E. SANBORN, Esq., ; slept
nearly all day ; got the Colt shod, and left at sunset. There is
no track of the Horses beyond this place.

☞ HODGE went from Lowell, Mass. to Kingston, N. H. on
Wednesday **26th** Aug. and in the afternoon of the same day passed through Epping, and went to visit his friends in Nottingham
Square, Deerfield, Northwood and Barnstead ; he is now in one
of the above mentioned places.

☞ $50 will be paid to any one who will secure HODGE so
that he may be brought to Justice.

$50 will be paid to any one who will return the HORSES, or
One Hundred Dollars FOR BOTH.

Sept. 2, 1835.

WILLIAM HALE, *Barrington.*
WILLIAM HALE, Jr. *Dover.*

Broadside offering reward for return of horses stolen from the William Hale farm, Barrington, N.H., 1835. Horsetheft was more common on New Hampshire highways than more violent crimes. This broadside, intended for posting at local stage stops, contains a particularly vivid description of the suspected thief and his escape route.

NHHS Collections   Photographer, Ernest Gould

Engraving from broadside, H[u]ds[o]n's Speech from the Pillory, *(detail), circa 1762, by Nathaniel Hurd. This early cartoon represents Joshua Howe, a notorious counterfeiter from Westmoreland, N.H., receiving as punishment seventy-eight lashes at the public whipping post in Boston. Howe and his accomplice, Dr. Seth Hudson, had obtained their tools from the infamous Glazier Wheeler, who headed a gang of counterfeiters in the upper Connecticut Valley.*

Courtesy, The Trustees of the Boston Public Library   Photographers, Geoffrey Stein Studio, Inc.

spread of other types of crime into New Hampshire, particularly the making and passing of counterfeit money. As early as the 1680s, an English immigrant, known to his contemporaries as the "Chymist of Cocheco," faced trial for counterfeiting coins in Dover.[157] And, in 1774, "the infamous Glazier Wheeler, the Money-Maker of Cohoss, and Peter Hubbart his Accomplice" were apprehended and brought to trial in Plymouth.[158] Frequently, counterfeit money was passed to an unsuspecting public at the local tavern. Around 1755, counterfeiter Benjamin Winn unwisely drew attention to himself at a Windham tavern by treating all who entered and paying with an eight-pound bill.[159]

During the American Revolution, counterfeiting served political, rather than purely economic, purposes: loyalists in New Hampshire as elsewhere undertook to discredit the new American economy by circulating spurious notes obtained from New York City.[160] It is perhaps significant that the leader of the Tory counterfeit ring in New Hampshire was himself a prominent tavernkeeper, Colonel Stephen Holland of Londonderry. Predictably, Henry Tufts

also became entangled in this counterfeiting operation. At a Claremont tavern towards the end of the Revolution, Tufts happened to share a bed with a stranger who claimed in the night to have "long been an agent for the British, who had now employed him . . . to explore the country, and circulate counterfeit money." Tufts "found not the slightest difficulty in passing [the spurious notes he received]," his first purchase being, naturally, a horse.[161]

Counterfeiting flourished in the nineteenth century as well, although for purely pecuniary motives. As a youth in the 1840s, the notorious Bill Dow had worked in Concord stables and "eating houses," where "he not infrequently met with strangers and travellers passing up and down the country . . . who often left behind them questionable looking bank bills, which he subsequently discovered in his master's money-drawer." Inspired by their example, Dow eventually became one of the most skillful counterfeit dealers in America. He traveled back and forth from New York to New England, where, in the jargon of the counterfeiter, he "readily found plenty of 'boodle carriers' anxious to assist him and take the 'stuff' into the interior, at figures

Manuscript fifteen-shilling Crown Point bill (counterfeit), Province of New Hampshire, 1755. In 1760, this false bill, apparently made by hand with a pen, was used by William Brown, a Madbury farmer, to make a purchase from a Portsmouth baker. The following year, it was displayed as evidence in Brown's trial. Another counterfeit bill, surviving among court records into the twentieth century, was originally detected in 1755 when used to make a payment at Denison's tavern in Windham, N.H.

Photograph, NHHS Collections

Engraved portrait of Bill Dow, captioned "The Noted N.E. 'Boodle Carrier,' " from Three Years with Counterfeiters, Smug[g]lers, and Boodle Carriers, *published circa 1875. Central New Hampshire inns and taprooms played a major role in the notorious career of Bill Dow, who was responsible for distributing counterfeit notes (or "boodle") from New York along a network of New Hampshire highways.*

Courtesy, Robert Wester   Photographer, Ernest Gould

that paid him generously, and afforded them large profits. 'Hod Bonney' of New Hampshire, was one of his chief boodle men. These agents parcelled the bogus notes out to 'peddlers,' or itinerant dealers, who 'shoved' it every where in the country towns, liberally." It is fitting that Dow's career, centered as it was on the highway, ended near where it had begun when he was arrested in Hooksett, apparently in a tavern taproom.[162] By the late nineteenth century, new methods of engraving banknotes did much to discourage counterfeiters.[163] And, in 1864, a Bow native, Laban Heath, devised an "Infallible Counterfeit Detector" to protect the public from this prevalent crime.[164]

The tavern, which played a prominent role in some criminals' activities, was fittingly used, at other times, as a temporary prison. When New Hampshire experienced a plague of counterfeiters in 1768, those who were sent to apprehend the suspects and take them to Portsmouth jail made use of taverns along their routes as stopping places at night. When Abiel Chandler took suspect Simeon Miller fifty miles from Derryfield to Portsmouth, the jailer employed four keepers to accompany the prisoner and tarried at five taverns along the way.[165] When Lieutenant James Taylor took other prisoners from Merrimack to Portsmouth on the same charges, he worked nine days without ceasing, even on the Sabbath. Taylor may have pursued his quarry tirelessly, but he at least gave himself and his helpers some worldly comfort; his bill at Jacob Tilton's tavern in Portsmouth, for example, includes three breakfasts, five dinners, two suppers, a dram, and four-and-a-half bowls of punch.[166]

The tavern did not always provide the security necessary to restrain a wily prisoner. The master criminal Henry Tufts recounts outwitting two keepers who succumbed to the tavern's temptations.

> Riding a few miles we called in at Ray's tavern in Gilmanton, where I treated my keepers so profusely with spirits, that both became excessively mellow. The waiting maid, observing their tippling propensity, advised my *treating* them freely; in which case she would warrant me out of their clutches before morning. I thought her advice apropos, and plied my conductors so warmly, that, before leaving the house, they both grew *reeling ripe*, and were scarce able to remount their horses.

After stopping at yet another Gilmanton tavern, Tufts brought his captors to such a state that he was able simply to ride away in the night, leaving the keepers to pay the liquor bills and find an explanation for his absence.[167]

Theft and counterfeiting were not the only illegal activities associated with the tavern and highway in early America. In the largest cities such as Boston, taverns operated by women were occasionally accused of allowing, if not actually encouraging, prostitution. As early as the seventeenth century, Boston widow Alice Thomas—described as "a common Baud"—was found guilty of "frequent secret and unseasonable Entertainm^t in her [tavern of] Lewd Lascivious & notorious persons of both Sexes, giving them opportunity to commit carnal wickedness."[168] According to surviving evidence, the "disorderly" conduct which New Hampshire tavernkeepers, both men and women, were sometimes accused of allowing, does not seem to have been generally of this nature. However, according to testimony in one child-support case of 1750, the alleged father claimed of Portsmouth tavernkeeper Mary Ayers that "he never intended to make one that he knew to be a hore [sic] his wife." Speaking to the deponent (Catharine Rymes), he continued to criticize the tavernkeeper: "Catey you know what she is & what she has been."[169]

A large percentage of the paternity cases tried in eighteenth-century New Hampshire courts involved the house of a third party. Although this was at times the local tavern—the main public gathering place of the community—no discredit seems to have reflected on the innkeeper. In 1774, for example, Rachel Terrell of Bedford, then "big with child," accused Enoch Emery of Dunbarton of having "at the Dwelling house of Capt. William Stark in said Dunbarton, Through Wheedlings and promises of Marriage offer[ed] to lie with her. . . ."[170] Stark, who appears to have been a tavernkeeper, was unquestionably a prominent man in his community.[171]

Evidence suggests that stage travel also may have tempted illicit activities. Speaking of American customs in general, a French traveler explained:

When there are women in the stages, they are not

obliged to share in the expense incurred for wine, liquors or other spirituous drinks served with a meal. Politeness requires this expense to be borne entirely by the men. I will whisper this: that this courtesy is sometimes extended to courtesans who figure that a stage can be made to serve purposes quite foreign to modesty.[172]

Taverns were also the setting for travelers' amorous adventures of a less incriminating nature. In a coastal town well south of New Hampshire, a Polish visitor watched while "two young Frenchmen, enticing a young and pretty American girl, repaired to a tavern . . . where, according to the . . . opinion of a third Frenchman, the faint-hearted virtue of the American girl was to expire on the laps of the Frenchmen."[173] Only Henry Tufts, however, confessed to such adventures. On one occasion, in a tavern near Charlestown around 1790, he "scraped acquaintance" with a female guest and "so contrived matters, that one bed sufficed for us both until morning." Only a few weeks later, he claims to have stopped at another tavern operated by a "beautiful young and debonair widow. Finding this woman approachable, I made immediate love to her cheek . . . and obtained her favor to the utmost latitude of my wishes."[174]

For every Henry Tufts whose daily activities violated the usual standards of behavior and threatened the routine of travel, countless other "people of the road" quietly worked to ease the traveler's way. These long-forgotten men and women, serving as tavernkeepers, stage drivers, ferry operators, and tollgate keepers, left no colorful memoirs. Yet the important public service they performed in maintaining the safety and comfort of life on the road earned them the gratitude of travelers and the respect of their communities.

TAVERNS AND GOVERNMENT

CHAPTER 7

UNTIL WELL INTO the nineteenth century, governmental activity across New Hampshire took place primarily in the tavern and the meetinghouse. Of the two, the tavern was by far the more important and hospitable home to politics. Provincial government in New Hampshire began in the tavern and remained centered there until after 1750. Local government might use the meetinghouse or (by the mid-1800s) the specially built town hall for its important annual or special town meetings, but the tavern remained the seat of its daily business of democratic discussion, speech-making, and committee meetings.

New Hampshire's provincial Council and House of Representatives had no official rooms until the State House on Portsmouth's Parade was sufficiently completed for occupancy in 1762. Before that time, the Council would sometimes meet in the home of the appointed governor. Such meetings are said to have taken place in the relatively spacious chambers of the house of Lieutenant Governor John Wentworth on "the Creek" (Puddle Dock) in Portsmouth during the 1720s. When Benning Wentworth rented the brick Macpheadris house in Portsmouth between 1741 and the mid 1750s, it is thought that the Council sometimes met in one of the elegantly paneled rooms of that dwelling, which the Governor endeavored unsuccessfully to acquire with public funds as a province house. After Wentworth fitted out his country farm at Little Harbor as his permanent seat, the Council undoubtedly met on occasion in the large, imposing room still called the Council Chamber. The same may have been true of a well-paneled room in the wing of the house of Councilor Peter Gilman in Exeter.

But even with these impressive private rooms available, both Council and Assembly met most often in public houses, and almost until the inauguration in 1767 of John Wentworth, New Hampshire's last royal governor, most of the public business of the province was carried out in a succession of Portsmouth taverns. This was in spite of explicit instructions issued by the King in 1682 to Lieutenant Governor Edward Cranfield: ". . . you are to take care that no meetings of the Councill or Assembly be held at Taverns or Ordinarys, nor that any part of the Revenue levied for Defraying the charge of the Government be spent in feasting or publique Entertainments."[1]

The most prominent among the taverns which served the government during the early 1700s was that owned first by Dr. Thomas Packer and, later, by Thomas Packer, Jr., the provincial sheriff. The building stood at the northeast corner of present-day Court and Pleasant streets and remained a tavern during most of its existence, which ended when the great Portsmouth fire of 1813 began in a stable across the street. When George Washington stayed in Portsmouth in 1789, this was the public house he selected as his headquarters. By that time, the house had been enlarged repeatedly, and in 1764, it was handsomely embellished by Joseph Burbeck, a Boston carver. It had served for a few years as the residence of John Langdon, and when Langdon entertained the Marquis de Chastellux there in 1782, the French visitor described the building as "elegant and well furnished, and the apartments admirably wainscotted."[2]

Packer's tavern was constructed some time after 1696. By the very early 1700s, with the shift of government activities from New Castle to Portsmouth, the building served increasingly both as meeting place for the governor and Council, for the Assembly or House of Representatives, and as a courthouse, with occasional use by Dr. Packer as a hospital as well.[3] Packer may have made architectural changes to the building to accommodate these functions, because it is clear that by the time of his death in 1723, one end of the tavern, containing at least two well-finished rooms, was referred to specifically as the "Court House and Council Chamber." In recognition of the importance of the house as a seat of government and as a potential place of refuge, the Council ordered that the tavern be fortified as a garrison in 1705.[4]

Packer's daughter Susanna inherited lifetime tenancy of the property in 1723, together with the tavern license associated with the house. This license was later exercised by her second husband, Benjamin Rust, a former cooper. Rust made further improvements to the building and bought new furniture for it in 1731.[5] The building continued to serve at least some governmental functions until the 1740s.

Although Packer's home was a licensed tavern, its owner's provision of special rooms for the government may have represented an attempt to overcome the objections to another public house in which the Assembly had been

Sign from the General Wolfe Tavern, Rochester, N.H., circa 1770. Bearing a bust-length portrait of French and Indian War hero General James Wolfe, this sign marked the tavern of Stephen Wentworth on the road from Dover to Wolfeboro. Political and military figures or emblems frequently embellished early tavern signs, symbolizing the interdependence of taverns and government.
NHHS Collections   Photographer, Bill Finney

meeting. In July 1701, the Assembly resolved that:

> The Publicque Afairs of the House of Representatives being much Obstructed by Persons Sitting and Lying on the bed, Voted That Whosoever hence forward Either Sitt or ly Down Shall forfeit three pence To the house. . . .

Whereas the Publicque Affairs of this House Is much

obstructed by Reason of several Members thereof Soe offten withdraw themselves Into the Chimney to take tobacco and sitt Talking And not Attend the Afairs of the House. Voted that Whoesoever Shall Soe doe for the future Shall pay A fine of three pence. . . . Except leave be givein &c.[6]

Even with the provision of special chambers, the use of a public house for governmental activities was not without its drawbacks. Sessions held in such a building would lack a certain symbolic dignity, seeming more like committee meetings than legislative deliberations. In one case in 1726,

> Mr. Theodore Atkinson Complained to the house that he was answered verry affrontingly while he was Debating in the house by Some one under the windows (which he Supposed was mr Justice Odiorn): the house Sent for mr Justice Odiorn: who came into the house & Declad. that what he Spoak was not Designedly don to affront any Member of the honble house: & that was the finall end of the matter.[7]

Lack of privacy and dignity eventually combined to suggest the advantage of building a state house to be used by House of Representatives, Council, and courts of law. The subject was first broached as early as 1718, and in 1725, the Council again recommended the idea, noting that "the sitting of the General Assembly and holding the Court of Justice at a Common Inn or Tavern as has been heretofore used within this province is not only a dishonour to the Government but attended wth Inconveniences too well known to need a mention. . . ."[8]

Despite these understandable objections, the province was not to have a proper state house for more than thirty years. Meanwhile, government and courts continued to depend on Portsmouth taverns. In 1750, roughly a decade before the building of the first true state house, traveler James Birket noted sourly that the court house was "a scandalous old building ready to tumble down."[9] At this time, it appears, the government was meeting in two rooms in Sarah Priest's tavern, although it would soon move to "two rooms in the western end" of the inn of David Horney on present-day Court Street, next door to provincial secretary Theodore Atkinson's house.[10]

It was natural, therefore, that government affairs even of transatlantic concern might be quartered in taverns. When the legislatures of New Hampshire and Massachusetts sent commissions to negotiate over the boundary between the two provinces in 1737, the delegates convened in John Brown's Georges Tavern in Hampton Falls, near the disputed line. Their deliberations were not merely of local concern, but had been referred to the King in Council and eventually involved appointees from several other colonies. The decision of the boundary commission eventually created the New Hampshire we know today, with the addition of the "New Hampshire Grants" west of the Connecticut River.[11] Much later, in 1781, representatives of the "Grants" likewise met in a tavern, the Evans House in

Photograph of the Horney Tavern (formerly the Underwood House), Court and Washington streets, Portsmouth, N.H., circa 1900. Possibly dating from as early as 1700, this house was operated as a tavern during the mid-eighteenth century by David and Hannah Horney at the Sign of the Ship, and was the meeting place of the provincial government during the 1750s and the early 1760s.
Courtesy, Strawbery Banke, Inc.,   Patch Collection

Charlestown, New Hampshire, to begin the organization of the new state of Vermont.[12]

Given this propensity to use taverns for the discussion of even the most weighty affairs of state, it is not surprising that town government, too, made constant use of public houses. Even when town affairs were decided in meetinghouses, as they often were, the preliminary committee work had probably been conducted in a tavern. Since annual town meetings take place in March, often with several feet of snow still standing on the frozen ground, and since meetinghouses were seldom if ever heated except by footstoves until the nineteenth century, there were frequent adjournments to neighboring taverns for refreshment and warmth. In Keene, for example, it was noted that town meetings of the 1760s were convened at the still-unfinished meetinghouse, but immediately adjourned to one of several neighboring taverns after the moderator was chosen.[13]

For reasons of convenience and comfort, the meetinghouse was often ignored altogether, especially if a tavern had a hall sufficiently large to accommodate all of the town's voters. New Hampshire town records are filled with innumerable references to the selection of inns for annual meetings, often on an alternating basis for fair distribution of the considerable profit involved. The atmosphere of one of these all-male gatherings in a pre-temperance age is described in a memoir written around 1870 in the town of Wentworth, recalling the typical meeting of half a century earlier:

Their first rendezvous is the "old Bar Room," where in a little square enclosure, and flanked by an array of glass decanters, glittering with shining labels attached to their long necks with small chains, stands the now-smiling landlord "en trim" for a hard day's work as each recruit goes directly for "a treat." . . . The bar room is becoming hot and steamy. Sharper and sharper is the jingle of those long-necked decanters. . . . The crisis is approaching: the Charge is to be made. The *Representative* to their *General Court is to be voted for*. The floor is crowded—the old wooden benches are crowded —the old *"bunk box"* is doubly crowded, its width giving sitting room for two rows. . . . Messengers from the "hall" descend to the bar room and give the rallying cry and with a hurrah which anon drowns the music of those long-necked decanters, they all rush for the "old hall" again. . . . The hall windows drip with condensed steam and the whole atmosphere of the room smells rank with the breath of those necklaced long-necked decanters. . . .[14]

Liquor was considered essential even when such meetings were held at a meetinghouse, in which case licenses were sometimes given for the convenient sale of drink outside the building. In Poplin (now Fremont), town meetings had been held in taverns before the construction of the meetinghouse in 1801; during the 1820s, two tavernkeepers were licensed to sell liquor on town meeting and militia days in the two end "porches" (stairhalls) of the building or close by.[15]

The ready availability of liquor at town meetings was not always conducive to the decision-making process. Political patronage was easily exercised in the atmosphere of "treating" to drink, as described in the town of Wentworth in the 1820s and commonplace everywhere. In 1776, a Tamworth election was challenged when it was asserted that Jonathan Moulton had bought votes with food and drink. Voters of Tamworth and Moultonborough denied

> that said Moulton or any of his Friends made any Entertainments or distributed any Victuals or Liqors with the least View of obtaining Votes for him; But on the close of the Day of Election the Inhabitants of Moultonborough & Tamworth being [far] from their own Homes, procured such Refreshment as they wanted at their own Cost & Charge, in a Sober & peacible Manner.[16]

The legislature recognized the danger of such bribery in a law of 1813 which mandated a fine of up to forty dollars for anyone convicted of giving "spirituous liquors to the voters of any town on the day of election, or at any prior or subsequent period [if] it shall . . . appear that the same was done with a view to influence the election, or as a treat for their suffrage."[17]

High emotions were stirred in the overheated atmosphere of liquor and partisanship. When the leaders of Marlborough met in Tucker's tavern about 1792 to transact some committee business, the meeting degenerated into a general carouse, according to an eyewitness, the committee "acting . . . as though they were 'bedeviled.' " John Rogers, one of the party, so offended the rest that he was pulled from the tavern and tied to a stake in a pile of shavings. Rogers and his persecutors were saved from tragedy by the fact that the confused mob had chosen green shavings for their fuel.[18]

Despite such aberrations, it is clear that most public committees commonly met in taverns and found there the comfort, hospitality, and refreshment that public business required, especially in an age when travel was slow and difficult and when committee members might live far apart and need several days away from home to conclude their affairs. When a committee for establishing a new table of governmental fees met in Portsmouth in 1742, their deliberations required a total of eight days at Ann Slayton's tavern, during which time they consumed thirty dinners, two breakfasts, and a bowl of punch.[19] Five years later, when the Province needed to negotiate with the Masonian Proprietors (a group of private investors who had purchased much of the territory of present-day New Hampshire), the government committee met the Proprietors at Slayton's tavern.[20]

Writing in 1765, famous Indian-fighter Robert Rogers complained that "there is but one place in the province at which the Courts of Justice are held, viz. at Portsmouth, one of the extremities, for which reason many of the inhabitants often have to travel 150 to 200 miles on very trifling occasions."[21] When it was decided in 1769 that New Hampshire should be divided into counties, the committee to draft a map and enabling legislation met at Jacob Tilton's Marquis of Rockingham Tavern near the State House in Portsmouth, even though all the committee members lived within walking distance of the center of town and most possessed spacious houses in which they might have hosted such meetings.[22] Once the division into counties was accomplished, towns were newly designated as county seats and still other taverns were pressed into the service of the courts. After the division took effect in 1771, Amherst emerged as the shire town of Hillsborough County and six court sessions convened each year at the tavern of Jonathan Smith.[23] Prominent taverns in the other shire towns were selected for similar uses.

In the absence of specially constructed courthouses, taverns also served as the seat of law. We have seen that the Province rented rooms for the courts in such Portsmouth taverns as Packer's, Slayton's, and Horney's. But courts might be convened in any house, and the quarterly sessions held before justices of the peace were especially likely to move from one convenient place to another. In 1730, when a slave named Sambo, belonging to a New Market family, threatened to "split out the brains" of Edward Hilton and "bury him in the Swamp," Hilton complained before a justice of the peace at the Portsmouth tavern of Henry Sherburne.[24]

Such sessions could expose a tavern to the usual hazards accompanying any large and excited crowd, but at least the tavernkeeper was likely to secure reimbursement for damages inflicted during the court session. When Ann Slayton submitted her bills for providing "house room, firewood & candles" to the Inferior Court of Common Pleas, the Superior Court, and the juries from 1753 to 1755, she included a £5.0.0 charge for "Breaking windows,

Chairs, &c."[25] Clearly, juries entertained in such unruly circumstances might not be properly sequestered, and this sometimes led to the offense of "watering": buying jurors drinks to sway their deliberations.

In rural areas, justices of the peace and probate judges, who frequently needed to travel considerable distances, could hardly have performed their duties without relying heavily on taverns. The diary of Matthew Patten of Bedford is filled with accounts of his holding courts at various taverns. Under orders from the Inferior Court of Common Pleas, Patten frequently acted with others as referee in minor legal disputes, almost always at some convenient inn. Patten used rooms in taverns for the serious business of taking depositions from witnesses in legal cases, often in the dead of winter when warmth, candlelight, and privacy were essential.

The rural justice's expenses for lodging at a tavern were usually compensated for by his legal fees, as in the fall of 1784 when Patten secured a promissory note for three dollars after a two-day court session at Underhill's tavern in Chester. Sometimes the country justice was not so promptly paid; earlier in 1784, Patten had spent more than half a day at a tavern to settle an estate, had charged a dollar for his time, and had been informed that the heir "could not pay it."[26] Patten often traveled to Amherst to rendezvous with the Register of Probate at Jonathan Smith's tavern, frequently settling his own outstanding debts while there.

Following the same pattern, country probate courts long continued to convene in any suitable tavern, often with a newspaper advertisement to publicize the time and place. Almost any New Hampshire paper from the mid-eighteenth century on contains several notices like the one that appeared in the Amherst Farmer's Cabinet in November 1810:

The Subscribers . . . have been appointed Commissioners, by the Judge of Probate for the County of Hillsborough, to receive and examine the Claims against the Estate of ALPHEUS GOODWIN, late of Amherst, deceased, represented insolvent—and that they will meet at the dwelling house of Aaron Cilley, Innholder in Amherst . . . for the purpose aforesaid.[27]

Even as late as 1908, Judge Charles R. Corning of Concord noted his conduct of probate proceedings in Henniker: "I held a simple Court in the Tavern parlor & soon completed my work. . . . The Tavern keeper is Hale, formerly of Perkins Inn, Hopkinton, who sets a good table & maintains a clean & attractive house. The pitcher of cream & milk he set before me was worth the journey."[28]

Because the tavern was of crucial importance to the conduct of public business, prospective tavernkeepers were quick to try to license dwellings which stood near political centers. Sometimes, if the need went unmet, taverns were created and licensed near the focus of government activity as a deliberate public service. The conjunction of taverns and government was especially noticeable in Portsmouth, where both the provincial Assembly and the courts of law convened until the 1770s, bringing many sojourners from distant towns. When the State House (also containing a courtroom) was built on Portsmouth Parade between 1758 and 1766, taverns ceased to serve a direct role in housing the functions of government. Yet the tavern retained its traditional role of housing delegates and petitioners, and taverns near the State House assumed new importance as political forums.

A number of taverns stood literally within sight of the State House. Across King (now Congress) Street from the North Meeting House was Jacob Tilton's Marquis of Rockingham Tavern, advertised by its shrewd proprietor as

Steel engraving, Main Street, Concord, N.H., mid 1850s. After the seat of state government moved to Concord, hotels clustered around the new State House. Published separately and as a vignette on a five-dollar note of Concord's Mechanicks Bank, this view shows the American House at the center, and the Eagle Hotel at the right, behind the flagpole.

NHHS Collections   Photographer, Bill Finney

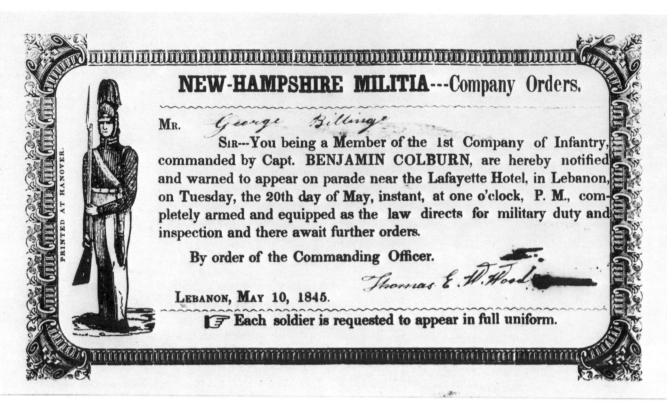

Militia order, Hanover, N.H., 1845. This summons to a spring muster in Lebanon, to be held near the Lafayette Hotel, shows an idealized uniform perhaps more complete than those actually worn during a period when the state militia was in decline.
NHHS Collections   Photographer, Ernest Gould

standing virtually at the western door of the State House. Later known under other proprietors as the Bell, this house had been built in 1743 by Paul March. About ten years later, Zachariah Foss built a neighboring tavern on King Street, symbolizing its convenient location by raising "the Sign of the State House" as soon as the capitol was constructed. A short distance east, on Daniel Street, stood James Stoodley's house, built about 1753, distinguished by "the Sign of the King's Arms," and quickly rebuilt after a fire in 1761. Just south, with a view of the eastern door and balcony of the State House, stood Packer's tavern, which had long served as the meeting place of the general court and the courts of law.

Country tavern sites, too, were regarded as particularly choice if they stood near government headquarters. In 1816, Lewis Hunt's "elegant" brick tavern and stage house in Charlestown was advertised for sale, its special virtue being that it stood "in front of the Court-House."[29] Three years later, a house at Smith's Bridge in Wolfeboro was advertised as an excellent prospect for a tavern, standing as it did "on a public road in a very flourishing village which will probably soon be established as the seat of one of the county Courts."[30]

Just as it served civil government, the tavern played a crucial military role. In the tenuous early years of settlement, taverns in a number of communities were strengthened as garrisons. As early as 1705, the Council voted to fortify the Portsmouth tavern of Thomas Packer (who was a colonel of the militia as well as a physician), partly because it stood as an outpost on what was then regarded as the remote western fringe of the compactly settled portion of the town.[31] Perhaps it was this early use as a garrison that gave present-day Pleasant Street, in front of the house, where militia drills were held, its original designation as "the Parade."

In 1732, the inhabitants of Hampton Falls registered a strong objection when a provincial court suspended the license of their former tavern and licensed a new house. The citizens not only asserted that the owner of the old stand "has substance by him, and [is] well supplied to keep the house, with suitable necessaries for entertaining Strangers and travellers," but also noted that the house

> was Bult with Logs, after the manner of a Garrison, and on purpose for a publick hous of Entertainment for travellers &c, and was veary sarvesable, for the Security of Travellers and the Inhabitants in the troublesome time of war. . . .[32]

Similarly, the first tavern in Concord was established in the venerable garrison house of James Osgood.[33]

New Hampshire's charter of 1679 had required the creation and periodic training of a militia, and this duty continued under both royal and constitutional government until the eve of the Civil War. The purpose of militia musters never varied from that designated under the law of

Termination of a Militia Sham Fight, 1833, watercolor on paper, by David Claypoole Johnston. This satire recalls the all-too-frequent conclusion to the sham battles staged at New England musters. Antics such as this had cast the militia into disrepute in the decades before the Civil War, leaving the military tradition of New England largely in the hands of elite volunteer companies.
Courtesy, American Antiquarian Society   Photographer, Marvin Richmond

1718: "to exercise [troops] in motions, the use of arms, and shooting at marks, or other military exercises." Although military discipline and organization changed over the decades, the laws evolved by the nineteenth century to call for spring and fall musters, and these events became fixtures in the social life of every community.

Musters were held on large, flat, mowed fields suitable for the marching and wheeling maneuvers of large bodies of men and horses. The methods of town planning practiced by both the Masonian Proprietors and the New Hampshire government from the mid eighteenth century ensured that such tracts of public land were allocated at town centers, usually adjacent to the meetinghouse. Such sites were also chosen by wise tavernkeepers, so that one or more taverns almost inevitably stood near both training field and meetinghouse. Even when a town's shifting population caused the abandonment of the earliest center, as often happened, new taverns would certainly appear at the relocated center of political and social activity. In many cases, if a public training field was not available at some newer town center, a shrewd tavernkeeper would make his own hayfield available for the semiannual musters.

To prevent bribery in the election of militia officers, the new State of New Hampshire passed a stern law in 1776 forbidding officers, on penalty of court-martial, from treating with victuals or drink on any training or muster day. Nevertheless, the provision of refreshment was always seen as essential at musters. Few if any musters, therefore, were held at sites far from one or more convenient taverns. By 1808, the law had evolved to require that "suitable meats and drinks, or thirty-four cents in lieu thereof,

should be furnished each non-commissioned officer and private" at public expense.[34] The expectation of such entertainment, combined with the chance to see seldom-met neighbors, to don military garb, to march to the stirring music of fife and drum, to burn the public supply of gunpowder in mock battles with musket and cannon, and to leave the routine of daily work, made the muster an eagerly awaited event in nineteenth-century life, one that gave wives and children as entertaining a holiday as it did the men.

The pomp and excitement of the muster was never more clearly seen than through the eyes of local children. Looking back in 1903, J. Trask Plumer recalled his youthful impressions of the autumn maneuvers at Goffstown:

The pen can but poorly portray the impressive grandeur of the scene as it appeared to the eyes of the country boy of half a century ago. How those fiery, mettlesome steeds reared and plunged beneath their martial riders as the inspiring music of fife and drum swelled and rolled out on the crisp autumn air. What an embodyment of stately dignity was that group of officers with their gay trappings, gold epaulettes and waving plumes. . . . Most of the forenoon was occupied in drilling and inspecting the troops. In the afternoon came the sham fight or mock battle. This was the great event of the day. . . . These sham battles not unfrequently developed into real fights owing to the ambition of some of the companies to establish their reputation for valor and bravery. I am not aware, however, that the fertility of the soil upon that field of Mars at Goffstown was very materially enhanced by the blood there shed.[35]

The Militia Muster, *1828, watercolor on paper, by David Claypoole Johnston. Another of Johnston's satirical views captures the ridiculous qualities which often earned the enrolled or general militia the epithets of "slam-bang," "string bean," or "flood wood" units. The caricatured disarray of the soldiers is close enough to the descriptions of contemporary observers to have made this painting an embarrassing commentary in 1828.*

Courtesy, American Antiquarian Society   Photographer, Marvin Richmond

The child's mixed excitement and apprehension at such maneuvers was recalled by Susan Blunt of Merrimack:

> When [the company] would halt before our house and give a salute, I would run down celer, for I was affraid of the guns. After dinner at the tavern, they would go on a little hill in the rear of the village and have a sham battle. They had a small cannon which they would fire off, and it would attract many spectators.[36]

Since the law required youths of sixteen or eighteen to join a local company, many raw recruits were nearly as distracted as the local children. Plumer tells the sad story of Jonathan Dighton, who "loaded his musket every time the order was given, but in the excitement of the fray" did not notice that it failed to fire. Finally, "having two or three charges in the old musket, well rammed down," Dighton unfortunately succeeded in priming the gun effectively. The result was such that "if Jonathan had received his wounds in legitimate warfare, in defense of this country, he would have been entitled to a pension for total disability."[37] In another incident in 1789, Joseph Bell of Bedford wounded his leg so seriously "in the training Field" that he required four visits by Dr. Zephaniah Kittredge of Amherst to dress the wound and no less than 162 later visits, many of them twice daily, by Dr. Nathan Cutler of Bedford.[38]

Alcohol and gunpowder make a dangerous combination, and sometimes the presence of the tavern must have contributed more to the mishaps that frequently marked muster day than did youthful inexperience. One Vermonter, reminiscing in 1901, recalled an incident when a befuddled young militiaman accidentally fired his musket, with the ramrod still in the barrel, in the basement kitchen of a house. The rod "tore up through the floor of the room above, exactly where the captain was standing . . . ripped a hole through the back of his coat and came out at the back of his neck without leaving a scratch."[39] An attempt to curb such dangerous behavior was made in 1795 when the New Hampshire legislature passed an act forbidding any noncommissioned officer or private from firing a gun "on the day or evening of a muster, in or near any public road, or any house, or on or near the place of parade, without permission of a commissioned officer."[40]

If lack of military training sometimes marked districtwide regimental musters, worse was all too often seen at the "little trainings" or local company musters usually held in the spring. The cynical attitude that sometimes accompanied these gatherings is reflected in a 1798 summons to an Antrim sergeant: "You are hereby required to warn all the training band . . . to meet at my house on Thursday the 7th day of this instant in order to drink some grog."[41] As Plumer recalled in 1903, "It is said that on some of these occasions, as the day advanced, and the men had partaken freely of the refreshments, that the only way the captain could succeed in forming his company into the semblance of a straight line was to back them up against some resisting barrier like a fence or barn."[42]

These springtime trainings, composed of ill-equipped men without uniforms, gave rise to the derisive descriptions of local companies as "slam bang," "string bean," or "flood wood" militia. In 1837, the traveler Marryat noted in his diary that "the militia service is not in good odour with the Americans just now . . . [and] they do all they can to make it ridiculous." At one muster he attended,

> not only were the men of all sorts and sizes, but the uniforms also, some of which were the most extraordinary I ever beheld, and not unlike the calico dresses worn by the tumblers and vaulters at an English fair. As for the exercise . . . they faced every way, and made mistakes on purpose. . . . When they marched off single file, quick time, they were one half of them dancing in and out of the ranks to the lively tune which was played—the only instance I saw of their keeping time.[43]

However amusing or embarrassing such musters may have been to spectators, many sought to avoid them as a waste of time. The only way to do so without incurring a fine was to seek certification as an invalid, exempt from military duty. An act of 1813 specified that certificates of disability could be obtained only from selectmen or designated regimental surgeons, and fines were levied on officials who took pay for issuing such certificates. Advertisements in the 1823 New-Hampshire Statesman named the official surgeons and surgeons' mates for the Thirtieth Regiment, and forbade company commanders from excusing " 'invalids' from military duty in consequence of certificates signed by other persons." The surgeons, in turn, advertised their presence at several taverns and at the North Sutton meetinghouse to "attend to examining all Invalids for Certificates to excuse them from doing Military duty" during April and May of that year.[44]

The carnival spirit that frequently characterized militia musters attracted not only family members seeking a holiday, but others looking for profit or mischief. As Plumer recalled, militia gatherings "were often infested by gangs of gamblers and light-fingered gentry who fleeced the unsuspecting farmer most unmercifully."[45] The Amherst Cabinet commended the discipline of the fall maneuvers of 1834, but noted that an "assemblage of peddlers, loafers, rum-drinkers, and gamblers was present, whose ill-conduct was a disgrace to the place, and to all concerned in it."[46] It was common for peddlers and hucksters to pitch tents around the margins of training fields or to occupy the taprooms of nearby taverns, and to entice locals into games in which the laws of chance played little part.

Yet sometimes even these itinerant rogues were outclassed. The notorious Seth Wyman began his life of crime in earnest at the Goffstown muster at the age of fourteen when he plucked a loaf of sugar from a table occupied by a group of officers "whose valor had become somewhat excited by copious draughts from the rum noggin [and who] were engaged in a loud dispute with tongue and fist."

VOLUNTEERS.

WANTED fome able Volunteers, to complete the Number in the Garrifon of His Majefty's Caftle of William and Mary, in the Province of New Hampfhire ;———— the Men in this Garrifon are provided with a compleat Suit of Regimentals once a Year ;—They alfo receive three Dollars per Month pay, and five fhillings lawful Money per Week for billeting;—Any Perfons inclineable to enter into this Service, are defired to apply to John Cochran, Efq; Commander of the faid Caftle at the Earl of Halifax Tavern in Portfmouth.

Portfmouth, March 1772.

Recruiting notice from the New-Hampshire Gazette *(Portsmouth), 1772. Seeking soldiers to garrison Fort William and Mary in New Castle, John Cochran used Stavers' Earl of Halifax Tavern as his recruiting office.*
NHHS Collections   Photographer, Bill Finney

Wyman followed that success with the rifling of a desk in a tavern bedchamber while the militiamen were at supper downstairs. Returning for the fall training, Wyman

> soon had my eye on the money they were taking in the tents around the field, which was placed in box covers, bowls, plates, &c. While their backs were turned, I generally managed to dip my hand into their coffers, and extract one or more piece of money.

By this straightforward thievery, not expected from a mere boy, Wyman enriched himself to the total of twelve dollars.[47]

Since, for better or worse, the tavern was indelibly associated in the public mind with the martial life, it is not surprising that the tavern was pressed into service for other military needs. When John Cochran, commander of Fort William and Mary in New Castle, sought to build up his garrison in 1772, he made the Earl of Halifax Tavern in Portsmouth his recruiting office.[48] When the federal government advertised in the Amherst area for enlistees for the War of 1812, Emerson's tavern was selected as the point of rendezvous.[49] In an age when militiamen elected their own officers, the tavern also served as a place for general meeting and balloting. And, since many of the best-disciplined and most resplendent militia companies were private, often sponsored by some local merchant or political figure, the tavern served as a place for dinners, speech-making, and general preparation for maneuvers among these elite units.[50]

While the modern mind imagines the soldier on military campaign as quartered in barracks or tents, eighteenth-century practice called for the soldier, at least on the way to and from battle, to be housed at public expense under a more permanent roof. Except under extreme conditions, that roof belonged to a tavern—the one type of dwelling designated by law to provide shelter to any traveler. Indeed, it became a matter of outrage to citizens in North America, and one against which they eventually protected themselves under Article III of the Bill of Rights, that soldiers might be "quartered in any [private] house without the consent of the owner."

New Hampshire laws of various periods specified the amounts to be reimbursed by the government to the tavernkeeper for billeting soldiers. A law of 1758 specified that the rate of reimbursement should reflect the current "act of Parliament for quartering and billeting Officers and Soldiers in England, Wales and the Town of Berwick upon Tweed," and further noted that officers and soldiers should be provided "with Diet & Small beer or Cyder." The law went on to specify a fine of five pounds sterling against any tavernkeeper who "shall refuse to receive and Victual any such officer or soldier so quartered and billeted upon him or her."[51]

The provincial treasurer's records are filled with bills from tavernkeepers for the housing of soldiers. Many of these statements make it abundantly clear why the tavernkeeper might regret the necessity of housing so rough and careless a clientele as the common soldier. Although the billeting of soldiers might guarantee both a full house and eventual payment from the government, such service was also likely to result in damage to both building and contents. When Portsmouth tavernkeeper John Stavers boarded a dozen soldiers for three days in 1769, he had the benefit of reimbursement from the selectmen for their lodging plus a total of 108 breakfasts, dinners, and suppers. But he also added a surcharge of six shillings to his bill for "my trouble of Cleaning, Scouring & Airing the house, &c., by keeping said soldiers."[52]

Soldiers were prone to rowdy behavior. Exeter tavernkeeper Theodore Carlton housed soldiers during the Revolution, and as a consequence his house sustained "42 squares of glass broke, 2 stairs broke, 6 doors gone, several others broke, and plaistering [sic] broke down in several rooms."[53] The military propensity for fighting was not confined to sham battles or actual warfare. When a company of soldiers was housed in Isaac Emery's tavern in East Concord during the War of 1812, Aaron Austin, a rival tavernkeeper and a Federalist who opposed the war, led a belligerent mob to Emery's barroom. The fight that ensued between civilians and soldiers was only quelled when John McNeil of Hillsborough, the six-foot-six company captain, seized the rival innkeeper and "threw him out of an open window upon the green."[54]

Surviving bills and diaries document the course of soldiers as they moved from tavern to tavern on their way to join their regiments. The diary of John Calfe of Hampstead records his progress toward Ticonderoga in February of 1777. The trip took twelve days, during which Calfe's normal routine was to march about five miles; to breakfast at a tavern; to march another five miles or so and then stop at a second tavern for refreshment; and finally to march a final five to nine miles and put up for the night at a third tavern.[55] Apparently at no point on this journey from eastern New Hampshire to western Vermont did absence of a tavern force Calfe to shift for himself outdoors or seek shelter at a private home.

While town and province records abound with bills for victualing of soldiers on their way to and from active duty, the same records reveal that the tavern was occasionally required to serve as a resting place, or even a hospital, for the sick or injured soldier. In 1754, a soldier named Samuel Houston rested for forty-one days at Osgood's tavern in Concord while recovering from a fractured leg.[56] Benjamin York, a New Hampshire soldier in the 1756 expedition against Crown Point, suffered wounds and was hospitalized for four months in the Chester tavern of Jonathan Blunt. Blunt's charges against the Province of New Hampshire included room and board, the "Keeping a fire for his Use Night & Day" for sixteen weeks, "the Bed on which he Lay[d], almost Spoil[d], feathers & all," "Linnen cloth & tow," and "Eight Gallons of Rum to Dress his wounds with." A year later, Blunt submitted a bill for nursing a second soldier.[57] In 1759, two other soldiers, "being Sick of the Measles" in Exeter, each recuperated for six days in the taverns of Jonathan Gilman and Benjamin Hanson.[58]

In the late autumn of 1760, eight hundred New Hampshire troops were returning from service at Crown Point and Canada when a smallpox epidemic struck. Many of the ill soldiers could not continue and had to seek care in taverns along the way. Tavernkeeper Reuben Spaulding of Nottingham West (later Hudson) gave shelter for three days to a soldier sick with the disease, providing food and nursing, followed by transportation to the home of Jonathan Hills of Londonderry for a four-week convalescence.[59] Tavernkeeper Nathan Kendall of Litchfield billed the province for the care of Nicholas Mariner, a soldier who "in his march homwards from Canady was Taken Sick at my house and there tarry[d] five weakes Before he was able to Travel. 3 weakes of the time he kept his bed."[60] Innholders Andrew Balch and Oliver Sanders of Salem provided rum, sugar, molasses, and candles for the care of their stricken townsman John Bedel as he lay dying of smallpox.[61] Tavernkeepers elsewhere in the province submitted bills for similar services during the Seven Years' War and, later, during the Revolution. When four New Hampshire riflemen were traveling toward Cambridge in December 1775, two of their number, Isaac Thomson and Sherman Shattuck, fell ill in Portsmouth and required ten days of nursing at Jacob Tilton's tavern.[62]

In coastal towns, seafarers often depended upon the humanity of tavernkeepers; tavernkeepers, in turn, sought reimbursement from the provincial government for the care of helpless strangers. In October 1759, a Jerseyman named John Jacob Joven, "a Passenger . . . from Antigua," lodged at the tavern of John King at Portsmouth Plains and died there at the end of the following January. King provided the wanderer with room and board, clothing, washing, attendance by a physician, and "rum at Sundry times to wash his Leggs." When Joven died, the tavernkeeper provided a winding sheet, a cap, a coffin, gloves, and liquor for the bearers, and the services of a sexton to dig the grave and ring the bell.[63] In 1766, a traveler named John Swenson came to Portsmouth "with Capt. Michael Pursell from North Carolina" and stayed at the tavern of Foster Trefetheren. Since "Both his feet & Legs was frost Bitten," Swenson had to have both limbs amputated by Dr. Joshua Brackett, followed by no fewer than 142 visits by the physician. The patient required eight weeks of board and nursing, firewood and candles, five-and-a-half yards of half-worn sheeting for bandages, and prodigious quantities of rum both for dressing and to dull his pain.[64]

Inland travelers also depended upon the innkeeper as agent of the government's charity. In 1771, a "stranger" named James McMahon was taken sick at the Goffstown tavern of Captain James Karr. Karr provided board, nursing, and attendance by a doctor for the invalid; when McMahon died eight weeks later, the tavernkeeper paid for "watchers" for the corpse, for a grave, a coffin, a shirt and winding sheet, and for funeral services.[65]

If the tavern provided for the parliamentary, military, and humanitarian needs of government, it likewise provided a stage for those who held or aspired to office. Most communities contained no other building so well suited for the exchange of ideas and frequently acrimonious debate between elected officials or candidates for office and the public. The tavern was the natural forum for the male electorate and traveling politicians in the eighteenth and nineteenth centuries.

As early as 1737, when a royally appointed commission met at Hampton to begin the settlement of the boundary line between New Hampshire and Massachusetts, Jonathan Belcher, governor of both provinces, used the occasion to profess his impartiality in a speech to the New Hampshire Assembly at John Brown's Georges Tavern in Hampton Falls. From that point forward, governors and presidents alike used the New Hampshire tavern as a forum to cultivate the good will of the populace.

Washington's tour of New Hampshire in 1789 was virtually a procession from tavern to tavern. In July 1817, recently inaugurated President James Monroe likewise made a tour of parts of New Hampshire, and the short notice provided of his itinerary pressed the ever-ready taverns along his route into impromptu service as the President's meeting places with his welcoming committees and the general public.

Monroe was first entertained at Wyatt's inn in Dover, where he dined and "gratified a great concourse of attending citizens by making his appearance" in the neighboring streets.[66] The following day, seven hours' notice was given that the President would travel to Concord along the First New Hampshire Turnpike. There, "the whole Village moved with the greatest activity and with perfect unanimity" to furnish Barker's inn "as handsomely as was in the power of the inhabitants." After refreshment at Piper's tavern in Northwood, Monroe and his entourage progressed westward to Concord, where they found Barker's Washington Tavern provided with "a stage about four feet high, erected under venerable elms in front of the Inn, which was covered with carpets, furnished with chairs, and tastefully decorated with evergreens and flowers." From this simple podium, on a hot afternoon, the President met and addressed the citizens of the capital and surrounding towns.[67]

Even at the time, it was remarked that one of the blessings enjoyed by the citizens of the United States was the fact that in this peaceful democracy, the tavern and the private home provided an adequately safe haven for a President. Despite strong political partisanship,

> such is the confidence of his fellow-citizens in their chief magistrate, presiding over eight millions of people, that he can travel 2000 miles in the interior of our country, unattended, except by two or three of his select friends while in other countries, no king or petty prince dare leave his threshold without a corps of life-guards.[68]

The same hospitality was accorded President Andrew Jackson when in June 1833, he stayed in Concord for four days with Vice President Van Buren and the two New Hampshire natives in his Cabinet, secretaries Cass and Woodbury. On that occasion the Eagle Coffee House served as the President's headquarters, and from its balcony Jackson addressed a concourse of ten thousand people.[69]

Aspiring officeholders likewise made use of the tavern. In 1836, vice-presidential candidate Richard M. Johnson of Kentucky was received with great pomp at the Dartmouth Hotel in Hanover; from its balcony, he addressed an enthusiastic crowd wearing the bullet-riddled waistcoat in which he had fought the Battle of the Thames in 1813.[70] Native son Daniel Webster made similar use of Keene's Cheshire House while campaigning for the Whig platform in 1840.[71]

The tavern served as a point of refreshment and official greeting for newly elected governors on their way to inauguration. This tradition had its origins along the seacoast in the seventeenth century. When Governor Samuel Allen's commission was proclaimed at the fort in New Castle in 1698, the celebrants consumed a punch containing four gallons of rum, eighteen pounds of sugar, a hundred limes, and three nutmegs, plus a dinner provided by the widow Hannah Purmort, a local innholder.[72] In 1716, Packer's tavern in Portsmouth was selected as the place where the

Assembly and Council would greet Governor Eliseus Burgess; Burgess, however, never left England to visit his New England dominions.[73] When Lieutenant Governor David Dunbar's commissions were published in 1731, Elizabeth Cross' Portsmouth tavern provided rooms and refreshments for the ceremony.[74]

After government moved to Concord in the early nineteenth century, it became customary for a committee of the legislature, usually with an honor guard of the militia, to greet each new governor at some tavern near the Concord town line, to enjoy a brief ceremonial stop with him there, and then to escort him in procession to his lodgings in town and then to the State House for the ceremony of inauguration. In Concord's early days as state capital, when most governors had their farms or homes in the eastern part of the state, a tavern in Pembroke was usually selected for the rendezvous; later, as governors arrived from different parts of the state, Hubbard Weeks' tavern on Hopkinton Road, Ambrose's tavern in Boscawen, or Brown's tavern in West Concord were used as the occasion might demand.[75]

The tavern served the partisan needs of government as well. Specific taverns became solidly identified with one political party or another, providing a hospitable environment for the quiet planning of strategy or the more raucous rallying to the party banner. Taverns were notorious nests of political intrigue during the years preceding the Revolution, and sometimes individual buildings were so closely associated with political machinations as to become hateful to the opposing faction. When, for example, "a large number of the most respectable Inhabitants" of Greenland erected a liberty pole at John Folsom's tavern in 1774, it was alleged in the newspaper that this conduct "being very disagreeable to Col. March, he enter'd his Dissent, and said none but lazy, idle Fellows . . . would have any Thing to do with such Business, and that he would indemnify any one that would cut the Pole down."[76]

Perhaps the earliest important act of political rebellion associated with a tavern occurred in 1734 in Exeter. Samuel Gilman's tavern was the focus of the so-called Mast Tree Riot, one of countless skirmishes between the authority of the crown and New Hampshire's rapacious lumbermen. Learning that mast trees were being felled illegally and sawed into lumber at the Copyhold Mill and other sawmills within Exeter's bounds, Lieutenant Governor David Dunbar, who was also Surveyor General of the King's Woods, sent a party to investigate. Dunbar's deputies spent the night at Gilman's tavern, while the outlaw sawyers assembled at another public house kept by Zebulon Giddinge to decide their strategy. Then, disguised as Indians, some thirty lumbermen surprised the official party in their beds, and, as James Pitman related,

> broke into the Room, & put out their candles; & immediately fell upon [Pitman and three others] & did then & there Beat us & Dragged us about, & at length got us to the Head of the chamber stairs & pulled us down, one over another headlong 'till they got us to the Door

& pulled us out then with a clubb did knock [me] down upon the Ground giving [me] several blows with wch [I] was in great danger of [my] life having recd several wounds, & lost a great deal of blood. . . .[77]

Thereupon, the painted marauders disappeared into the countryside, never to be brought to justice despite Dunbar's earnest efforts.

A similar occurrence took place in Weare in April 1772. Governor John Wentworth, who also held the office of Surveyor, had commenced with renewed vigor to enforce the law against cutting mast trees. Benjamin Whiting, sheriff of Hillsborough County, and John Quigley, his deputy, arrested millman Ebenezer Mudgett of Weare, agreeing to await his bail in the morning. The officers spent the night at Aaron Quinby's inn. "Early the next Morning," according to a newspaper account, Mudgett

> came to the Chamber Door, and told Mr. Whiting he had got Bail; to which the Sheriff answered it was very well, but added, he need not have hurried quite so much, but have stopped till it was lighter. However, that he would get up, and wait on him. While he was dressing, thirty or forty Persons, in Disguise, with black[ened] Faces, Rushed into the Room with Clubs, upon which Mr. Whiting retreated back to the Wall, and having got his Pistols, declared he would Shoot the first man that approached him, and its thought would thus have defended himself, but some of these Fellows having got up in the Garret, took up the Floor, and soon overpowered the Sheriff and his Assistant, whom they abused and beat in a most Shameful Manner, and then went to the Barn and cut the Ears, Tails and Mains [sic] off both of their Horses, and ordered the Sheriff and his Man to mount, and go off; which they prudently complied with. . . . [78]

The upshot of Weare's Pine Tree Riot was that the offenders were finally brought to trial, but after submitting themselves to the grace of "our Lord the King" were punished with a token fine of twenty shillings each.[79]

As the Revolution approached, New Hampshire taverns, like others up and down the Eastern seaboard, increasingly became scenes of political activity and protest. In November 1765, the Globe Tavern at Portsmouth Plains was the rallying point for "some Hundreds of Persons from the Country" who marched toward town to stop the distribution of stamped paper, but who "return'd to their respective Homes . . . in Peace and Quietness" after learning that Portsmouth's citizens would permit none of the paper to be unpacked.[80] When tea, rather than excise stamps, became the focus of public outrage, New Hampshire saw several minor "tea parties" akin to the more famous one in Boston. In August 1774, news reached Portsmouth from Haverhill that

> some Time last Week, a Number of honest Savages, Friends of the Rights of America, having Information of a small Quantity of Bohea-Tea, lodg'd by a pedling Trader, at the House of an Innholder in Haverhill, entered the same without Ceremony, and having

ON THE ROAD NORTH OF BOSTON

seized on the execrated Weed, convey'd it into the public Road, and immediately made a burnt Offering of the Whole. A Proof this, that the same Spirit of Freedom pervades & enlivens the remotest Parts of our English Settlements.[81]

Certain Portsmouth taverns became known as hotbeds of sedition. James Stoodley's tavern, ironically called the Sign of the King's Arms, and Jacob Tilton's Marquis of Rockingham Tavern were both recognized points of rendezvous for rebels. Both played a role on the fateful days of December 14 and 15, 1774, when the first overt act of revolution followed directly upon Paul Revere's arrival in Portsmouth. Revere brought news that Secretary of State Lord Dartmouth had sent a letter to all American governors ordering them to seal every port against the importation of munitions that might aid in rebellion. At midday on December 14, some four hundred men led by John Langdon went downriver to New Castle, where the fort had been infiltrated by a few of their allies. The party surrounded the fort and, after a brief skirmish, subdued the guard of five men and the captain, John Cochran. The raiders then carried off about a hundred hundred-pound barrels of all-important gunpowder.[82]

Their work was not yet done. The following morning, more armed men began to appear in town. Led by John Sullivan of Durham, the men gathered on the Parade directly below the second-floor council chamber of the State House, where the Governor and Council were meeting in emergency session. Demanding to know whether royal troops were on the way to regarrison the fort, the men were answered in the negative by Governor Wentworth. Sullivan and his men then gathered at Tilton's tavern, across the street from the State House, to await nightfall. That afternoon, Wentworth ordered another tavernkeeper, James Stoodley, a commanding officer of the First Regiment of Militia, "to enlist or Impress Thirty effective men to serve his Majesty as a Guard & Protection to his Fort William and Mary in New Castle." Stoodley, whose duty conflicted with his private convictions, later testified that he had followed orders, having "Paraded the streets, caused the Drums to be Beat, & Proclamation to be made at all the Publick corners, & on the Place of Parade." Despite the armed men who filled the town, however, Stoodley was singularly unsuccessful in his recruiting, "No Person appearing to Enlist."[83]

Later that night, Sullivan and his men left Tilton's, boarded boats, and returned to the fort. There they removed some sixteen cannons, sixty muskets, and other military equipment, and loaded the armaments on gundalows. Awaiting a turn of tide to transport the guns upriver, Sullivan and his men remained temporarily immobile. During the same night, however, the raiding party was protected by still other men, led by Nathaniel Folsom, who traveled by dark from Exeter. Among them was Gideon Lamson, who recounted his experience some fifty years later:

We rode into Portsmouth after daybreak, and stopped at Major Stoodley's inn, [revealing] no appearance of the design. . . . We had coffee about sunrise. Major Stoodley looked queer upon such guests, with guns and bayonets. . . . At nine, Colonel Langdon came to Stoodley's and acquainted General Folsom and company with the success of the enterprise,—that General Sullivan was then passing up the river with the loaded boats of powder and cannon.[84]

If Stoodley's and Tilton's taverns were well-known haunts of rebels, John and Bartholomew Stavers' Earl of Halifax Tavern was equally known as a meeting place of loyalists. In 1777, with the Revolution underway, Stavers' tavern at last suffered for its connections. Bartholomew Stavers, who had returned to England, testified that he had suffered because "his House was a tory house, because he kept a house of entertainment for the King's Officers & the friends of Government, at which they used to meet. . . ."[85] More was known of the Stavers' activities than merely that; the rebels had planted a spy there. Nathaniel Odiorne later revealed that "he frequented Staver's Tavern with a view of finding out the Principles of sundry Persons who used to associate there."[86]

Trouble began in late January 1777, when the tavern was under the sole proprietorship of John Stavers. A sailor named John Wheelwright arrived with James Sheafe at Stavers' tavern to find "a mob with one Ward a barber with an ax in his hand." Despite the commotion, Wheelwright and Sheafe entered the tavern, where "Mistress Stavers Came into the room and told Mister Stivers [sic] that mister Marck Nobell had had sum Lickur and refused to Pay for it." According to Wheelwright, Stavers then told Noble

to go about his Business, he did not want any Destirbunce; he went out and I understand he went to Cut the [sign] Post Down. Sum Person Came in and Said to mister Stiver "Nobell is Cuting your Post Down." He Sais, "James, go drive them away." Sum time after I heard murder Caled out. We all Quit the room and went out where theare was a man Laid in the Streate and . . . the Post was Cut Down.[87]

Local tradition says that Stavers' slave seized an axe and struck Noble on the head, rendering him insane for most of the rest of his life, and that John Langdon stepped in to prevent the complete wreckage of the house.[88] Stavers was arrested and imprisoned in the Exeter jail for a few days, but was released when Noble, in a period of lucidity, wrote the Committee of Safety to say that it was by his own "Bad Luck or misfortune [that] I have Received A Bad Blow," and that Stavers was "in gaol upon my account contrary to my desire."[89] Within a few weeks, Stavers placed a notice in the New-Hampshire Gazette thanking "the Gentlemen of the town who were active in suppressing the late tumult at his house [and] who exerted themselves in preserving so great part of his Interest from the violence of an enraged populace."[90] Shortly thereafter, Stavers changed the name of his tavern from The Earl of Halifax to William Pitt, after the great British defender of liberty.

Because of the extralegal nature of much activity leading up to the Revolution, the tavern was pressed into service to provide a home for those committees which in effect were the kernels of a second government with nowhere else to meet. When members of the New Hampshire Assembly formed a committee of correspondence and laid plans to elect delegates to a Continental Congress, Governor Wentworth attempted to stop their activity by adjourning, and finally dissolving, the Assembly. Dissolved or not, the Assembly convened in their accustomed middle chamber of the State House in June 1774. They were met by the Governor and the county sheriff, who proclaimed that only the King through his appointed deputy could call the Assembly together, and ordered the representatives to disperse. The Assembly obeyed, but only to the extent that they quit the State House and reconvened across the street in Jacob Tilton's tavern, returning to chambers much like the ones they had met in before the State House was readied for occupancy in 1762.[91]

Other towns followed suit to the extent that at the outbreak of the Revolution, New Hampshire was held together by a government of committees centered in taverns. Among the taverns in which local committees of safety are known to have met were those of John Paine in Hanover and Colonel Isaac Wyman in Keene. In Exeter, the committees for accounts and safety met in the house of Samuel Brooks, who billed them not only for rooms, firewood, and candles, but also for a "Box of Wafers" with which to seal their documents and for a not unusual "two chairs broke."[92]

Some of these inland taverns became places of dread for local Tories. From such buildings might storm a mob, usually heated with drink, to arrest and sometimes mistreat those deemed to be loyalists. When David McClure visited Pembroke in 1774, he was forced to apply for lodging at a fellow minister's house. McClure reported that he

> could not get lodging at the tavern, on account of the great number of people there, who are engaged in the business of taking up Tories. In the morning, they compelled one Dicks to make a long Confession, from the head of a large Cask, to about 300 sons of Liberty.[93]

Abner Sanger of Keene noted in his diary that he was roughly arrested in 1777 and "carried before a violent committee setting at the house of Mr. Nathan Blake," a Keene tavernkeeper. Sanger was thereupon confined to the house of Alexander Ralston, another tavernkeeper (who, oddly, was generally regarded as keeping a "Tory hall").[94] Two years later, Captain Elisha Mack of Gilsum made his own Tory-hunting incursion into Keene. Meeting at Partridge's tavern outside of town, Mack sent his men to surround the houses of suspected loyalists. In the morning, Mack rode into town, collected his suspects, and paraded them to Hall's tavern where they were confined in a chamber. Before Mack could do any further mischief to his

Wood engraving from Zadock Thompson's History of Vermont, *1842. In the incident pictured, the sentence of being "tied in an armed chair and hoisted to the sign" of the Green Mountain Tavern was carried out against a New Yorker in Bennington, Vermont, in 1775. Such summary punishment, however, was often directed against enemies of the Revolution at New Hampshire taverns during the same period.*

NHHS Collections   Photographer, Ernest Gould

prisoners, he and his men were driven away by two local companies of militia.[95] The more partisan colonel of the Ninth New Hampshire Regiment of militia, innkeeper Moses Kelley of Goffstown, was locally famous for making his house the starting point for many "forays against the Tories of the neighborhood."[96]

In Concord, a group of men gathered at "Mother Osgood's" tavern in 1777 and threatened to pull down the house of a suspected Tory, Peter Green. Two more moderate citizens, Timothy Walker, Jr., and John Bradley, plied the mob with punch until drowsiness overcame them near nightfall and they were persuaded to depart, "every man to his tent."[97] Matthew Patten recalled that Colonel Atherton of Amherst similarly mollified a mob who came to "visit" him in 1774; upon signing a declaration of loyalty, Atherton invited his guests "to go to Mr. Hildreth's and drink what they pleased," after which they departed about midnight with no further mischief.[98]

ON THE ROAD NORTH OF BOSTON

PHŒNIX HOTEL.

ABEL HUTCHINS,

CONCORD, NEW-HAMPSHIRE,

A FEW RODS SOUTH OF THE STATE-HOUSE,

INFORMS his Friends and the Public, that he has added, during the past summer, to his former accommodations, at the Sign of the

PHŒNIX HOTEL,

three new commodious PARLORS, and eighteen LODGING ROOMS, which will enable him to accommodate his customers with still more convenience than heretofore; and it will be his continual endeavor to render the PHŒNIX HOTEL a pleasant asylum for the Traveller, and an agreeable residence for the man of business or leisure.

Stages from Boston, Burlington, Vt. Stanstead, L. C. Haverhill and Hanover, arrive and depart every day, Sundays excepted;—from Portsmouth, Newburyport, Dover and Exeter, three times a week.

Stage Books kept for every Stage arriving in town.

MARCH, 1830.

Wood engraving of the Phoenix Hotel, Concord, N.H., 1830, by Abel Bowen. Newly enlarged in 1830, Concord's Phoenix was a favorite lodging place and stage depot, and became a popular meeting place of the Whig coalition.

NHHS Collections   Photographer, Bill Finney

The linkage between certain taverns and political partisanship long outlived the Revolution. In the early nineteenth century, Federalists and Jeffersonian Republicans tended to identify themselves with certain favorite inns in most towns, sometimes to the extent that members of the opposing party dared not enter those houses, at least at times of high political excitement. Later, the Democrats and Whigs—and still later, the "new" Republicans—likewise used chosen taverns for informal gatherings and official conventions to select candidates for office. Victory celebrations were held in the favored tavern, and sometimes were moved tauntingly close to the rival inn where political losers had retreated.

The polarization of parties around rival taverns was well illustrated in Dover in the early 1800s. A sarcastic letter from a Jeffersonian Republican to the Dover *Sun* in 1802 identified Nathaniel Ela's tavern as the place where the Federalists, a " 'self-sufficient' Gentry," assembled and "after appointing a 'wise' moderator, they 'wisely' agreed (all but one!) that 'wise men' should hold the reins of government in this state for the present year."[99] A few years later, Daniel Waldron, a Federalist, noted that,

> the grog shops of Esq. Williams and A. Pierce have been the rendezvous of democracy [i.e., Jeffersonians] for several weeks. . . . Tobias [Tuttle] has been guilty of the grossest lying and his shop has been continually filled with the Back River and [Dover] Neck people—he preaching democracy.[100]

The Republicans gathered in other "grog shops" in other towns. When Jefferson was inaugurated in 1801, his followers in Amherst celebrated by firing cannons, ringing bells, and enjoying a public dinner in the hall of Watson's tavern.[101] In Poplin (now Fremont), they met at Asa Woods' tavern; in Greenland, at Marshall's tavern; in Epping, at Pike's tavern; and in Amherst, at Emerson's tavern. The Federalists took notice of these meetings, and in Amherst, in 1812, a number of them went to Emerson's inn and proceeded to dominate the caucus in a meeting that the Concord *Patriot* called "one of the most scandalous, outrageous, and aggravating affairs" within memory.[102] Bands of roving party-members also tended to keep watch for rivals to intimidate. In Concord, in 1810, Republican George Connell was first

> greatly insulted at the court house by one Roggers, for daring to support his principles. On going into Stickney's to obtain some refreshment he was assaulted by a party of Federalists, from the other side of the river, and abused in a shameful manner. He was brought home . . . considerably injured.[103]

After the Whig coalition was formed in 1834, its adherents likewise used taverns to build their political strength. During the 1830s and 1840s, the Whigs met at Brown's tavern, Smith's Hotel, Little's tavern, Pike's tavern, and the Rockingham House in Epping; at Dearborn's and Dunbar's in Hampton; at Dodge's in Rochester; at Blake's in Raymond; at Goodrich's in Kingston; at the Squamscot in Exeter; at the Franklin House in Portsmouth; and at Tilton's in Meredith Bridge.[104] In Concord, the Whigs made the Phoenix their headquarters, while in Amherst they celebrated the election of Harrison as President in 1840 with a supper at Nutt's tavern. In Hanover, the Whigs commemorated the election of Zachary Taylor in 1848 with a grand dinner at the Dartmouth Hotel, punctuated by a salute of fifty guns and by "twenty-one regular and several volunteer toasts."[105]

The "spoils system" was much in evidence during the nineteenth century. Since postmasterships were among the choice rewards for political support, and since innkeepers sought to bring post offices and their associated business into their taverns, post offices tended to move from tavern to tavern as the administration in Washington changed from party to party. In Plymouth, the post office was moved after the election of different Presidents from David Webster's tavern to another building; then back to the Pemigewasset House (which had replaced Webster's tavern); then away; then back to the Pemigewasset site for a third time.[106]

The association between taverns and politics did not end with the Civil War and the advent of the modern Republican and Democratic parties. As late as 1874, the Democrats of Fremont celebrated the reelection of Governor James A. Watson by firing a cannon several times on the outskirts of the village. Fearing that this did not sufficiently impress the Republicans, gathered in Warren True's hotel (formerly Lovering's tavern), the celebrants "moved the gun directly in front of the 'True Hotel' and putting in an extra charge blazed away again. This discharge brought out twenty three lights of glass from said hotel," for which the triumphant Democrats magnanimously reimbursed the owner.[107]

The Fremont celebration may have been a mere relic of a dying tradition, however. In the later years of the nineteenth century, the tavern as an institution was in decline, many of its traditional functions being better served by specialized institutions. Political activity moved increasingly to larger city hotels, especially to the rebuilt Eagle Hotel in Concord, facing the State House, and to the Rockingham in Portsmouth, rebuilt by Democrat Frank Jones.

In its day, the tavern provided important service to government. Despite its sometimes rough and boisterous nature, the tavern provided a young and changing democracy with a meeting place, a forum for debate and parliamentary procedure, and a center for the free exchange of information and opinion with the electorate. In short, the tavern was to the institutions of government what it was to the individual citizen or traveler: a public house.

TAVERN ENTERTAINMENT: FOOD AND DRINK

CHAPTER 8

IN ADVERTISING HAVERHILL'S Grafton Hotel in 1830 as "a house of public entertainment," tavernkeeper Jonathan Sinclair was offering not amusement and diversion, but refreshment and lodging. Early tavernkeepers whose painted signboards and printed advertisements promised "entertainment" were simply announcing their willingness to accommodate strangers in their homes and to provide them with food and drink. Tavern "entertainment" extended not only to travelers, but also to their horses and other animals. A Greenland innkeeper, for instance, offered in 1782, at his hospitable "Sign of the Salutation," the very "best Entertainment for Gentlemen and their Horses."[1]

Just as expectations of public hospitality have changed through the years, so too have the customs associated with dining and drinking, as well as the varieties of food and drink served to travelers. Fortunately, European visitors in the late eighteenth and early nineteenth centuries found American tavern fare and table service sufficiently unusual to justify recording. As a result, the collective accounts of travelers succeed in transmitting a lucid picture of mealtime at the typical tavern.

With apparently few exceptions, tavern guests ate their meals with the innkeeper's family, just as if they were friends rather than strangers. "It is the custom in all the American taverns, from the highest to the lowest, to have a sort of *table d'hôte*, or public table, at which the inmates of the house and travellers dine together at a certain hour."[2] Whenever James Birket, a mid-eighteenth-century Portsmouth visitor, did not eat out at the home of an acquaintance, he noted in his journal: "dined with my Landlady Sla[y]ton."[3] A French traveler in America found it worth noting that, on one particular evening for unknown reasons, his innkeeper did not join the tavern guests for supper.[4]

In large establishments, the tavernkeeper's table, almost invariably referred to as the *table d'hôte* (the host's table), was, in a literal sense, extensive. When dinner was announced at one Boston establishment, guests "were shewn into a room where [they] found a long table covered with dishes, and plates for twenty persons."[5] A visitor to

> JONATHAN SINCLAIR,
>
> **H**AS recently repaired and enlarged the **GRAFTON HOTEL,** his former establishment at *Haverhill Corner N. H.*, and has re-opened the same as a house o **Public Entertainment.**
>
> To his friends and former customers he would only say, that his accommodations are much superior to what they formerly were, and *inferior* to none in the country. To the public generally he would observe, that his house shall never become the *haunt* of tiplers, gamblers and idlers, but shall on all occasions be found a pleasant and commodious resort for the weary traveller, the man of business, and the gentlemen of pleasure. On the subject of *charges*, *attendants* and fare, the proprietor would remark that, *fair dealing*, *trusty servants*, *and good living* shall ever be found *inmates* of his establishment. He also professes to be a connoisseur in the article of *Coffee*—and can well disitnguish the *Coos Domestic*, from the—Java Coffee.
>
> His bar is well furnished with the best 'of liquors and *one toddy stick* for the accommodation of customers—and with *none* for *family use*.
>
> Haverhill Feb. 24, 1830.

Newspaper advertisement for Jonathan Sinclair's Grafton Hotel, Haverhill, N.H., New-Hampshire Post *(Haverhill), 1830. Tavernkeepers "entertained" friends and strangers alike with food and drink in a homelike atmosphere. Sinclair, owner of a three-story brick tavern, described himself as a connoisseur of coffee as well as of liquors.*

NHHS Collections   Photographer, Ernest Gould

northern New England described the "landlord and landlady" at one tavern (possibly in neighboring New York) as taking "their places at the two ends of a board large enough to have dined a regiment of infantry."[6] Exceptionally crowded conditions, especially in smaller taverns, could result in a particular meal being served in successive sittings. At a Concord stage inn one evening in 1821, for instance, "supper was three times spread, for at least twenty people."[7]

At least through the early nineteenth century, it was not a custom for meals to be provided separately for guests in their chambers or other private quarters. One disgruntled European noted in the mid-1830s that "dinners served at private rooms, or served at particular hours, are nearly as expensive as in London; but are seldom called for by native Americans."[8] And, as late as 1861, another of the many foreign travelers unhappy with this situation commented: "It is possible to hire a separate room and have one's meals served in it; but in doing so a man runs counter to all the institutions of the country, and a woman does so equally."[9]

Not only did European visitors to America bemoan the lack of private eating facilities, but they also denounced the relative inflexibility of mealtimes. As early as the 1790s, a tourist claimed, while discussing tavern dining: "It is seldom that a private parlor or drawing room can be procured at any of the taverns, even in the towns; and it is always with reluctance that breakfast or dinner is served up separately to any individual."[10] As a general rule, tavern guests assembled at the *table d'hôte* at stated hours for their meals.[11] One British visitor found that, in smaller American inns even during the 1860s:

> If you happen to arrive too late for one meal it is only with great difficulty, and as a matter of favour, that you can get anything to eat till the next one is ready, which may not be for some hours. . . . How curious it seems, to one fresh from Europe, to hear a party of newly-arrived travellers at an inn humbly craving: say for some breakfast—the landlord raising objections, making difficulties, perhaps remaining inexorable, perhaps at last graciously consenting.[12]

Another traveler offered some timely advice on the subject: "No man should travel in the United States without one of Baraud's best chronometers in his fob. In no other country can a slight miscalculation of time be productive of so much mischief. Woe to him whose steps have been delayed, by pleasure or business, till the fatal hour has elapsed, and the dinner-cloth been removed!"[13]

Although strict mealtimes were adhered to in most early American inns, rural New Hampshire innkeepers may have been more accommodating. In the 1830s, a European visitor, who claimed to "have gone through a great portion of the most unsettled country in New York, Vermont, and New Hampshire," stated that he had "never had reason to complain of want of cleanliness, good victuals, or civility." He continued, more specifically to the point: "I have asked at the most unseasonable hours, both early and late, for breakfast, dinner, and supper; and in the course of ten minutes have always been supplied with a beefsteak, potatoes, bread and cheese, butter, eggs, and tea or coffee."[14]

Sign from the tavern of Nathan Merrill, Rumney, N.H., 1806. Tavern signboards depicting punch bowls, wine glasses, and teapots enticed travelers and natives alike to accept the innkeeper's hospitality. A surviving document from 1814 shows that Merrill no longer served only imported rum and brandy, but had begun also to make his own gin according to a special patented recipe.

Courtesy, Private Collection   Photographer, Bill Finney

Perhaps in the more rural areas characteristic of New Hampshire, guests arrived at such infrequent intervals that they could not be "entertained" according to a rigid schedule.

Reminiscences concur, however, that the sound of a bell usually announced tavern mealtimes.[15] The tavern staff may have used a hand bell, such as those listed in the 1797 probate inventory of Portsmouth tavernkeeper John Stavers, or a larger bell hung outdoors.[16] Upon the sound of the bell, American tavern guests, from all accounts, lost little time in attending to the business of eating. British visitors often expressed "shock" at the "hurried manner in which [Americans] perform those services over which Englishmen so devoutly linger."[17] A mealtime guest typically found himself "form[ing] one of a long row of eaters who proceed through their work with a solid energy that is past all praise."[18] Foreign visitors sometimes lamented their own inability to follow the example of their American hosts: "[The Englishman's] utmost efforts are required, to keep pace with his neighbours; I was never so much at a

Stereograph, "Interior of Tip-Top House," Mount Washington, N.H., circa 1860. Our earliest look at public dining and drinking areas in New Hampshire reveals a single long dining table in the far room similar to the table d'hôte of earlier taverns.
Courtesy, Douglas A. Philbrook   Photographer, S. F. Adams; photograph courtesy of Mount Washington Observatory

loss how to conduct myself properly, as at an American table."[19] Some travelers felt the reason for this behavior was that "Americans know the value of time too well to waste it at the table."[20]

There were apparently few exceptions to this standard dining behavior in New Hampshire. According to a late-nineteenth-century reminiscence about early New Hampshire inns: "Little time was wasted at the table of one of these old taverns. A good square meal was usually finished, by the active aid of a two tined fork and a broad case knife, in about ten or twelve minutes."[21] In 1850, a traveler, stopping near Center Harbor for a meal, recorded meticulously in his diary not only that he had eaten supper between his arrival at half past six and departure at seven o'clock, but also that, while his hostess was preparing supper, he had had time to browse through her "album" or guest book.[22]

One recorded exception to this atmosphere of "hurry

and bustle" was found at Portsmouth's Rockingham House, a Federal-style mansion which had been transformed into a more comfortable inn than was common at the time. In the late 1830s, at least one group of European visitors was pleased to find "a leisure and repose among the guests, who sit half an hour at breakfast, and sometimes an hour at dinner—that is quite remarkable, and made us feel more at home than in any hotel in which we had ever lived since we landed in the country."[23]

It is difficult to determine the customary schedule for serving meals in New Hampshire taverns. Travelers sometimes noted the time at which they ate particular meals. Scattered evidence suggests that dinner, the main meal of the day, was either at two or three o'clock. In Bradford on a certain day in 1803, Timothy Dwight, for example, described himself in the midst of dining at two o'clock; two decades earlier, William Bentley recorded dining at Hampton Falls at three.[24] In fashionable private homes, such as that of Portsmouth's John Langdon, invited guests arrived for dinner at two o'clock.[25] The fact that one traveler reached a Tamworth tavern at noon for dinner, but did not depart until after four o'clock suggests that, even in the country, standard mealtimes were adhered to whenever possible.[26] The common occurrence of this surprisingly late hour for the midday meal is confirmed by early-nineteenth-century travelers in Boston and New York, who inform us that it was not customary for the *table d'hôte* at their respective hotels to be served until two or three o'clock.[27]

The custom of three meals a day was not yet established. Even though breakfast was usually served from seven to nine in the morning and the last meal of the day from seven to nine in the evening, there was greater flexibility in the timing of these less formal meals. Tea often constituted a fourth meal, as substantial as at least two of the others. Certain Boston and New York establishments are known to have served their *table d'hôte* four times a day.[28] Whenever travelers mentioned only three meals being served, supper is as likely as tea to be the one omitted. When both tea and supper were served, the latter was often delayed until after nine. In the late eighteenth century, distinguished travelers in Portsmouth often visited the home of John Langdon, who seems to have followed the local custom in providing his guests both tea and supper.[29] One Langdon guest commented in his journal two nights in a row that it was not until eleven o'clock that he "retired to [his] tavern."[30]

The three or four daily meals differed from what is common today not only in their timing, but also in their content. It seems that regardless of when the meals were served, similar foods were offered, varying primarily in quantity. One traveler, describing American hotels in general in the 1830s, noted: "There are four good meals served every day, viz. breakfast, dinner, tea, and supper, at each of which a profusion of meat is brought on the table."[31] Likewise, the northern New England traveler does not appear to have questioned the propriety of receiving "beef-steak, potatoes, bread and cheese, butter, eggs, and tea or coffee"—whether for "breakfast, dinner, [or] supper"—as long as this hearty fare was placed before him promptly.[32] A perceptive Concord native, recalling local tavern practice, expressed his opinion that the term "dining room" was peculiarly appropriate for a tavern's eating quarters, because dinner was there "repeated three times each day."[33]

With the exception of travel accounts and diaries, surviving documents do not itemize the specific foods served three or four times daily in early New Hampshire taverns. Innkeepers usually entered food sales in their account books by meal name alone. Often they were even less specific, describing a customer's charge as simply for "entertainment" or, redundantly, for "meals of victuals." The tavernkeeper's own purchases of food supplies, entered on the opposite side of his ledger page, are no more enlight-

ening; many worked also as storekeepers, buying food products for resale as well as for tavern use, and others were farmers whose own food products met many tavern needs without registering in any financial accounts. Furthermore, all early tavernkeepers lived in the complex world of a barter economy, in which any family's acquisitions were as likely to be for potential exchange as for immediate use.

Printed menus or "bills of fare" were not common until the mid-nineteenth century. Selection from a variety of entrees was a privilege as yet unknown. Bills of fare, listing foods being served, first appeared in connection with special catered dinners, rather than as a daily feature. When Dudley Lull of Weare was given a menu at the Manchester House, probably in the 1850s, tradition states "he put it in his pocket and said he guessed he would read that after he had got through eating."[34] A Russian traveler's 1857 description of "large sheets printed especially for dinner," suggests that even an intercontinental traveler at that period might have considered menus a novelty.[35] Although printed tavern bills appeared three-quarters of a century before menus, the specific foods were not itemized. Alcoholic beverages were listed and separately priced, but food was classified merely by the name of the meal served, if not even more generically as "victuals."

Fortunately, articulate travelers conscientiously described many of their tavern meals, compensating somewhat for the lack of more specific documentation. According to an English visitor in 1807:

> At the better sort of American taverns or hotels . . . they breakfast at eight o'clock upon rump steaks, fish, eggs, and a variety of cakes, with tea or coffee. . . . Formerly, pies, puddings, and cyder used to grace the breakfast table: but they are now discarded from the genteeler houses, and are found only at the small taverns and farm-houses in the country.[36]

An English traveler stopping for breakfast at a Connecticut tavern in the same year was "greatly surprized to see a hot beef-steak, swimming in grease and onions, brought upon the table; and still more so to find this substantial dish followed by another of fried eggs and bacon."[37] Other breakfasts described by travelers included hash, cheese, salt fish, dried beef, bread or toast, pickles, and potatoes.[38] As late as 1857, a Russian visitor considered the meal his hotel served for breakfast "about right for a good dinner."[39]

The distinctive characteristic of an American dinner, in the late eighteenth and early nineteenth centuries, seems to have been a specially prepared meat dish, ideally a roast—available, however, only at slaughter time—and a selection of vegetables, which do not seem to have been an important part of other meals.[40] A French visitor described a typical American dinner in the 1790s:

> About two o'clock they dine without soup. Their dinner consists of broth, with a main dish of an English roast surrounded by potatoes. Following that are boiled green peas, on which they put butter which the

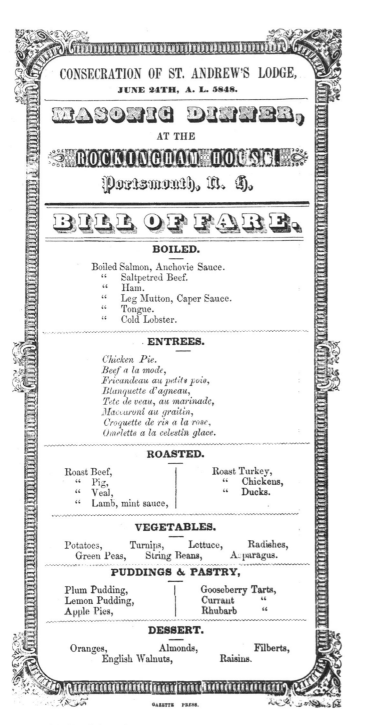

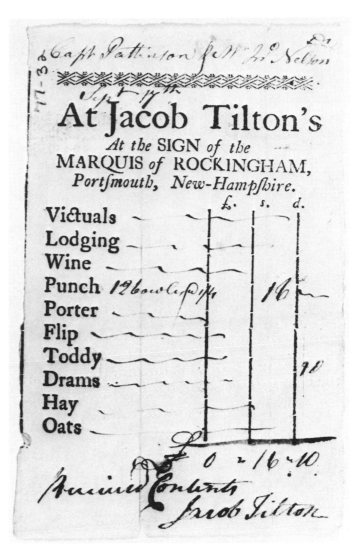

Printed bill, Jacob Tilton's tavern, Portsmouth, N.H., circa 1775. Printed tavern bills often show a greater range of offerings in beverages and animal feed than in the "victuals" offered travelers. Each day, guests shared the family's own meals, enjoying little individual choice except in drink. Since the selection of beverages affected charges, such items appeared separately on the bill.

NHHS Collections   Photographer, Ernest Gould

Printed bill of fare for Masonic dinner, Rockingham House, Portsmouth, N.H., 1848, printed by Gazette Press. The earliest printed menus were those accompanying special catered dinners in the mid-nineteenth century. Menus as a daily feature appear to have become common only after 1850. The year on this bill of fare reflects the Masonic dating system.

NHHS Collections   Photographer, Ernest Gould

heat melts, or a spicy sauce; then baked or fried eggs, boiled or fried fish, salad which may be thinly sliced cabbage seasoned to each man's taste on his own plate, pastries, sweets. . . . For dessert, they have a little fruit, some cheese and a pudding.[41]

Although dinners did not vary drastically from the usual breakfast or supper in the kind of foods offered, the quantities served appear to have been greater.[42] This difference, together with the more extensive food preparations involved, affected the dinner prices charged at taverns. Portsmouth tavernkeeper Elizabeth Packer, for instance, charged twice as much in 1704 for dinner as for breakfast or supper.[43]

As their similarity in price suggests, breakfast and supper, at this early period, were almost identical meals. Tourists and other commentators often made comparisons between them.[44] A German visitor, arriving in Springfield, Massachusetts, one evening in the mid-1840s, found "on the elegantly decorated table . . . coffee and two kinds of tea, two kinds each of warm and cold bread, fried sausage, beefsteaks, fried chicken, fried ham, fried doves, eggs on butter and soft-boiled eggs, black raspberries and blueberries, . . . two kinds of *torte*, several kinds of cake, and, finally, cheese and butter.''[45] Leftovers from dinner were also featured, as they often were at breakfast as well.[46] Meats, however, were not consumed in quantities as large as at dinner.[47] As one traveler explained: ''The meats used at breakfast and supper are generally intended to be dainties.''[48] Supper meats, when not served cold, were heated by the relatively quick methods of frying or broiling.

Tea, when served as an additional meal, often included cold meats, as well as cake, pies, cheese, bread and butter, doughnuts, jelly, jam and other ''sweet preserves.''[49] As a Newburyport woman recalled: ''Tea was served at six. . . . If the gentlemen came to tea, and this was the only refreshment, sliced ham or tongue were usually added, but often there would be a hot meat supper at nine or ten o'clock.''[50]

Between-meal snacks obtained at New Hampshire taverns are often documented more thoroughly than planned meals. Travelers sometimes enjoyed sweets at a local tavern as a break from the tedium of the road. In 1808, a seventeen-year-old girl traveling by chaise recorded stopping at Hill's tavern in Newtown (now Newton), where she and her driving companion were ''entertained with Apple pie, and cheese.''[51] And, in 1832, Andrew Jackson himself supposedly sampled the cook's doughnuts at a Hooksett tavern.[52] Occasional entries for ''gingerbread,'' ''pye & cheese,'' ''brandy & biscuit,'' and ''bread & cheese'' appear in the account books of the same New Hampshire tavernkeepers who customarily recorded their sales in such general terms as ''meals of vitals [*sic*]'' and ''dinner.''[53] Like alcoholic beverages, also often itemized, snacks were optional and varied in price; however, because the content and cost of a tavern meal on any particular day was the same for all diners, its detailed description was not essential for accounting purposes.

Lunch, first mentioned by travelers staying at large city hotels in the 1850s and 1860s, did not at first replace any of the other meals, but was considered a ''second breakfast'' or fifth meal. Consisting of cold foods, its purpose was to bridge the gap between an early breakfast and the mid-afternoon dinner.[54]

Travelers' reaction to New Hampshire tavern fare varied widely, determined in part by the section of the state they happened to visit. In 1836, a party of travelers from the South, passing briefly through the fertile and well-settled southwest corner of the state, praised the meals served them at Walpole and Fitzwilliam as ''the richest on [their] whole route.''[55] In 1797, however, at the remote northern outpost of Jefferson—still at that time called Dartmouth—tavern guests from southern New England dined ''on fare so bad that with difficulty we swallowed a little part of it.''[56] More than one late-nineteenth-century memoir, recalling the Crawford family's original inns from the perspective of

a later day, described early mountain fare as ''primitive'' —''not exactly suited to the fastidious taste of present excursionists, but wholesome and good.''[57] At a more sophisticated urban establishment such as Portsmouth's Rockingham House, however, even a British visitor could find little to criticize: ''The table is as well supplied as in any town in Europe.''[58]

Both the location of the inn and the season of the year had an immeasurably greater effect on New Hampshire tavern cuisine than is conceivable today. Certain phrases appearing repeatedly in the advertisements of urban and rural tavernkeepers alike indicate their unavoidable dependence on the availability of food supplies. Advertising differed significantly from city to country, with Portsmouth tavernkeepers promising to keep their tables supplied with ''the best the season and *market* affords,'' while their rural counterparts offered, somewhat less ambitiously, either ''such fare as is *common* to taverns in the country'' or ''the best of provisions the *country* affords.''[59]

The seasonal nature of early New Hampshire diet derived only partly from the short growing period for vegetables and fruits, depending as much on the annual butchering schedule. All but the wealthiest families consumed fresh meats only at slaughter time, which—in order to avoid both warm-weather spoilage and winter-feeding costs—was usually planned for the late fall.[60] The development of New England's famous ice industry, together with the related popularity of ice houses, was a phenomenon of the second quarter of the nineteenth century.[61] Prior to this time, a combination of drying, smoking, salting, and pickling techniques was sufficient to ensure the preservation of the products of an autumn's slaughter through the following summer.[62]

It is not surprising that visitors to New Hampshire often recorded dining upon preserved meats, such as ''ham, tongues, [and] dried beef'' (at Whipple's in Jefferson in 1784); ''corned beef'' (at Thomas Crawford's in 1829); and ''broiled ham'' (at the Lafayette House in Franconia Notch in 1838).[63] Moreover, the frequent mention of fried and boiled meats indicates the heavy dependence on preserved meat; fresh meat was generally prepared either by roasting or broiling.[64] A meal of ''fried pork,'' such as a traveler in Londonderry criticized around 1800, was, therefore, almost certainly of the salted, smoked, or pickled variety.[65] Tavernkeepers, including Portsmouth's John Stavers, kept their cellars well stocked with barrels of preserved pork, long one of the chief staples of the New England diet.[66]

The amount of meat Americans consumed seems to have impressed European travelers, who not infrequently proclaimed their surprise at the ''use of animal food at every meal.''[67] Although Europeans may have exaggerated to some extent, the importance of meat, whether fresh or preserved, in the New Hampshire tavern diet is indisputable. Portsmouth innkeeper Eliphalet Daniels, for instance, bought 735 pounds of beef from one supplier between September 1769 and the following February.[68]

Dried and salted fish were another staple of tavern and domestic cuisine, both along the coast and inland. When Portsmouth tavernkeeper John Stavers died in a travel accident in 1797, estate appraisers counted in his "Store Room" forty-two pounds of dunfish—a high-quality cod dried partly underground.[69] Early nineteenth-century visitors to the White Mountains referred to the Crawfords' dependence on salt fish, which, coupled with corned beef, constituted the "wholesome" but somewhat "primitive" mountain fare.[70] Throughout the state and region in this early period, the imported salt used for food preservation was both an essential and valuable commodity. Each year, Ethan Allen Crawford spent much of his winter transporting salt from Portland, Maine, to Lancaster and Colebrook, where he exchanged much of it for grain.[71]

Fresh fish, game, and poultry often supplemented the usual diet of preserved meat and fish. From an early date, the White Mountain region was noted for its plentiful and tasty trout, which countless travelers recorded enjoying at Jefferson and Crawford Notch taverns. As a Concord woman recalled of her 1831 visit at Ethan Crawford's: "The brooks then furnished, what they do not now, an *abundance* of delicious trout—which greatly helped along the cold corned beef and salt fish which were the only articles of animal food afforded us."[72]

Salmon, shad, and eels, when in season, were also a staple of regional diet. Until the construction of dams in the nineteenth century, salmon abounded in both the Merrimack and Connecticut rivers, although forced to abandon the Piscataqua at an early date probably because of sawmill construction.[73] No doubt, Atkinson's Reverend Stephen Peabody was just one of many who frequently "dined upon salmon" while on the road.[74] Seasonally, Amoskeag Falls in Derryfield (now Manchester) yielded tremendous quantities of eels, which formed such an important part of the local diet that they became known as "Derryfield beef."[75] Popular particularly among the Scotch-Irish population in the area, eels became a leading commodity of exchange in their community. One fisherman, for example, offered his Amoskeag tavernkeeper freshly caught eels in payment for his rum and lodging. "Derryfield beef" undoubtedly dominated local tavern cuisine, at least seasonally.[76]

Along the seacoast, shellfish helped to diversify an otherwise bland diet. Lobsters, which mid-eighteenth-century Portsmouth residents "bake[d] in abundance near their wharfs," were purchased at the local market by one English visitor in 1807 for as little as "two-pence . . . per pound."[77] And, in 1805, Portsmouth tavernkeeper James Geddes, appealing to what one traveler in the 1790s had described as the American "passion for oysters," sought to increase his clientele by featuring in his advertisement of tavern fare "an oyster-supper in all its perfection."[78]

With the apparent exception of urban Portsmouth, hunting, like fishing, supplemented the basic diet. Only a single deer bone numbered among 629 identifiable animal bones excavated in recent years from eighteenth-century Portsmouth house sites.[79] In the Connecticut Valley, however, Jeremy Belknap enjoyed "venison for dinner" at Chase's tavern in Cornish in 1774; two decades later, Timothy Dwight was served partridge at Williams' Littleton inn.[80] And, as late as 1836, a meal of "potted pigeons" and steak greeted stage passengers in Merrimack.[81] In 1821, Ethan Crawford contemplated building a deer park, partly to amuse his visitors, but also to allow him "now and then, [to] spare one for the table, if requested."[82]

During most seasons of the year, vegetables and fruits, like meat and fish, appeared on New Hampshire tables in preserved form only. Despite intervening centuries, it is possible to sense even today the enthusiasm that New Hampshire's summertime abundance once inspired both in travelers and others. Tavernkeepers, even in the city, often cultivated their own vegetable gardens. One of the earliest Europeans to travel in New Hampshire described Portsmouth's "abundance of Garden Culture" as including carrots, onions, cabbages, cauliflowers, beans, peas, parsnips, turnips, radishes, asparagus, potatoes, sweet potatoes, and squashes.[83] In 1784, Jeremy Belknap delighted in "full-grown cucumbers" at McMillan's in Conway.[84] In 1825, Concord's *New-Hampshire Patriot & State Gazette* proudly reported that the "table of the Columbian Hotel on the 4th of July was furnished with a bountiful supply of new potatoes, apparently full grown, from the field of Jonathan Eastman, jun. Esq. of this town."[85] Root crops appear to have dominated the local produce, and in the colder seasons, together with dried corn, beans, and peas, were generally the only vegetables appearing in estate inventories, including those of tavernkeepers.[86]

As early as 1750, Portsmouth boasted "Apples[,] Pears, Plumbs, Cherries, & Peaches in . . . Abundance . . . also Apricots & Nectrines from England . . . likewise Gooseberrys, Currant[s,] Rasberries, Strawberries, Huckleberries[,] Water & Muskmellions."[87] In more rural areas, wild berries were the fruit that most commonly graced the tavern table. According to one guest at the Notch House in 1842, "blackberries seem the prevailing dessert."[88] A few years earlier a traveler at the nearby tavern of Abel Crawford enjoyed "huckleberries with milk."[89] And, at Whipple's in Jefferson in 1784, "a sauce composed of raspberries, cream, and maple sugar" accompanied one guest's dinner.[90] Many rural tavernkeepers were also farmers, with orchards of their own. Although apple pies were a common tavern snack, many of the apples produced were not eaten or cooked fresh, but preserved for winter use, either by being pressed into cider or cut into quarters for drying.[91] Until canning in sealed containers became popular in the mid-nineteenth century, only those fruits and vegetables which could be dried or preserved in sugar or vinegar solutions were eaten year round.

Travelers often admired both New Hampshire's flourishing apple orchards and extensive fields of maize—the state's leading grain crop. Bread, the one food always

Plate, English, tin-glazed earthenware with polychrome decoration, owned by Hezekiah Hutchins, a tavernkeeper of Hampstead, N.H., 1750-70. Although ceramic shards from dinnerware used at New Hampshire taverns have been unearthed by archeologists, this is a rare example that has survived intact through the centuries. Other New Hampshire taverns, including James Stoodley's in Portsmouth and Thomas Leavitt's in Hampton, are known to have contained imported delftware similar to this plate.

NHHS Collections   Photographer, Bill Finney

present in the tavern diet, most often consisted of corn meal, rye, or a combination of both. Except in parts of the Connecticut Valley, little wheat was grown locally, being generally imported from New York or Philadelphia.[92]

Tavernkeeper James Underwood of Swanzey obtained his flour (presumably wheat) from Boston in the early nineteenth century.[93]

Evidence suggests that the food served in taverns was all brought to the table at once, rather than in separate courses. As the daughter of a Nashua tavernkeeper recalled: "roasts, boiled meats, fruit, puddings, pan dowdies, turnover pies, and pancakes were all placed on the board when the guests sat down."[94] Similarly, "on the elegantly decorated table" of a Springfield, Massachusetts, tavern, supper guests found everything from bread, beefsteaks, and fried doves, to blueberries, cheese, and cake.[95]

Not all travelers stopping at taverns partook of the meals offered, however. Teamsters and less wealthy natives, traveling relatively short distances, often carried with them meals which innkeepers allowed them to eat in the tavern and sometimes to heat at the tavern fireplace.[96] According to one local tradition, even those dining at the *table d'hôte* might, for the sake of economy, bring along "their own bread and cheese."[97] Quite unintentionally, one notorious New Hampshire criminal-turned-author has given us an intimate look at the food carried by local teamsters. Searching for something worth stealing from a pair of unattended sleighs, Goffstown's Seth Wyman was delighted to find "in one corner [of the sleigh] a pillar [sic] case filled with the food of the teamster." While not hesitating to do "ample justice to [his] fare," this practiced thief proudly itemized the tasty contents of the pillow case as "nuts, Yankee turnovers, pork and beans—all of them cooked and ready for the eating."[98] Teamsters and drovers often carried animal feed with them as well, sometimes depositing supplies with "reliable landlords" along the route for use during their return journey.[99]

Tavernkeepers also occasionally supplied guests with edibles to carry with them on the next stage of their journey, particularly if they were headed through unsettled ter-

Spoon, brass with a residue of tin plating, probably English, 1650-75. This seal-handled spoon was found in Dover, N.H., in 1857, during excavations for a cellar at a site believed to have been that of the first tavern in Dover. The spoon reflects the form of more expensive silver of the same period.

NHHS Collections   Photographer, Bill Finney

ritory. In 1754, Exeter tavernkeeper John Light provided three unidentified guests on a government mission with both chocolate and rum "to carry into the Woods."[100] In October 1775, Conway tavernkeeper Andrew McMillan packed "provysions to go through the woods" and eight months later, "provision to go hom[e]" for John Peirce and Jotham Rindge, both of Portsmouth; the supplies consisted in part of "nine pounds of Beef to go through the woods" and "Bread to d[itt]o."[101]

In the more settled parts of New Hampshire, however, providing refreshments for social events was a more typical part of an innkeeper's job than packing provisions for small groups of adventurers. Surprisingly little is known, though, about the types of delicacies prepared for such special occasions. Innkeepers advertised their willingness to accommodate "Societies and Private Parties" with "suppers at the shortest notice."[102] Newspapers reported on "sumptuous" dinners such as that presented to President Monroe in 1817 at Barker's tavern in Concord.[103] Even in rural Wilmot, a local tavernkeeper successfully provided a "highly gratifying collation" on the occasion of a military academy's excursion through town.[104] Banquets were praised as "sumptuous" and "gratifying," but, unfortunately, were not described in detail. In most cases, all record of the refreshments served at special "entertainments" appears to have vanished with the last delectable bite.

When the event was a dance or other celebration not requiring a meal, the few surviving bills suggest that the usual accompaniment to a wide array of alcoholic beverages was cheese, served with bread, biscuits, or cake. James Underwood of Swanzey, for instance, charged one party $12.37 for toddy, brandy, gin, and sangaree, $6.50 for "Cake & cheas," as well as $4.50 for a "fidlar."[105]

Lavish preparations were made for Lafayette's return to America in 1824, a momentous event in the early-nineteenth-century tavern world described in many recollections. Lafayette was served turkey at Pattee's tavern in Salem, and roast pig with an apple in its mouth, at a meal catered by Dover tavernkeeper Samuel Wyatt. However, judging from the wide variety of dishes served daily at a tavern *table d'hôte*, the identity of even the main entree cannot give an adequate impression of any meal then served. In fact, according to one reminiscence, the table prepared for Lafayette in Dover "was fairly groaning with food it was so heavily laden."[106]

One special dinner, more fully documented than most, was that celebrating John Wentworth's reception as royal governor of the province in 1767, for which many of the food-purchase bills survive. This exceptional meal, intended for one hundred guests and catered by tavernkeeper James Stoodley, required the special fattening of a dozen turkeys, two dozen ducks, and three dozen "dunghill fowles." Fifty pounds of pork, supplemented by tongue, bacon, veal, and cod, were consumed as well. Twelve pounds of rice and twenty pounds of sugar also fig-

ured in the preparations as well as the judicious use of lemons, salt, capers, rose water, pepper, bottled mustard, oil, vinegar, and miscellaneous spices. Pickles, cranberries, currants, and raisins accompanied the main dishes served. A charge for "28 days Labour for Sundry persons," appearing on one of the surviving bills, probably represents in actuality only a fraction of the total manpower involved in preparing and serving this dinner.[107]

Holiday cooking also required efforts extending well beyond the daily tavern routine. A Nashua innkeeper's daughter recorded the "Fourth of July specialty at the Indian Head House [as] roast pig with a lemon in its mouth."[108] A traveler from the South, spending her Thanksgiving Day in 1828 at one of the Crawford family taverns, unfortunately mentioned only the pumpkin pies.[109] By its very nature, however, holiday fare is more predictable than daily diet. The meal served for Thanksgiving in a nineteenth-century tavern, with its emphasis on root crops and preserved fruits, would appear less unusual to us today than the daily tavern fare even though the turkey would have been just one among several meat dishes served.[110]

Since the height of the tavern era, changes in eating and dining customs have taken place so gradually that to this day their significance has not been fully grasped. Continual improvements in the means of food storage and preparation allowed a wider range of foods to be offered; modifications in daily work hours led to changes in meal times. The continuing use still today of the term "dinner" for the midday meal, even when no longer the main meal of the day, demonstrates the almost imperceptible nature of these changes. Food customs form such a basic part of our heritage that they provide "one of our most intimate glimpses into our past."[111] As Jefferson recommended in 1787, to comprehend the underlying nature of a people, you must "ferret [them] out" at home, "look into their kettles [and] eat their bread."[112]

American drinking customs, on the contrary, underwent such a deliberate transformation during the first half of the nineteenth century that hardly a writer of the period failed to chronicle the dramatic result. As documents of the time illustrate, observers did not exaggerate the magnitude of the change.

From the seventeenth through the early nineteenth centuries, alcoholic beverages were an essential part of the daily fare of all New Hampshire residents. In fact, until the temperance movement of the second quarter of the nineteenth century revolutionized prevailing attitudes, alcohol was an accepted part of daily life and considered a proper accompaniment to work. In the 1820s, both Concord and Rochester calculated their per capita alcohol consumption —based on store sales alone and not including the considerable domestic cider production—as four and one half to five gallons each year "to every man, woman and child in the town"![113] In Concord in 1827, "the cost of this liquor to the consumers was [estimated at] not less than $9,000, which was more than twice the amount of all the taxes the year previous, for town, county and state expenses, and for the support of schools."[114] Although the average orchard yielded twenty-five to fifty barrels of cider, which quickly fermented and became alcohol, farmers who purchased supplies from at least one New Hampshire store in the early nineteenth century almost always invested in additional liquor as well.[115] In one typical case, the four members of an Andover farm family began purchasing liquor in May, having consumed the thirty barrels of cider placed in their cellar the previous November.[116]

Worker satisfaction and productivity depended as heavily on daily liquor rations then as on coffee at a later time. As an apprentice in a Walpole printing shop in 1796 recalled: "Before I was in the office two hours, I was called upon to treat the whole crowd, on brandy, wine, sugar, cheese, eggs and crackers."[117] Construction accounts always indicated a certain allotment of rum for the workmen. Public records, moreover, show that towns consistently provided rum to surveyors, road and bridge laborers, and others undertaking work for the community.[118]

Surviving farm records also reflect an increase in rum purchases whenever mowing was underway.[119] Since "the idea was universal, that no laborer could sustain summer-work without rum," farmers or their young sons, at certain times of the day, carried "well-filled bottles" into the field for the benefit of their help.[120] According to the business records of a North Charlestown merchant dealing heavily in rum, more liquor customers patronized his store during the haying season than at any other time of the year.[121]

Besides preparing men to feel "strong and able to work," alcohol was believed to promote relaxation.[122] Innkeepers' account books prove that local customers often made regular stops at the tavern to share a bowl of toddy while catching up on the news. Typically, the village store, also licensed to sell liquor in small quantities, was another favorite gathering place. Evidence suggests, however, that the home was the primary site for social enjoyment of liquor either produced on the farm or bought (usually at the local store) in quantities varying from pints to barrels.[123] Many stories tell of the hospitable treatment of guests at local family sideboards.

Drinking while traveling was another early custom as generally accepted then as it is frowned upon today. According to a Polish traveler, journeying from Boston to Albany just before 1800, "Taverns occur practically as frequently as shops. A traveling American stops in front of nearly every one, if not for punch, at least for water with whisky."[124] Another traveler offered an even more colorful analysis of highway customs: "The American stage coach stops every five miles to water the horses, and *brandy* the *gentlemen*."[125] According to local tradition, a stage line operating through Newport in the 1830s attempted to compete with a rival company by offering to cover passengers' "grog bills" at "wayside taverns."[126] At a Concord stage

John Goatam,
Innholder,
HEREBY informs the Publick,

That he has remov'd his Residence from where he lately liv'd, to the PLAINS TAVERN, known by the Name of the GLOBE, a very convenient House, every Way calculated for the same, about two Miles from the Town-House, on the Great Road to BOSTON, in a very pleasant Place;— where he shall provide every Requisite for the Entertainment of GENTLEMEN and LADIES, Travellers and others, who shall do him the Honor to use his HOUSE; who may rely upon his exerting himself to the utmost of his Ability, to serve them in an elegant and bountiful Manner.— He begs Leave to signify to all those who have a true Relish for that chearing and delicious Fluid call'd PUNCH, compos'd of genuine Materials, that they may be always gratified by repairing to his FOUNTAIN,— And such as prefer the all-animating Juice of the Grape, may, at the same Place, find a Source suitable for the Gratification of the nicest Palate,—These admirable Liquors, exhilirating the Spirits, and creating a good Appetite, a true Criterion of Health, may be accompanied with many Dishes of high Renown, whenever wanted, either for Necessity or Repast, by Day or by Night, served up in a genteel Manner, and on the shortest Notice.——— And for all this, he will content himself with a moderate Profit.———He has a good Stable, woll provided with the best of Hay, for HORSES. Portsmouth *April* 3d, 1765.

Newspaper advertisement for John Goatam's Globe Tavern, Portsmouth Plains, New-Hampshire Gazette, 1765. Goatam prided himself on the quality of the "entertainment" he was able to offer, whether in providing "Dishes of high Renown," "the best of Hay," or "genuine" punch. As suggested in his advertisement, alcohol was highly valued in the eighteenth century for its "exhilirating [sic]" and health-sustaining effects.
NHHS Collections   Photographer, Ernest Gould

stop in 1828, a female missionary, one of the passengers, apparently felt no qualms about asking the bartender "to bring her a little drap [sic] of gin."[127] The great variety and number of pocket flasks and traveling liquor cases surviving from this period suggest, furthermore, that travelers did not depend solely on the local tavern. A Swedish visitor to New England during the 1830s, sharing a stagecoach with four elderly gentlemen, observed that "out of their coat-pockets peeped modestly the necks of a couple of well-filled bottles."[128]

Traveling liquor case or cellaret owned by Major-General Joseph Cilley of Nottingham, N.H., late 18th century. Following a distinguished military career during the Revolution, Cilley served as justice of the peace, state legislator, governor's councilor, and major-general of the state militia. In his era, a convenient supply of alcohol was considered essential to any activity ranging from travel to war.

NHHS Collections   Photographer, Bill Finney

In these early days, almost the entire New Hampshire population, including children, consumed alcohol to a surprising degree. One Westmoreland tavernkeeper, who moved to Vermont in 1807, is said to have lined up his twenty children twice daily to share rum toddy from a common bowl.[129] And, when a young Goffstown boy followed his mother to the house of a woman in labor, the doctor's advice was to "give him some rum and molasses and send him home." He drank as much rum as he desired before departing alone.[130]

From all accounts, it was a breach of etiquette not to offer the minister alcohol if he came to visit. In 1827, when the Reverend Nathaniel Bouton was a candidate for Concord's Congregational ministry, he spent a day, as he later recalled, "in visiting through a portion of three school districts in the West Parish: and in every family which I visited, I was either offered and solicited to drink ardent spirits, or received an apology for their not happening to have any on hand."[131] In 1706, an Anglican missionary preaching in Dover acknowledged receiving the usual hospitality even from a "Quaker-Woman," who, though she had spoken out against his beliefs, "did invite [him] to her House, and did kindly entertain [him] both with Victuals and Drink."[132] Tavern as well as store records show that ministers, like their contemporaries in other professions, regularly purchased liquor for their own family use.[133]

A story survives concerning an Andover woman who objected to a church being erected near her residence on the grounds that "if the meeting house is built here . . . we shall be expected to keep a bar for the accommodation of the ministers."[134]

Until about 1830, rarely did a special occasion pass in the history of an institution, business, or community without the sharing of alcohol. Large quantities were purchased by churches for the celebration of ordinations, dedications, and pastoral conferences.[135] As more than one foreign traveler noted, a private business agreement usually concluded with the parties concerned agreeing to "liquor on it."[136] Alcohol was an expected accompaniment to community events, ranging from town meetings and military musters to the signing of contracts and other documents. Even a prisoner's release from jail could prompt the sharing of "a bowl or two of grog"—such a ceremony, as we have learned from one articulate New Hampshire criminal, being considered "a matter of course on these occasions."[137]

The ritual sharing of rum played an indispensable part in properly solemnizing not only weddings but also funerals. Charges for "liquor att the funeral" appearing in town, provincial, and other financial accounts prove that alcohol was a customary part of funeral rites.[138] According to Jeremy Belknap's 1792 state history, an alcohol shortage during the Revolution temporarily discouraged the custom of giving "drams" at funerals.[139] As late as 1819, however, Francestown voted to dismiss an article from its town warrant which would have discontinued the public practice of "giving Spirituous Liquors at Funerals."[140]

The community event most frequently associated in later years with ceremonial drinking was the raising of building frames. Large quantities of rum and cider, accumulated specifically for the occasion, supposedly fortified the workers at various stages of their enormous task. At least one New Hampshire town, erecting its meetinghouse in 1801, voted to "treat with Liquor the Spectators" as well.[141]

Alcohol also served a variety of medicinal purposes. Handwritten medical bills, surviving from the eighteenth century, document the heavy reliance on rum as an antiseptic for "dressing . . . wounds." As much as eight gallons of rum could be required to dress the wounds of an injured patient.[142] Until the introduction of ether and chloroform as anesthetics in the 1840s, alcohol and opium were the most powerful pain-killers available to patients undergoing an operation, giving birth, or suffering from a terminal illness. Success in surgery depended largely on the physician's dexterity and speed; some American surgeons by 1800 claimed to have "become skillful enough to amputate a leg through the thigh so rapidly that the patient felt pain for no more than two minutes."[143]

Alcohol consumption by those caring for the sick was taken for granted as an aid to their work. When a North Carolina resident suffering from frostbite received treatment at a Portsmouth tavern in 1766, his bill included a charge for "1/2 pint rum [and] 3 Boles punch to ye Docters

& Assistan[ts] in Cutting of[f] his Legs."[144] When recovered, a patient was responsible for paying not only the expense of his medical care, but also the cost of "drink" for the "watchers" who had nursed him to health.[145]

During the Revolution, a steady supply of alcohol proved so indispensable to the Continental Army, both for medical purposes and for the nourishment of fighting soldiers, that rum stockpiled by Portsmouth merchants was confiscated and each town in the state required to provide a given amount of rum to the army—the town of New Ipswich, for example, was assessed the quantity of 122 1/2 gallons.[146] The fact that, in this early period, liquor attained value of its own simply as a commodity of exchange is not surprising.

Acceptable for most occasions, alcohol seems also to have been socially permissible at all hours of the day. In his diary for 1783, Matthew Patten of Bedford did not attempt to conceal the fact that he had enjoyed at MacGregor's tavern, while fishing at Amoskeag, "a jill of W[est] I[ndia] Rum last night and another this morning."[147] One European traveler visiting New England in 1807 described his steak breakfast as accompanied by "Yankee rum" and "sour cyder."[148] And charges for "Breakfast & Rum," "brackfast & a gill sling [a rum-based drink]" and "1 pt wine Egs & bacon" are typical of those appearing in the accounts which early New Hampshire tavernkeepers maintained for their customers.[149]

Travelers' descriptions of tavern meals suggest that liquors sometimes automatically accompanied dinner and were included in the meal charge. Speaking of the "better sort of American taverns," one early-nineteenth-century New Hampshire visitor carefully noted: "Brandy, hollands [Dutch gin], and other spirits, are allowed at dinner; but every other liquor is paid for extra."[150] According to a European visiting America in the 1830s, "In many instances cider, beer, and even brandy are handed round, without any additional charge."[151] And, during the 1790s, a certain Boston establishment, which one Englishman described as "more properly a lodging house than a tavern," set a pint of Madeira before each of its satisfied diners.[152]

The typical tavern—in New Hampshire as elsewhere in early America—offered a tremendous variety of alcoholic beverages, prepared according to a confusing array of popular recipes, little appreciated today. Although cider was the "common drink" in New Hampshire, made in such "great Plenty" in the mid-eighteenth century that it was shipped both to Canada and the Carolinas, it figures relatively little in tavern records and appears to have been enjoyed primarily at home.[153] Rum and rum-based drinks usually dominated the sales of any New Hampshire tavern. Similarly, the freight records of a North Charlestown storekeeper from shortly after 1800 show that he ordered about five times more rum for his local customers than all other types of liquor combined.[154] Much of the rum consumed in New Hampshire originated in the West Indies, but New Englanders, particularly in the Boston area, also produced great quantities locally from imported molasses. New

Hampshire sales records often specified in abbreviated form whether the rum bought was of West India or New England origin, since the imported variety was usually more expensive. At least one New Hampshire tavernkeeper —James Underwood of Swanzey—transported hogsheads of rum directly from Boston, although it is not clear whether he was purchasing the imported or local variety.[155]

Brandy and wine also rated high in popularity as local tavern beverages. In addition to 129 gallons of rum, the typical storage cellar of one Portsmouth tavern contained in 1797, 33 gallons of brandy, 13 of Madeira, and 26 of sherry wine.[156] Taverns relied on an extensive trade network for more specialized liquors. Local merchants' advertisements listing alcoholic beverages include wines from Madeira, Málaga, Lisbon, and Tenerife as well as brandies from Cognac and gin from Holland. The wine which one mid-eighteenth-century Portsmouth visitor called the "most commonly Drunk here" was "Oidonia," obtained from "the Canaries & Western Islands." This wine, perhaps more properly identified as "Vidonia," was obscure enough at the time to require the traveler's detailed description: "tis of a pale coll[o]r tasts [sic] harsh and is inclined to look thick."[157] The popularity of such all-but-forgotten varieties suggests a wine selection in early New Hampshire taverns very different from that available today. Local vintages, such as the cherry wine which a French traveler enjoyed at a Sandown tavern in 1788, supplemented the exotic imports.[158]

Beer and other malt liquors appear infrequently in tavern sales except in the form of a very popular hot drink called flip made primarily from beer and sugar with a relatively small quantity of rum. In the earliest days of settlement, beer consumption had been relatively heavy. But, as New England's orchards gradually matured, cider replaced beer as the region's primary fermented beverage.[159] In 1766, a newly established "brew-house" in Portsmouth proudly advertised "New-Hampshire ale and small-beer."[160] However, even though the province was producing "Good Hops" in 1750, "malt liquor" was considered by some at the end of the century as "not so frequent as its wholesomeness deserves; and as the facility with which barley and hops may be raised, seems to require."[161] Portsmouth merchants imported Dorchester ales from London, and most of the beer drunk even in New York City was brewed abroad. Neither the breweries in Portsmouth nor New York succeeded. The reason given in the latter situation was that "the farmers do not care to cultivate [barley and] do not drink much beer themselves, preferring cyder and whiskey, which they get without buying."[162]

Grain-based distilled liquors never became common in eighteenth-century New Hampshire, despite the contemporary popularity of gin in England and of whiskey in Scotland. Not a single whiskey transaction appears in ten years of surviving financial accounts (1800-1810) from Robert Rand's North Charlestown store, although purchases of gin were occasionally recorded.[163]

ON THE ROAD NORTH OF BOSTON

In 1792, the only "distil-house" in the state was producing rum from West Indian molasses.[164] The commercial manufacture of distilled liquors in New Hampshire appears to have increased dramatically, however, in the first decades of the nineteenth century. Keene, for instance, was just one among several towns in the upper Connecticut Valley suddenly boasting its own gin distillery, and two Newport firms were distilling cider brandy by the 1820s.[165] This phenomenon, together with the eventual decline in the predominance of rum, can be traced to the interruption of foreign commerce during the Embargo and War of 1812, as well as to the legal termination in 1808 of slave importation—inextricably tied to the rum trade.[166] If the temperance movement had not occurred, the types of liquors consumed in taverns might have changed noticeably.

Tavernkeepers themselves often became involved in liquor production on a small scale. In 1814, Nathan Merrill, a Rumney publican, obtained the "exclusive right and liberty of making GIN" for a term of fourteen years, using a special patented recipe.[167] Concord taverner William Stickney operated a malt house; Samuel Barnes, a Hillsborough tavernkeeper, purchased hops every May in preparation for the summer beermaking season. Barnes also operated a cider mill; and, according to one traveler, Abel Crawford cultivated an orchard of seven hundred apple trees for the primary purpose of making cider.[168]

The drinks typically served in New Hampshire taverns bore such picturesque names as flip, sling, bounce, grog, toddy, and sangaree. When first encountering the confusing array of American beverages in 1832, a Swedish traveler exclaimed: "Of such a variety are the different mixtures composed, that it requires a long time and no ordinary degree of acuteness to get acquainted with their denomination."[169] With a few exceptions, these drinks were primarily rum- or brandy-based, as were both the eggnog and punch still familiar today. Surviving records show a distinction in price between "brandy punch" and "rum punch."[170] Also, "brandy tody [sic]," such as diarist Matthew Patten enjoyed at an Amoskeag tavern in 1783, was presumably more expensive than the common rum toddy.[171] The popular hot drink called flip accounted for most of the beer consumed in early taverns. Nathan Stickney, the son of a Concord tavernkeeper, recalled helping convert two barrels of beer into flip for an occasional public event.[172]

Other basic ingredients which these drinks shared in subtle combinations were a lump of sugar, nipped with a special implement from a cone-shaped loaf; flavorings such as lemon juice, nutmeg, herbs, or essence of peppermint; and either cold or boiling water. The addition of milk resulted in drinks known as milk toddy or milk punch.[173] The detail with which mid-nineteenth-century local historians described the toddy and eggnog sticks, among other early utensils employed in mixing drinks, suggests that surviving examples of these tools already were rare by that point.[174] Even the term "loggerhead"—a lengthy iron tool

Punch bowl, Chinese, porcelain with polychrome decoration, 1750-70, owned by the Reverend Paine Wingate of Hampton Falls and Stratham, N.H. Until late in the eighteenth century, tavernkeepers sold punch and toddy by the bowl. It seems to have been customary for friends to pass the bowl from one to another and drink directly from it.

NHHS Collections   Photographer, Bill Finney

heated in the fire and used to produce a foaming mug of warm flip—did not appear in this specialized sense in dictionaries of the time.[175] Nevertheless, a "loggerhead," along with a "tavern syn," were among the items sold in 1828 and 1829 in the estate settlement of Deerfield tavernkeeper Benjamin Butler.[176]

The type of drinking vessels in which the popular beverages were served evolved during the eighteenth century from the tankards, bowls, and "potts" listed in earlier tavern bills to glasses and mugs at a later date. Toddy, in particular, once available by the bowl, was later offered in mugs and glasses. Part of the reason for this change may have been a trend away from the customary sharing of common drinking vessels. As one observer wrote, "There was no suspicion of impoliteness, when all the guests successively partook of . . . drink from the same vessel."[177] As late as 1821, a traveler being entertained at a private home in the vicinity of Springfield, New Hampshire, where he had stopped to inquire the distance to the next inn, described tankards "brimming full" and "the mug of cider circulat[ing]."[178] And, in the 1790s, militia officers in a Goffstown tavern on training day, to one New Hampshire criminal's delight, "had become somewhat excited by copious draughts from the rum noggin." Since this single mug, together with a loaf of sugar, were the only objects observed by the watchful pilferer on the officers' table, individual drinking vessels were apparently not supplied.[179]

At the same time, however, a change in customs was starting to occur. The well-known Worcester printer Isaiah Thomas, in his 1792 almanac intended for all the New England states, gave the following "Advice to Country Tavern Keepers": "When you bring on liquors, endeavor to give

Firing glass, from John Stavers' William Pitt Tavern (previously the Earl of Halifax), Portsmouth, N.H., late 18th century. With a heavy base especially designed to endure the pounding that accompanied ceremonial toasts, this wine glass is believed to be one of three "masons" glasses listed in the tavernkeeper's 1797 household inventory. Probably used by the Masonic lodges which met in Stavers' "long room," this glass is remembered more specifically for its use during Washington's visit of 1789.

Courtesy, St. John's Lodge No. 1, F. & A.M., Portsmouth
   Photographer, Bill Finney

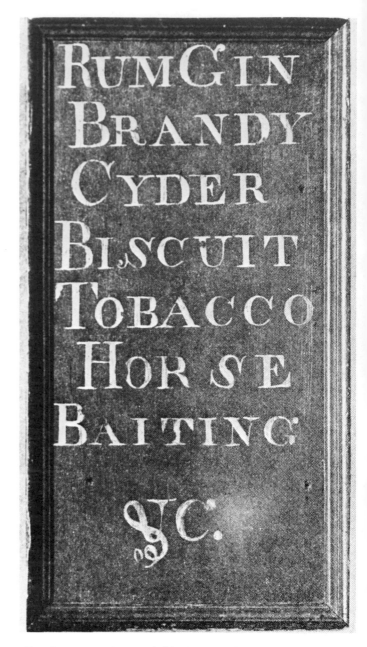

Sign from tavern in Deerfield, N.H., 18th century. Tobacco was as regular a part of tavern entertainment as food and drink. Typical handwritten tavern bills itemize pipes and tobacco alternately with "Dinners," "Potts of Flip," "Half Pints of Rum," "Horses Hay," and "Pecks of Oates."

Photograph from Russell Hawes Kettell, *The Pine Furniture of Early New England*, 1929

everyone a separate glass; if you have not enough in the house you will be excused; but gentlemen do not like that all the company should drink out of the same glass."[180]

The custom of "shar[ing], in [the] company [of friends], a bowl or two of grog," as Henry Tufts, Matthew Patten, and others often did, symbolizes the social nature of early drinking habits.[181] Toasting was another drinking custom, reinforcing the camaraderie of the occasion. In earlier times, when a formal gathering occurred, fifteen or twenty toasts might be proposed. In 1810, for instance, a non-partisan political assembly in Bow drank to the militia ("a wall to the republic, that the blood hounds of Europe cannot pass"); to the Merrimack ("one of the principle arteries of the nation"); to the Clergy ("may they 'preach peace on earth and good will to men' "); to the memory of Washington; to an "independent South America"; and to Temperance ("may we this day show an example")—but

not before ten concluding toasts.[182] Such ceremonial drinking served a social purpose in reinforcing the community's underlying cohesiveness.

Tavern fellowship was further enhanced by the ritual of smoking. Tobacco was as much a part of public hospitality as food or drink, with both pipes and tobacco appearing as early as 1704 in the bill of Portsmouth tavernkeeper Elizabeth Packer for entertaining the Governor.[183] More than a century later, a young Concord woman admired a "tempt-

Tobacco box, inscribed: "The Memory of all Those who have Fallen in The Cause of America," tin with painted decoration, 1780-1830, from the Thorne family of Pembroke, N.H. In a society that valued the fellowship they fostered, the pipe and wine glass were also used to symbolize the most exalted patriotic and commemorative feelings.

NHHS Collections   Photographer, Bill Finney

ing display of pipes and tobacco on the mantel shelf" at Abel Crawford's tavern; another traveler observed one day in 1842 that the male members of the staff of a Conway inn, without exception, held "cigars in their mouths—the landlord, waiter, ostler, groom, driver, porter, and stable-boy," filling the inn with tobacco-smoke.[184]

Chewing tobacco, as well as smoking it, provided a popular pastime during at least part of this period. One New Hampshire resident captured the attention of a European traveler in 1846 by the "unusual vehemence" with which he chewed and "by the unerring certainty with which he expectorated . . . into a spittoon, which lay between two sleepers on the floor. He occasionally varied his amusement by directing his filthy distillations against the stove, from the hot side of which they sometimes glanced with the report of a pistol."[185] Tavern accounts show that women also bought tobacco.[186] Their purchases were not necessarily intended for the men in their families: according to a boy growing up in Goffstown in the late eighteenth century, his mother "chewed, smoked and snuffed, and [his] sister helped her in the smoking department."[187]

While the popularity of tobacco continued, the age of unquestioning acceptance of alcohol was, by the early nineteenth century, rapidly approaching its end. Although many later remembered the era as one in which individuals drank large quantities of alcohol without undue influence on their behavior, the effects of intoxication were often devastating. In the early nineteenth century, inebriated New Hampshire citizens were guilty of profaning the sabbath, lying on the side of the road, and leaving their family's table "lean, naked and destitute . . . oftener replenished with N[ew] E[ngland] Rum than the comforts of life."[188] In 1808, a stage driver on the route from Windsor, Vermont, to Hanover became so intoxicated, "owing to his frequent and long stops at taverns," that he indulged in "singing vulgar songs and shouting at passers-by."[189]

Throughout the eighteenth century, attempts to control such behavior by limiting the number of licensed retailers continued, despite the conviction of one leading provincial authority that neither "scarcity[,] distance or dearness, or any other difficulty attending the acquisition of [rum] would . . . wean the wicked topers from their Idol, while it is upon ye face of ye Earth."[190]

It is not surprising that ministers, physicians, and others professionally concerned with the welfare of the public provided leadership in the earliest stages of the nationwide reaction against the heavy consumption of alcohol. In his 1792 account of New Hampshire, Reverend Jeremy Belknap called "the free indulgence of spirituous liquors . . . one of the greatest faults of many of the people of New Hampshire."[191] Elsewhere, the state's first historian bemoaned the extent to which New Hampshire residents had become dependent on a supply of liquor: "The thirst for spirits in the back country is so ardent, that in the fall & winter they will sell their wheat for this sort of pay, & then in the spring & summer following go 40 or 50 miles after bread."[192]

Belknap, having moved to Boston, corresponded on the subject with Philadelphia's Dr. Benjamin Rush, one of the national leaders in the earliest stages of temperance reform. Rush hoped, with the help of Belknap and a South Carolina physician, to initiate a long-term movement that would result by "1915" in a drunkard being "as infamous in society as a liar or a thief, and the use of spirits as uncommon in families as a drink made of a solution of arsenic." About 1790, Belknap distributed over 150 copies of Rush's writings on this subject to New Hampshire clergymen.[193] Belknap argued as well that "the disuse of ardent spirits would also tend to abolish the infamous traffic in slaves, by whose labour this baneful material is procured."[194]

The goal of this early generation of temperance reformers was the substitution of beer, cider, and other fermented liquors for the stronger distilled substances. In Belknap's view, "the juice of the apple, the fermentation of barley, and the decoction of spruce are amply sufficient for the refreshment of man, let his labor be ever so severe, and perspiration ever so ex[t]ensive."[195] Indeed, this attitude was so prevalent that, in 1792, the state legislature, with the express purpose of "diminish[ing] the Use of Ardent Spirits, and preserv[ing] the Morals and Health of the People," offered to exempt from all state and poll taxes anyone operating "works for the Manufacture of Malt and Malt Liquors."[196]

The introduction of coffee, tea, and chocolate into the English-speaking world in the late-seventeenth century had provided invigorating alternatives to distilled liquor and led to the development of the coffeehouse as a new form of gathering place in England. By the late eighteenth century, coffeehouses provided an alternative to the tavern in urban

Robert Calder,

LATE FROM LONDON ;

CUTS and Dreſſes, LADIES and GENTLEMEN's HAIR in the genteeleſt Faſhions, either at his Houſe, or attends at the Time and Place directed by thoſe that will favor him with their Cuſtom. He alſo begs Leave to inform the Public, That he has open'd a COFFEE HOUSE, oppoſite the South Side of the Reverend Mr. HAVEN's Meeting Houſe in Portſmouth, where may be had COFFEE, TEA and CHOCOLATE in the beſt and moſt agreable Manner.——Care will be taken to have all the the Engliſh and American News Papers, Magazines, and political Pamphlets, as early as poſſible ; and every other Means aſſiduouſly purſued to give Satisfaction, and obtain the Encouragement and Favor of the Public.

Newspaper advertisement for Robert Calder's coffeehouse, Portsmouth, New-Hampshire Gazette, 1767. Calder, in addition to bringing the latest in hair fashions directly from London, opened a coffeehouse in Portsmouth similar to those thriving in England. Following London precedent, Calder served non-alcoholic beverages and offered his patrons the most recent newspapers and magazines.

NHHS Collections   Photographer, Ernest Gould

Illustration, captioned: ''His Father Was a Lazy, Shiftless Fellow,'' frontispiece of The Old Tavern, *and Other Stories, 1886, by Mary Dwinnell Chellis. This opening illustration set the mood for one of a series of novels written by a Newport, N.H., resident and published by the National Temperance Society. The ending of chapter four demonstrates the intensity of the reaction against former ways and institutions: ''Liquor has been the curse of all our farming towns, and the old-fashioned taverns did a big business in making drunkards.''*

NHHS Collections   Photographer, Ernest Gould

New Hampshire, where they imitated their famous London counterparts in serving as forum and news center. Although wine, ale, and punch sometimes appeared in advertisements of coffeehouse fare, tea, coffee, and chocolate remained the specialty of these newer establishments. The growing popularity of non-alcoholic stimulants helped reinforce the movement away from distilled liquor. New Hampshire tavernkeepers responded to the trend by offering tea and coffee as well as stronger beverages, and the distinctions between coffeehouses and contemporary taverns began to dissolve.[197]

Despite the increased emphasis on fermented and non-alcoholic beverages as an alternative to distilled spirits, the New Hampshire temperance movement did not gain full strength until the late 1820s. In 1827, Jonathan Kittredge, a Lyme lawyer and reformed alcoholic, delivered so powerful a lecture on ''the effects of ardent spirits'' that it was translated into several languages and republished throughout Europe.[198] The description of another such lecture in Bath as ''pretty fiery'' probably applied to many of the numerous temperance lectures that followed.[199] Concord's

Reverend Nathaniel Bouton alone delivered more than thirty lectures on the subject.[200]

The lectures quickly inspired a proliferation of temperance organizations—at the town, county, regional, and state level. Special temperance newspapers championed the cause. Eventually, locally produced plays and regionally written novels dramatized the subject. In Dover, intemperance was blamed for producing ''seven eights of the pauperism, more than three fifths of the widowhood, two thirds of the orphanage, and *one tenth of the mortality* in [the] town.''[201] In the rural town of Stoddard, as late as 1846, ''several criminal, and one civil prosecution within a few years past [were found] traceable to rum.''[202]

In general, the effects of the reform activity were astound-

ROCKINGHAM HOUSE,
AT EPPING CORNER.

STEVENS DOCKHAM, respectfully informs the public, that he has taken the well known Brick Tavern, at Epping Corner, which has been thoroughly renovated and furnished with entire *new furniture*; that he has entered upon its duties as its *Landlord;* has re-opened it upon strict TEMPERANCE PRINCIPLES, and is prepared with every thing necessary for the convenience of the travelling community.

Permanent and transient boarders can be accommodated. Likewise *Parties of Pleasure*, will find the Rockingham House always in readiness to receive company.

The Stable is very extensive, and well stocked; good and trusty hostlers will be at all hours on hand, and pains or expense will not be spared to make the Rockingham House truly the 'traveller's home.'

S. D. invites a call from old friends and the public generally, and by strict attention to his business and a determination to please, hopes to *merit* and *receive* a fair patronage.

Epping Corner, July 6.   27-3w.

Newspaper advertisement for Stevens Dockham's Rockingham House, Epping, N.H., Manchester Memorial, *1843. The owner of the brick tavern at Epping Corner was one of the many innkeepers who pledged adherence to the new "temperance principles" by closing their bars in the late 1830s and early 1840s.*

NHHS Collections   Photographer, Ernest Gould

ing. In 1829, as a result of just one year's publicity about the dangers of alcohol, a Newport temperance group could report an 18.5 percent decrease in the town's liquor sales.[203] In the six years between 1824 and 1830, moreover, the importation of "spirits" into the country as a whole dropped from just over five million gallons to just over one million, with the number and production of American distilleries declining as well.[204] And, in the case of one typical New Hampshire merchant, liquor sales diminished from one-quarter of his store's business in the early 1820s to one-tenth of total sales a decade later.[205]

Other results of the temperance movement are less easily quantified. As early as 1792, Belknap had objected to the daily rum " 'allowance' which is usually given to labouring people."[206] In 1817, a Chester minister shocked his listeners by preaching that "ardent spirit was entirely useless; that a man could do more work without it than with it."[207] In 1828, the Hillsborough County Agricultural Fair held at Amherst offered an award to any individual "performing the labor on his farm . . . without rum."[208] That year only five farms in the entire county earned the prize, but by 1833, the Connecticut Valley town of Acworth could boast forty farms within its bounds alone being operated without the use of distilled spirits.[209] Early Francestown historians recorded that Aaron Draper's barn, erected in 1834, had the distinction of being the first building raised in that town without rum.[210] Similarly, the raising of the Eagle Coffee House in 1827 proved the last occasion for a "rum-ceremony" of this type in the capital city.[211]

Even in the early 1820s, individual towns had begun to vote their disapproval of the sale of liquor within the meetinghouse on town meeting day.[212] Some churches began to require that new members sign a temperance pledge.[213] In 1827, the state's Masonic Grand Lodge recommended to subordinate lodges "that they dispense with the use of ardent spirits at their regular and other meetings."[214] And, as late as 1846, Sarah Josepha Hale, well-known editor of a national woman's magazine, found it worthy of note, during a visit to her hometown of Newport, that the Fourth of July celebration was "conducted on strict temperance principles."[215] As the movement strengthened, temperance advocates began to denounce fermented beverages along with the distilled varieties, resulting eventually in the most unfortunate aspect of New Hampshire's temperance era: in 1833, Thomas Coffin of Boscawen was just one among countless farmers throughout the state to deliberately destroy his own apple orchard, which until then had produced nearly one hundred barrels of cider annually.[216]

In the late 1830s and throughout the 1840s, one tavern after another, in response to the new attitudes, announced its conversion to a "temperance house." In Dover, the Wyatts claimed to have established New England's first temperance house in 1835, having experimented in their Boston hotel two years earlier by doing away with liquor during dinner.[217] Both the Phoenix in Concord and Veasey's in Northwood, however, had closed their bars as early

Sign from the tavern of Simeon Atkinson, Boscawen, N.H., 1793. Atkinson's tavern served travelers on a major early route along the Merrimack Valley and, from 1804, on the newly completed Fourth New Hampshire Turnpike running between Concord and Haverhill. At this time, the decanter and wine glass originally decorating the sign were ideal symbols of tavern hospitality. Replaced by a stylized star, most likely during the height of the temperance movement, the elements of the original design have become visible again because of the worn condition of the later paint.
NHHS Collections   Photographer, Bill Finney

as 1833.[218] In 1845, Thomas J. Crawford, keeper of the Notch House, wrote to Reverend John G. Adams of Malden, Massachusetts, that he had "adopted the plan of keeping a strictly temperance house." In an informal manner, Crawford continued: "You can say to your friends that the *creature* is not kept or to be found in our house—you will not find it behind the door."[219]

At a much earlier date, a small number of individual tavernkeepers, like Keene's Isaac Wyman in 1788, had, for

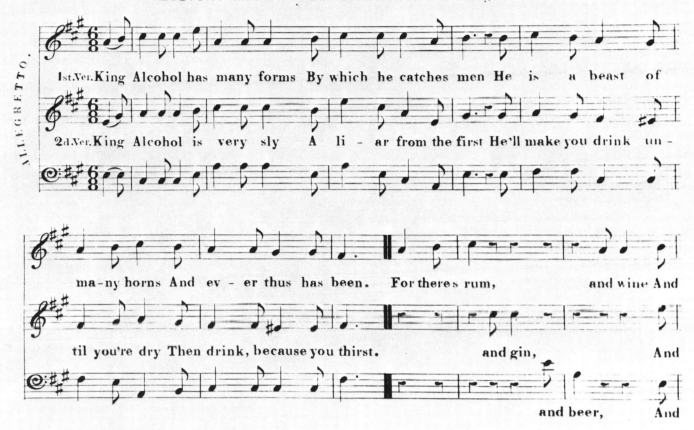

Sheet music, ''King Alcohol,'' lyrics by Jesse Hutchinson, Sr., published by Oliver Ditson, 1843. The Hutchinson Family Singers from Milford, N.H., were well-known entertainers who promoted a variety of popular reforms. According to the St. Louis Democrat in 1861: ''The Hutchinsons have with their eloquence of truth and music, doubtless converted thousands whom arguments less inspired could not have reached.''

NHHS Collections   Photographer, Ernest Gould

one reason or another, decided that they would ''not in future vend any liquors—but would be glad to serve Travellers with Boarding and Lodging, and the best of Horsekeeping.''[220] Others, as late as 1830, however, continued to advertise a bar ''well furnished with the best of liquors,'' though with the added promise that this ''house shall never become the *haunt* of tiplers.''[221]

Coffeehouses continued in popularity, but the features which distinguished them from typical taverns had become increasingly vague. As early as 1786, Portsmouth's William Brewster opened what he referred to as a ''coffee-house-tavern.''[222] And, in 1832, Concord's Eagle Coffee House, its name reflecting the new temperance fervor, nevertheless boasted a ''BAR . . . with the choicest liquors and wines

Daguerreotype, male members of the Hutchinson Family of Milford, N.H., circa 1845. New Hampshire's Hutchinson Family Singers were strong temperance advocates and social reformers. With a sentimentality typical of its era, this daguerreotype records the close-knit family in mourning both for their eleventh brother and a brother-in-law, who had died within two days of each other from typhoid fever. As itinerant performers, the Hutchinsons frequently suffered the "fatigue of constant speaking and singing in school houses, barns, mills, depots, and the open air."
Courtesy, Private Collection

of every description."[223] Despite the early success of coffeehouses, it was not until the late 1830s that large numbers of taverns renounced liquor in an effort to preserve their more basic meal and accommodation business.

The temperance movement in New Hampshire was not without opposition. Portsmouth's *New-Hampshire Gazette* claimed in 1841 that being temperate, in the strict sense of the word, required moderation rather than abstinence.[224] As late as 1846, the town of Walpole, in response to a survey on the association between the number of taverns and pauperism in any given town, replied almost defiantly that "Walpole has the honor and ability to support five rumselling taverns."[225] And, around 1833, when fifty Dover-area merchants signed a pledge not to sell intoxicating liquors, an opposed group "resolved, that we consider the attempt made by some temperance societies to proscribe all who differ from them in opinion, and to trade and deal exclusively with members of their own society and those who favor their views, as the emanation of an unjust and wicked spirit of intolerance."[226]

Despite such opposition and perhaps somewhat spurred on by it, the original quest for temperance evolved by the 1840s into a movement for total abstinence. The eventual result was a state law passed in 1849, allowing the sale of "wine and spirituous liquors" for medicinal purposes only. This was followed by more stringent legislation in 1855 prohibiting all sales of "spirituous or intoxicating liquors," with the exception of domestic wine or cider. Further legislation in 1877 and 1878 banned retail sales of both fermented cider and malt liquor.[227]

This legislation does not seem to have discouraged the large brewing industries that began to flourish in Portsmouth in the 1860s. In fact, because New Hampshire was one of only thirteen states to pass prohibition laws at this period, the local situation may have forced the development of the national market that "Portsmouth ale" eventually commanded.[228] Statewide prohibition, in connection with other developments of the mid-nineteenth century, did affect the tavern world, however, threatening to undermine its basic foundations.

TAVERNS IN THE AGE OF TOURISM

CHAPTER 9

ALTHOUGH IN THE COURSE of daily life and work, early New Englanders frequently traveled for the purpose of conducting business, marketing local produce, buying imported goods, visiting friends and relatives in communities they had left behind, and speculating in distant property for future needs, few visited New Hampshire's lake and mountain region before the 1820s for pleasure. When James Duncan, a Haverhill, Massachusetts, merchant, for instance, undertook an extensive journey northward through Gilmanton, Meredith, Plymouth, Haverhill, and Lebanon in 1806, his purpose was to strengthen both his family's country trade and land holdings.[1] The remarks of a French traveler, as recorded in 1799, illustrate this early attitude toward travel:

> We were asked every where, whether we travelled with a view to buy lands. There is hardly a person in America, who has the least idea of gentlemen travelling with any other design; and when we told them, that we traveled with no other purpose than to gratify our curiosity, they thought we were fools, or, at best, liars.[2]

One part of the state that did attract a small number of tourists at a relatively early period was the Connecticut River region. According to the Reverend Timothy Dwight, it was largely because "the roads in this valley were generally good throughout . . . [that] a multitude of strangers have at all times been induced to make this valley the scene of their pleasurable traveling."[3] As early as 1799, the hotel at Walpole Bridge was advertising the advantages of its location as "a retreat from the feverish air of a city, or as an agreeable temporary retirement from the confusion and bustle of the town."[4]

Another reason for the early development of tourism in this agriculturally fertile region was that, in an era dominated by settlement activity, the open, cultivated landscape of the river valley was aesthetically more appealing than the wilderness dominant elsewhere. The Massachusetts merchant who kept a diary of his journey through the state's lake and mountain region in 1806 seldom commented on the landscape except to note systematically the condition of mountain roads and the varieties of trees on each of his individual lots. But, upon reaching the western border of the state at Piermont, even this confirmed businessman could not resist pausing "to view the country," noting that

Engraving, View of Bellows Falls, and Mansion-House Hotel, Taken from the Western Bank, *Walpole, N.H.; detail from Edward Ruggles' map,* New Hampshire, From Late Survey . . . , *Walpole, 1817, engraved by Oliver Tarbell Eddy. Built about 1799, this elegant hotel was one of the first large taverns constructed to serve an already substantial tourist traffic in the Connecticut River valley. The hotel, offering an unsurpassed view of the waterfalls, contained two halls and twenty chambers, and had many outbuildings, including a smokehouse and dovecote.*

NHHS Collections   Photographer, Ernest Gould

he was "very much delighted with the prospect of the land on Connecticut River."[5]

A definite increase in the number of tourists in New Hampshire both in the mountains and at the ocean gained attention for the first time in the 1820s. In 1825, a Portsmouth newspaper editor learned from a friend who had recently visited Hampton Beach that "on one day nearly one hundred persons had been counted there seeking health or amusement."[6] Simultaneously in the mountains, the Crawford family saw their "summer company" increasing yearly.[7] Already by 1828, the White Mountains were noted for "attract[ing] large companies of the gay and the fashionable in the summer season."[8] The Crawfords and other mountain innkeepers began to supplement their services to guests by acting as "guides to every accessible point in the neighborhood."[9]

By the 1830s and 1840s, a new attitude toward nature had begun to prevail. As cities developed and the lives of much of the population became removed from the daily struggle with nature, it became fashionable for travelers, along with artists and writers, to seek aesthetic pleasure in the uncultivated, untamed terrain, rather than remain intimidated as before. Discriminating travelers deliberately began to seek out the "picturesque" in the landscape, along with the more serenely "beautiful." A visitor to Carroll County in 1848 pointed out that, despite the fact that the surrounding countryside "possess[ed] no attractions in the agricultural way, yet the wild and sublime character of the mountains is admired by all."[10] Included among the travelers were a group of artists, later referred to as the White Mountain School, who attempted to capture on canvas the "grand and sublime display of Nature." Benjamin Champney, John F. Kensett, Asher B. Durand, Jasper Cropsey, Albert Bierstadt, and others portrayed both the pastoral and the untamed aspects of mountain scenery through close observation and a high degree of technical skill.[11] Other visitors attempted to put their impressions into words:

> The deeper you go into the Notch, the wilder it becomes—the Mts. tower more & more, & the vallies and gullies beneath the road deepen, & blacken into mysterious windings where only cascades roll almost unheard. . . . Here an old white stump would rise from some angle in the road, & thrust out dragon-like claws into the air between the giant hills.[12]

In keeping with this new appreciation of the wilderness, Caroline Gilman, a Southerner visiting the Connecticut Valley in 1836, bemoaned the fact that there was "but little remaining of natural beauty at Bellows' Falls." Ironically, the man-made marvels which she criticized were the very features which a previous generation had found most attractive: "The dashing waters have gone to aid a slow canal; mills are working over the rocks, and a bridge hides the most beautiful portion of the cascade."[13]

The preoccupation throughout the nineteenth century with the benefits of fresh air, healthful water, and moderate exercise—particularly for invalids and convalescents from crowded cities—provided another impetus for the development of tourism. Summertime advertisements, as early as the mid-1820s, invited "invalids, and all those who value health," especially from Boston, to take advantage of the "salubrious sea-air and picturesque scenery" at Hampton Beach, or else the "cool and bracing" atmosphere of the White Mountains.[14] In 1833, a Haverhill, New Hampshire, newspaper suggested:

> Could we prevail upon more of the inhabitants of our cities, who, during the summer months, drag out a miserable existence, "half dead and half alive,["] in the dust, heat and foul air of narrow and confined streets . . . to come quietly up our river and spend a few days with friend Crawford; eat of his "fresh trout;" drink of his "clear cold water:" and now and then, for a tonic, take a tramp with him up the mountains, we have no doubt they would return with a general tone of improvement of health, which, independent of the delight and enjoyment to be derived from a view of the *grandest* scenery, would infinitely more than compensate for all the time and expense it would require.[15]

Even before the 1840s when Rye began to develop into a summer resort or "watering place," it had become customary for "persons out of health, from the interior of the State, to make their way to Rye, and engage an abiding-place with some one of the seaboard farmers during the warm months. . . . Invalids were accustomed to render such assistance as was in their power toward ordinary farm labor, and generally returned to their home in firmer health, and but a trifle out of pocket."[16] The Isles of Shoals, about ten miles beyond New Hampshire's coastline, gained widespread recognition as a health-restoring environment before achieving fame as the home of a summer literary colony. According to tradition, a sea voyage provided the ultimate tonic; and, in one expert's opinion, the Isles of Shoals "more nearly than almost any other inhabited island in the Western Atlantic [approximated] the atmospheric conditions found in a ship at sea."[17] "Botanic infirmaries" and mineral-spring resorts, scattered throughout the state, catered even more specifically to the health requirements of guests.[18] In the 1860s, "fear of the ravages of the Cholera" led even healthy urban residents to vacate "the large cities and towns of New England and the Middle States" during the summertime in favor of New Hampshire's seashore and mountains.[19]

The coming of the railway to New Hampshire by mid-century brought ever greater numbers of visitors, whether for health or amusement, to the state's seashore and mountains. The "flock of summer tourists" which by 1838 was annually "tak[ing] wing through the region" had become by 1852 a steady "current": "The railroad routes which are opening more and more into the centre of the state pour in their carloads of visitors who sweep in a continuous stream through the Notch, meeting quite as strong a current from the opposite side of the hills."[20] By the early 1850s, visitors came to the White Mountains from all parts of New England, New York, Philadelphia, and Baltimore, as well as from elsewhere in the United States and Canada.[21] In the early 1860s, Thoreau estimated that one hundred visitors daily ascended Mount Monadnock, while Rye hotels and

Lithograph, Ocean House, Rye Beach, N.H. . . . , circa 1855, by John H. Bufford after H. Harnden. An increasing interest in romantic scenery and a healthful environment made the seashore as popular as the mountains among mid-century tourists. The Ocean House, opened in 1847, was one of the first grand hotels built on the New Hampshire shore. Accommodating guests in more than a hundred rooms by the time of this picture, the hotel was said to be especially suited to "gentlemen with their families, parties of pleasure, or invalids."

NHHS Collections   Photographer, Ernest Gould

boarding houses accommodated four hundred "strangers" at a time.[22] In fact, there was not a train on the Eastern Railroad in the summer of 1865 that did not leave passengers at the local depots to visit the Rye coast.[23]

A number of New Hampshire railroad corporations were formed in 1835 and 1836; during the first decade, however, only ninety-five miles of track—all in the southern part of the state—actually reached the point of construction.[24] Editor Sarah Josepha Hale, on returning to her hometown of Newport in 1846, diagnosed "an improvement fever . . . now raging in New Hampshire, melting down the 'everlasting hills,' smoothing the granite precipices, and fusing, as in a crucible, the varied interests of the people into one burning desire for steam power and a railroad to pass through every town in the state."[25] Although she then discovered that these "improvements" were not yet complete and that travel was "still chiefly by stage-coach," the local determination she had sensed succeeded by 1860 in multiplying the state's railroad access at least sixfold.[26] The railroad, in effect, considerably shortened travel distances, enabling Thoreau, for instance, in 1852 to reach Concord, Massachusetts, only "four hours from the time [he was] picking blueberries on [Monadnock], with the plants of the mountain fresh in [his] hat."[27]

Although the tourists visiting New Hampshire's White Mountain area in 1825 found "the accommodations at most of the [region's] public houses . . . as good as can be found any where in the interior," from the 1830s onward, the constant refrain was the need for "larger houses" with more convenient features.[28] In 1833, Ethan Allen Crawford proudly announced that his inn, recently expanded especially to serve tourists, could accommodate "28 couple[s] and more if *necessary*."[29] By August 1851, however, shortly after the first railroad reached the mountain area, one hundred passengers could arrive in a single day by train only to discover that every room at Gorham's White Mountain Station House had already been taken. On one such occasion, 140 additional passengers arrived the two following days, making the situation even more intolerable.[30] Despite continual expansion and renovation of existing structures, the problem of space continued. Following its construction in 1847, the Ocean House at Rye was expanded for its second season to fifty-five rooms. The number of rooms more than doubled by 1853, but even expansion to this extent was not enough to keep the proprietor that year from having "to lodge visitors in cottages in the neighborhood."[31]

In 1865, with White Mountain tourism once again so "immense [that it] tasks to the utmost the capacity of all the hotels and boarding houses," the proprietors of the Crawford House—completely rebuilt in 1859—announced that two hundred more rooms were to be added by the next season.[32] The eventual result of such rapid growth was the

Lithograph, Pemigewasset House, Plymouth, N.H., *circa 1865, by John H. Bufford. Constructed in 1863 by the Boston, Concord, & Montreal Railroad, the great T-shaped Pemigewasset House symbolized the replacement of the mountain tavern by the grand hotel. Its predecessor had been a small gambrel-roofed tavern built in the eighteenth century by Colonel David Webster or his son William. The Webster tavern, enlarged after 1841 by Denison Rogers Burnham, served as Plymouth's principal public house until it burned down in 1862 and was replaced by the great hotel.*

NHHS Collections   Photographer, Bill Finney

splendid era of the grand hotel. In 1861, when Anthony Trollope, the English novelist, visited the White Mountain region, he was astonished to find a "district in New England containing mountain scenery superior to much that is yearly crowded by tourists in Europe [and] dotted with huge hotels, almost as thickly as they lie in Switzerland."[33]

Any of the old-fashioned taverns which had failed to keep up with the expansion fervor found it difficult to compete with the "mountain houses," whose proprietors, Thoreau claimed regretfully, were making the region "as much like the city as they can afford to."[34] In the state's largest cities, changes in accommodations followed the same general pattern as in the major tourism centers. Large and luxurious hotels gradually replaced even the most fashionable public houses. By 1863, in comparison with the "towering height and liberal accommodations" of Con-

cord's relatively new Eagle Hotel, for instance, the once popular Eagle Coffee House which it replaced had, in the public eye, "dwindle[d] into a mere Turkey-buzzard."[35]

But the new standards in lodging that tourism and urbanization together had imposed were only partly responsible for the decline of the tavern in the mid-nineteenth century. The ascendancy of the railroad by the 1850s, as well as the culmination of the temperance movement in statewide prohibition, finally resulted in the end of the tavern era. Ironically, although railroad corporations often held their formative meetings in local taverns, railroad tracks throughout the state typically bypassed both existing routes and the public houses that had developed to serve them.[36] As recorded by a local historian in New Ipswich, writing in 1852 during the midst of this change: "travel took a direction which had never before been

ON THE ROAD NORTH OF BOSTON

Lithograph, Rockingham House, Portsmouth, N.H., 1873-74, by Charles H. Crosby & Co., after Dominick I. Drummond. The brick mansion built around 1785 by Woodbury Langdon had served since 1833 as one of Portsmouth's finest hotels. In 1870, local brewing-magnate Frank Jones bought the hotel and expanded it into the grand mansard-roofed hotel seen here—one of the first great city hotels in New Hampshire. This building was partly destroyed by fire in 1884 and rebuilt on a still larger scale the following year, with opulent interiors that emphasized the change from earlier taverns.

NHHS Collections   Photographer, Ernest Gould

dreamed of."[37] Furthermore, because of the increased speed of travel made possible by steam, overnight accommodations were less steadily in demand. As early as 1842 when the tracks first reached Concord, it was possible to eat breakfast in Plymouth and supper in Boston, after traveling over one hundred miles easily in a single day.[38]

The temperance movement, having gained in strength since the 1820s, exerted a negative impact on the tavern's future. By the mid-1830s, conscientious tavernkeepers were beginning to "clear [their] bar[s] of the usual *labelled array* of decanters."[39] In 1836, a committee of influential Concord citizens visited each of the remaining liquor-dealing taverners and retailers in town "to plead, with tears, that the dreadful traffic might cease."[40] By 1843, it was claimed that no hotel in the capital city "can long have a reputation without throwing out its bar."[41] In 1841, the

reform movement reached Dartmouth College; the students that year boycotted the Dartmouth Hotel, foregoing the commencement ball usually held there.[42]

The effect of temperance reform on the state's taverns was astounding. Even before state prohibition was enacted in the 1850s, individual towns often succeeded in "purging" their own communities of the "coveted poisons." By 1846, the "grogshop" had become a totally "discarded institution" in the town of Dublin, while, in the same year, Roxbury—also in Cheshire County—could proudly report: "No rumselling store or tavern curses this favoured town."[43] Even New Castle, once noted for its taverns catering to fishermen, claimed in 1852 to have "no public house—no place where the traveller can feel the warm welcome which the inn presents."[44]

Ultimately, the mention of a tavern began to evoke an

House Where Dan[ie]l Webster Was Born, mid-19th century, pencil on paper. An unknown political opponent of Daniel Webster's, taking advantage of the fact that Webster's father had kept a tavern, used the prevailing temperance sentiment of the era to impugn the statesman's character. This cartoon portrayed the tavern as seen by the temperance movement: a dirty and dilapidated saloon, the home of vice and dissipation.

NHHS Collections   Photographer, Ernest Gould

entirely different image than it once conveyed. In 1845, the traditional tavern complete with bar, formerly one of the key focal points of a community, was officially "deemed" by the citizens of Keene to be nothing less than "a public nuisance."[45] A tavern, once required by law to provide beds and stabling for guests, was now defined merely as a "drinking house," with a "few bottles of whiskey" the only necessities. A tavern became distinct from an "inn, or house of entertainment for travellers."[46] And, tavernkeeping, once an essential and honorable occupation, was seen as "a business which, however gainful, must have been followed by many compunctions at the misery and wretchedness it was entailing . . . and the pauperism and crime which it daily and hourly created."[47]

Yet the sentiment against alcohol was not universal, and many turned away in disgust from those communities and inns which advocated temperance. In 1848, the Howes and Company Great United States Circus, not being able to obtain a license in Concord where little or no liquor had been sold since 1844, set up across the town line in Bow, near the railroad crossing.[48] And, in 1839, when the tavern long associated with the famous Londonderry fair became a temperance house, "a number of persons on assembling at the usual time, and finding this to be the case, at once withdrew, and [as of 1851] no traces of the Fair remain[ed] in Derry, where for more than a century it had been observed."[49]

The conversion of a tavern to a temperance house—especially in the early years of the reform movement—often caused the tavernkeeper financial hardship. Sophia Wyatt of Dover recalled that when she and her husband decided to make their hotel a strict temperance house, "some of our customers stood by us, but a larger proportion turned away."[50] And, in 1845, the keeper of the Mansion House in neighboring Portsmouth, after having observed temperance principles for more than two years, announced regretfully his intention to reintroduce a bar. This proved financially necessary because, as the proprietor had warned earlier, "The bar is one of the most profitable sources of the income of a public house [and] . . . Temperance principles cannot be sustained even in these times without the tangible assistance of the temperance community."[51]

Rail-Road House.
HAMPTON, N. H.

THE Subscribers would respectfully inform their friends and the public that they have taken the *DEARBORN TAVERN*, which has been fitted up where they will be happy to wait on the public.

This house is situated in the centre of the pleasant village of Hampton, half way from Newburyport to Portsmouth, on the great stage road, about 20 rods East of the Eastern Rail-Road, ¼ of a mile from the Academy, and 2 miles from Hampton Beach. The visitors at the Beach will find that the facilities of communication with Boston and elsewhere afforded at this stand are such as to render it the most desirable place of residence in this vicinity.— We are also prepared to accommodate a number of Boarders through the season.

The Table and Bar will be well supplied. The Stables are large and commodious, and every attention will be paid to them. The public may rest assured that the subscribers will use every exertion to give satisfaction to their customers and to render them in every way comfortable. The patronage of travellers is respectfully solicited.
BATCHELDER & GODFREY.
Jan 21, 1840.

Newspaper advertisement for Alfred J. Batchelder and Oliver Godfrey's Rail-Road House (formerly the Dearborn Tavern), Hampton, N.H., New-Hampshire Gazette (Portsmouth), *1840. Those taverns fortunate enough to be located close to a new railroad line found their futures secure even as more remote taverns suffered from the diversion of their traditional traffic. The proximity of the Rail-Road House to the ocean also favored business.*
NHHS Collections   Photographer, Ernest Gould

By mid-century, a number of New Hampshire's taverns were forced out of business. When statewide prohibition was enacted in 1855, Edwin Carleton of Bath "took his sign down and nailed up his door," complaining that he was no longer able to obtain a license to sell liquor.[52] Only those public houses which happened to be near railroad depots thrived. In keeping with the times, Hampton's Dearborn Tavern, one of the few fortunate in its location, began in 1840 to promote itself as the "Rail-Road House."[53] As early as 1869, the *Nashua Telegraph* calculated that "the era of railroads stripped the public houses . . . of three-fourths of their importance and patronage."[54]

According to an 1887 account, many "inns, deserted by their former patrons, were converted to farmhouses, and are still used as such."[55] Others in more urban settings were subdivided into apartments, as was the Dover Hotel in 1854.[56] Deliberate destruction by fire or demolition was the fate of many tavern structures when business failed. Some, it was claimed, were "burned at the expense of the insurance companies," while the dilapidated condition of others tempted incendiaries.[57] In 1858, the village tavern in Wentworth, after being closed for two years, was torn down and replaced by an elegant private dwelling.[58] The Reverend Dr. Jonathan French of North Hampton also erected a new home in the early 1850s on the site of an old tavern, perhaps hoping to erase memories of pre-temperance customs.[59]

Although large numbers of tavern buildings were destroyed during the decade of the 1850s, some survived—often in dilapidated condition—into the next century. One of the oldest taverns of the Grafton Turnpike did not face demolition until the winter of 1908-9.[60] Not far from this Canaan example, a stone Greek Revival tavern in Hanover, with a reputation for being haunted that often kept it unoccupied, survived into the 1920s, when vandals with no respect for its imposing style finally destroyed it.[61]

During the 1860s, a new era began with the construction throughout the state of large and fashionable town and village hotels. Communities such as Amherst, once known for their hospitality, suddenly discovered during this decade that, after the village taverns had succumbed one by one to the "torch of the incendiary," not a single "place of public entertainment" remained in the entire town.[62] Beginning in the late 1850s, citizens in one town after another joined together in private corporations "for the purpose of purchasing, repairing, or building a house of public entertainment" to serve their community.[63] In Amherst, an extensive three-story hotel was erected near the site of the Golden Ball Tavern in 1869.

The buildings specifically designed for hotel purposes during this period brought the higher standards in accommodations expected by tourists to even the smallest New Hampshire towns. While occasionally taverns had offered "separate sitting, eating, and sleeping rooms" for each party of guests as early as the 1790s, "private rooms" or "suites of rooms" had not been common even in larger cities except in the most fashionable establishments.[64] By the 1860s and 1870s, many small towns had replaced defunct taverns with new hotels containing fifty to one hundred bedchambers.[65] Even many of those public houses which had survived because of their proximity to the railroad eventually had to be replaced by more up-to-date structures because of rapid increases in business.[66]

The tavern's demise also reflected a demand for specialization in a society increasing in size and complexity. As the nineteenth century progressed, no single institution could satisfy all the varied social needs of the typical community. The tavern's multi-purpose role diminished as restaurants, livery stables, lecture halls, opera houses, dance pavilions, and eventually barrooms, became established businesses—each performing just one of the many functions formerly managed by the tavern.

Although restaurants (then called "victualling cellars") appeared in the largest towns as early as the 1820s, their numbers had increased significantly throughout the state by the 1840s. During this decade, "refreshment rooms" and "eating saloons" typically flourished in the vicinity of railroad depots. In keeping with temperance standards, the "refreshments" offered generally excluded "rum and its kindred poisons."[67] Although the tavern once had

Photograph, Muzzey Tavern, Hampstead, N.H., circa 1900. The late nineteenth century was a time of drastic change for New Hampshire's economy. Abandoned farms were a common sight in rural areas, and with the dwindling of rural population and traffic, many taverns were doomed.

NHHS Collections   Photographers, Halliday Historic Photograph Company

Photograph, the livery stable of William W. Davis, Warner, N.H., 1890s. The diverse functions of the tavern were gradually assumed by specialized businesses during the late nineteenth century. The array of vehicles and horses belonging to this Warner livery stable indicates the range of service available in a small town.

NHHS Collections

served as the local place to board horses, rent vehicles, and hire drivers, independent livery establishments took over the business during the nineteenth century. Specialized stables were among the many services eventually clustered around the depot to cater to railway and tourist traffic.[68] Separate barrooms appropriately called saloons (from the French word for "reception room") had been popular elsewhere in the country since the 1850s and emerged legally in New Hampshire following the repeal of state prohibition in 1903 as the modern substitute for the tavern taproom.[69]

Independent barrooms and even fashionable hotels occasionally retained the name "tavern" into the twentieth century, but they bore little resemblance to the multi-faceted inns of earlier times.[70] Originally, in the finer taverns, once the focal point of all community activities, every citizen was a personal acquaintance and every traveler a welcomed guest. Although certain restrictions governed tavern operation and visitors had to adapt their needs to the family's schedule, a warm, hospitable spirit usually dominated the tavern atmosphere. The hotels that took the place of taverns during the nineteenth century were often owned and operated impersonally by corporations rather than individuals prominent in the community. Although guests typically enjoyed a greater degree of both freedom and privacy, most remained basically anonymous, having little or no direct contact with the hotel management. In the mid-nineteenth century, visitors to Boston, where New England's hotel movement originated, described both their pleasure in being able to "eat, drink, or sleep, at what time, in what manner, and on what substances [they] might prefer" and their dismay on being given "a key with a corresponding number attached" and led to "a small clean room on the third story, where to all intents and purposes [their] identity was lost—merged in a mere numeral."[71]

Because of the greatly improved efficiency of the railroad, travel also assumed a more uniform, routine, and impersonal nature. As early as 1846, Sarah Josepha Hale captured the essence of railroad travel while approaching Nashua by train: "On and on, straight and almost as swift as a carrier pigeon would fly, we go through the country, and hardly have a reminiscence to record, except some serious disaster occurs."[72] From the viewpoint of the bystander as well as the traveler, a new homogeneity replaced the diversity once characteristic of highway traffic. Herds of animals, circuses, military troops, tourists, immigrants, and everything "freightable" were suddenly, in the words of a Wentworth citizen, "hurried through the Town, by the magic influence of *Steam*."[73] Despite the earlier flurry of canal-building activity, the slow but picturesque river traffic also experienced a steady decline following the rise of the railroad.[74] Even the individual contact between inland farmers delivering their produce or livestock and coastal merchants came to an end, this change being noted as early as 1858 by the historian of Mason, New Hampshire: "The farmer need not leave his own premises to find a ready

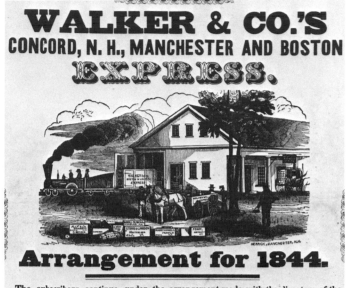

Broadside advertising Walker & Co.'s Concord, N.H., Manchester and Boston Express, 1844, printed by Morrill, Silsby, & Co., with wood engraving by Henry Walker Herrick. The advent of the railroad ended employment for many drivers on major stage routes. Taking advantage of their hard won reputations for honesty and reliability, some of these drivers banded together to establish express companies which offered the secure delivery of goods and packages from the relatively few railroad depots to any destination.

NHHS Collections   Photographer, Bill Finney

market at remunerating prices, for all the surplus products of his farm."[75]

Another aspect of highway life traditionally involving close relationships between travelers and the "people of the road" was also entering by mid-century a period of decline and change. As railway tracks were laid, stage service between certain points became superfluous; fortunately, stage proprietors and drivers were flexible enough to modify existing stage routes to meet the new needs of railroad passengers. As the railroad was extended into New Hampshire, the points of intersection between stage and railway were in a constant state of evolution. During this period of transition, stage proprietors were repeatedly announcing "New Arrangement[s]" in the local newspapers.[76]

The Crawford Notch, White Mountains, 1883, oil on canvas, by Frank Henry Shapleigh. Although the railroad ended stage travel on many principal routes, the stagecoach remained an important shuttle vehicle between railroad depots and centers not served by the train. Large hotels on the coast, in the mountains, and in the centers of cities, in particular, long maintained coaches to ensure frequent transportation between railroad centers and their establishments.

Courtesy, Mr. and Mrs. Frederic A. Sharf   Photographer, Robert Swenson

As the railroad network expanded further, eventually serving most of the state, the stage driver's occupation became obsolete. Many of the coachmen continued in travel-related professions, often becoming conductors, brakemen, or station agents for the railroads that had eclipsed the less efficient but more colorful stage service.[77] Others, capitalizing on the stage driver's reputation for trustworthiness in transporting "papers, Packages, Deeds, [and] Bundles," as well as large sums of money, established their own express services—manifesting in yet another way the trend toward specialization.[78] In 1841, Gideon Walker and John Mendum publicized their services as " 'ancient knights of the whip,' [who] having been thrown from their former employment by the opening of the *Rail-Road,* have associated themselves together for the purpose of running an Express Car, from Boston to Portsmouth, for the carrying of Bundles and small Packages, and the transaction of any other business that may be entrusted to their care."[79] One former New Hampshire stage driver, Benjamin Pierce Cheney, eventually helped to found the United States and Canada Express Company, one of the leading subsidiaries of American Express.[80]

The transition from horse to steam power was, of course, never a complete one. Most New Hampshire travelers, by the mid-nineteenth century, took advantage of different modes of transportation on any one journey. As early as 1836, Caroline Fitch, on a visit to Lyme, New Hampshire,

left Boston by railway, transferred to steamboat in Lowell, and to stagecoach in Nashua.[81] The stage appears to have survived for a longer time in New Hampshire than in some locales. Sarah Josepha Hale, on her return to New Hampshire in 1846, claimed to have "almost forgotten the old-fashioned stage-coach, but we found it again in the 'Old Granite State.' "[82] Particularly in New Hampshire's developing tourist regions, coaches continued to see service into the early twentieth century as private hotel vehicles, carrying passengers back and forth to the depot, and supplementing the electric trolleys that had begun to carry passengers from the cities to nearby resorts. Already by the late 1840s, the Ocean House at Rye Beach, for instance, had a coach running "to meet the cars at the Greenland Depot" three times a day during the summer.[83] During the 1880s and 1890s in the White Mountains, great coaching parades were held annually in which resort hotels entered their own stagecoaches elaborately decorated for the occasion; these parades represented the final flourish of the stagecoach era.[84]

Economic changes began to affect New Hampshire's turnpike network well before the railroad altered the entire transportation system of the state. The roads had never produced a great profit; few attained, even briefly, the 6 percent annual earnings which most charters established as a fair minimum level. Beginning in 1816, the First Turnpike began to show an annual loss.[85] The Fourth Turnpike,

Photograph of coach parade, Bethlehem, N.H., circa 1895. One of the favorite spectacles of the White Mountain resort communities in the late nineteenth century was the coach parade. Coaches belonging to different hotels were decorated as parade floats and pulled by matched teams driven by experienced old-time drivers, their roofs adorned with pretty girls from each hotel. Hotels and houses were decorated with bunting and flags, and the day ended with a baseball game and fireworks. Held in late summer, the parades were especially successful in Bethlehem and North Conway.
NHHS Collections

even with its "Great Feeder," the Grafton Turnpike, returned an average annual profit of only 2.15 percent between 1820 and its demise in 1842.[86] Stock in the Coos Turnpike, from Warren to Haverhill, showed an annual profit of 2 percent until 1819, and the road managed to pay a dividend of a dollar a share until 1834.[87] But persisting as long as they did, at a consistent if small profit, the Fourth and the Coos turnpikes were easily among the most successful of New Hampshire's toll roads. Others began to succumb to economic pressures within twenty years of their opening, or even sooner. Stock in the Third Turnpike had depreciated from the original $200 a share to a mere $12 by 1813.[88]

Attorney John M. Shirley of Andover, who wrote an extended history of the Fourth Turnpike in 1881, attributed the demise of toll roads to several factors, foremost among them being lack of public spirit among those who might have supported such enterprises:

The tavernkeepers with their retainers and dependents, who wielded a great deal of influence, felt that a free road would bring a large increase of public travel and consequent profits to their pockets. The general public felt that the corporation was made up of a few men, some of whom had acquired blocks of stock at pauper prices . . . and summed up their opposition in the ugly word *monopoly*. A war was made upon the turnpikes. . . .[89]

The character of this war was revealed by the traveler Marryat, when he recounted in 1837 that the citizens of Charlestown, deciding that the Cheshire Turnpike was "*monarchical*," gathered "one fine night . . . with a hawser and a team or two of horses, made the hawser fast to the [toll]house at the gate, dragged it down to the river, and sent it floating down the stream, with the gate and board of tolls in company with it."[90] Other roads suffered because of collusion among town officials in the widespread practice of "shunpiking," or bypassing the tollgates. In 1821, the town of Piermont threatened to build a road parallel to the Coos Turnpike.[91] In 1823, the directors of the First Turnpike sued the selectmen of Concord "for laying out a highway in Concord running along by the side of & near to the turnpike road at & opposite the turnpike gate numbered six."[92]

One of the problems suffered by turnpike corporations

Photograph, road-building crew, probably New Hampshire, circa 1890. Bypassing a steep hill, the route chosen for this highway illustrates Frank West Rollins' maxim that a winding road was more picturesque than a straight one, added little to the distance traveled, and was far easier on draft animals.

NHHS Collections

arose from their initial zeal to lay out their roads along the straightest possible line between two points. However beautiful such a route might be to the mathematical eye of the surveyor or the efficient mind of the turnpike director, the fact is that the road-building equipment of the early 1800s permitted only limited cutting and filling in hilly, ledge-filled terrain. Drivers quickly found that their teams were exhausted by long, straight hauls up endless hills. Much of the "shunpiking" noted in New Hampshire took place because of the concern of teamsters to save their animals rather than from an avaricious desire to bypass toll-gates. Many years later, in a speech he gave widely throughout the state, Frank West Rollins commented on the folly of arrow-straight roads in New Hampshire:

> . . . a straight line has its advantages; but I think they are more than counterbalanced by the advantages of a winding road. It is not very much longer, and it is certainly less expensive to build, and saves heavy grades or an immense amount of excavation. . . . The old illustration of the handle of a pail is the best illustration I know of. It is no [shorter] when you hold it up straight, which is the direct route over the hill, than it is when the handle is down at the side, which is the road around the hill. . . . And just think what the expense and waste of strength is, and what it means in wear and tear when spread over hundreds of years.[93]

As profits decreased, some turnpike directors began to feel the effect of the clause, common to all the charters, which stipulated that the corporation, "may be indicted for defect of repairs of said road, after the toll gates are erected, and fined in the same way and manner as towns are by law finable for suffering roads to be out of repair." The legislature passed a law in 1826 compelling the Ashuelot Turnpike to surrender its charter unless it made immediate repairs to the road, and stipulating that any attempt to collect further tolls before repairs were made would result in the award of a ten-dollar fine to anyone who had been charged to use the road.[94]

Given this discouraging climate, it was inevitable that turnpike directors began to seek ways to unburden themselves of properties that threatened to ruin them. Long before their charters expired, most corporations approached the legislature with proposals to transform their turnpike into a free road. The First and Third turnpikes became free in 1824; the Grafton in 1827; the Second in 1837; the Chester in 1838; the Dover in 1840; and the Fourth, section by section, in the years up to 1845. Most others quietly abandoned their tollgates and relinquished their rights-of-way to the communities through which they passed.[95] The directors of some turnpikes, like the First, were able to collect substantial sales prices from the towns along their

Engraving, The Mount Washington Road (White Mountains), *engraved by Samuel Valentine Hunt after Harry Fenn for William Cullen Bryant, ed.,* Picturesque America, *published 1872, vol. 1. Commemorating the construction of a turnpike to the top of the highest peak in New England by the Mount Washington Summit Road Company, this popular print portrayed the mountain with an exaggerated alpine ruggedness to emphasize both the sublime scenery and the herculean accomplishment.*

NHHS Collections   Photographer, Ernest Gould

Wood engraving, Summit of Mount Washington, *engraved by Nathaniel Orr after C. G., for* Ballou's Pictorial Drawing-Room Companion, *1856; second state (with telegraph poles added), published in Benjamin G. Willey's,* Incidents in White Mountain History, *1856. Reflecting the dreams of early planners more than the road as actually built, this print shows the summit crowned by a vast hotel with an astronomical observatory in one tower; the entire complex is linked to the base by telegraph. The proposed omnibuses had bodies that pivoted on curved frames which were supported by steel springs and were fitted with screws to allow either the front or the back of the coach to be elevated.*

NHHS Collections   Photographer, Ernest Gould

routes; the directors of others, like the Second and Third, seem to have been grateful for legislative permission simply to relinquish their charters. In any case, most accounts agree that the immediate result of freeing each turnpike was identical with what occurred to the Fourth Turnpike: "the great highway thereafter swarmed with travel as it never had done before."[96]

Only those toll roads which served the tourist survived the bleak years of the "war upon the turnpikes." Private mountain-top roads, built to provide the pleasure-seeker with sweeping views of New Hampshire's scenery, thrived to the extent that some were incorporated as late as the 1880s. The first of these was also the longest-lived: the Mount Washington Summit Road Company, chartered in 1859 to supplant a similar corporation of 1853, built the toll road which still carries traffic to the "top of New England" from the Glen House. While the *Portsmouth Journal* had grumbled in 1852 that "we hope the extortion of toll as a ticket to the Notch [on the Tenth Turnpike] will soon be obsolete," the same paper greeted the prospect of a turnpike to the summit of Mount Washington a year later with unequivocal approval. Noting that 15,000 people were estimated to have visited the White Mountains during the summer of 1853, and that no fewer than 3,400 had climbed Mount Washington, the *Journal* enthusiastically described the proposed turnpike:

It is to be fifteen feet wide, clear of all obstructions, McAdamized in the best manner, and the average grade will be a rise of from one foot to eight and a half, with level spots at various points of interest, where travelers may rest and enjoy the scenery. Wherever the road is on the side of declivities, strong walls will be erected, the road itself inclining inward. The carriages are to be peculiarly constructed; they will be broad and low, and so arranged with screws that whether going up or down, the body of the coach will be on a perfect level.[97]

After the opening of the Summit Road in 1861, other mountaintops were viewed as worthy prizes by turnpike speculators. Among the mountain toll roads chartered, many of them in conjunction with summit hotels, were the Kearsarge Summit Road (1864), the Mount Lafayette Road (1866), the Mount Hayes Turnpike (1866), the Warner and Kearsarge Road (1866), the Mount Willard Turnpike (1869), the Moosilauke Mountain Turnpike (1870), the Wilmot and Kearsarge Road (1873), the Uncanoonuc Road (1877), the Starr King Mountain Road (1881), the Chocorua Mountain Road (1889), and the Mount Prospect Turnpike (1893).

Not all of these roads were built, and not all that were built were successful. Yet it is significant that New Hampshire's turnpikes, the first highways to reflect economic reality, finally dwindled to a service for the tourist. After the mid-nineteenth century, the influence of the summer visitor would make itself felt not only in road-building, but in all aspects of the state's economy.

New Hampshire's economy underwent drastic and painful changes during the last half of the nineteenth century. Many young men who fought in the Civil War, having seen or heard of the rich lands of the Midwest, decided that their best hope for a future in farming lay a thousand miles away from the rocky hills of the Granite State. Even sheep-raising, which had provided many marginal New Hampshire farms with their last vestige of success, soon began to wither in the face of western competition. The great manufacturing cities of the Merrimack Valley exerted an increasingly powerful pull on ambitious young people. By 1870, New Hampshire had a work force of 120,000, of whom 46,500 were engaged in manufacturing—virtually equal to the number working in agriculture.[98] And the railroad, driven as much by engines of economics as by steam, favored those few villages that lay in the pathways between cities, or that could provide labor, food, and raw materials for the cities, and left many communities bereft of the only transportation that could ensure continued prosperity.

The effect on New Hampshire's countryside, at first slow, was powerful, and was watched anxiously. Statistics soon revealed that New Hampshire faced a threat with the potential to be devastating. Although the state's population

Photographic postcard, "Old Turnpike, New Ipswich, N.H.," circa 1905. Looking southeast along the Third Turnpike from Clark's Hotel (on the right), this photograph records the decline of both tavern and turnpike in a village which had been bypassed by the railroad. The hotel, the bandstand, and the cast-iron watering trough with its street lamp (patented by Henry W. Clapp of Concord, N.H., in 1890), once the scene of bustling activity, stand deserted.

Courtesy, John Preston

as a whole did not decline except in the terrible decade of the Civil War, which registered a loss of nearly 8,000 people, the figures for some counties and many individual towns pointed to the extinction of an entire way of life. Between 1870 and 1900, the population of Carroll County dropped by 437 people, while Sullivan County remained stagnant. The majority of hill towns in Merrimack, Sullivan, Grafton, and Carroll counties declined in population after 1860. Some towns, once regarded as among the most prosperous agricultural centers in the state, showed frightening losses. Gilmanton dwindled from 3,800 people in 1830 to a mere 1,100 in 1900, although some of that loss was attributable to the splitting off of other townships from its territory. Strafford declined from 2,000 in 1860 to half that number in 1900; Nottingham, from 1,300 to 600; Weare, from 2,300 to 1,500.

Despite their rich soils, some of the long-settled towns along the Connecticut River were equally threatened. Piermont, Orford, Lyme, Plainfield, Cornish, and Charlestown all lost high percentages of their populations. Many communities with established villages—prosperous regional centers in the heyday of agriculture—found their former importance diminishing. Effingham, Freedom, New Boston, Sandwich, Warner, Francestown, Dublin, Fitzwilliam, Temple, and New Ipswich were among the many towns whose beautiful and once-thriving centers were no defense against the exodus.[99]

The reversal of New Hampshire's tradition of slow but steady growth elicited many reactions. Some showed the timeless human tendency to blame a decadent present generation for not sustaining the virtues of its forebears. Writing in 1878, the Reverend Elliott C. Cogswell satirized those "men with soft hands and well-trimmed mustache" and those "delicate ladies from city homes" who found the town of Deerfield, formerly one of the most prosperous farming towns in the state, to be "nothing and nowhere, because, forsooth, the railroad does not pass through it with its rumbling roar!"[100]

Others placed the blame less on the effete city dweller than on the New Hampshire farmer himself. In 1870, Alonzo Fogg provided statistics showing that much New Hampshire land actually exceeded that of the West in fertility.[101] In 1889, the *Plymouth Record* spoke of "the farming problem" as rooted in the fact that "the old time farmer has almost ceased to exist among us." Even though the new farmer demanded "pianos, organs, handsome furniture, fine carpets, pictures and engravings," the article claimed, he was unwilling to copy the self-disciplined efficiency of the businessman, whose life he wished to imitate.

In the same year, the *Manchester Mirror* published an article, reprinted by other papers, purportedly written by "An Astonished Westerner." The Westerner registered his amazement at the cheap price at which New Hampshire farmers were willing to sell their inherited lands. The situation, he wrote, "speaks not only of poor farming and poor farmers, but excites wonder that the descendants of those who had the courage and energy to clear the wild lands and destroy the wild beasts . . . should deliberately abandon the homes of their fathers, allow them to become covered with weeds and underbrush, and then offer them for sale for the low price of $1 or $5 an acre!" In agreement with other writers, the Westerner felt that New Hampshire's agricultural problem called mainly for backbone:

> . . . it is foolish for the farmer of New Hampshire or any other locality to desert his post and lose his birthright on the supposition that he can better his condition by going somewhere else. . . . The true way is to buckle on the armor anew, study the situation, ascertain what is needed to restore the fertility of the soil and bring returning prosperity, and then set to work with renewed vigor to do the needed thing. The great fact is that the demands of the hour are for a higher style of farming and a more educated class of farmers.[102]

Steps were taken to meet this need. The New Hampshire College of Agriculture and Mechanic Arts, a land-grant school, was chartered at Hanover in 1866. The legislature reestablished a long-defunct Board of Agriculture in 1870, and beginning in 1872, provided for series of lectures on farming. But while these measures might ensure New Hampshire's most prosperous farms a brighter future, they did nothing to help the hundreds of marginal farms, many of them struggling to survive in the hands of an aging generation whose children had moved away to seek a better life.

The sad, pervading image of this era of New Hampshire's history was the abandoned farm. New Hampshire's self-regard as a land of hardy farming men and women, and of fruitful if rugged hills, was deeply shaken by these changes. In 1889, the legislature created the office of State Commissioner of Immigration, appointing Nahum J. Bachelder of East Andover, already the Commissioner of Agriculture, to the new post. Bachelder's task was to repopulate the deserted farms of New Hampshire, and toward that end he immediately surveyed the extent of abandonment.

The results were not encouraging. In the 160 towns reporting, there were no fewer than 936 abandoned farms which might be reclaimed by quick reoccupation. In addition, half again as many still-occupied farms were then for sale. Some towns, like Canaan, Hillsborough, New Boston, Moultonborough, Sandwich, and Bath, listed between twenty and thirty empty farms within their borders.[103]

No one could fail to see in this situation a portent of widespread disaster. Thousands of acres of abandoned land, paying no revenue, were an immediate threat to the entire governmental structure in a state where most public works were paid for by property taxes. But of far more than local concern was the looming collapse of an entire agricultural civilization, abandoned by its youth and maintained by elderly couples and equally aged hired men. The farmhouse in disrepair alongside neglected, overgrown fields became a pervasive image in New England literature of the late nineteenth century.

All joy, all tragedy of life,
All toil, all suffering, hardship, strife,
And whate'er made New England great,
E'er fed the sinews of our State,
Are writ upon thy crumbling wall,—
Upon thy wall.[104]

Against all of this, there was one hope. Those myriads of tourists who had sought out New Hampshire's healthful food and water, fresh air, and incomparable scenery had developed more than a passing interest in the state. Many of them were ready to return again and again as their time and money might allow, not necessarily to the grand resort hotels, but to humble and wholesome boarding houses where they could enjoy both tranquility and the personal attention of a kindly family. Summer boarders might individually leave only a few dollars with a farming family, but their aggregate contribution to the state's economy was recognized by the 1890s to represent one of New Hampshire's largest sources of income. In 1899, 174,280 summer visitors came to the state, resulting in a direct income to their hosts of $540,000. The total cash they left behind, not including railroad, steamboat, and stage fares, had totaled nearly $5,000,000. All but about thirty of the state's 235 communities had benefited from this newly recognized industry.[105]

New Hampshire quickly adopted strategies to nurture this source of income. In the 1880s, among the first roads to receive state aid for highway improvement, in areas where local government was nonexistent or too poorly funded to undertake the important work, were highways leading to and through the notches of the White Mountains. At the same time, Thomas J. Walker, editor and publisher of the *Plymouth Record*, set an example by using his paper and his fortunate location in the foothills of the mountains to "boom" New Hampshire. Walker believed that "Advertising is what does the business now[a]days and persistent advertising at that."[106] His example was widely commented upon elsewhere in the state. The *Farmington News* admired Walker's efforts, regretting only that the *Record* focused its promotion on a single region of New Hampshire: "Our State is too small to sectionalize and its advantages in its entirety had better be brought forward than to try to lift up any one section at the expense possibly of some other equally as good."[107]

Other papers quickly reinforced Walker's efforts. The *Concord Monitor* editorialized in 1890:

... the most important work to be done is to let people of other states know what attractive places the mountains and hills and valleys of New Hampshire are, and what boundless opportunities for sojourning here pleasantly during the summer months are yet unimproved. For each boarder entertained in the farm houses of the state this season there is room for a hundred, and for each boarding house and small hotel doing a profitable business there is room for ten—perhaps twenty—to do likewise.[108]

The *Monitor* pointed to New London as particularly successful in advertising, crediting the local publication, *Summer Rest*, with having brought no fewer than 1,500 summer boarders to the vicinity of Lake Sunapee in 1890.[109] The late 1800s was a period of intense belief in the value of fresh air and wholesome food as a tonic for world-weary city dwellers whose bodies and minds had been attenuated by their artificial environment. As the *Monitor* proclaimed, "New Hampshire has become one of the great lungs of the public, giving life and strength to the weary and afflicted, yet keeping back enough for her own children. As a joyous traveller once remarked, the Granite State owns an ozone factory that furnishes nerve food for everybody."[110]

Thanks to the railroads, the *Monitor* editor pointed out, the White Mountains had become more easily accessible to Bostonians than they had been twenty years earlier to those living within sight of them. Pursuing the theme of New Hampshire as a place of healing for the city-weakened constitution, the editor saw the urban areas to the south as the source of endless patronage for New Hampshire's life-giving hospitality:

New Hampshire is the map beautiful of the East. It has a thousand sanitariums, large and small, skirting the sea, lurking amid the mountains, or fringing the lakes, all offering rest and quiet, peace and health. The summer work [of promotion] has just begun, and one of these years New Hampshire will be the foremost state of the Atlantic coast, not because it is wealthy or powerful, but because health and innocent pleasure live in her mountains and hills and waters. The estimated money paid by these summer boarders reaches high figures, going among the millions, and yet the state has no harvested charms; nothing has been worn out or lost; the exquisite topography is still here and in many places untouched.[111]

The "booming" of New Hampshire at first emphasized the patronage of the transient boarder, who could be transported from a local depot to a farmhouse or inn and provided with both sustenance and a pleasant environment for his summer vacation. In the spring of 1891, Walker's *Plymouth Record* organized a campaign to send 25,000 specially illustrated copies of the paper to "leading bankers, brokers, merchants, manufacturers, public officers and others who may be attracted to the White Mountains for a summer's pleasure or induced to invest money in our local schemes for development." One advertisement urged readers: "Help! Help! Help! Sound the Tocsin for Summer Boarders. Invite them to the White Mountains. Tell them of the attractions of the Mountains, Lakes and Streams of Northern New Hampshire. Where to find Good Board and what it will cost them."[112]

But not everyone had a taste for the rugged mountain terrain; many were content to spend their vacations at a farm near the coast or amid the fields and ponds and rolling hills of southern New Hampshire. The primary requisites for a successful boarding house seem to have been a spacious

Photograph showing Penacook House, Boscawen, circa 1915. A number of old taverns in favored locations were transformed into popular boarding houses at the turn of the century; still later, in the automobile era, some became tearooms or restaurants. The Penacook House, returning to its former name of the Bonney Tavern, remained popular for its steak and chicken dinners until its demolition in 1937.
Courtesy, Dr. Dorothy M. Vaughan

piazza from which one could enjoy a pleasant view of fields, mountains, or water; good wholesome food—all the better if it was grown on the property; and plenty of shade trees. The state soon had thousands of modest boarding houses where ordinary people sought a summer's rest. Nahum Bachelder of East Andover, Commissioner of Immigration, set an example when he renovated several village homes and built a boarding house, called The Halcyon, on his own property for the entertainment of summer people.[113] The heyday of this movement was best chronicled by former governor Frank West Rollins in his 1902 publication, *The Tourist's Guide-Book to the State of New Hampshire.*

Many old taverns, long abandoned by their traditional clientele, were transformed into boarding houses: Underwood's tavern in Swanzey became the Elm House; Sanderson's tavern in Stoddard, the Central House; Hoyt's tavern in Bridgewater, the Elm Lawn Inn; Drew's tavern in Walpole, the Mountain House; the Penacook House in Boscawen, the Old Bonney Tavern; Hall's tavern in Hooksett, Pinnacle Inn (in recognition of the nearby hill with its observatory); and Harvey's tavern in Northwood, the Harvey House.

But something more was needed if New Hampshire's vast numbers of abandoned farms were ever to return to the tax rolls. The key to rescuing these derelict properties,

as Commissioner of Immigration Nahum J. Bachelder and his successors knew, was to induce summer visitors to become property owners—to convince them to buy and repair old houses across the state either as working farms or as summer homes. Bachelder began his great campaign in 1890 with the publication of a pamphlet whose title summarized his argument: *Secure a Home in New Hampshire, Where Comfort, Health and Prosperity Abound.* Noting that the state offered no less than 1,442 abandoned farms with tenantable buildings, Bachelder emphasized that these properties had not been vacated because the soil had been exhausted or was considered worthless for agriculture. Rather,

> They have become vacated in some instances by the death of the former occupant, who left no children to take up and till the ancestral acres. In other instances the children have sought employment in the neighboring city or village, and have now become engrossed in other business and cannot return. In other cases the owner has accumulated a sufficient property on the farm to invest in a more extensive business than the farm would afford, and the land and the buildings are still there offering equal inducements to the next occupant.

In all cases, "we claim that there is no section of the country where a small investment in a farm will secure more for the purchaser than in one of the vacated farms of New Hampshire."[114]

Bachelder and his successors carried on their publications until after 1920. The original pamphlet was renamed *New Hampshire Farms Available for Farming or Summer Homes*. It was supplemented after 1902 by a larger publication, *New Hampshire Farms for Summer Homes*, skillfully but anonymously edited by Harlan C. Pearson, with essays in praise of New Hampshire's scenery and wholesome life.[115] Other writers blatantly tried to appeal to readers' sentiments, as did the editor of *Granite State Magazine*:

> What bright dreams have arisen above these spots of neglect. What memories center here. . . . Here came the pioneer and his good wife to hew themselves homes out of the cheerless wilderness. He came in the elastic strength of manhood, filled with ambition and hopefulness. She came in the faith of woman's sacrifice of parental ties, giving into the keeping of her husband her beauty, her hopes, her happiness, her young life, her future. Here has rung the childish prattle and the merriment of childish laughter, innocent of guile. Here the fond mother's heart beat quicker as baby lips first uttered that precious name, *mother*![116]

Popular literature of the day aided the cause. In 1900, Helen Albee of New Castle published *Mountain Playmates*, recounting her efforts with her husband, also a writer, to reclaim an abandoned Tamworth farm in the shadow of Mount Chocorua. Beginning in 1907, the persuasive arguments for a simple country life offered by the nationally famous author Ray Stannard Baker, writing under the pseudonym David Grayson, began to captivate New England readers. Taking advantage of this growing sentiment, Governor Frank West Rollins instituted Old Home Week in 1899, with Nahum Bachelder as secretary of the Old Home Week Association. Recognizing that among those most vulnerable to the tug of the old homestead were the children who had left it to "become engrossed in other business," Rollins sought, often successfully, to induce these prosperous natives to repurchase the family farm, or one nearby, as a summer place. Some sixty towns held Old Home Week reunions in 1899 and seventy-two the following year, and the event soon became an institution in many towns.

It was immediately obvious to all who were interested in the welfare of rural New Hampshire that there was one absolute prerequisite to the success of the movement. Without good roads, there could be no hope of inducing people to return to the land. Without good roads, many working farms would remain isolated from any market for their products. Even though New Hampshire saw the development of many local creameries during the late nineteenth century, as well as a network of railroads to transport milk to larger centers, only those farmers who could carry their bulk milk safely and quickly to some market could benefit from this new source of livelihood. Similarly, owners of many old farms found that the second-growth forest on their long-unused fields had matured into a marketable crop, but again, only those who could haul heavy loads of logs to the mill, or sawn boards to a buyer, could benefit from this opportunity for new income. New Hampshire also saw a resurgence of interest in apple orchards during the late 1800s, with apples now marketable as whole fruit rather than merely as raw material for hard cider for local consumption, but even those growers willing to plant orchards of choice grafted trees were wasting their time and money if they could not carry their wagon-loads of barrels to market.

Americans had long known, in theory, how to build good roads. Rees' *Cyclopaedia*, an English publication reprinted in Philadelphia between 1810 and 1824, contained a 23,000-word essay on road-building which was virtually a manual of the most advanced British theory on the subject. The turnpike era had provided practical experience with diverse terrain. American engineers published many books and articles on the subject before 1850, notably Bloodgood's *Treatise on Roads* (1838) and W. M. Gillespie's *A Manual of the Principles and Practice of Road-Making* (1847). Readers in the United States were familiar with the two major British systems of road construction, the first developed by Thomas Telford, in which a highway surface of broken rock was underlaid with a bed of large, closely laid stones, and the other by John Loudon McAdam, in which a well-rolled layer of crushed stone was laid over the local gravel without an underlying pavement.

The problem of both British road types was their expense. As long as stone had to be broken by men with hammers, labor costs were prohibitive except where convicts were employed in the work. If a proper stone could not be obtained locally, its transportation was costly. If roads could be prepared and maintained only with picks, shovels, hoes, and horse-drawn plows and scrapers, the work was too inefficient for the vast distances of the United States. If only horse-drawn rollers, having a maximum weight of less than ten tons, were available to compact the road surface, a solid bed could be obtained only on limited lengths of highway.

Technical advances soon led to the improvement of roads, whether stone roads of the McAdam and Telford types or the traditional New Hampshire road of native gravel. The first advance was the development after the Civil War of the relatively inexpensive "road machine," a horse-drawn grader. With large steel blades adjustable to any height or angle, these vehicles could do the work of many men, plows, and scrapers in pulling trampled road material from the ditches to the center of the highway, in filling wheel ruts and rough horse tracks, and in building a perfect crown on a road. The excellent results achieved with one such machine, called Fisher's Road Machine, invented in Walpole and manufactured in Keene, were described glowingly by the selectmen of Newport: "It does good business on rough as well as smooth roads, usually turnpiking from one to two and one half miles per day,

Photograph of a four-horse road machine in use in Weare, N.H., circa 1890. The road machine, a grader drawn by horses or oxen, offered a marked advance in gravel-road maintenance in the late nineteenth century. By pulling loose and trampled road material to the center of the highway, the adjustable blade of the machine re-crowned roads rapidly and with far less labor than with the older method of using horse-drawn scoops and teams of men with shovels.

Courtesy, George Hollis

leaving the road in much better condition than the old method, smoother, more even, and *made all the way.*"[117]

The second major advance leading to highway improvement was the development of portable steam machinery. Rock crushers became increasingly available and affordable following the Civil War, offering the realistic possibility in more prosperous towns of the construction of stone roads of the best type. Many towns found, too, that they could afford to rent or buy a steam roller, a ponderous machine often weighing twenty tons and capable not only of making McAdam (soon referred to as macadam) roads but of rendering ordinary gravel roads far harder and more permanent.

One of the first protagonists of good roads in New Hampshire was *Plymouth Record* publisher and editor Thomas J. Walker. By the late 1880s, Walker was filling nearly every issue of his paper with straightforward pleas for road improvement, with historical and technical articles on road building, with articles by civil engineers from other states with more advanced road programs, and with persuasive arguments for the role of roads in New Hampshire's new campaign for increased summer boarders and for the reclamation of abandoned farms. As a tireless anthologist of nearly every article or speech written on the subject of highway improvement in the eastern United States, Walker was one of the most influential forces in the early years of New Hampshire's campaign to pull itself

FISHER'S ROAD MACHINE.

CHARLES FISHER, Pat'ee,   Manuf'dby Humphrey Machine Co.,
Walpole, N. H.   Keene, N. H.

Wood engraving from advertising brochure for Fisher's Road Machine, patented in 1874 by Charles Fisher of Walpole, N.H., and manufactured by Humphrey Machine Co., Keene, N.H.; brochure printed by Charles C. Davis, circa 1875. This lightweight, three-wheel machine, drawn by "two good heavy yoke of cattle or their equivalent," gained popularity throughout New Hampshire. One customer exclaimed: "We are satisfied that your machine will change the whole system of repairing, and give us good turnpiked highways that we shall take pride in riding over."

NHHS Collections   Photographer, Ernest Gould

Photograph of an ox-drawn road machine in the vicinity of Plymouth, N.H., circa 1900. The four yoke of oxen attached to this four-wheel grader are indicative of the motive power needed for larger road machines. Such machines had a seat used by a driver when pulled by horses, but required men with goads when pulled by cattle; a man on the machine guided the blade in either case.
NHHS Collections

Photograph of gravel sorter, probably Hopkinton, N.H., circa 1905. Usually powered by a portable steam engine, gravel-sorting machines lifted road material to the top by conveyor belt; there, it passed through rotating tubular screens of varying sizes and fell into bins from which a wagon could be filled in two to five minutes. This sorter appears to be fed by a steam-powered rock crusher at the right, into which men may be dropping stones from a nearby wall. The steam engine is not shown.
Courtesy, New Hampshire Antiquarian Society
  Photographer, Leown H. Kelley

from the mire of bad roads. In 1890, for example, Walker published statistics showing that a pulling force of 200 pounds was required to move one ton over a "common earth road," while the same load could be pulled with only 46 pounds of tractive effort on a well-rolled macadam highway. He then quoted from a report by the United States Department of Agriculture in terms that any farmer or selectman could understand:

> By the improvement of these common roads . . . every article brought to market would be diminished in price, the number of horses necessary as motive power would be reduced, and . . . the thousands of acres of land . . . now wasted in feeding unnecessary animals in order to carry on this character of transportation, would be devoted to the production of food for the inhabitants of the country.[118]

Walker's task was made far easier by the fact that the "Good Roads" movement had become a national phenomenon of concern to individual states, to the federal government, and to special-interest groups. Chief among the latter was the League of American Wheelmen, a national fraternity of bicyclists who lobbied hard and successfully for roads that would not pitch them headlong over the handlebars of their high-wheeled machines. Founded in 1880, the League began to publish *Good Roads Magazine* in 1892.[119] The introduction in the 1880s of the "safety" bicycle, with its chain drive and two wheels of equal size, made cycling

Photograph of the Concord Wheel Club in front of Hannibal Bonney's tavern, Penacook (Boscawen), N.H., 1888. The national League of American Wheelmen and local bicycle clubs became strong advocates of the Good Roads movement in the late nineteenth century. The movement gained considerable strength after the high-wheeled ''standard'' bicycle was superseded by the low-wheeled ''safety'' bicycle.

NHHS Collections

a sport for long-skirted women as well as men, and the bicycle lobby gained in economic power and influence. It was no accident that Walker's paper frequently contained bicycle advertisements alongside editorials for highway improvement. Nor was it coincidental that Walker found some of his best arguments in the writings of Colonel Albert A. Pope of Boston. Pope, who proposed and endowed a course in highway engineering at the Massachusetts Institute of Technology in 1890, was also America's leading bicycle manufacturer, the developer of the famous Columbia bicycle, one of the best in the world, and the founder of the Good Roads campaign of the League of American Wheelmen.[120]

By the 1890s, because of the efforts of many progressive minds focused on the single problem of road building, New Hampshire was beginning to catch up with more prosperous states. In 1891, attorney and historian Albert Stillman Batchellor of Littleton, recently appointed as editor of the *New Hampshire State Papers*, showed himself to be practi-

cal as well as scholarly when he proposed that the New Hampshire College of Agriculture and the Mechanic Arts, about to move from Hanover to Durham, institute a department for ''scientific instruction in road making.''[121] Batchellor's idea soon took form in the work of the Agricultural Experiment Station in Durham, which began to issue useful bulletins on road-making.[122]

Beginning in 1897, the New Hampshire Board of Agriculture began to hold Good Roads institutes in various parts of the state. The papers presented at these conferences were uniformly practical, based less on theory than on experience and aimed directly at the realities faced by New Hampshire selectmen and road agents. Several, indeed, focused on the knotty problem of finding and keeping good road agents in every town. Many dealt with the great bane of New Hampshire roads, springtime mud, demonstrating its reduction through proper drainage by culverts rather than by the all-too-common waterbar or ''thank-you-ma'am''—a V-shaped ditch and ridge to shed water on

Series of three photographs showing the construction of a Telford road, Main Street, Durham, N.H., 1895. In 1895, Charles H. Pettee of the New Hampshire College of Agriculture and Mechanic Arts used Durham's Main Street near the Agricultural Experiment Station for a demonstration of the laying of a Telford base of large stones, covered with a pavement of crushed stone. The experiment was intended to show farmers and rural road agents that urban methods of paving were practical on country roads.

Courtesy, U.N.H. Collection—Media Services

Photograph of snow roller, Jackson, N.H., 1925. Country roads had long been ''broken out'' with teams of cattle and horses, often pulling a log drag to smooth the surface. Beginning in the late 1800s, many New Hampshire towns began to pack snow-covered roads with large, horse-drawn wooden rollers, providing a hard and compact surface for sleighs and pungs.

Courtesy, Winston Pote   Photographer, Winston Pote

downhill slopes. Other reports recognized that macadam roads would long be beyond the reach of many towns, and dealt in a practical way with road improvements using local gravel and horse-drawn equipment. One paper by Professor John D. Quackenbos of New York, a summer resident of New Hampshire and lifelong friend of Nahum Bachelder, was entitled "The Aesthetic Side of Farm Life." Perhaps heard more sympathetically by other summer people than by native farmers, the paper described one highway problem that was already out of hand by 1900:

> Ruthless advertisers, in deliberate contempt of our feelings and our property rights in the scenery, are everywhere disfiguring the face of nature with the flaring placards of nostrum proprietors, dry goods and hardware dealers, agents for farm machinery. Huge field boards intercept the most inspiring views with disgusting portraitures in color of stage and circus brutalities; barn-sides, painted black, proclaim in colossal saffron letters the virtues of . . . sarsaparilla; and

every fence rail commends to the passer-by the comforts of Duchess trousers or the sedative effects of L. M. Cough Drops. Time was when the scenery and the outlook needed no protection; now there exists an organized intent to destroy both—the inalienable birthright of the community, with the object of adding to the gains of a handful of traders.[123]

The concerted efforts of individuals and groups had its effect shortly after 1900. Since the mid-1800s, the State of New Hampshire had made occasional appropriations for the improvement of individual highways, especially in the White Mountains. Most legislators, however, had felt that highway improvements should rest with individual towns, as they had since the provincial period. In 1903, however, with Nahum J. Bachelder as governor, the legislature passed two laws which radically changed the state's relationship with highway improvements. These laws created the new post of state highway engineer, called for a general highway survey of the entire state, designated certain

Photograph, "The Arrival at Twin Rivers: The Governor and the Commissioners Inspecting the Southern Division of the Jefferson Notch Highway," 1901. The Jefferson Notch Highway, running north from the Crawford House at Crawford Notch to the town of Jefferson, was built with state funds to provide easy travel between two White Mountain resort areas. In November 1901, Governor Chester B. Jordan and his party inspected the southern section of the road in a mountain wagon pulled by six horses and driven by "several old-time stage drivers."

NHHS Collections   Photographer, probably Walter R. Merryman

roads as state highways, and prepared the way for a bill at the next legislative session which would detail the methods by which the state would construct roads in its own right or in partnership with towns.[124] In keeping with precedent, the first state highways were in the region of the White Mountains, part of which was about to be designated in 1911 a National Forest under an act introduced by Senator John Wingate Weeks, a native of Lancaster.

The first engineer appointed by Governor Bachelder and Council was John W. Storrs of Concord. A man of vision who later became a leading designer of steel truss bridges, Storrs immediately proposed a system of three "trunk line" state highways to run from the Massachusetts border in the Piscataqua, Merrimack, and Connecticut river valleys and converge on the White Mountains. Storrs' system was intended to establish three major points of entry to New

Hampshire, providing both access to the mountains and arteries of commerce between the major towns and cities in the southern part of the state.

Storrs advocated state acquisition of the major private toll bridges, especially several that crossed the Connecticut River, and he urged their replacement with steel spans. He predicted that state improvements to roads would encourage heavier loads, and that many of the old wooden bridges would be unable to bear the weight of the new traffic. Even as early as 1905, Storrs predicted a new challenge both to road surfaces and to bridges: the automobile. "The impact caused by automobiles is a serious strain on bridges, the effect being similar to that of a train of [railroad] cars," he noted. "This will prove a new factor that must be taken into consideration by town officials, who must see to it that bridges are constructed on a sufficiently scientific basis to

Photograph, "Opening of the New State Highway over the Jefferson Notch Pass," 1902. Costing about $10,000, the Jefferson Notch Highway was completed and inspected by Governor Jordan in September 1902, opening a "route at once convenient for public traffic and a delightful drive for tourists." Governor and Council rode to the summit of Jefferson Notch in a mountain wagon driven by Ethan A. Crawford III, builder of the northern section of the road and descendant of Abel Crawford. There they were met by a "cavalcade of ladies and gentlemen" on horseback, shown here.

NHHS Collections   Photographer, probably Walter R. Merryman

meet the conditions created by it and the additional weights of the increased loads."[125]

As required by one of the laws of 1903, a bill was introduced in 1905 elaborating upon the new system of state roads and state aid to towns. The bill became law under Governor John McLane. The new law established regular state highway appropriations which were shared with towns in proportion to amounts they were required to raise locally. The law reaffirmed the state's commitment to a system of state roads. Soon after, the state commenced development of the first of several systems of "trunk line" highways—wide, well-surfaced, state-owned roads running from village to village and connecting with village

roads similarly improved through financial aid from the state. By 1911, the state highway department had experimented with bituminous macadam, an early form of asphalt pavement which was found to be necessary to prevent damage from the rubber tires of an ever-increasing number of automobiles.

By the turn of the twentieth century, New Hampshire was poised to enter the age of paved roads, steel bridges, and the automobile. Much remained from the past, yet much was changed. Old habits, old institutions, and old conditions melted away as the state entered a new century. A few of those who looked to the future with confidence paused a while to acknowledge that the way of life of their

Photograph, Cheshire Bridge, Charlestown, N.H., 1896. Even before the advent of the automobile, increased highway loads required the replacement of old, weakened wooden bridges with scientifically designed steel spans. This photograph shows the dismantling of the Town lattice bridge at Charlestown, with one section of the new steel truss, built at a cost of $65,000, in the distance.

NHHS Collections

Photograph, Livermore Falls Bridge, Campton, N.H., 1895. Civil engineers of the late nineteenth century had perfected many light yet strong iron and steel truss types, preparing the way for increased highway loads after 1900. The rugged gorge at Livermore Falls on the Pemigewasset River was spanned by one of the most impressive bridges in New Hampshire, a double lenticular truss carrying the highway deck above a supporting framework of wrought iron. The bridge was built in 1885 by the Berlin Iron Bridge Company of East Berlin, Connecticut.

NHHS Collections   Photographer, Edward A. Richardson

Photograph, Crawford House, Crawford Notch, N.H., 1909. In 1904, the first "Climb to the Clouds" proved that many types of automobiles had the capability to climb the Mount Washington Summit Road. The following year, Boston automobile-enthusiast Charles J. Glidden instituted the first "Glidden Tour" of the American Automobile Association, also including a climb of Mount Washington in the itinerary. By 1910, the automobile was becoming a common sight at grand White Mountain hotels, proving that the motor age was here to stay.

NHHS Collections

Photograph of steam automobile at the residence of Richard Gove, Laconia, N.H., (detail), circa 1880. Several New Hampshire inventors experimented with horseless carriages in the late nineteenth century. This steam-powered vehicle was built by Enos Merrill Clough of Springfield, N.H., in 1869, and was later bought by Richard Gove, a wealthy jeweler of Laconia.

Courtesy, Laconia Public Library

parents and grandparents would soon be as irretrievably lost as the people who had lived that life. The quaint reminders of that way of life—the old taverns and stables, the milestones and guideposts along the road, the abandoned highways leading nowhere—would be mere curiosities to a generation that would never guess the labor, the sacrifice, and the pride that had once suffused these now useless relics of a vanished society.

In 1903, Henry McFarland of Concord said his own farewell to a way of life:

> Seven hundred travellers' horses can no longer find nightly shelter in our tavern stables. The last of the old stagemen, who not many months ago gave us a page of his recollections, has gone to the country whence no traveller returns. The portly landlord no longer stands in Macgregor's place and carves the roast. The bar where decanters stood in as plain sight as were the andirons on the hearth is banished. . . . If one could find the shelter of the old Eagle Coffee House, it would be proper now to select a pair of sheepskin slippers from the public supply in the half-open bar-room drawer, light a candle, and go quietly to bed.[126]

Footnotes

CHAPTER 1
The Tavern in Society

1. Anthony Trollope, *North America* (New York: Harper & Bros., 1862), p. 552.

2. Jeremy Belknap, *The History of New-Hampshire*, 2d ed., vol. 3, ed. with an Introduction by G. T. Lord (Dover, N.H.: O. Crosby & J. Varney, 1812; reprint ed., Hampton, N.H.: Peter E. Randall, 1973), p. 251.

3. Joseph B. Walker, "Penacook House and the Old Time Taverns of the State," *Proceedings of the New Hampshire Historical Society*, 1 (1872-88):389; Duke de La Rochefoucault-Liancourt, *Travels through the United States of North America, The Country of the Iroquois and Upper Canada in the Years 1795, 1796, and 1797, with an Authentic Account of Lower Canada* (London: R. Phillips, 1799; American Culture Series 2, reel 192.1, Ann Arbor, Mich.: University Microfilms, n.d.), p. 53.

4. New Hampshire, [*Provincial and State Papers*], 40 vols. (Concord: State of New Hampshire, 1867-1943), 12:444-45 (hereafter cited as *NHPP*).

5. Ibid., 21.26.

6. Ibid., 12:674.

7. Kenneth Scott, "Colonial Innkeepers of New Hampshire," *Historical New Hampshire* 19 (Spring 1964):21, citing petition from Exeter selectmen.

8. *NHPP*, 3:620.

9. Scott, "Colonial Innkeepers," pp. 18 and 27-28; *NHPP*, 3:717 and 719, 12:444-45, 13:274-75.

10. Based on statistical tables in John Farmer and Jacob B. Moore, *A Gazetteer of the State of New-Hampshire* (Concord: Jacob B. Moore, 1823), pp. 50-63.

11. Scott, "Colonial Innkeepers," pp. 14, 20, and 30; *Portsmouth Journal*, April 26, 1823; *Farmer's Cabinet* (Amherst), May 8, 1810.

12. Scott, "Colonial Innkeepers," pp. 38 and 47; *The Vade Mecum for America, or a Companion for Traders and Travellers* (Boston: D. Henchman, 1732), p. 195; New Hampshire, Laws, May 6, 1708, "Orders, Resolves, and Votes of Legislative Nature Passed During This Session, [1708]"; *NHPP*, 32:632.

13. Scott, "Colonial Innkeepers," pp. 15, 35, and 47.

14. *NHPP*, 12:673-74.

15. *New-Hampshire Gazette* (Portsmouth), October 22, 1805.

16. Scott, "Colonial Innkeepers," p. 24.

17. Ibid., p. 22.

18. Ibid., p. 35.

19. *New Hampshire Sentinel* (Keene), October 26, 1816; *Portsmouth Journal*, October 13, 1821; and *Dartmouth Gazette* (Hanover), August 22, 1801.

20. P. Stansbury, *A Pedestrian Tour of Two Thousand Three Hundred Miles in North America to the Lakes, the Canadas, and the New-England States Performed in the Autumn of 1821* (New York: J. D. Myers & W. Smith, 1822), p. 247.

21. Scott, "Colonial Innkeepers," pp. 11 and 41.

22. Ibid., p. 25.

23. Ibid., pp. 11, 17, 22, 30, and 36.

24. Tavern license granted to Richard Abbot of New Castle, 1683, New Hampshire Historical Society, Miscellaneous Manuscripts, V16A-15; bond acknowledged by Richard Webber of Portsmouth, 1683 (privately owned).

25. *The Colonial Laws of Massachusetts Reprinted from the Edition of 1672 with the Supplements through 1686* (Boston: By Order of the City Council, 1887), p. 80.

26. *NHPP*, 3:818.

27. New Hampshire, Laws, January 6, 1715/16, chapter 2.

28. Scott, "Colonial Innkeepers," pp. 15 and 45.

29. *The New Hampshire Register and United States Calendar with an Ephemeris for the Year of Our Lord 1812* (Exeter, N.H.: C. Norris & Co., [1812]), p. 32.

30. Abbie L. Phelps, comp. and ed., *Historic New Ipswich: A Collection of Papers Written for the Historical Society of New Ipswich, New Hampshire, and Read at Society Meetings* (Milford, N.H.: Cabinet Press, 1936), pp. 45-46; A. Allen, *Allen's New England Almanack for 1821*, Hartford, reprinted in Seymour Dunbar, *A History of Travel in America*, 4 vols. (Indianapolis: Bobbs-Merrill Co., 1915), 1:213.

31. Timothy Dwight, *Travels in New England and New York*, ed. Barbara Miller Solomon with the assistance of Patricia M. King, new ed., 1st pub. 1821-22, 4 vols. (Cambridge: Harvard University Press, Belknap Press, 1969), 2:170.

32. J. P. Brissot de Warville, *New Travels in the United States of America, 1788*, trans. Mara Soceanu Vamos and Durand Echeverria, ed. Durand Echeverria (Cambridge: Harvard University Press, Belknap Press, 1964), p. 368; William Bentley, *The Diary of William Bentley, D.D., Pastor of the East Church, Salem, Massachusetts*, 4 vols. (Salem, Mass.: Essex Institute, 1907-14), 2:390.

33. Anne Royall, *The Black Book, or a Continuation of Travels in the United States*, 3 vols. (Washington, D.C.: By the Author, 1828-29), 2:354.

34. Timothy Dwight, *Travels*, 2:96.

35. La Rochefoucault-Liancourt, *Travels through the United States,* in *Two Centuries of Travel in Essex County, Massachusetts: A Collection of Narratives and Observations Made by Travelers, 1605-1799,* comp. George Francis Dow (Topsfield, Mass.: Topsfield Historical Society, 1921), p. 178; Luigi Castiglioni, *Luigi Castiglioni's Viaggio: Travels in the United States of North America, 1785-87,* trans. and ed. Antonio Pace (Syracuse, N.Y.: Syracuse University Press, 1983), p. 121.

36. Isabella Lucy Bird, *The Englishwoman in America,* with a Foreword by Andrew Hill Clark (London: John Murray, 1856; reprint ed., Madison: University of Wisconsin Press, 1966), p. 99; Frederick Marryat, *A Diary in America with Remarks on Its Institutions,* ed. with an Introduction by Sydney Jackman, new ed., 1st pub. 1839 (New York: Alfred A. Knopf, 1962), p. 374.

37. James Fenimore Cooper, *Notions of the Americans Picked up by a Travelling Bachelor,* with an Introduction by Robert E. Spiller, 2 vols. (London: H. Colburn, 1828; reprint ed., New York: Frederick Ungar Publishing Co., 1963), 1:68.

38. Julian Ursyn Niemcewicz, *Under Their Vine and Fig Tree: Travels through America in 1797-1799, 1805 with Some Further Account of Life in New Jersey,* trans. and ed. with an Introduction by Metchie J. E. Budka (Elizabeth, N.J.: Grassman Publishing Co., 1965), p. 161.

39. Timothy Dwight, *Travels,* 4:250.

40. Lavinia Bailey Kelly, Diary, John Kelly Papers, New Hampshire Historical Society.

41. New Hampshire, Laws, October 11, 1680-81, "General Laws," article 39; January 6, 1715/16, chapter 2; June 18, 1686, chapter 17; June 14, 1791, chapter 6.

42. John Wentworth to Eleazar Wheelock, February 19, 1774, in Frederick Chase, *A History of Dartmouth College and the Town of Hanover, New Hampshire,* ed. John K. Lord (Cambridge, Mass.: John Wilson & Son, University Press, 1891), pp. 264-65.

43. John King Lord, *A History of Dartmouth College, 1815-1909: Being the Second Volume of A History of Dartmouth College and the Town of Hanover, New Hampshire, Begun by Frederick Chase* (Concord, N.H.: Rumford Press, 1913), pp. 267-68, 282-83, 592, citing College Laws; Stansbury, *Pedestrian Tour,* p. 243.

44. New Hampshire, Laws, March 16, 1679, "Criminal Laws," article 22.

45. Ibid., May 2, 1719, chapter 11.

46. Ibid., June 14, 1791, chapter 6, as printed in *New-Hampshire Gazette,* April 30, 1816.

47. New Hampshire, Laws, January 6, 1715/16, chapter 2.

48. Ibid., November 14, 1682, chapter 1, article 10; July 19, 1700, chapter 3; January 6, 1715/16, chapter 2.

49. Scott, "Colonial Innkeepers," p. 34.

50. New Hampshire, Laws, July 19, 1700, chapter 3.

51. David McClure, *Diary of David McClure, Doctor of Divinity, 1748-1820,* with Notes by Franklin B. Dexter (New York: Knickerbocker Press, 1899), p. 144; "Journal of Colonel Alexander Harvey of Scotland and Barnet, Vermont," *Proceedings of the Vermont Historical Society,* 1921-23, p. 223.

52. *NHPP,* 12:478, 551, 13:150-51 and 715-18.

53. see *Portsmouth Journal,* January 14, 1826; New Hampshire, Laws, December 23, 1842, chapter 118; Trollope, *North America,* p. 40.

54. New Hampshire, Laws, December 15, 1797, chapter 21.

55. William Little, *History of the Town of Warren, N.H. From Its Early Settlement to the Year 1854* (Concord, N.H.: McFarland & Jenks, 1854), p. 82.

56. New Hampshire, Laws, May 14, 1718, chapter 40.

57. Ibid., January 22, 1766, chapter 15.

58. *NHPP,* 8:500; New Hampshire, Laws, January 12, 1787, chapter 25.

59. New Hampshire, Laws, March 3, 1753, chapter 2 and January 14, 1772, chapter 8; broadside requiring tavernkeepers to render account, 1775, New Hampshire Historical Society.

60. New Hampshire Province Treasury Records, 1762—"The Account of Payments of Excise by Tavernkeepers & Innholders to George Jaffrey Receiver of Excise from September 1760 to September 1761," New Hampshire Division of Records Management and Archives.

61. *NHPP,* 17:758, 3:818.

62. New Hampshire, Laws, December 26, 1778, chapter 2.

63. Ibid., January 6, 1715/16, chapter 2.

64. C. C. Benton, "The Lafayette Hotel, with Memories of Earlier Days," *Granite State Free Press* (Lebanon), November 24, 1871, included in Allan Burritt Downs, comp., "Reminiscences of Lebanon," 1935 (typewritten), pp. 12-13.

65. Alexander Hamilton, *Gentleman's Progress: The Itinerarium of Dr. Alexander Hamilton, 1744,* ed. with an Introduction by Carl Bridenbaugh (Chapel Hill: University of North Carolina Press for the Institute of Early American History and Culture, 1948), p. 125.

66. *New-Hampshire Gazette,* July 19, 1771.

67. Charles J. Fox, *History of the Old Township of Dunstable Including Nashua, Nashville, Hollis, Hudson, Litchfield, and Merrimac, N.H.; Dunstable and Tyngsborough, Mass.* (Nashua, N.H.: Charles T. Gill, 1846), p. 270; Warren Brown, *History of the Town of Hampton Falls, New Hampshire, from the Time of the First Settlement within Its Borders, 1640 until 1900,* 2 vols. (Manchester, N.H.: John B. Clarke Co., 1900-1918), 1:402-3; S. G. Griffin, *A History of the Town of Keene from 1732, When the Township Was Granted by Massachusetts, to 1874, When It Became a City* (Keene, N.H.: Sentinel Printing Co., 1904), p. 292; Emma P. Boylston Locke, comp., *Colonial Amherst: The Early History, Customs, and Homes* (Milford, N.H.: W. B. & A. B. Rotch, 1916), p. 36.

68. Moultonborough Town Records, 2 vols. (microfilm, New Hampshire State Library), 2:487-90, 495, 507-11, 517, 522-23, 528-30, 536, 538, 553-54, 558, 616, 635-36, 677-78, 683, 696, 699; Milton Town Records, 2 vols. (microfilm, New Hampshire State Library), 2:130, 183, 185-86, 198-99; *The Records of the Town of Hanover, New Hampshire, 1761-1818* (Hanover, N.H.: By the Town, 1905), pp. 267-68.

69. *New-Hampshire Gazette,* September 1, 1801.

70. Gerald D. Foss, *Three Centuries of Freemasonry in New Hampshire* (Concord, N.H.: Grand Lodge of New Hampshire, 1972), pp. 44-45, 96; Charles W. Brewster, *Rambles About Portsmouth: Sketches of Persons, Localities, and Incidents of Two Centuries, Principally from Tradition and Unpublished Documents* (Portsmouth, N.H.: C. W. Brewster & Son, 1859), 1st ser., pp. 311-12; Raymond A. Brighton, *They Came to Fish: A Brief Look at Portsmouth's 350 Years of History,* 2 vols. (Portsmouth, N.H.: Portsmouth 350, Inc., 1973), 2:46-47, 67; and Gerald D. Foss, "The Globe Tavern, Portsmouth Plains," *St. John's Lodge No. 1 Trestle Board,* January 1986, p. 4.

71. *Proceedings of the Grand Lodge of New-Hampshire from July 8, 5789 [1789] to June 8, 5841 [1841], Inclusive* (Concord, N.H.: McFarland and Jenks, 1860), p. 76.

72. Ibid., pp. 101, 119, 131, 160.

73. Ibid., p. 113.

74. Ibid., pp. 138-39.

75. "Records of the Proprietors' Meetings," NHPP, 29:403-644, passim.

76. New-Hampshire Gazette, January 22, 1800 (First Turnpike); Farmer's Cabinet (Amherst), August 28, 1810 (Second); New-Hampshire Gazette, January 16, 1810 (Fourth); August 21, 1810 (Jefferson), July 3, 1810 (Dover), July 2, 1793, June 13, 1794 (Piscataqua Bridge); Federal Mirror (Concord), May 31, 1796 (Concord Bridge); New-Hampshire Gazette, July 1, 1800 (New Castle Bridge).

77. Farmer's Cabinet (Amherst), January 16, 1810, February 13, 1810, April 17, 1810, December 11, 1810; B. T. Whitehouse, comp., " 'Dover Cotton Factory' No. 1," Granite Chips, no. 2 (n.d.), p. 1.

78. New-Hampshire Gazette, October 22, 1805.

79. Portsmouth Town Records (microfilm, New Hampshire State Library), 18:535, 550, 552, 696, 706, 712, 791; 19:5, 192, 199, 305.

80. Daniel J. Smith, Rambles About the Dover Area, 1623-1973 (Lexington, Mass.: Hancock Press, 1973), p. 44; Griffin, History of Keene, p. 348; Farmer's Cabinet (Amherst), March 27, 1810; New Hampshire Statesman (Concord), December 22, 1823.

81. Griffin, History of Keene, pp. 155-56.

82. Records of the New Hampshire Medical Society (Concord, N.H.: By the Society, 1911), pp. 7, 10, 33, 40, 56-57, 95; New-Hampshire Gazette, April 13, 1801, January 16, 1810; Farmer's Cabinet (Amherst), January 16, 1810; New Hampshire Statesman (Concord), September 15, 1823.

83. New Hampshire Historical Society, Minutes, 1:4 and 21.

84. New Hampshire Statesman (Concord), September 15, 1823.

85. Belknap, History, 3:198.

86. New-Hampshire Gazette, August 26, 1774.

87. Nathaniel Bouton, The History of Concord from Its First Grant in 1725 to the Organization of the City Government in 1853 (Concord, N.H.: Benning W. Sanborn, 1856), p. 404.

88. James O. Lyford, ed., History of Concord, New Hampshire, from the Original Grant in Seventeen Hundred and Twenty-five to the Opening of the Twentieth Century, 2 vols. (Concord, N.H.: Rumford Press, 1903), 2:856.

89. Allan Forbes and Ralph M. Eastman, Taverns and Stagecoaches of New England, 2 vols. (Boston: State Street Trust Co., 1953-54), 1:29-38.

90. New-Hampshire Gazette, June 3, 1800.

91. Ibid., November 21, 1766; September 8, 1769.

92. Ibid., April 13, 1841.

93. Ibid., November 3, 1769; November 10, 1769.

94. NHPP, 13:276-77.

95. George B. Bryan, "As the Actors Saw Us: John Durang, John Bernard, and Tyrone Power on Vermonters and Their Neighbors," Vermont History 54 (Spring 1986): 93-94; B. T. Whitehouse, " 'Dover Cotton Factory,' " p. 4; Griffin, History of Keene, p. 384; Bouton, History of Concord, p. 403; Lyford, History of Concord, 2:861.

96. Bouton, History of Concord, p. 321; Lyford, History of Concord, 2:855.

97. William Allen Wallace, The History of Canaan, New Hampshire (Concord, N.H.: Rumford Press, 1910), p. 150.

98. Griffin, History of Keene, p. 276.

99. C. C. Lord, Life and Times in Hopkinton, N.H. (Concord, N.H.: Republican Press Association, 1890), p. 258.

100. New-Hampshire Gazette, May 1, 1767; September 11, 1772.

101. Ibid., February 29, 1760; May 3, 1771.

102. Ibid., September 29, 1801; December 29, 1801; April 24, 1810.

103. New Hampshire Province Treasury Records, 1761, New Hampshire Division of Records Management and Archives.

104. W. R. Cochrane and George K. Wood, History of Francestown, N.H. (Nashua, N.H.: James H. Barker, 1895), p. 159.

105. New-Hampshire Patriot (Concord), July 17, 1810, quoted in David A. Bundy, 100 Acres More or Less: The History of the Land and People of Bow, N.H. (Canaan, N.H.: Bow Town History Committee, 1975), pp. 176-77.

106. NHPP, 9:345-47.

107. New-Hampshire Gazette, April 9, 1762.

108. Peter L. Hoyt, Hoyt's History of Wentworth, New Hampshire, transcribed from original manuscript by Frances A. Muzzey (Littleton, N.H.: Courier Printing Co., 1976), p. 326.

109. Farmer's Cabinet (Amherst), December 16, 1806.

110. New-Hampshire Gazette, August 21, 1761; November 20, 1761; December 4, 1761.

CHAPTER 2
The Tavern Building

1. New Hampshire Province Probate Records, New Hampshire Division of Records Management and Archives, 3:73-74.

2. Records and Files of the Quarterly Courts of Essex County, Massachusetts, 8 vols. (Salem, Mass.: Essex Institute, 1911-21), 6:432.

3. Warren Brown, History of the Town of Hampton Falls, New Hampshire, from the Time of the First Settlement within Its Borders, 1640 until 1900, 2 vols. (Manchester, N.H.: John B. Clarke Co., 1900-1918), 1:403-5.

4. James Leo Garvin, "Academic Architecture and the Building Trades in the Piscataqua Region of New Hampshire and Maine, 1715-1815" (Ph.D. dissertation, Boston University, 1983), pp. 28-29.

5. New Hampshire Province Court Records, New Hampshire Division of Records Management and Archives, 18234-35.

6. Ibid., 13202.

7. Thomas Packer to John Jackson, May 11, 1764, New Hampshire Historical Society, Miscellaneous Manuscripts, 17B-30.

8. William Bentley, The Diary of William Bentley, D.D., Pastor of the East Church, Salem, Massachusetts, 4 vols. (Salem, Mass.: Essex Institute, 1907-14), 1:64; New-Hampshire Gazette (Portsmouth), November 18, 1786.

9. Henry Tufts, The Autobiography of a Criminal, ed. with an Introduction by Edmund Pearson, new ed., 1st pub. 1807, Dover, N.H. (New York: Duffield & Co., 1930), p. 98.

10. John Adams, Diary and Autobiography of John Adams, ed. L. H. Butterfield, 4 vols. (Cambridge: Harvard University Press, Belknap Press, 1961), 1:359-60.

11. New-Hampshire Gazette, January 19, 1833.

12. New Hampshire Province Court Records, 25751.

13. Peter Livius, Copy-Book, New Hampshire Historical Society, p. 29.

14. Rockingham County Probate Records, docket no. 4586.

15. Ibid., docket no. 6384.

16. Francisco de Miranda, *The New Democracy in America: Travels of Francisco de Miranda in the United States, 1783-84*, trans. Judson P. Wood, ed. John S. Ezell (Norman: University of Oklahoma Press, 1963), p. 179; John Adams, *Diary*, 1:359.

17. Duke de La Rochefoucault-Liancourt, *Travels through the United States of North America, The Country of the Iroquois and Upper Canada in the Years 1795, 1796, and 1797, with an Authentic Account of Lower Canada* (London: R. Phillips, 1799; American Culture Series 2, reel 192.1, Ann Arbor, Mich.: University Microfilms, n.d.), p. 464.

18. Jeremy Belknap, *The History of New-Hampshire*, 2d ed., vol. 3, ed. with an Introduction by G. T. Lord (Dover, N.H.: O. Crosby & J. Varney, 1812; reprint ed., Hampton, N.H.: Peter E. Randall, 1973), 3:195.

19. New Hampshire, [*Provincial and State Papers*], 40 vols. (Concord: State of New Hampshire, 1867-1943), 24:776-77 (hereafter cited as NHPP).

20. Ibid., 28:407, 29:392-93.

21. Timothy Dwight, *Travels in New England and New York*, ed. Barbara Miller Solomon with the assistance of Patricia M. King, new ed., 1st pub. 1821-22, 4 vols. (Cambridge: Harvard University Press, Belknap Press, 1969), 2:96.

22. John Carver, *Sketches of New England, or Memories of the Country* (New York: E. French, 1842), p. 87, quoted in Peter B. Bulkley, "A History of the White Mountain Tourist Industry, 1818-1899" (M.A. thesis, University of New Hampshire, 1958), p. 14.

23. Stephen Burroughs, *Memoirs of the Notorious Stephen Burroughs of New Hampshire*, with a Preface by Robert Frost, new ed., 1st pub. 1811 (New York: Lincoln MacVeagh, Dial Press, 1924), pp. 35-36.

24. Asa McFarland, *An Outline of Biography and Recollection* (Concord, N.H.: Republican Press Association, 1880), p. 72.

25. [Theodore Dwight], *The Northern Traveller and Northern Tour with the Routes to the Springs, Niagara, Quebec, the Tour of New-England, and the Routes from the South*, 5th ed., rev. (New York: Goodrich & Wiley, 1834), p. 305.

26. Harriet Martineau, *Society in America*, 2 vols. (New York: Saunders & Otley, 1837), 1:168.

27. Belknap, *History*, 3:175-76.

28. Ibid., p. 178.

29. Timothy Dwight, *Travels*, 2:96-97.

30. *Oracle* (Portsmouth), April 16 and April 23, 1803.

31. *New-Hampshire Gazette*, April 12, 1814.

32. Ibid., January 14, 1840; *Portsmouth Directory*, 1821, pp. 11 and 65.

33. *Portsmouth Journal*, May 10, 1879.

34. *New Hampshire Sentinel* (Keene), October 26, 1816.

35. Martha McD. Frizzell et al., *Second History of Charlestown, N.H.: The Old Number Four* (Littleton, N.H.: Courier Printing Co., 1955), p. 59.

36. Keene History Committee, *"Upper Ashuelot": A History of Keene, New Hampshire* (Keene, N.H.: By the City, 1968), p. 63.

37. Ibid., p. 74.

38. *New-Hampshire Spectator* (Newport), February 7, 1826.

39. William F. Witcher, *History of the Town of Haverhill, New Hampshire* (Concord, N.H.: Rumford Press, 1919), p. 339; Katharine Blaisdell, *Over the River and through the Years*, 6 vols. (Bradford, Vt. and Woodsville, N.H.: Journal Opinion, 1979-84), 5:60-61.

40. Rockingham County Probate Records, docket no. 6384.

41. Keene History Committee, "Upper Ashuelot," p. 63; Bryant F. Tolles, Jr., "Abel Hutchins and the Building Contract for the Phenix Hotel, Concord, New Hampshire," *Historical New Hampshire* 27 (Winter 1972): 224-34; *Concord Directory* (1830), pp. 26-27.

42. New Hampshire Province Probate Records, 20:251, printed in *Historical New Hampshire* 24 (Spring & Summer 1969):34-42.

43. *New-Hampshire Patriot and State Gazette* (Concord), June 4, 1832.

44. Charles William Janson, *The Stranger in America* (London: Albion Press, 1807), p. 83.

45. Jean Lipman, *Rufus Porter, Yankee Pioneer* (New York: Clarkson N. Potter, 1968), pp. 89-158.

46. *New-Hampshire Statesman* (Concord), December 15, 1823.

47. *New-Hampshire Patriot and State Gazette* (Concord), June 4, 1832.

48. William Thayer Smith et al., *Hanover Forty Years Ago: Recollections of Hanover, New Hampshire, in the Sixties and Seventies* (Hanover, N.H.: Dartmouth Press, 1904), p. 4.

49. M. O. Hall, *Rambles About Greenland in Rhyme* (Boston: A. Mudge, 1900; reprint ed., Hampton, N.H.: Peter E. Randall, 1979), pp. 177-78.

50. Lucy Crawford, *The History of the White Mountains from the First Settlement of Upper Coos and Pequaket* (White Hills: n.p., 1846), p. 76.

51. *New-Hampshire Patriot and State Gazette* (Concord), June 4, 1832.

52. Bentley, *Diary*, 2:47.

53. Julian Ursyn Niemcewicz, *Under Their Vine and Fig Tree: Travels through America in 1797-1799, 1805 with Some Further Account of Life in New Jersey*, trans. and ed. with an Introduction by Metchie J. E. Budka (Elizabeth, N.J.: Grassman Publishing Co., 1965), p. 275.

54. *New-Hampshire Gazette*, September 18, 1798.

55. *Portsmouth Journal*, December 19, 1846.

56. *New-Hampshire Gazette*, February 17, 1769.

57. Ibid., December 2, 1774.

58. New Hampshire, Laws, May 24, 1694, chapter 3; April 25, 1721, chapter 4; December 26, 1778, chapter 2.

59. NHPP, 11:554-55.

60. *Phoenix* (Dover), March 9, 1793.

61. *New-Hampshire Gazette*, October 10, 1814 and February 18, 1817; Frizzell, *Second History of Charlestown*, pp. 269-70.

62. *Portsmouth Journal*, April 24, 1852.

63. *Ibid.*, November 19, 1836; *New-Hampshire Gazette*, March 27, 1841.

64. Catherine Fennelly, *Life in an Old New England Country Village* (New York: Thomas Y. Crowell Co., 1969), pp. 102-3.

65. Albert Annett and Alice E. E. Lehtinen, *History of Jaffrey (Middle Monadnock), New Hampshire: An Average Country Town in the Heart of New England*, 3 vols. (Jaffrey, N.H.: By the Town, 1934-1971), 1:348.

66. *New Hampshire Sentinel* (Keene), October 26, 1816; *New-Hampshire Gazette*, November 18, 1817.

67. *Portsmouth Journal*, January 27, 1866.

68. *The Colonial Laws of Massachusetts Reprinted from the Edition of 1672 with the Supplements through 1686* (Boston: By Order of the City Council, 1887), p. 79.

69. Harold Kirker, "The Boston Exchange Coffee House," *Old-Time New England* 52 (July-September 1961): 11-13.

70. Elizabeth Fitzpatrick Jones, "Hotel Design in the Work of Isaiah Rogers and Henry Whitestone," in *Victorian Resorts and Hotels: Essays from a Victorian Society Autumn Symposium*, ed. Richard Guy Wilson, published as *Nineteenth Century* 8 (1982):33-35.

71. *New-Hampshire Patriot and State Gazette* (Concord), March 21, 1831; *New-Hampshire Spectator* (Newport), April 2, 1831.

72. *New-Hampshire Patriot and State Gazette* (Concord), July 12, 1830. Gass' pride in the State House and prison arose from the fact that he had begun his Concord career by supplying cut granite for both structures.

CHAPTER 3
The Road System

1. Timothy Dwight, *Travels in New England and New York*, ed. Barbara Miller Solomon with the assistance of Patricia M. King, new ed., 1st pub. 1821-22, 4 vols. (Cambridge: Harvard University Press, Belknap Press, 1969), 2:205.

2. Wentworth Papers, New Hampshire Historical Society, box 1, folder 2; see also New Hampshire, [*Provincial and State Papers*], 40 vols. (Concord: State of New Hampshire, 1867-1943), 9:87-89, 5:235, 412, 803 (hereafter cited as *NHPP*).

3. Jeremy Belknap, *The History of New-Hampshire*, 2d ed., vol. 3, ed. with an Introduction by G. T. Lord (Dover, N.H.: O. Crosby & J. Varney, 1812; reprint ed., Hampton, N.H.: Peter E. Randall, 1973), 3:58.

4. *NHPP*, 6:350.

5. Belknap, *History*, 3:61.

6. *NHPP*, 9:87-88.

7. William Bentley, *The Diary of William Bentley, D.D., Pastor of the East Church, Salem, Massachusetts*, 4 vols. (Salem, Mass.: Essex Institute, 1907-14), 2:50.

8. Timothy Dwight, *Travels*, 2:90.

9. James L. Garvin, "The Range Township in Eighteenth-Century New Hampshire," *New England Prospect: Maps, Place Names, and the Historical Landscape: The Dublin Seminar for New England Folklife Annual Proceedings, June 27 through 29, 1980*, ed. Peter Benes and Jane Montague Benes (Boston: Boston University, [1982]), pp. 47-55.

10. Ibid., pp. 62-68.

11. *NHPP*, 9:89.

12. New Hampshire, Laws, April 3, 1742, chapter 18; May 20, 1746, "Orders, Resolves, and Votes of Legislative Nature Passed During this Session [1746]"; *NHPP*, 9:89, 5:412, 803.

13. Elliott C. Cogswell, *History of Nottingham, Deerfield, and Northwood* (Manchester, N.H.: John B. Clarke, 1878; reprint ed., Somersworth, N.H.: New Hampshire Publishing Co., 1972), p. 90.

14. *NHPP*, 6:350.

15. Belknap, *History*, 3:57-58.

16. Ibid., p. 57.

17. Ibid., p. 58.

18. Timothy Dwight, *Travels*, 2:206-7.

19. Vernon Briggs, *History and Genealogy of the Cabot Family, 1475-1927* (Boston: Charles E. Goodspeed & Co., 1927), p. 175; Benjamin Franklin Parker, *History of Wolfeborough* (Wolfeboro: By the Town, 1901), pp. 82-95.

20. J. Leander Bishop, *A History of American Manufactures from 1608 to 1860* (Philadelphia: Edward Young & Co., 1868), pp. 55-57.

21. Jeremy Belknap, "Tour to the White Mountains," *Collections of the Massachusetts Historical Society*, ser. 5, vols. 2-3 (1877): *Belknap Papers*, pt. 2, p. 183.

22. Timothy Dwight, *Travels*, 2:83.

23. [Benjamin Silliman], *Remarks Made on a Short Tour between Hartford and Quebec in the Autumn of 1819* (New Haven: S. Converse, 1820), pp. 74-75; E. S. Abdy, *Journal of a Residence and Tour in the United States of North America from April 1833 to October 1834*, 3 vols. (London: John Murray, 1835), 1:117.

24. New Hampshire, Laws, September 23, 1743, "Orders, Resolves and Votes of Legislative Nature Passed During this Session [1743]"; *NHPP*, 9:103-5.

25. *NHPP*, 9:181-85; New Hampshire Province Treasury Records, New Hampshire Division of Records Management and Archives, 1770-71.

26. *NHPP*, 9:87-89.

27. New Hampshire, Laws, December 6, 1752, "Orders, Resolves, and Votes of Legislative Nature Passed during this Session [1752]."

28. Ibid., February 21, 1754, chapter 2; February 12, 1760, chapter 3.

29. *NHPP*, 18:555.

30. New Hampshire, Laws, December 17, 1763, chapter 12; January 25, 1765, chapter 13.

31. *New-Hampshire Gazette*, January 17, 1766; August 5, 1768; June 9, 1769; *NHPP*, 18:584.

32. *New-Hampshire Gazette*, July 6, 1770.

33. Ibid., March 15, 1771.

34. Ibid., October 1, 1773.

35. James W. Goldthwait, "The Governor's Road, from Rochester to Wolfeboro," *New Hampshire Highways* 9 (May 1931):2-3.

36. *NHPP*, 27:500-516; for work done by the Rochester proprietors on the Middleton Road, see New Hampshire Province Treasury Records, New Hampshire Division of Records Management and Archives, 1771.

37. James W. Goldthwait, "The Road from Wentworth House to Dartmouth College," *New Hampshire Highways* 9 (July 1931):5; see also Nathaniel L. Goodrich, "The Governor's Road," *Dartmouth Alumni Magazine* 14 (April 1922):414-26; Eva Augusta Speare and Catherine Norwood Winters, *The Saga of the Dartmouth College Road* (n.p., 1974).

38. Lucy Crawford, *The History of the White Mountains from the First Settlement of Upper Coos and Pequaket* (White Hills: n.p., 1846), p. 18.

39. Belknap, "Tour to the White Mountains," pt. 1, p. 392.

40. *NHPP*, 11:414; New Hampshire, Laws, June 17, 1780, chapter 5; Belknap, "Tour to the White Mountains," pt. 1, p. 396.

41. *NHPP*, 18:791-92, 9:801; New Hampshire, Laws, February 2, 1788, chapter 1.

42. *New-Hampshire Gazette*, May 21, 1789; see also *NHPP*, 11:46-47; New Hampshire, Laws, June 23, 1780, chapter 11; July 4, 1781, chapter 10.

43. *New-Hampshire Gazette*, May 21, 1789.

44. *NHPP*, 20:542-43.

45. New Hampshire, Laws, February 12, 1791, "Votes, Resolves, etc., of a Legislative Nature Passed at this Session [1791]."

46. Frederic J. Wood, *The Turnpikes of New England and Evolution of the Same through England, Virginia, and Maryland* (Boston: Marshall Jones Co., 1919), pp. 14-18.

47. Ibid., p. 15.

48. Ibid., p. 215; Hobart Pillsbury, *New Hampshire: Resources, Attractions, and Its People, A History*, 8 vols. (New York: Lewis Historical Publishing Co., 1927-28), 2:421-51.

49. Martha McDanolds Frizzell, *A History of Walpole, New Hampshire*, 2 vols. (Walpole: Walpole Historical Society and the Town, 1963), 1:25.

50. *New-Hampshire Gazette*, November 25, 1800.

51. *Farmer's Weekly Museum* (Walpole), November 24, 1801.

52. Timothy Dwight, *Travels*, 4:120.

53. *New-Hampshire Gazette*, November 25, 1800.

54. *New-Hampshire Gazette*, February 15, 1771, December 6, 1771; James Hill Fitts, *History of Newfields, New Hampshire, 1638-1911* (Concord, N.H.: Rumford Press, 1912), p. 182.

55. New Hampshire, Laws, June 23, 1785, chapter 7.

56. Ibid., January 12, 1790, chapter 11; December 24, 1803, chapter 31.

57. Ibid., June 11, 1807, chapter 16.

58. Broadside, "Dixville Road Lottery," 1808, New Hampshire Historical Society.

59. *New-Hampshire Gazette*, May 12, 1791; June 23, 1791.

60. "New Hampshire Turnpike Directors' Records," New Hampshire Historical Society, p. 46, quoted in W. Dennis Chesley, "The New Hampshire Turnpike, 1796-1825," [Durham], 1982 (typewritten), p. 42.

61. "New Hampshire Turnpike Directors' Records," p. 117.

62. Contract between Henry Wiggin and the Proprietors of the Stratham and Newmarket Bridge, August 11, 1807, "Stratham-Newmarket Bridge Company Records, 1807-1850," New Hampshire Historical Society.

63. New Hampshire, Laws, June 14, 1796, chapter 13.

64. Wood, *Turnpikes of New England*, pp. 215-48.

65. *New-Hampshire Gazette*, October 7, 1800; *Oracle* (Portsmouth), October 18, 1800.

66. "New Hampshire Turnpike Directors' Records," New Hampshire Historical Society, p. 13.

67. Accounts, "The Proprietors of the Dover Turnpike," Old Berwick Historical Society, South Berwick, Maine.

68. "New Hampshire Turnpike Directors' Records," pp. 8, 113, 115; see Chesley, "New Hampshire Turnpike," pp. 21-22, 29, 31.

69. W. R. Waterman, "The Fourth New Hampshire Turnpike," *Historical New Hampshire* 15 (November 1960):11.

70. Patrick Shirreff, *A Tour through North America, Together with a Comprehensive View of the Canadas and United States as Adapted for Agricultural Emigration* (Edinburgh: Oliver & Boyd, 1835), p. 37.

71. E. T. Coke, *A Subaltern's Furlough: Descriptive of Scenes in Various Parts of the United States, Upper and Lower Canada, New-Brunswick, and Nova Scotia during the Summer and Autumn of 1832*, 2 vols. (New York: J. & J. Harper, 1833), 2:156.

72. Ibid.; Shirreff, *Tour through North America*, p. 37.

73. *The New-Hampshire Highway Surveyor's Account Book, Containing the Law Relating to Their Official Duties* (Concord, N.H.: G. Parker Lyon, 1855), p. 8.

74. Printed road maintenance agreement between the Third New Hampshire Turnpike Corporation and William and Archibald Tenney, October 18, 1816, Miscellaneous Papers of John Preston, Treasurer, Third New Hampshire Turnpike Corporation, New Hampshire Historical Society, Folder 1.

75. Timothy Dwight, *Travels*, 1:308.

76. Chesley, "New Hampshire Turnpike," p. 28.

77. New Hampshire, Laws, March 11, 1899, chapter 91; see also July 7, 1866, chapter 4263.

78. Waterman, "Fourth New Hampshire Turnpike," pp. 13-14; John M. Shirley, "The Fourth New Hampshire Turnpike," *The Granite Monthly* 4 (May 1881):352-53.

79. New Hampshire, Laws, December 31, 1783, chapter 3.

80. *New-Hampshire Mercury* (Portsmouth), February 8, 1785; Robert Fletcher and Jonathan P. Snow, "A History of the Development of Wooden Bridges," in *American Wooden Bridges*, American Society of Civil Engineers Historical Publication No. 4 (New York: By the Society, 1976), pp. 39-40, 72-73, 112; Lyman Simpson Hayes, *History of the Town of Rockingham, Vermont* (Rockingham, Vt.: By the Town, 1907), pp. 264-74; Timothy Dwight, *Travels*, 2:62-64; and John Farmer and Jacob B. Moore, *A Gazetteer of the State of New-Hampshire* (Concord, N.H.: Jacob B. Moore, 1823), p. 17.

81. *New-Hampshire Gazette*, October 18, 1792; New Hampshire, Laws, June 16, 1792, chapter 7; see also December 15, 1796, chapter 31.

82. *New-Hampshire Gazette*, April 28, 1795.

83. Ibid., December 9, 1794; Nathaniel Adams, *Annals of Portsmouth* (Portsmouth, N.H.: By the Author, 1825; reprint ed., Hampton, N.H.: Peter E. Randall, 1971), pp. 306-8; for a full study of the Piscataqua Bridge, see W. Dennis Chesley, "A History of Piscataqua Bridge, 1793-1855" (M.A. thesis, University of New Hampshire, 1984).

84. *Oracle* (Portsmouth), June 21, 1794.

85. Timothy Dwight, *Travels*, 1:316; documentation on the design of the Piscataqua Bridge was destroyed when the records of the proprietors were consumed in the Portsmouth fire of December 22, 1813 (see "Record Book of the Proprietors of Piscataqua Bridge," 1814-55, Peirce Estate papers, Sanderson & Dudley, attorneys, Portsmouth, N.H.).

86. Timothy Dwight, *Travels*, 1:292-93.

87. New Hampshire, Laws, December 18, 1792, chapter 22; *Examination Relative to the Original Expense of the Improvement at Bellows Falls* [1832], New Hampshire Historical Society; Hayes, *History of the Town of Rockingham, Vermont*, p. 278-92.

88. *Amoskeig Canal*, broadside, 1803, New Hampshire Historical Society.

89. *Statements Concerning the Blodget Canal at Amoskeag Falls on Merrimac River* (n.p., 1805), p. 5.

CHAPTER 4
Travel Conditions

1. William Bentley, *The Diary of William Bentley, D.D., Pastor of the East Church, Salem, Massachusetts*, 4 vols. (Salem, Mass.: Essex Institute, 1907-14), 2:43.

2. New Hampshire, [*Provincial and State Papers*], 40 vols. (Concord: State of New Hampshire, 1867-1943), 28:284 (hereafter cited as NHPP).

3. Bentley, *Diary*, 2:46.

4. John Bernard, *Retrospections of America, 1797-1811*, ed. Mrs. Bayle Bernard, with an Introduction by Laurence Hutton and Brander Matthews (New York: Harper & Bros., 1887), p. 346.

5. [Theodore Dwight], *The Northern Traveller and Northern Tour with the Routes to the Springs, Niagara, Quebec, the Tour of New-England, and the Routes from the South*, 5th ed., rev. (New York: Goodrich & Wiley, 1834), p. 306.

6. Timothy Dwight, *Travels in New England and New York*, ed. Barbara Miller Solomon with the assistance of Patricia M. King, new ed., 1st pub. 1821-22, 4 vols. (Cambridge: Harvard University Press, Belknap Press, 1969), 2:87, 206.

7. Ibid., 2:87.

8. Isaac Fidler, *Observations on Professions, Literature, Manners, and Emigration in the United States and Canada, Made during a Residence There in 1832* (London: Whittaker, Treacher, & Co., 1833), pp. 202-203.

9. Timothy Dwight, *Travels*, 2:87.

10. Jeremy Belknap, *Jeremy Belknap's Journey to Dartmouth in 1774*, ed. Edward C. Lathem (Hanover: Dartmouth Publications, 1950), pp. 24-25.

11. Edward Augustus Kendall, *Travels through the Northern Parts of the United States in the Years 1807 and 1808*, 3 vols. (New York: I. Riley, 1809), 3:187.

12. Timothy Dwight, *Travels*, 2:84, 106, 203, 211.

13. Jeremy Belknap, "Tour to the White Mountains," *Collections of the Massachusetts Historical Society*, ser. 5, vols. 2-3 (1877): Belknap Papers, pt. 1, p. 400; pt. 2, p. 186.

14. David Sutherland, *Address Delivered to the Inhabitants of Bath on the Evening of January 23, 1854, Being the Fiftieth Anniversary of the Author's First Preaching in the Town* (Boston: Geo. C. Rand & Avery, 1855), p. 119; Joseph B. Walker, "Penacook House and the Old Time Taverns of the State," *Proceedings of the New Hampshire Historical Society*, 1 (1872-88):400; Benjamin Chase, *History of Old Chester from 1719 to 1869* (Auburn, N.H.: By the Author, 1869), pp. 428-29; William Little, *The History of Weare, New Hampshire, 1735-1888* (Lowell, Mass.: S.W. Huse & Co., 1888), p. 185; John J. Dearborn, comp., *The History of Salisbury, New Hampshire, from Date of Settlement to the Present Time* (Manchester, N.H.: William E. Moore, 1890), p. 415.

15. George Whitefield, *A Continuation of the Rev. Mr. Whitefields' Journal . . . Containing an Account of the Work of God at Georgia, Rhode Island, New-England* (London, 1741), in *Two Centuries of Travel in Essex County, Massachusetts: A Collection of Narratives and Observations Made by Travelers, 1605-1799*, comp. George Francis Dow (Topsfield, Mass.: Topsfield Historical Society, 1921), p. 72.

16. NHPP, 36:478-79; *New-Hampshire Gazette* (Portsmouth), September 9, 1763.

17. Timothy Walker, *Diaries of Rev. Timothy Walker: The First and Only Minister of Concord, N.H., from His Ordination November 18, 1730 to September 1, 1782*, ed. Joseph B. Walker (Concord, N.H.: Ira C. Evans, 1889), p. 23.

18. Sutherland, *Address to the Inhabitants of Bath*, pp. 114 and 119.

19. Henry Tufts, *The Autobiography of a Criminal*, ed. with an Introduction by Edmund Pearson, new ed., 1st pub. 1807, Dover, N.H. (New York: Duffield & Co., 1930), pp. 124, 148.

20. Estwick Evans, *A Pedestrious Tour of Four Thousand Miles through the Western States and Territories during the Winter and Spring of 1818* (Concord, N.H.: Joseph C. Spear, 1819).

21. Susan Baker Blunt, Memoir, 1913, Manchester Historic Association, typewritten transcript, pp. 13-14.

22. *New-Hampshire Argus and Spectator* (Newport), June 15, 1839.

23. Fidler, *Observations on the United States and Canada*, p. 197.

24. Frederick Hall, *Letters from the East and from the West* (Washington, D.C.: F. Taylor & Wm. M. Morrison, 1840), pp. 15-16.

25. *A Journal of an Excursion Made by the Corps of Cadets of the American Literary, Scientific, and Military Academy under Capt. Alden Partridge, June 1822* (Concord, N.H.: Hill & Moore, 1822), p. 34 and *passim*; John Calfe, Diary, 1777, reprinted in *A Memorial of the Town of Hampstead, New Hampshire*, comp. Harriette Eliza Noyes (Boston: George B. Reed, 1899), p. 288; Evans, *Pedestrious Tour*, p. 8.

26. Tufts, *Autobiography*, p. 223.

27. Belknap, *Journey to Dartmouth*, *passim*; Belknap, "Tour to the White Mountains," pt. 1, p. 400 and *passim*.

28. John Macgregor, *The Progress of America from the Discovery by Columbus to the Year 1846*, 2 vols. (London: Whittaker & Co., 1847), 2:125, citing *Boston Evening-Post*, April 6, 1761.

29. Tufts, *Autobiography*, p. 238.

30. Robert Gilmor, "Memorandums Made in a Tour to the Eastern States in the Year 1797" in Dow, *Two Centuries of Travel in Essex County*, pp. 182-83.

31. *New-Hampshire Gazette*, November 25, 1800.

32. E. T. Coke, *A Subaltern's Furlough: Descriptive of Scenes in Various Parts of the United States, Upper and Lower Canada, New-Brunswick, and Nova Scotia during the Summer and Autumn of 1832*, 2 vols. (New York: J. & J. Harper, 1833), 2:144.

33. Timothy Dwight, *Travels*, 4:112.

34. New Hampshire, Laws, December 23, 1771, chapter 1.

35. *New-Hampshire Statesman* (Concord), February 24, 1823.

36. Hall, *Letters from East and West*, p. 15.

37. *New-Hampshire Gazette*, April 28, 1801.

38. P. Stansbury, *A Pedestrian Tour of Two Thousand Three Hundred Miles in North America to the Lakes, the Canadas, and the New-England States Performed in the Autumn of 1821* (New York: J. D. Myers & W. Smith, 1822), p. 248.

39. Timothy Dwight, *Travels*, 2:87; Marquis de Chastellux, *Travels in North America in the Years 1780, 1781, and 1782*, trans. Howard C. Rice, Jr., 2 vols. (Chapel Hill: University of North Carolina Press for the Institute of Early American History and Culture, 1963), 2:484.

40. Francisco de Miranda, *The New Democracy in America: Travels of Francisco de Miranda in the United States, 1783-84*, trans. Judson P. Wood, ed. John S. Ezell (Norman: University of Oklahoma Press, 1963), p. 178.

41. Anne Royall, *The Black Book, or a Continuation of Travels in the United States*, 3 vols. (Washington, D.C.: By the Author, 1828-29), 2:372.

42. Harriet Martineau, *Retrospect of Western Travel*, 3 vols. (London: Saunders & Otley, 1838), 3:71.

43. Coke, *Subaltern's Furlough*, 2:144.

44. Tufts, *Autobiography*, pp. 109, 150, 164-65, 168.

45. [Theodore Dwight], *Sketches of Scenery and Manners in the United States* (New York: A. T. Goodrich, 1829), p. 31.

46. Samuel Johnson, " 'Journal of a Tour to the White Hills': An 1842 Chronicle by Samuel Johnson," ed. with an Introduction by Bryant F. Tolles, Jr., *Essex Institute Historical Collections* 120 (January 1984):4.

47. [Theodore Dwight], *Sketches*, p. 71.

48. Ibid., pp. 63, 72; [Benjamin Silliman], *Remarks Made on a Short Tour between Hartford and Quebec in the Autumn of 1819* (New Haven: S. Converse, 1820), p. 393; Coke, *Subaltern's Furlough*, 2:143 and 151; Timothy Dwight, *Travels*, 2:212-213 and 228; *Excursion Made by the Corps of Cadets under Capt. Alden Partridge*, pp. 9, 12-13, 32-33; Kendall, *Travels through Northern Parts*, 3:187, 204.

49. Timothy Dwight, *Travels*, 2:94-95.

50. Bentley, *Diary*, 2:43-48.

51. [Sarah Josepha Hale], "Editors' Table," *Godey's Magazine and Lady's Book* 33 (September 1846):142.

52. Blunt, *Memoir of Susan Baker Blunt*, p. 1.

53. Timothy Dwight, *Travels*, 2:216.

54. William Patten to Timothy Dwight, May 14, 1802, quoted in Dwight, *Travels*, 2:85.

55. *New-Hampshire Spectator* (Newport), November 19, 1831.

56. Alice Morse Earle, *Stage-coach and Tavern Days* (New York: Macmillan Co., 1901), p. 369, quoting letter.

57. *Oracle* (Portsmouth), October 7, 1797.

58. Harriet Martineau, *Society in America*, 2 vols. (New York: Saunders & Otley, 1837), 2:5.

59. Ibid., 1:165.

60. *Excursion Made by the Corps of Cadets under Capt. Alden Partridge*, p. 17.

61. Sarah Connell Ayer, *Diary of Sarah Connell Ayer: Andover and Newburyport, Massachusetts; Concord and Bow, New Hampshire; Portland and Eastport, Maine,* [ed. Margaret H. Jewell] (Portland, Me.: Lefavor-Tower Co., 1910), p. 88; Timothy Dwight, *Travels*, 2:155.

62. Martineau, *Retrospect of Western Travel*, 3:70.

63. Timothy Dwight, *Travels*, 2:107; see also Belknap, "Tour to the White Mountains," pt. 1, p. 392.

64. Earle, *Stage-Coach and Tavern Days*, p. 368.

65. Martineau, *Retrospect of Western Travel*, 3:60-61.

66. [Theodore Dwight], *Northern Traveller*, p. 305.

67. Esther A. Parker, Memoirs, 1906, typewritten (privately owned).

68. Sarah Anna Emery, *Reminiscences of a Nonagenarian* (Newburyport, Mass.: William H. Huse & Co., 1879), pp. 109-110.

69. Adam Hodgson, *Remarks during a Journey through North America in the Years 1819, 1820, and 1821 in a Series of Letters,* comp. Samuel Whiting (New York: Samuel Whiting, 1823), pp. 231-32.

70. *Boston News-Letter*, February 3, 1705, referring to the roads "beyond Newbury," and February 22, 1748, quoted in Joseph B. Felt, *The Customs of New England* (Boston: T. R. Marvin, 1853), p. 88.

71. Royall, *Black Book*, 2:352.

72. Thomas Hamilton, *Men and Manners in America*, new ed. (Edinburgh: William Blackwood & Sons, 1843; reprint of [2d] ed., New York: Johnson Reprint Corporation, 1968), p. 86.

73. Ayer, *Diary of Sarah Connell Ayer*, pp. 5 and 32.

74. Chastellux, *Travels in North America*, 1:85.

75. [John] Ogilby, *The Traveller's Guide, or, A Most Exact Description of the Roads of England Being Mr. Ogilby's Actual Survey* (London: W. B., [1712?]).

76. John Melish, *A Description of the Roads in the United States, Compiled from the Most Authentic Materials* (Philadelphia: G. Palmer, 1814); John Melish, *The Traveller's Directory through the United States* (Philadelphia: By the Author, 1816).

77. [Theodore Dwight], *Northern Traveller*, pp. 294 and 299.

78. New Hampshire, Laws, December 17, 1792, chapter 19.

79. Little, *History of Weare*, p. 581.

80. Bentley, *Diary*, 2:393.

81. Bernard, *Retrospections of America*, p. 322.

82. Ibid., p. 321.

83. Elias Alexander Bryant, "A Grandson's Recollections of Alexander Wilson and Family," in Elizabeth F. Billings et al., *Memories of a New England Homestead Gathered from Recollection and Family Tradition by Grandchildren of Alexander Wilson and Elizabeth Fairbanks Wilson of Francestown, N.H.* (Concord, N.H.: Rumford Press, 1917), p. 27.

84. Bernard, *Retrospections of America*, p. 320.

85. Helen R. Albee, *Mountain Playmates* (Boston: Houghton, Mifflin & Co., Riverside Press, 1900), pp. 32-34.

86. Bernard, *Retrospections of America*, p. 320.

87. [Theodore Dwight], *Northern Traveller*, p. 307; Kendall, *Travels through Northern Parts*, 3:180.

88. Coke, *Subaltern's Furlough*, 2:151; Johnson, "Tour to the White Hills," p. 15.

89. Bentley, *Diary*, 2:47.

90. See, for example, Belknap, *Journey to Dartmouth*, p. 1 and J. F. D. Smyth, *A Tour in the United States of America*, 2 vols. (London: G. Robinson, 1784), 2:364.

91. John Lambert, *Travels through Canada and the United States of North America in the Years 1806, 1807, & 1808*, 3d ed., 2 vols. (London: Baldwin, Cradock & Joy, 1816), 2:496.

92. Coke, *Subaltern's Furlough*, 2:144.

93. Bernard, *Retrospections of America*, p. 34.

94. Royall, *Black Book*, 2:390; Patrick Shirreff, *A Tour through North America, Together with a Comprehensive View of the Canadas and United States as Adapted for Agricultural Emigration* (Edinburgh: Oliver & Boyd, 1835), p. 50.

95. Ayer, *Diary of Sarah Connell Ayer*, p. 48.

96. Martineau, *Retrospect of Western Travel*, 3:64; Johnson, "Tour to the White Hills," pp. 13, 24, 28.

97. Carl David Arfwedson, *The United States and Canada in 1832, 1833, and 1834*, with an Introduction by Marvin Fisher, 2 vols. (London: Richard Bentley, 1834; reprint ed., New York: Johnson Reprint Corporation, 1969), 1:192.

98. Royall, *Black Book*, 2:353, 378; Shirreff, *Tour through North America*, pp. 49-50.

99. Royall, *Black Book*, 2:372.

100. Bernard, *Retrospections of America*, p. 34.

101. eg. *New-Hampshire Gazette*, October 7, 1800.

102. [Hale], "Editors' Table," p. 142.

103. New Hampshire, Laws, July 7, 1869, chapter 27.

104. *New-Hampshire Gazette*, October 7, 1800.

105. John Melish, *Travels through the United States of America in the Years 1806 & 1807, and 1809, 1810, & 1811* (Philadelphia: By the Author, n.d.; London: George Cowie & Co., 1818; reprint ed., New York: Johnson Reprint Corporation, 1970), pp. 87-88.

106. Thomas Hamilton, *Men and Manners in America*, p. 147.

107. *Concord Gazette* (possibly Massachusetts), quoted in *New-Hampshire Spectator* (Newport), September 1, 1829.

108. *New-Hampshire Spectator* (Newport), June 23, 1832.

109. Belknap, "Tour to the White Mountains," pt. 2, p. 178; *New-Hampshire Gazette*, August 26, 1774.

110. Charles Augustus Murray, *Travels in North America during the Years 1834, 1835, and 1836*, 2 vols. (London: Richard Bentley, 1839), 1:95.

111. Ayer, *Diary of Sarah Connell Ayer*, passim.

112. E. S. Abdy, *Journal of a Residence and Tour in the United States of North America from April 1833 to October 1834*, 3 vols. (London: John Murray, 1835), 1:118; Coke, *Subaltern's Furlough*, 2:141.

113. Miranda, *The New Democracy in America*, p. 185.

114. New Hampshire, Laws, June 25, 1858, chapter 2122; Martineau, *Retrospect of Western Travel*, 3:59.

115. Murray, *Travels in North America*, 1:100.

116. Blunt, Memoir of Susan Baker Blunt, p. 2; Allan Forbes and Ralph M. Eastman, *Taverns and Stagecoaches of New England*, 2 vols. (Boston: State Street Trust Co., 1953-54), 1:93 and 2:29.

117. Murray, *Travels in North America*, 1:95-96.

118. Johnson, "Tour to the White Hills," p. 27.

119. [Sophia Hayes Wyatt], *The Autobiography of a Landlady of the Old School* (Boston: By the Author, 1854), p. 43.

120. J. P. Brissot de Warville, *New Travels in the United States of America, 1788*, trans. Mara Soceanu Vamos and Durand Echeverria, ed. Durand Echeverria (Cambridge: Harvard University Press, Belknap Press, 1964), p. 369.

121. Johnson, "Tour to the White Hills," p. 27.

122. James Birket, *Some Cursory Remarks Made by James Birket in His Voyage to North America, 1750-1751* (New Haven: Yale University Press, 1916), p. 3.

123. Timothy Dwight, *Travels*, 2:234.

124. Belknap, *Journey to Dartmouth*, pp. 23-24; Hodgson, *Remarks during a Journey through North America*, pp. 232-33.

125. Frances Wentworth to Sarah Langdon, October 4, 1770, Wentworth Papers, New Hampshire Historical Society.

126. Miranda, *The New Democracy in America*, p. 179.

127. Royall, *Black Book*, 2:164-65; Anne M. Means, *Amherst and Our Family Tree* (Boston: By the Author, 1921), p. 36.

128. Bentley, *Diary*, 2:53.

129. *New-Hampshire Spectator* (Newport), April 23, 1831.

130. Kendall, *Travels through Northern Parts*, 3:189.

131. Petition relating to tavern license of Israel Blake of Nottingham, 1753, quoted in Kenneth Scott, "Colonial Innkeepers of New Hampshire," *Historical New Hampshire* 19 (Spring 1964):37.

132. Stansbury, *Pedestrian Tour*, p. 248.

133. Isaac Weld, *Travels through the States of North America and the Provinces of Upper and Lower Canada during the Years 1795, 1796, and 1797*, with an Introduction by Martin Roth, 2 vols. (London: John Stockdale, 1807; reprint ed., New York: Johnson Reprint Corporation, 1968), 1:28.

134. Blunt, Memoir of Susan Baker Blunt, p. 8.

135. Lucy Crawford, *The History of the White Mountains from the First Settlement of Upper Coos and Pequaket* (White Hills: n.p., 1846), p. 63.

136. Henry Reed Stiles, *Bundling: Its Origin, Progress, and Decline in America* (Albany: Knickerbocker Publishing Co., 1871; reprint ed., New York: AMS Press, 1974), passim; [Francis] Grose, comp., *Lexicon Balatronicum: A Dictionary of Buckish Slang, University Wit, and Pickpocket Eloquence* (London: C. Chappel, 1811; reprint ed., Chicago: Follett Publishing Co., 1971); Andrew Burnaby, *Travels through the Middle Settlements in North America in the Years 1759 and 1760, with Observations upon the State of the Colonies*, with an Introduction by Rufus Rockwell Wilson, 3d ed., rev. and enl. (London: T. Payne, 1798; reprint ed., New York: A. Wessels Co., 1904), pp. 141-42; Charles William Janson, *The Stranger in America* (London: Albion Press, 1807), p. 88.

137. Thomas Anburey, *Travels through the Interior Parts of America in a Series of Letters by an Officer*, new ed., 1st pub. 1789, with a Foreword by William Harding Carter, 2 vols. (Boston: Houghton Mifflin Co., Riverside Press, 1923), 2:25-26 and 57.

138. *New-Hampshire Republican* (Dover), November 9, 1824.

139. Chastellux, *Travels in North America*, 1:85.

140. Emery, *Reminiscences of a Nonagenarian*, p. 279; Thomas Hamilton, *Men and Manners in America*, p. 146.

141. Parker, Memoirs of Esther A. Parker; Ayer, *Diary of Sarah Connell Ayer*, p. 200.

142. Parker, Memoir.

143. Asa McFarland, *An Outline of Biography and Recollection* (Concord, N.H.: Republican Press Association, 1880), p. 72; Levi Hutchins, *The Autobiography of Levi Hutchins* (Cambridge: Riverside Press, 1865), p. 169.

144. Alexander Hamilton, *Gentleman's Progress: The Itinerarium of Dr. Alexander Hamilton, 1744*, ed. with an Introduction by Carl Bridenbaugh (Chapel Hill: University of North Carolina Press for the Institute of Early American History and Culture, 1948), p. 125.

145. Stansbury, *Pedestrian Tour*, pp. 247-48.

146. David McClure, *Diary of David McClure, Doctor of Divinity, 1748-1820*, with Notes by Franklin B. Dexter (New York: Knickerbocker Press, 1899), p. 142.

147. Belknap, *Journey to Dartmouth*, pp. 4-5.

148. Moreau de St. Méry, *Moreau de St. Méry's American Journey [1793-1798]*, trans. and ed. Kenneth Roberts and Anna M. Roberts, with an Introduction by Stewart L. Mims (Garden City, N.Y.: Doubleday & Co., 1947), p. 325.

149. Ibid., p. 121.

150. Tufts, *Autobiography*, p. 200.

151. Brissot de Warville, *New Travels*, pp. 369-70.

152. *The Colonial Laws of Massachusetts Reprinted from the Edition of 1672 with the Supplements through 1686* (Boston: By Order of the City Council, 1887), pp. 51, 80, 82; Edmund Wheeler, *The History of Newport, New Hampshire from 1766 to 1878* (Concord, N.H.: Republican Press Association, 1879), pp. 270-72.

153. Francis J. Grund, *The Americans in Their Moral, Social, and Political Relations*, 2 vols. in 1 (Boston: Marsh, Capen & Lyon, 1837), p. 327.

154. *Dover Gazette & Strafford Advertiser*, February 2, 1830.

155. Hutchins, *Autobiography*, p. 80.

156. Tufts, *Autobiography*, pp. 124, 331, 333-34; Bernard, *Retrospections of America*, p. 324.

157. New Hampshire, Laws, June 27, 1859, chapter 2230; Tufts, *Autobiography*, p. 132.

158. Abdy, *Residence and Tour in the United States*, 1:168.

159. New Hampshire, Laws, December 15, 1796, chapter 30; June 24, 1835, chapter 22; June 26, 1850, chapter 963; and September 11, 1883, chapter 91.

CHAPTER 5
Traffic and Commerce

1. *New-Hampshire Gazette* (Portsmouth), April 3, 1761.

2. Daniel Webster, "Autobiography," in *The Private Correspondence of Daniel Webster*, ed. Fletcher Webster, 2 vols. (Boston: Little, Brown & Co., 1857), p. 22, quoted in James O. Lyford, ed., *History of Concord, New Hampshire, from the Original Grant in Seventeen Hundred and Twenty-five to the Opening of the Twentieth Century*, 2 vols. (Concord, N.H.: Rumford Press, 1903), 2:844.

3. Sarah Anna Emery, *Reminiscences of a Nonagenarian* (Newburyport, Mass.: William H. Huse & Co., 1879), p. 75.

4. Frederick Marryat, *A Diary in America with Remarks on Its Institutions*, ed. with an Introduction by Sydney Jackman, new ed., 1st pub. 1839 (New York: Alfred A. Knopf, 1962), p. 364.

5. *Portsmouth Directory*, 1821, p. 11.

6. *Prominent Features of a Northern Tour, Written from a Brief Diary Kept in Travelling from Charleston, S.C., to and through Rhode-Island, Massachusetts, New-Hampshire, Vermont, Lower and Upper Canada, New-York, Maine, North-Carolina, South-Carolina, and Back to Charleston Again, Commencing on the 12th of June 1821 and Terminating the 12th of November Following* (Charleston, S.C.: C. C. Sebring, 1822), p. 40.

7. See [Theodore Dwight], *The Northern Traveller and Northern Tour with the Routes to the Springs, Niagara, Quebec, the Tour of New-England, and the Routes from the South*, 5th ed., rev. (New York: Goodrich & Wiley, 1834), opp. p. 399.

8. Broadside, "Depositions, Relating to the Portsmouth Bridge," 1841, New Hampshire Historical Society.

9. Lyford, *History of Concord*, 2:848-49.

10. *New-Hampshire Gazette*, April 28, 1801.

11. Ibid., February 25, 1774.

12. *New-Hampshire Spectator* (Newport), February 24, 1829; *Dartmouth Gazette* (Hanover), November 11, 1807.

13. *New-Hampshire Gazette*, July 6, 1782.

14. *Farmer's Cabinet* (Amherst), April 30, 1805.

15. *New-Hampshire Gazette*, April 3, 1761; April 22, 1763; May 13, 1768; July 19, 1771; Allan Forbes and Ralph M. Eastman, *Taverns and Stagecoaches of New England*, 2 vols. (Boston: State Street Trust Co., 1953-54), 2:28-29.

16. Harry N. Scheiber, "Coach, Wagon, and Motor-Truck Manufacture, 1813-1928: The Abbot-Downing Company of Concord," *Historical New Hampshire* 20 (Autumn 1965):3-6 and *passim*; *19th Century American Carriages: Their Manufacture, Decoration, and Use* (Stony Brook, N.Y.: Museums at Stony Brook, 1987), pp. 27-33; Lewis Downing, Ledger, 1813-24, Abbot-Downing Company Records, New Hampshire Historical Society, pt. 1, vol. 16.

17. [Theodore Dwight], *Northern Traveller*, p. 293; Mary Jane Thomas, "Reminiscences of the White Mountains," ed. with Foreword by Harriet S. Lacy, *Historical New Hampshire* 28 (Spring 1973):50.

18. New Hampshire, [*Provincial and State Papers*], 40 vols. (Concord: State of New Hampshire, 1867-1943), 17:651 (hereafter cited as *NHPP*); *New-Hampshire Gazette*, November 30, 1770.

19. New Hampshire, Laws, August 5, 1693, chapter 3.

20. Ibid., May 31, 1690, chapter 13; see also *NHPP*, 4:33.

21. *NHPP*, 18:697; *New-Hampshire Gazette*, November 25, 1800.

22. *Boston News-Letter*, February 5, 1705, quoted in James W. Goldthwait, "New Hampshire Post Roads," *New Hampshire Highways* 9 (November 1931):6.

23. *New-Hampshire Gazette*, May 25, 1759.

24. Ibid., December 18, 1772; February 25, 1774.

25. Carl H. Scheele, *A Short History of the Mail Service* (Washington, D.C.: Smithsonian Institution Press, 1970), p. 55.

26. Matthew Patten, *The Diary of Matthew Patten of Bedford, N.H., 1754-1788* (Bedford, N.H.: By the Town, 1903), p. 361.

27. Josiah Bartlett, *The Papers of Josiah Bartlett*, ed. Frank C. Mevers (Hanover, N.H.: University Press of New England for the New Hampshire Historical Society, 1979), p. 228.

28. See Richard Waldron, Jr., to his brother, May 6, 1745, Waldron Papers, New Hampshire Historical Society; Scheele, *A Short History of the Mail Service*, pp. 45ff.; and for legal aspects, New Hampshire, Laws, August 5, 1693, chapter 3.

29. Hugh Finlay, Journal Kept by Hugh Finlay, Surveyor of the Post Roads on the Continent of North America, 1773-74, transcript at Smithsonian Institution, Division of Philately and Postal History, entry for October 5, 1773, pp. 25-27, quoted in Scheele, *A Short History of the Mail Service*, p. 55.

30. E. T. Coke, *A Subaltern's Furlough: Descriptive of Scenes in Various Parts of the United States, Upper and Lower Canada, New-Brunswick, and Nova Scotia during the Summer and Autumn of 1832*, 2 vols. (New York: J. & J. Harper, 1833), 2:141.

31. [Frederic Kidder and Augustus Addison Gould], *The History of New Ipswich from Its First Grant in MDCCXXXVI to the Present Time* (Boston: Gould & Lincoln, 1852), p. 130.

32. Coke, *Subaltern's Furlough*, 1:220-21.

33. Lucy Crawford, *The History of the White Mountains from the First Settlement of Upper Coos and Pequaket* (White Hills: n.p., 1846), p. 61; Coke, *Subaltern's Furlough*, 2:153, 155.

34. William Little, *The History of Weare, New Hampshire, 1735-1888* (Lowell, Mass.: S. W. Huse & Co., 1888), p. 570.

35. Samuel Johnson, " 'Journal of a Tour to the White Hills': An 1842 Chronicle by Samuel Johnson," ed. with an Introduction by Bryant F. Tolles, Jr., *Essex Institute Historical Collections* 120 (January 1984):13-14.

36. Little, *History of Weare*, p. 570.

37. *Farmer's Cabinet* (Amherst), October 23, 1809, quoted in Leander W. Cogswell, *History of the Town of Henniker, Merrimack County, New Hampshire* (Concord, N.H.: Republican Press Association, 1880), p. 256.

38. Patten, *Diary*, p. 404.

39. *New-Hampshire Gazette*, March 1, 1765.

40. John Lambert, *Travels through Canada and the United States of North America in the Years 1806, 1807, & 1808*, 3d ed., 2 vols. (London: Baldwin, Cradock & Joy, 1816), 2:497-98.

41. *New-Hampshire Gazette*, March 16, 1770.

42. John Hughes to Jonathan Roberts, September 7, 1769, reprinted in Anna M. Holstein, *Swedish Holsteins in America from 1644 to 1892, Comprising Many Letters and Biographical Matter Relating to John Hughes, the "Stamp Officer"* (Norristown, Pa.: M. R. Wills, 1892), p. 56.

43. *New-Hampshire Spectator* (Newport), April 23, 1831 and Catherine Fennelly, *Life in an Old New England Country Village* (New York: Thomas Y. Crowell Co., 1969), p. 100.

44. Julian Ursyn Niemcewicz, *Under Their Vine and Fig Tree: Travels through America in 1797-1799, 1805 with Some Further Account of Life in New Jersey*, trans. and ed. with an Introduction by Metchie J. E. Budka (Elizabeth, N.J.: Grassman Publishing Co., 1965), p. 164.

45. *New-Hampshire Patriot & State Gazette* (Concord), July 18, 1825.

46. John Melish, *Travels through the United States of America in the Years 1806 & 1807, and 1809, 1810, & 1811* (Philadelphia: By the Author, n.d.; London: George Cowie & Co., 1818; reprint ed., New York: Johnson Reprint Corporation, 1970), p. 84; Jeremy Belknap, *The History of New-Hampshire*, 2d ed., vol. 3, ed. with an Introduction by G. T. Lord (Dover, N.H.: O. Crosby & J. Varney, 1812; reprint ed., Hampton, N.H.: Peter E. Randall, 1973), p. 61.

47. Emery, *Reminiscences of a Nonagenarian*, p. 280; Little, *History of Weare*, pp. 308-13.

48. "Depositions, Relating to the Portsmouth Bridge," 1841.

49. Everett S. Stackpole, Lucien Thompson, and Winthrop S. Meserve, *History of the Town of Durham, New Hampshire (Oyster River Plantation)*, 2 vols. (Concord, N.H.: Rumford Press, 1913), 1:331.

50. [Theodore Dwight], *Northern Traveller*, p. 297; [Theodore Dwight], *Sketches of Scenery and Manners in the United States* (New York: A. T. Goodrich, 1829), p. 31.

51. "Port of Piscataqua, Colonial Customs Records, 1770-1775," copy, Portsmouth [N.H.] Athenaeum.

52. Timothy Dwight, *Travels in New England and New York*, ed. Barbara Miller Solomon with the assistance of Patricia M. King, new ed., 1st pub. 1821-22, 4 vols. (Cambridge: Harvard University Press, Belknap Press, 1969), 1:305; *Dover Gazette & Strafford Advertiser*, September 2, 1834.

53. James L. Garvin and Donna-Belle Garvin, *Instruments of Change: New Hampshire Hand Tools and Their Makers, 1800-1900* (Canaan, N.H.: Phoenix Publishing for the New Hampshire Historical Society, 1985), pp. 52-53.

54. William Gilman Perry, *Exeter in 1830: Notes and Occasional Papers* (Exeter, N.H.: News-Letter Press, [1913]), p. 102.

55. *New-Hampshire Patriot & State Gazette* (Concord), July 18, 1825.

56. Anne Royall, *The Black Book, or a Continuation of Travels in the United States*, 3 vols. (Washington, D.C.: By the Author, 1828-29), 2:193; John Hughes to Jonathan Roberts, September 7, 1769, in Holstein, *Swedish Holsteins in America*, p. 56.

57. William Little, *The History of Warren: A Mountain Hamlet Located Among the White Hills of New Hampshire* (Manchester, N.H.: William E. Moore, 1870), p. 386; C.C. Benton, "The Lafayette Hotel, with Memories of Earlier Days," *Granite State Free Press* (Lebanon), November 24, 1871, included in Allan Burritt Downs, comp., "Reminiscences of Lebanon," 1935 (typewritten), p. 5.

58. Lawrence D. Butterfield, "Cattle Droving in New England at the Turn of the Century: A Personal Experience" (typewritten),

p. 29; "Excerpts from the Samuel Minot diaries," 1837, in Edward Chamberlin et al., *Historical Notes of Bath, New Hampshire, 1765-1965* (Littleton, N.H.: Courier Printing Co., 1965), p. 139.

59. William Bentley, *The Diary of William Bentley, D.D., Pastor of the East Church, Salem, Massachusetts*, 4 vols. (Salem, Mass.: Essex Institute, 1907-14), 3:518.

60. Benton, "Lafayette Hotel," p. 5.

61. Emery, *Reminiscences of a Nonagenarian*, p. 279.

62. Charles R. Corning, Diaries, New Hampshire Historical Society, v. 42.

63. *New-Hampshire Patriot & State Gazette* (Concord), January 2, 1832.

64. *Dover Gazette & Strafford Advertiser*, February 2, 1830.

65. Little, *History of Weare*, p. 311.

66. *Nashua Gazette*, December 23, 1843, quoted in S. Winship, "Concord Winters Often Defy Forecasts," *Concord Monitor*, December 26, 1987.

67. *New-Hampshire Gazette*, February 11, 1774.

68. Emery, *Reminiscences of a Nonagenarian*, p. 72.

69. Susan Baker Blunt, Memoir, 1913, Manchester Historic Association, typewritten transcript, p. 8.

70. Thomas Anburey, *Travels through the Interior Parts of America in a Series of Letters by an Officer*, new ed., 1st pub. 1789, with a Foreword by William Harding Carter, 2 vols. (Boston: Houghton Mifflin Co., Riverside Press, 1923), 2:57.

71. Royall, *Black Book*, 2:387.

72. Amos Kendall, *Autobiography of Amos Kendall*, ed. William Stickney (Boston: Lee & Shepard, 1872), p. 19.

73. Marryat, *Diary in America*, p. 140; Royall, *Black Book*, 2:389.

74. Sarah Clark, Diary, 1861-62, Fales Collection, New Hampshire Historical Society, entry for April 17, 1862.

75. Toll Book, 1836-43, Cornish Bridge Records, New Hampshire Historical Society, summarized in William H. Child, *History of the Town of Cornish, New Hampshire, with Genealogical Record, 1763-1910*, 2 vols. (Concord, N.H.: Rumford Press, n.d.), 1:214-15.

76. Peter L. Hoyt, *Hoyt's History of Wentworth, New Hampshire*, transcribed from original manuscript by Francis A. Muzzey (Littleton, N.H.: Courier Printing Co., 1976), p. 130.

77. Cornelius Weygandt, *November Rowen: A Late Harvest from the Hills of New Hampshire* (New York: D. Appleton-Century Co., 1941), pp. 281-82; Butterfield, "Cattle Droving in New England," p. 24; *Seabrook, N.H., 1768-1968: Commemorative Book* (Somersworth, N.H.: New Hampshire Publishing Co., 1968), p. 48.

78. Timothy Dwight, *Travels*, 4:117; Royall, *Black Book*, 2:393.

79. Steven R. Pendery, "The Archeology of Urban Foodways in Portsmouth, New Hampshire," *Foodways in the Northeast: The Dublin Seminar for New England Folklife Annual Proceedings, June 25 through 27, 1982*, ed. Peter Benes and Jane Montague Benes (Boston: Boston University, 1984), p. 23.

80. Belknap, *History*, 3:106.

81. *New-Hampshire Patriot & State Gazette* (Concord), July 18, 1825; "The Weston Cattle Drives of the 1880s," *The Mountain Ear* (Conway), November 6, 1987.

82. *New-Hampshire Patriot & State Gazette* (Concord), January 9, 1832.

83. Marquis de Chastellux, *Travels in North America in the Years 1780, 1781, and 1782*, trans. Howard C. Rice, Jr., 2 vols. (Chapel Hill: University of North Carolina Press for the Institute of Early American History and Culture, 1963), 1:84.

84. Timothy Dwight, *Travels*, 4:117.

85. Emery, *Reminiscences of a Nonagenarian*, p. 106; John Preston, "The Turnpike Road—Fortune or Folly," paper presented at the annual meeting of the New Ipswich Historical Society, August 1987 (typewritten), p. 4; *Seabrook, 1768-1968*, p. 48.

86. Elias Alexander Bryant, "A Grandson's Recollections of Alexander Wilson and Family," in Elizabeth F. Billings et al., *Memories of a New England Homestead Gathered from Recollection and Family Tradition by Grandchildren of Alexander Wilson and Elizabeth Fairbanks Wilson of Francestown, N.H.* (Concord, N.H.: Rumford Press, 1917), p. 27; Butterfield, "Cattle Droving in New England," pp. 2-3; and Weygandt, *November Rowen*, p. 281.

87. Butterfield, "Cattle Droving in New England," pp. 8 and 15.

88. Weygandt, *November Rowen*, p. 282.

89. Christopher Daniel Chamberlin, "The Business of Robert Rand, Merchant at North Charlestown, New Hampshire, 1800-1810" (M.A. thesis, University of Missouri-St. Louis, 1985), pp. 108ff.

90. *New-Hampshire Gazette*, June 22, 1764.

91. Lyford, *History of Concord*, 2:853; Chamberlin, "Business of Robert Rand," p. 115.

92. Frederic J. Wood, *The Turnpikes of New England and Evolution of the Same through England, Virginia, and Maryland* (Boston: Marshall Jones Co., 1919), p. 233.

93. Edgar Gilbert, *History of Salem, N.H.* (Concord, N.H.: Rumford Printing Co., 1907), p. 325.

94. Chastellux, *Travels in North America*, 1:84; Bryant, "A Grandson's Recollections," pp. 27-29; *Farmer's Weekly Museum* (Walpole), October 19, 1798; January 20, 1800; *Farmer's Cabinet* (Amherst), June 10, 1806.

95. John Livingston Wright and Abbie Scates Ames, *Mr. Eagle's U.S.A. As Seen in a Buggy Ride of 1400 Miles from Illinois to Boston* (Hartford, Conn.: Truman Joseph Spencer, 1898), p. 183; "Weston Cattle Drives," *The Mountain Ear*, November 6, 1987; Wood, *Turnpikes of New England*, p. 233; Chamberlin, "Business of Robert Rand," p. 114; Butterfield, "Cattle Droving in New England," p. 7.

96. Henry David Thoreau, *Thoreau in the Mountains: Writings by Henry David Thoreau*, with Commentary by William Howarth (New York: Farrar, Straus, Giroux, 1982), p. 228.

97. W. R. Waterman, "Locks and Canals at the White River Falls," *Historical New Hampshire* 22 (Autumn 1967):23.

98. Captain Nelson Richardson, Memoirs, *Vermont Phoenix* (Brattleboro), May 2, 1896, transcribed by Rosetta B. Lowe.

99. "Depositions, Relating to the Portsmouth Bridge," 1841.

100. Edward Augustus Kendall, *Travels through the Northern Parts of the United States in the Years 1807 and 1808*, 3 vols. (New York: I. Riley, 1809), 3:218.

101. Richard E. Winslow, III, *The Piscataqua Gundalow: Workhorse for a Tidal Basin Empire* (Portsmouth, N.H.: Portsmouth Marine Society, 1983), pp. 57-63; "Depositions, Relating to the Portsmouth Bridge," 1841; Caroline M. Fitch, Diary, Old Sturbridge Village, 1836; John P. Adams, *Drowned Valley: The Piscataqua River Basin* (Hanover, N.H.: University Press of New England for the University of New Hampshire, 1976), p. 141.

102. Richardson, Memoir, p. 7 (transcript).

103. Timothy Dwight, *Travels*, 4:107.

104. Frederick Hall, *Letters from the East and from the West* (Washington, D.C.: F. Taylor & Wm. M. Morrison, 1840), pp. 16-17.

105. Lyman S. Hayes, "The Navigation of the Connecticut River: Address before the Vermont Historical Society in the Hall of the House of Representatives, January 16, 1917," *Proceedings of the Vermont Historical Society*, 1915-16, pp. 63-70; Robert A. Whitehouse and Cathleen C. Beaudoin, *Port of Dover: Two Centuries of Shipping on the Cochecho* (Portsmouth, N.H.: Peter E. Randall for the Portsmouth Marine Society, 1988), pp. 25-27, 44.

106. New Hampshire, Laws, June 18, 1807, chapter 53; June 10, 1808, chapter 13.

107. Ibid., January 4, 1792, chapter 52.

108. Hayes, "Navigation of the Connecticut River," pp. 60-63, citing account of C. W. Bliss of West Fairlee, Vermont; Joseph Kidder, "Early Recollections of Manchester: An Address by Mr. Joseph Kidder, Delivered Before the Manchester Historic Association, October 16, 1901," *Manchester Historic Association Collections* 3 (1902-3):72-73.

109. Richardson, Memoir, p. 3 (in transcript); Hayes, "Navigation of the Connecticut River," p. 57.

110. Grace P. Amsden, "A Capital for New Hampshire," Concord, N.H., ca. 1950 (typewritten), vol. 3, chapter 29, p. 5.

111. Marjorie Whalen Smith, *Historic Homes of Cheshire County, New Hampshire*, 3 vols. (Brattleboro, Vt.: Griswold Offset Printing, 1968-1979), 2:36.

112. Rosetta B. Lowe, "Connecticut River at Hinsdale," (manuscript); Edward L. Parker, *The History of Londonderry* (Boston: Perkins & Whipple, 1851; reprint ed., Londonderry, N.H.: By the Town, 1974), p. xi.

113. Belknap, *History*, 3:199.

114. New Hampshire, Laws, January 27, 1688, chapter 15; May 15, 1714, chapter 21.

115. *Manchester Historic Association Collections* 3(1902-3):li; Richardson Wright, *Hawkers & Walkers in Early America: Strolling Peddlers, Preachers, Lawyers, Doctors, Players, and Others, from the Beginning to the Civil War* (Philadelphia: J.B. Lippincott Co., 1927), pp. 48, 60, and *passim*; Ernest Poole, *The Great White Hills of New Hampshire* (Garden City, N.Y.: Doubleday & Co., 1946), p. 172.

116. James Duncan Phillips, "James Duncan of Haverhill: Pack-Peddler, Storekeeper and Merchant," *Essex Institute Historical Collections* 88 (January 1952):1-18; *Manchester Historic Association Collections*, 3:li.

117. Ebenezer Graves, "Journal of a Peddling Trip Kept by Ebenezer Graves of Ashfield, Massachusetts," *Old-Time New England* 56 (January-March 1966):81-82.

118. John Bernard, *Retrospections of America, 1797-1811*, ed. Mrs. Bayle Bernard, with an Introduction by Laurence Hutton and Brander Matthews (New York: Harper & Bros., 1887), p. 42.

119. *New-Hampshire Gazette*, January 19, 1770.

120. *New-Hampshire Spectator* (Newport), December 22, 1829.

121. *New-Hampshire Gazette*, January 22, 1768.

122. George Keith, *A Journal of Travels from New-Hampshire to Caratuck on the Continent of North-America* (London: Joseph Downing, 1706), pp. 11-15.

123. William G. McLoughlin, *New England Dissent, 1630-1833: The Baptists and the Separation of Church and State*, 2 vols. (Cambridge:

Harvard University Press, 1971), 2:726-28, 745-49; David Marks, *Memoirs of the Life of David Marks, Minister of the Gospel*, ed. Marilla Marks, 2d ed. (Dover, N.H.: Free-will Baptist Printing Establishment, 1847), p. 62; and J. Bernard, *Retrospections of America*, p. 304.

124. Marks, *Life of David Marks*; Mark Fernald, *Life of Elder Mark Fernald, Written by Himself* (Newburyport, Mass.: Geo. Moore Payne & D. P. Pike, 1852).

125. Marks, *Life of David Marks*, pp. 62 and 115.

126. Nym Cooke, "Itinerant Yankee Singing Masters in the Eighteenth Century," *Itinerancy in New England and New York: The Dublin Seminar for New England Folklife Annual Proceedings, June 16 and 17, 1984*, ed. Peter Benes and Jane Montague Benes (Boston: Boston University, 1986), p. 28.

127. *New-Hampshire Gazette*, June 1, 1819.

128. Martha McD. Frizzell et al., *Second History of Charlestown, N.H.: The Old Number Four* (Littleton, N.H.: Courier Printing Co., 1955), p. 216; *New-Hampshire Spectator* (Newport), February 26, 1831; Benton, "Lafayette Hotel," p. 10.

129. Louis Pichierri, *Music in New Hampshire, 1623-1800* (New York: Columbia University Press, 1960), pp. 216, 218-19, 224-25, 229-30.

130. Ibid., pp. 144 and 234; [Kidder and Gould], *History of New Ipswich*, p. 263.

131. Augusta H. Worthen, *The History of Sutton, New Hampshire* (Concord, N.H.: Republican Press Association, 1890; reprint ed., Sutton, N.H.: By the Town, 1975), p. 538, quoted in Cooke, "Itinerant Yankee Singing Masters," p. 28.

132. Pichierri, *Music in New Hampshire*, pp. 183-84.

133. *Oracle* (Portsmouth), August 11, 1795.

134. *New-Hampshire Spectator* (Newport), April 20, 1833.

135. *Oracle* (Portsmouth), April 11, 1801.

136. *Dartmouth Gazette* (Hanover), March 28, 1806.

137. Bentley, *Diary*, 2:392.

138. James Guild, "From Tunbridge, Vermont, to London, England—The Journal of James Guild, Peddler, Tinker, Schoolmaster, Portrait Painter, from 1818 to 1824," *Proceedings of the Vermont Historical Society*, n.s., 5 (1937):268, quoted in Diane E. Forsberg, *A Useful Trade: 19th Century Itinerant Portrait Artists, An Exhibition* (Brattleboro, Vt.: Brattleboro Museum & Art Center, 1984), p. 4.

139. *New-Hampshire Gazette*, August 28, 1821.

140. *Farmer's Weekly Museum* (Walpole), July 17, 1797.

141. *New-Hampshire Gazette*, February 25, 1840.

142. Henry Tufts, *The Autobiography of a Criminal*, ed. with an Introduction by Edmund Pearson, new ed., 1st pub. 1807, Dover, N.H. (New York: Duffield & Co., 1930), p. 56; Kym S. Rice, *Early American Taverns: For the Entertainment of Friends and Strangers* (Chicago: Regnery Gateway in association with Fraunces Tavern Museum, 1983), p. 119; Joe Kindig, III, "The Perspective Glass," *Antiques* 65 (June 1954):466-68.

143. Broadside, "Rare Curiosities To Be Seen at Mr. Pattees Hall in Warner, Two Mummies from Egypt," 1827, New Hampshire Historical Society; Lavinia Bailey Kelly, Diary, John Kelly Papers, New Hampshire Historical Society, entry for October 23, 1828; *New-Hampshire Gazette*, April 22, 1774; *Dover Gazette & Strafford Advertiser*, January 8, 1828.

144. *New-Hampshire Gazette*, October 5, 1764; June 15, 1819; *Dover Gazette & Strafford Advertiser*, September 20, 1831; *The Impartialist* (Claremont), "Extra," [August] 1834.

145. *New-Hampshire Spy* (Portsmouth), September 5, 1789; Fennelly, *Life in an Old New England Country Village*, p. 101.

146. Sarah Lathrop Truman, "Reminiscences of Lebanon, N.H.," in Allan Burritt Downs, "Reminiscences of Lebanon," p. 7.

147. *New-Hampshire Gazette*, May 28, 1811; R. W. G. Vail, *Random Notes on the History of the Early American Circus* (Barre, Mass.: Barre Gazette, 1956), p. 83.

148. Emery, *Reminiscences of a Nonagenarian*, pp. 259-61; see also p. 269.

149. "The Village Tavern," *The Farmington News*, December 9, 1887.

150. Blunt, Memoir of Susan Baker Blunt, pp. 4-5.

151. New Hampshire, Laws, January 27, 1688, chapter 15; May 14, 1718, chapter 3; June 29, 1821, chapter 28.

152. Tufts, *Autobiography*, pp. 81, 105-106, 111, 124, 148-149, 194, 204-205, 220, 250, 252, 254, 306-307, 314, 316.

153. Pichierri, *Music in New Hampshire*, pp. 219-20, quoting *New-Hampshire Gazette*, September 10, 1773; *New-Hampshire Patriot & State Gazette* (Concord), January 9, 1832.

154. New Hampshire, Laws, May 14, 1718, chapter 15.

155. Ibid., June 29, 1821, chapter 28.

156. Emery, *Reminiscences of a Nonagenarian*, p. 280.

157. Lambert, *Travels through Canada and the United States*, 1:251.

158. Martha McDanolds Frizzell, *A History of Walpole, New Hampshire*, 2 vols. (Walpole: Walpole Historical Society and the Town, 1963), 1:359.

159. *History of Washington, New Hampshire, from the First Settlement to the Present Time, 1768-1886* (Claremont, N.H.: Claremont Manufacturing Co., 1886), p. 72.

160. R. R. Waldron to William Pickering, July 29, 1831, New Hampshire Historical Society, Miscellaneous Manuscripts, 18B-25.

161. Wilbur H. Siebert, *The Underground Railroad in Massachusetts* (Worcester, Mass.: American Antiquarian Society, 1936), pp. 27-28, 30-32, 35-36, 77, and *passim*.

162. Charles L. Blockson, *The Underground Railroad* (New York: Prentice Hall Press, 1987), p. 269; Luane Cole, ed., *Lyme, New Hampshire: Patterns and Pieces, 1761-1976* (Canaan, N.H.: Phoenix Publishing for the Lyme Historians, Inc., 1976), p. 312.

163. Jeremy Belknap, "Tour to the White Mountains," *Collections of the Massachusetts Historical Society*, ser. 5, vols. 2-3 (1877): *Belknap Papers*, pt. 1, p. 395; pt. 2, p. 184; Samuel J. May, *Memoir*, reprinted in "A Horseback Journey to the White Mountains in 1819," comp. Frederick Tuckerman, *Appalachia* 15 (November 1920), p. 61.

164. Benton, "Lafayette Hotel," pp. 5-6.

165. *Portsmouth Journal*, August 9, 1851; October 2, 1852.

166. Blunt, Memoir of Susan Baker Blunt, p. 12.

167. Mary E. Colby to Susan Colby, June 14, 1834, Colby-Colgate-Cleveland Collection (privately owned).

CHAPTER 6
People of the Road

1. Leaflet, "A Glorification of Stage-Drivers," in Abbot-Downing Company Records, New Hampshire Historical Society, pt. 1, vol. 17 (scrapbook, 1871-1897).

2. Allen Washington Dodge, quoted in Allan Forbes and Ralph M. Eastman, *Taverns and Stagecoaches of New England*, 2 vols. (Boston: State Street Trust Co., 1953-54), 1:92.

3. "Glorification of Stage-Drivers."

4. John Bernard, *Retrospections of America, 1797-1811*, ed. Mrs. Bayle Bernard, with an Introduction by Laurence Hutton and Brander Matthews (New York: Harper & Bros., 1887), p. 35.

5. Samuel Johnson, " 'Journal of a Tour of the White Hills': An 1842 Chronicle by Samuel Johnson," ed. with an Introduction by Bryant F. Tolles, Jr., *Essex Institute Historical Collections* 120 (January 1984):6.

6. Patrick Shirreff, *A Tour through North America, Together with a Comprehensive View of the Canadas and United States as Adapted for Agricultural Emigration* (Edinburgh: Oliver & Boyd, 1835), p. 49.

7. Bernard, *Retrospections of America*, p. 35.

8. Shirreff, *Tour through North America*, p. 49.

9. John Lambert, *Travels through Canada and the United States of North America in Years 1806, 1807, & 1808*, 3d ed., 2 vols. (London: Baldwin, Cradock & Joy, 1816), 2:498-99.

10. Shirreff, *Tour through North America*, p. 49.

11. James Silk Buckingham, *The Eastern and Western States of America*, 3 vols. (London: Fisher, Son, & Co., 1842), 3:216-17, quoted in Peter B. Bulkley, "A History of the White Mountain Tourist Industry, 1818-1899" (M.A. thesis, University of New Hampshire, 1958), p. 13.

12. Frederick Marryat, *A Diary in America with Remarks on Its Institutions*, ed. with an Introduction by Sydney Jackman, new ed., 1st pub. 1839 (New York: Alfred A. Knopf, 1962), p. 124.

13. Lyman S. Hayes, *The Connecticut River Valley in Southern Vermont and New Hampshire: Historical Sketches* (Rutland, Vt.: Tuttle Co., 1929), p. 123, quoting account, c. 1905, by Newman Weeks.

14. William Thayer Smith et al., *Hanover Forty Years Ago: Recollections of Hanover, New Hampshire, in the Sixties and Seventies* (Hanover, N.H.: Dartmouth Press, 1904), p. 15.

15. *New-Hampshire Gazette* (Portsmouth), December 25, 1772.

16. "From Stage Driver to Railroad Builder: B. P. Cheney," in Forbes and Eastman, *Taverns and Stagecoaches of New England*, 1:105-10.

17. P. Stansbury, *A Pedestrian Tour of Two Thousand Three Hundred Miles in North America to the Lakes, the Canadas, and the New England States Performed in the Autumn of 1821* (New York: J. D. Myers & W. Smith, 1822), p. 248; [Sophia Hayes Wyatt], *The Autobiography of a Landlady of the Old School* (Boston: By the Author, 1854), pp. 247-48; and Johnson, "Tour to the White Hills," pp. 32-35.

18. Forbes and Eastman, *Taverns and Stagecoaches of New England*, 1:92, quoting an unidentified recollection.

19. Caroline Gilman, *The Poetry of Travelling in the United States* (New York: S. Colman, 1838), p. 135; see also [Sarah Josepha Hale], "Editors' Table," *Godey's Magazine and Lady's Book* 33 (September 1846):142 and *New-Hampshire Argus and Spectator* (Newport), June 15, 1839.

20. Johnson, "Tour to the White Hills," pp. 9, 13, 36; Anne Royall, *The Black Book, or a Continuation of Travels in the United States*, 3 vols. (Washington, D.C.: By the Author, 1828-29), 2:191, 353, 372, 389.

21. Johnson, "Tour to the White Hills," p. 13.

22. [Hale], "Editors' Table," p. 142 and Bernard, *Retrospections of America*, p. 35.

23. Warren Brown, *History of the Town of Hampton Falls, New Hampshire, from the Time of the First Settlement within Its Borders, 1640 until 1900*, 2 vols. (Manchester, N.H.: John B. Clarke Co., 1900-1918), 1:448-49.

24. Marryat, *Diary in America*, p. 364.

25. E. T. Coke, *A Subaltern's Furlough: Descriptive of Scenes in Various Parts of the United States, Upper and Lower Canada, New-Brunswick, and Nova Scotia during the Summer and Autumn of 1832*, 2 vols. (New York: J. & J. Harper, 1833), 2:141.

26. Francisco de Miranda, *The New Democracy in America: Travels of Francisco de Miranda in the United States, 1783-84*, trans. Judson P. Wood, ed. John S. Ezell (Norman: University of Oklahoma Press, 1963), p. 178.

27. William Little, *History of the Town of Warren, N.H. from Its Early Settlement to the Year 1854* (Concord, N.H.: McFarland & Jenks, 1854), pp. 87-88.

28. Forbes and Eastman, *Taverns and Stagecoaches of New England*, 2:29.

29. Bernard, *Retrospections of America*, p. 35.

30. *Farmer's Cabinet* (Amherst), n.d., quoted in Nathaniel Bouton, *The History of Concord from Its First Grant in 1725 to the Organization of the City Government in 1853* (Concord, N.H.: Benning W. Sanborn, 1856), p. 577.

31. Alice Morse Earle, *Stage-coach and Tavern Days* (New York: Macmillan Co., 1901), p. 323.

32. *New-Hampshire Spectator* (Newport), May 7, 1831.

33. "Glorification of Stage-Drivers."

34. Bernard, *Retrospections of America*, p. 35.

35. Royall, *Black Book*, 2:387.

36. *New-Hampshire Patriot & State Gazette* (Concord), February 3, 1837, quoted in Forbes & Eastman, *Taverns and Stagecoaches of New England*, 1:32-34.

37. New Hampshire, Laws, January 29, 1789, chapter 32; April 14, 1784, chapter 7.

38. New Hampshire, [*Provincial and State Papers*], 40 vols. (Concord: State of New Hampshire, 1867-1943), 12:220-21 (hereafter cited as NHPP).

39. New Hampshire, Laws, June 7-10, 1680, chapter 1; May 14, 1718, chapter 21; Laws, July 3, 1703; May 19, 1704; October 18, 1707; May 4, 1722; "Orders, Resolves, Votes of Legislative Nature Passed during [These] Session[s], [1703-22]."

40. See, for example, New Hampshire, Laws, June 12, 1700, chapter 2.

41. Kenneth Scott, "Colonial Innkeepers of New Hampshire," *Historical New Hampshire* 19 (Spring 1964):33-34.

42. Timothy Dwight, *Travels in New England and New York*, ed. Barbara Miller Solomon with the assistance of Patricia M. King, new ed., 1st pub. 1821-22, 4 vols. (Cambridge: Harvard University Press, Belknap Press, 1969), 2:234.

43. *New-Hampshire Spectator* (Newport), November 5, 1831.

44. New Hampshire, Laws, June 22, 1813, chapter 30.

45. Ibid., June 22, 1820, "Orders, Resolves, and Votes of a Legislative Nature Passed during This Session [1820]."

46. Robert Ferguson, *America during and after the War* (London: Longmans, Green, Reader, & Dyer, 1866), p. 55.

47. Timothy Dwight, *Travels*, 1:309.

48. James Fenimore Cooper, *Notions of the Americans Picked up by a Travelling Bachelor*, with an Introduction by Robert E. Spiller, 2 vols. (London: H. Colburn, 1828; reprint ed., New York: Frederick Ungar Publishing Co., 1963), 1:65.

49. New Hampshire, Laws, May 25, 1687, chapter 26.

50. Scott, "Colonial Innkeepers," pp. 27 and *passim*.

51. Francis Brown Eaton, "The Story of Lake Massabesic," in *Manchester Historic Association Collections* 3 (1902-3):130-31.

52. Biographical sketch of John Hall, in *Colonial Tavernkeepers: Qualifying Ancestors of Flagon and Trencher Members*, ed. Harriet Stryker-Rodda (n.p.: By the Author, 1976), 1:8.

53. *Dictionary of American Biography*, s.v. "Pierce, Benjamin," by Roy F. Nichols; *General Jonathan Chase (1732-1800) of Cornish, New Hampshire: His Papers* (Cornish, N.H.: Cornish Bicentennial Commission, 1977), preface.

54. *NHPP*, 17:36, quoted in Edwin Colby Byam, comp., *Descendants of John Hutchins of Newbury and Haverhill, Massachusetts*, ed. Jack Randolph Hutchins (Washington, D.C.: Goetz Press, 1975), pp. 51-52.

55. Charles H. Bell, *History of the Town of Exeter, New Hampshire* (Boston: J. E. Farwell & Co., 1888), p. 395 and James Burley, *Company Discipline* (Exeter, N.H.: Francis Grant, 1820).

56. Shirreff, *Tour through North America*, p. 49.

57. Cooper, *Notions of the Americans*, 1:82 and 84.

58. Nathaniel Adams, *Annals of Portsmouth* (Portsmouth, N.H.: By the Author, 1825; reprint ed., Hampton, N.H.: Peter E. Randall, 1971), pp. 154-55; Scott, "Colonial Innkeepers," p. 40; Matthew E. Thomas, "Taverns & Inns of Fremont, New Hampshire—Olde Poplin," Fremont, N.H., 1986 (typewritten), p. 2; Charles S. Parsons, *New Hampshire Silver* (n.p.: Adams Brown Co., 1983), p. 93; and Charles S. Parsons, "New Hampshire Joiner Cabinetmakers," Goffstown, N.H., 1981 (typewritten), pp. 90 and 227.

59. [Theodore Dwight], *The Northern Traveller and Northern Tour with the Routes to the Springs, Niagara, Quebec, and Tour of New-England, and the Routes from the South*, 5th ed., rev. (New York: Goodrich & Wiley, 1834), p. 304 and Andrew McMillan, Account Book, 1774-1805, New Hampshire Historical Society.

60. Royall, *Black Book*, 2:392.

61. *New-Hampshire Gazette*, December 19, 1766; March 13, 1767; November 13, 1767; September 26, 1775; see also *Exeter News-Letter*, August 29, 1837.

62. *New-Hampshire Gazette*, April 9, 1762; February 5, 1768; October 27, 1769; August 28, 1772.

63. *New-Hampshire Gazette*, October 4, 1765; February 26, 1773.

64. Patricia Riley, Background Research for Pitt Tavern Restoration, Strawbery Banke, Inc., Portsmouth, N.H., 1982-84 (typewritten), pp. 7-8 and *New-Hampshire Gazette*, February 24, 1769.

65. *New-Hampshire Gazette*, April 26, 1771, transcribed in Riley, Pitt Tavern Restoration, p. 8.

66. *Dollar Weekly Mirror* (Manchester), September 22, 1860.

67. Jeremiah Fellows, Account Book, 1772-1832, New Hampshire Historical Society, and David McCrillis, Daybook, 1787-1824, New Hampshire Historical Society.

68. *New-Hampshire Gazette*, October 2 and 9, 1810.

69. Rockingham County Superior Court Records, docket no. A-864, quoted in James Leo Garvin, "Academic Architecture and the Building Trades in the Piscataqua Region of New Hampshire and Maine, 1715-1815" (Ph.D. dissertation, Boston University, 1983), pp. 127-28.

70. *A Journal of an Excursion Made by the Corps of Cadets of the American Literary, Scientific, and Military Academy under Capt. Alden Partridge, June 1822* (Concord, N.H.: Hill & Moore, 1822), *passim*.

71. Scott, "Colonial Innkeepers," pp. 15, 22, 24-25, 29, 33-35, 40, 42, 46-47.

72. *NHPP*, 17:675.

73. Timothy Dwight, *Travels*, 2:95-96.

74. Royall, *Black Book*, 2:191.

75. *Dartmouth Gazette* (Hanover), August 2, 1805, illustrated in Jerold Wikoff, *The Upper Valley: An Illustrated Tour Along the Connecticut River before the Twentieth Century* (Chelsea, Vt.: Chelsea Green Publishing Co., 1985), p. 72.

76. Frank Burnside Kingsbury, *History of the Town of Surry, Cheshire County, New Hampshire* (Surry, N.H.: By the Town, 1925), pp. 260-61; Henry Tufts, *The Autobiography of a Criminal*, ed. with an Introduction by Edmund Pearson, new ed., 1st pub. 1807, Dover, N.H. (New York: Duffield & Co., 1930), pp. 160-62; and Raymond A. Brighton, *They Came to Fish: A Brief Look at Portsmouth's 350 Years of History*, 2 vols. (Portsmouth, N.H.: Portsmouth 350, Inc., 1973), 2:47.

77. Timothy Dwight, *Travels*, 4:242.

78. Alexander Hamilton, *Gentleman's Progress: The Itinerarium of Dr. Alexander Hamilton, 1744*, ed. with an Introduction by Carl Bridenbaugh (Chapel Hill: University of North Carolina Press for the Institute of Early American History and Culture, 1948), p. 127.

79. Anthony Trollope, *North America* (New York: Harper & Bros., 1862), p. 37.

80. Harriet Martineau, *Retrospect of Western Travel*, 3 vols. (London: Saunders & Otley, 1838), 3:60 and Coke, *Subaltern's Furlough*, 2:148-49.

81. Johnson, "Tour to the White Hills," pp. 14-15.

82. Duke de La Rochefoucault-Liancourt, *Travels through the United States of North America, The Country of the Iroquois and Upper Canada in the Years 1795, 1796, and 1797, with an Authentic Account of Lower Canada* (London: R. Phillips, 1799; American Culture Series 2, reel 192.1, Ann Arbor, Mich.: University Microfilms, n.d.), p. 464.

83. *New-Hampshire Post* (Haverhill), February 24, 1830.

84. Buckingham, *Eastern and Western States*, 3:216-17, quoted in Bulkley, "History of the White Mountain Tourist Industry," p. 12.

85. Esther A. Parker, Memoirs, 1906, typewritten (privately owned).

86. Thomas Hamilton, *Men and Manners in America*, new ed. (Edinburgh: William Blackwood & Sons, 1843; reprint of [2d] ed., New York: Johnson Reprint Corporation, 1968), p. 146.

87. Martineau, *Retrospect of Western Travel*, 3:69.

88. J. P. Brissot de Warville, *New Travels in the United States of America, Performed in 1788* (Boston: Joseph Bumstead, 1797), p. 254.

89. Martineau, *Retrospect of Western Travel*, 3:67-68.

90. *NHPP*, 32:197-98.

91. Bill of sale, December 13, 1769, quoted in Ezra S. Stearns, *History of Plymouth, New Hampshire*, 2 vols. (Cambridge, Mass.: University Press, 1906), 1:404-5.

92. Isaac Weld, *Travels through the States of North America and the Provinces of Upper and Lower Canada during the Years 1795, 1796, and 1797,* with an Introduction by Martin Roth, 2 vols. (London: John Stockdale, 1807; reprint ed., New York: Johnson Reprint Corporation, 1968), 1:29.

93. Garvin, "Academic Architecture in the Piscataqua Region," pp. 127-29.

94. Henry Wadsworth Longfellow, "Lady Wentworth," in *Tales of a Wayside Inn* and Charles W. Brewster, *Rambles About Portsmouth: Sketches of Persons, Localities, and Incidents of Two Centuries, Principally from Tradition and Unpublished Documents* (Portsmouth, N.H.: C.W. Brewster & Son, 1859), 1st ser., pp. 103-5.

95. Charles William Janson, *The Stranger in America* (London: Albion Press, 1807), p. 85.

96. Buckingham, *Eastern and Western States,* 3:207, quoted in Bulkley, "History of the White Mountain Tourist Industry," p. 12.

97. Timothy Dwight, *Travels,* 2:104.

98. Cooper, *Notions of the Americans,* 1:64.

99. [Benjamin Silliman], *Remarks Made on a Short Tour between Hartford and Quebec in the Autumn of 1819* (New Haven: S. Converse, 1820), pp. 33-34, paraphrasing advice offered an English traveler.

100. James Stuart, *Three Years in North America,* 2d ed., rev., 2 vols. (Edinburgh: Robert Cadell, 1833), 1:123; Thomas Hamilton, *Men and Manners in America,* p. 146; Moreau de St. Méry, *Moreau de St. Méry's American Journey [1793-1798],* trans. and ed., Kenneth Roberts and Anna M. Roberts, with an Introduction by Stewart L. Mims (Garden City, N.Y.: Doubleday & Co., 1947), pp. 298-99; Brissot de Warville, *New Travels in the United States,* p. 254; Isaac Fidler, *Observations on Professions, Literature, Manners, and Emigration in the United States and Canada, Made during a Residence There in 1832* (London: Whittaker, Treacher, & Co., 1833), p. 200; Francis J. Grund, *The Americans in Their Moral, Social, and Political Relations,* 2 vols. in 1 (Boston: Marsh, Capen & Lyon, 1837), pp. 326-27.

101. Cooper, *Notions of the Americans,* 1:96.

102. Isabella Lucy Bird, *The Englishwoman in America,* with a Foreword by Andrew Hill Clark (London: John Murray, 1856; reprint ed., Madison: University of Wisconsin Press, 1966), p. 98.

103. Henry David Thoreau, *Thoreau in the Mountains: Writings by Henry David Thoreau,* with Commentary by William Howarth (New York: Farrar, Straus, Giroux, 1982), p. 212.

104. Stansbury, *Pedestrian Tour,* p. 243.

105. Mrs. Amos G. Draper, comp., "Pension Papers of New Hampshire Soldiers in the Revolutionary War: Abstracts from the Original Documents in the Archives of the United States at Washington," 64 vols., Washington, D.C., 1917-22 (typewritten), 35:343.

106. Henry Wansey, *An Excursion to the United States of North America in the Summer of 1794,* 2d ed. (Salisbury, England: J. Easton, 1798), p. 20.

107. Johnson, "Tour to the White Hills," pp. 13-14.

108. Bernard, *Retrospections of America,* p. 350.

109. Martineau, *Retrospect of Western Travel,* 3:66.

110. Harriet Martineau, *Society in America,* 2 vols. (New York: Saunders & Otley, 1837), 1:165.

111. Janson, *Stranger in America,* pp. 19-20.

112. Ibid., p. 19.

113. J. F. D. Smyth, *A Tour in the United States of America,* 2 vols. (London: G. Robinson, 1784), 2:364.

114. Sarah Anna Emery, *Reminiscences of a Nonagenarian* (Newburyport, Mass.: William H. Huse & Co., 1879), p. 297.

115. Alexander Hamilton, *Gentleman's Progress,* pp. 124-25 and [Francis] Grose, comp., *Lexicon Balatronicum: A Dictionary of Buckish Slang, University Wit, and Pickpocket Eloquence* (London: C. Chappel, 1811; reprint ed., Chicago: Follett Publishing Co., 1971).

116. Tufts, *Autobiography,* pp. 200-201.

117. Rockingham County Court Records, docket no. A-3991 (Ebenezer Dearing vs. Philip Barker).

118. Broadside, "Life and Dying Speech of Elisha Thomas, Who Suffered At Dover, June 3, 1788—for the Murder of Capt. Peter Drowne," New Hampshire Historical Society.

119. *NHPP,* 40:190 and Brighton, *They Came to Fish,* 1:9.

120. John King Lord, *A History of the Town of Hanover, N.H.* (Hanover, N.H.: By the Town, 1928), p. 151.

121. Walter Newman Dooley, "Lafayette in New Hampshire" (M.A. thesis, University of New Hampshire, 1941) and Elwyn L. Page, *George Washington in New Hampshire* (Boston: Houghton Mifflin Co. for the George Washington Bicentennial Commission of New Hampshire, 1932).

122. Edgar Gilbert, *History of Salem, N.H.* (Concord, N.H.: Rumford Printing Co., 1907), p. 361; Jeremy Belknap, "Tour to the White Mountains," *Collections of the Massachusetts Historical Society,* ser. 5, vols. 2-3 (1877): *Belknap Papers,* pt. 1, p. 400.

123. *NHPP,* 9:479.

124. Scott, "Colonial Innkeepers," *passim.*

125. *NHPP,* 40:177.

126. Martineau, *Retrospect of Western Travel,* 3:61.

127. Royall, *Black Book,* 2:343-44, 377, 387-89 and Sarah Connell Ayer, *Diary of Sarah Connell Ayer: Andover and Newburyport, Massachusetts; Concord and Bow, New Hampshire; Portland and Eastport, Maine* (Portland, Me.: Lefavor-Tower Co., 1910), p. 85.

128. [Susanna Willard Johnson Hastings], *A Narrative of the Captivity of Mrs. Johnson,* new ed., 1st pub. 1796, Walpole, N.H. (Springfield, Mass.: H.R. Huntting Co., 1907), pp. 136, 141-42, 144-45.

129. Royall, *Black Book,* 2:372-92.

130. Ayer, *Diary of Sarah Connell Ayer,* pp. 25, 47-48, 221, and *passim.*

131. Ibid., pp. 25, 105.

132. Ibid., p. 221.

133. Hale, "Editors' Table," p. 142.

134. Amos Kendall, *Autobiography of Amos Kendall,* ed. William Stickney (Boston: Lee & Shepard, 1872), p. 41.

135. Ayer, *Diary of Sarah Connell Ayer,* p. 106.

136. Aleksandr Borisovich Lakier, *A Russian Looks at America: The Journey of Aleksandr Borisovich Lakier in 1857,* trans. and ed., Arnold Schrier and Joyce Story (Chicago: University of Chicago Press, 1979), p. 25.

137. Bird, *Englishwoman in America,* p. 94.

138. E. S. Abdy, *Journal of a Residence and Tour in the United States of North America from April 1833 to October 1834,* 3 vols. (London: John Murray, 1835), 1:168.

139. Gilman, *Poetry of Travelling,* p. 134.

140. Lucy Crawford, *The History of the White Mountains from the First Settlement of Upper Coos and Pequaket* (White Hills: n.p., 1846), pp. 54-56 and 62.

141. Abdy, *Residence and Tour in the United States*, 1:167-68.

142. Ibid., 1:121-22.

143. John Melish, *Travels through the United States of America in the Years 1806 & 1807, and 1809, 1810, & 1811* (Philadelphia: By the Author, n.d.; London: George Cowie & Co., 1818; reprint ed., New York: Johnson Reprint Corporation, 1970), p. 87.

144. New Hampshire, Laws, January 6, 1715/16, chapter 2.

145. Ibid, June 18, 1686, chapter 17.

146. Tufts, *Autobiography*, pp. 180, 291-94.

147. Stephen Burroughs, *Memoirs of the Notorious Stephen Burroughs of New Hampshire*, with a Preface by Robert Frost, new ed., 1st pub. 1811 (New York: Lincoln MacVeagh, Dial Press, 1924), p. 45 and Tufts, *Autobiography*, p. 109.

148. Seth Wyman, *The Life and Adventures of Seth Wyman, Embodying the Principal Events of a Life Spent in Robbery, Theft, Gambling, Passing Counterfeit Money, &c., &c.* (Manchester, N.H.: J. H. Cate, 1843), pp. 12-13, 126-27.

149. *New-Hampshire Gazette*, May 3, 1771.

150. James Riddle to [William] Richardson, July 17, 1832 (privately owned).

151. Bernard, *Retrospections of America*, p. 34.

152. William Little, *The History of Weare, New Hampshire, 1735-1888* (Lowell, Mass.: S. W. Huse & Co., 1888), p. 608.

153. Tufts, *Autobiography*, p. 180.

154. Gilbert, *History of Salem*, p. 361.

155. Leander W. Cogswell, *History of the Town of Henniker, Merrimack County, New Hampshire* (Concord, N.H.: Republican Press Association, 1880), pp. 94-95.

156. Martha McDanolds Frizzell, *A History of Walpole, New Hampshire*, 2 vols. (Walpole: Walpole Historical Society and the Town, 1963), 1:593-97.

157. Kenneth Scott, "Counterfeiting in Colonial New Hampshire," *Historical New Hampshire* 13 (December 1957):3-4, quoting New Hampshire Province Court Records, New Hampshire Division of Records Management and Archives, vol. 9.

158. *New-Hampshire Gazette*, February 11, 1774.

159. Scott, "Counterfeiting in Colonial New Hampshire," p. 20.

160. Kenneth Scott, "New Hampshire Tory Counterfeiters Operating from New York City," *The New-York Historical Society Quarterly* 34 (January 1950):31-57.

161. Tufts, *Autobiography*, pp. 168-70.

162. *Three Years with Counterfeiters, Smuglers [sic], and Boodle Carriers; with Accurate Portraits of Prominent Members of the Detective Force in the Secret Service* (Boston: John P. Dale & Co., [ca. 1875]), pp. 90-100.

163. Waterman Lilly Ormsby, *A Description of the Present System of Bank Note Engraving Showing Its Tendency to Facilitate Counterfeiting: To Which Is Added a New Method of Constructing Bank Notes to Prevent Forgery* (New York: W. L. Ormsby, 1852), and Robert Wester, "Engraving Art, Science in Book," *The Asylum*, Spring 1985, pp. 4-8.

164. Laban Heath, *Heath's Infallible Counterfeit Detector At Sight* (Boston: Laban Heath, 1864).

165. New Hampshire Province Treasury Records, 1769, New Hampshire Division of Records Management and Archives.

166. Ibid., 1768.

167. Tufts, *Autobiography*, pp. 130-32.

168. Kym S. Rice, *Early American Taverns: For the Entertainment of Friends and Strangers* (Chicago: Regnery Gateway in association with Fraunces Tavern Museum, 1983), pp. 55 and 139, based on Boston court records.

169. Deposition of Catharine Rymes, December 1750, New Hampshire Province Court Records (Mary Ayers vs. George Massey), transcribed in Thomas Marsh, Research Material Relating to Mary Frost and Hopely Ayers, Durham, N.H. (typewritten), 1988.

170. Deposition of Rachel Turril, March 3, 1774, Matthew Patten Papers, New Hampshire Supreme Court.

171. Matthew Patten, *The Diary of Matthew Patten of Bedford, N.H., 1754-1788* (Bedford, N.H.: By the Town, 1903), p. 232; Alice M. Hadley, *Dunbarton, New Hampshire: Where the Winds Blow Free* (Canaan, N.H.: Phoenix Publishing for the Dunbarton History Committee, 1976), pp. 28, 31, 40; and Caleb Stark, *History of the Town of Dunbarton, Merrimack County, New-Hampshire, from the Grant by Mason's Assigns, in 1751, to the year 1860* (Concord, N.H.: G. Parker Lyon, 1860), p. 72.

172. Moreau de St. Méry, *American Journey*, p. 122.

173. Julian Ursyn Niemcewicz, *Under Their Vine and Fig Tree: Travels through America in 1797-1799, 1805 with Some Further Account of Life in New Jersey*, trans. and ed. with an Introduction by Metchie J. E. Budka (Elizabeth, N.J.: Grassman Publishing Co., 1965), p. 275.

174. Tufts, *Autobiography*, pp. 250-51. See also Laurel Thatcher Ulrich and Lois K. Stabler, " 'Girling of it' in Eighteenth-Century New Hampshire," *Families and Children: The Dublin Seminar for New England Folklife Annual Proceedings, June 29 and 30, 1985*, ed. Peter Benes and Jane Montague Benes (Boston: Boston University, 1987), pp. 24-36. For possible tavern setting of the incident described, see Abner Sanger, *Very Poor and of a Lo Make: The Journal of Abner Sanger*, ed. Lois K. Stabler (Portsmouth, N.H.: Peter E. Randall for the Historical Society of Cheshire County, 1986), pp. 237, 306, and 409-10.

CHAPTER 7
Taverns and Government

1. Albert Stillman Batchellor and Henry H. Metcalf, eds., *Laws of New Hampshire*, 10 vols. (Concord: State of New Hampshire, 1904-22), vol. 2: *Province Period, 1702-45*, p. 763.

2. New Hampshire, [*Provincial and State Papers*], 40 vols. (Concord: State of New Hampshire, 1867-1943), 2:486, 488, 563; 3:343, 551; 4:279-80, 291, 440, 451, 455, 466, 519, 526, 547, 554-55, 571, 582, 619, 693, 723, 768 (hereafter cited as NHPP); James Leo Garvin, "Academic Architecture and the Building Trades in the Piscataqua Region of New Hampshire and Maine, 1715-1815" (Ph.D. dissertation, Boston University, 1983), pp. 191-92, 278.

3. NHPP, 3:341, 346, 527.

4. Ibid., 2:465, 467, 477-78.

5. New Hampshire Province Court Records, New Hampshire Division of Records Management and Archives, 18234-35.

6. NHPP, 19:736-37.

7. Ibid., 4:433.

8. Ibid., 18:1.

9. James Birket, *Some Cursory Remarks Made by James Birket in His Voyage to North America, 1750-1751* (New Haven: Yale University Press, 1916), p. 9.

10. New Hampshire Province Treasury Records, 1742-47 (Priest); 1753-62 (Horney), New Hampshire Division of Records Management and Archives.

11. Warren Brown, *History of the Town of Hampton Falls, New Hampshire, from the Time of the First Settlement within Its Borders, 1640 until 1900*, 2 vols. (Manchester, N.H.: John B. Clarke Co., 1900-1918), 1:402.

12. Martha McD. Frizzell et al., *Second History of Charlestown, N.H.: The Old Number Four* (Littleton, N.H.: Courier Printing Co., 1955), p. 75.

13. S. G. Griffin, *A History of the Town of Keene from 1732, When the Township Was Granted by Massachusetts, to 1874, When It Became a City* (Keene, N.H.: Sentinel Printing Co., 1904), pp. 148-49.

14. Peter L. Hoyt, *Hoyt's History of Wentworth, New Hampshire*, transcribed from original manuscript by Francis A. Muzzey (Littleton, N.H.: Courier Printing Co., 1976), pp. 267-70.

15. Poplin Town Records, Town of Fremont, 1822-26.

16. *NHPP*, 13:539.

17. New Hampshire, Laws, June 23, 1813, chapter 33.

18. Charles A. Bemis, *History of the Town of Marlborough, Cheshire County, New Hampshire* (Boston: Geo. H. Ellis, 1881; reprint ed., Marlborough, N.H.: Frost Free Library, 1974), p. 190.

19. New Hampshire Province Treasury Records, 1742.

20. Ibid., 1747.

21. Robert Rogers, *A Concise Account of North America* (London: By the Author, 1765), p. 51.

22. New Hampshire Province Treasury Records, 1770.

23. John Farmer, *An Historical Sketch of Amherst, in the County of Hillsborough, in New-Hampshire* (Amherst, N.H.: Richard Boylston, 1820), p. 12.

24. *NHPP*, 13:11.

25. New Hampshire Province Treasury Records, 1755.

26. Matthew Patten, *The Diary of Matthew Patten of Bedford, N.H., 1754-1788* (Bedford, N.H.: By the Town, 1903), p. 480.

27. *Farmer's Cabinet* (Amherst), November 27, 1810.

28. Charles R. Corning, Diary, 1906-8, New Hampshire Historical Society, entry for March 2, 1908.

29. *New Hampshire Sentinel* (Keene), October 26, 1816.

30. *New-Hampshire Gazette* (Portsmouth), March 30, 1819.

31. *NHPP*, 2:465, 467, 477-78.

32. Brown, *History of Hampton Falls*, 1:404.

33. James O. Lyford, ed., *History of Concord, New Hampshire, from the Original Grant in Seventeen Hundred and Twenty-five to the Opening of the Twentieth Century*, 2 vols. (Concord, N.H.: Rumford Press, 1903), 2:853.

34. Chandler E. Potter, *The Military History of the State of New-Hampshire, 1623-1861*, 2 pts. in one vol. (Concord, N.H.: McFarland & Jenks, 1866-68; reprint ed., Baltimore: Genealogical Publishing Co., 1972), pt. 1, p. 388.

35. J. Trask Plumer, "The Old Times Muster," *Manchester Historic Association Collections* 3 (1902-3):175-76.

36. Susan Baker Blunt, Memoir, 1913, Manchester Historic Association, typewritten transcript, p. 9.

37. Plumer, "Old Times Muster," p. 176.

38. New Hampshire State Treasury Records, 1791.

39. Anthony Marro, "Vermont's Local Militia Units, 1815-1860," *Vermont History* 40 (Winter 1972):31.

40. Potter, *Military History*, pt. 1, p. 380.

41. Plumer, "Old Times Muster," p. 179.

42. Ibid., p. 178.

43. Ibid.; Frederick Marryat, *A Diary in America with Remarks on Its Institutions*, ed. with an Introduction by Sidney Jackman, new ed., 1st pub. 1839 (New York: Alfred A. Knopf, 1962), pp. 124-25.

44. Potter, *Military History*, pt. 2, pp. 242-43; *New-Hampshire Statesman* (Concord), April 21, 1823.

45. Plumer, "Old Times Muster," p. 177.

46. Daniel F. Secomb, *History of the Town of Amherst, Hillsborough County, New Hampshire*, with a Foreword by Richard F. Upton (Concord, N.H.: Evans, Sleeper & Woodbury, 1883; reprint ed., Somersworth, N.H.: New Hampshire Publishing Co., 1972), p. 428.

47. Seth Wyman, *The Life and Adventures of Seth Wyman, Embodying the Principal Events of a Life Spent in Robbery, Theft, Gambling, Passing Counterfeit Money, &c., &c.* (Manchester, N.H.: J. H. Cate, 1843), p. 13.

48. *New-Hampshire Gazette*, March 6, 1772.

49. *The Town of Amherst, New Hampshire, 1760-1960, 200th Anniversary Celebration*, June 1960 (n.p., 1960), p. 13.

50. Plumer, "Old Times Muster," p. 174; Potter, *Military History*, pt. 2, pp. 367-77; *Farmer's Cabinet* (Amherst), April 14, 1807.

51. New Hampshire, Laws, January 10, 1758, chapter 2.

52. New Hampshire Province Treasury Records, 1769.

53. [Charles H. Bell], *Exeter in 1776. Sketches of an Old New Hampshire Town As It Was a Hundred Years Ago* (Exeter, N.H.: News-Letter Press, 1876), p. 35.

54. Lyford, *History of Concord*, 1:331-32.

55. Harriette Eliza Noyes, comp., *A Memorial of the Town of Hampstead, New Hampshire* (Boston: George B. Reed, 1899), p. 288.

56. New Hampshire Province Treasury Records, 1755.

57. Ibid., 1758.

58. Ibid., 1757.

59. Ibid., 1761.

60. Ibid.

61. Ibid.

62. Ibid., 1775.

63. Ibid., 1760.

64. Ibid., 1766.

65. Ibid., 1771.

66. *New-Hampshire Gazette*, July 29, 1817.

67. Ibid.; Lyford, *History of Concord*, 2:1097-98.

68. *New-Hampshire Gazette*, July 29, 1817.

69. Lyford, *History of Concord*, 2:1102.

70. John King Lord, *A History of Dartmouth College, 1815-1909: Being the Second Volume of A History of Dartmouth College and the Town of Hanover, New Hampshire, Begun by Frederick Chase* (Concord, N.H.: Rumford Press, 1913), p. 272.

71. Griffin, *History of Keene*, pp. 434-35.

72. *NHPP*, 17:679, 681.

73. Ibid., 19:83.

74. New Hampshire Province Treasury Records, 1731.

75. Lyford, *History of Concord*, 2:1110.

76. *New-Hampshire Gazette*, December 30, 1774; January 6, 1775.

77. *NHPP*, 18:52-53; Charles H. Bell, *History of the Town of Exeter, New Hampshire* (Boston: J. E. Farwell & Co., 1888), pp. 72-75.

78. *New-Hampshire Gazette*, April, 24, 1772; Edward D. Boylston, comp., *Historical Sketch of the Hillsborough County Congresses, Held at Amherst, (N.H.), 1774 & 1775: With Other Revolutionary Records* (Amherst, N.H.: Farmers' Cabinet Press, 1884), pp. 12-13; William Little, *The History of Weare, New Hampshire, 1735-1888* (Lowell, Mass.: S.W. Huse & Co., 1888), pp. 185-91.

79. *New-Hampshire Gazette*, May 1, 1772; Little, *History of Weare*, p. 190.

80. *New-Hampshire Gazette*, November 8, 1765.

81. Ibid., August 26, 1774.

82. Bell, *History of Exeter*, pp. 241-42; Charles L. Parsons," The Capture of Fort William and Mary, December 14 and 15, 1774," *Proceedings of the New Hampshire Historical Society* 4 (1899-1905):18-47; Elwin L. Page, "The King's Powder, 1774," *The New England Quarterly* 18 (March 1945):83-92; Elwin L. Page, "What Happened to the King's Powder?" *Historical New Hampshire* 19 (Summer 1964): 28-33; Paul Wilderson, "The Raids on Fort William and Mary: Some New Evidence,"*Historical New Hampshire* 30 (Fall 1975):178-202.

83. Parsons, "Capture of Fort William and Mary," p. 23.

84. Bell, *History of Exeter*, p. 240.

85. "New Hampshire Loyalists: Transcripts from the Records of the Commission for Enquiring into the Losses and Services of American Loyalists, 1783-1790, Preserved in the Public Record Office, London, England," 5 vols., New Hampshire State Library, Concord, N.H., 4:1709-10, quoted in Patricia Riley, Biographical Sketch of John Stavers, Strawbery Banke, Inc., Portsmouth, N.H., 1982-84 (typewritten).

86. Deposition, January 30, 1777, Otis G. Hammond Papers, New Hampshire Historical Society, "Transcripts—Loyalists," under Isaac Rindge et al.

87. Ibid., February 3, 1777.

88. Charles W. Brewster, *Rambles About Portsmouth: Sketches of Persons, Localities, and Incidents of Two Centuries, Principally from Tradition and Unpublished Documents* (Portsmouth, N.H.: C. W. Brewster & Son, 1859), 1st ser., pp. 192-94.

89. Mark Noble to the Committee of Safety, Exeter, February 3, 1777, "Transcripts—Loyalists," under John and Bartholomew Stavers, transcribed in Brewster, *Rambles About Portsmouth*, 2d ser. (Portsmouth, N.H.: Lewis W. Brewster, 1869), p. 85.

90. *New-Hampshire Gazette*, February 18, 1777.

91. Parsons, "Capture of Fort William and Mary," p. 18; Josiah Bartlett, *The Papers of Josiah Bartlett*, ed. Frank C. Mevers (Hanover, N.H.: University Press of New England for the New Hampshire Historical Society, 1979), p. 11.

92. John King Lord, *A History of the Town of Hanover, N.H.* (Hanover, N.H.: By the Town, 1928), pp. 152-53; *NHPP*, 11:332; New Hampshire Province Treasury Records, 1775.

93. David McClure, *Diary of David McClure, Doctor of Divinity, 1748-1820*, with Notes by Franklin B. Dexter (New York: Knickerbocker Press, 1899), p. 155.

94. Abner Sanger, *Very Poor and of a Lo Make: The Journal of Abner Sanger*, ed. Lois K. Stabler (Portsmouth, N.H.: Peter E. Randall for the Historical Society of Cheshire County, 1986), pp. 126-27.

95. Griffin, *History of Keene*, pp. 241-42; Sanger, *Very Poor and of a Lo Make*, p. 248.

96. Potter, *Military History*, pt. 1, p. 346; William E. Moore, "Early Settlement of Kelley's Falls," *Manchester Historic Association Collections* 2 (1900-1):89-91.

97. Nathaniel Bouton, *The History of Concord from Its First Grant in 1725 to the Organization of the City Government in 1853* (Concord, N.H.: Benning W. Sanborn, 1856), pp. 272-73.

98. Patten, *Diary*, p. 330.

99. *The Sun* (Dover), March 6, 1802, quoted in Gordon F. Grimes, "A History of Dover, New Hampshire, 1790-1835," [Brunswick, Me.], 1971 (typewritten), p. 29.

100. Daniel Waldron to William Hale, March 14, 1814, Hale Papers, New Hampshire Historical Society, quoted in Grimes, "History of Dover," p. 69.

101. Emma P. Boylston Locke, comp., *Colonial Amherst: The Early History, Customs, and Homes* (Milford, N.H.: W.B. & A. B. Rotch, 1916), p. 37.

102. Secomb, *History of Amherst*, p. 123.

103. Sarah Connell Ayer, *Diary of Sarah Connell Ayer: Andover and Newburyport, Massachusetts; Concord and Bow, New Hampshire; Portland and Eastport, Maine* [ed. Margaret H. Jewell] (Portland, Me.: Lefavor-Tower Co., 1910), p. 146.

104. *Portsmouth Journal*, January 20, 1838; October 20, 1838; January 19, 1839; December 12, 1840; December 23, 1843; January 6, 1844; December 26, 1846; January 19, 1839; March 2, 1844; December 26, 1840; January 7, 1843; January 18, 1845; Ibid.; October 17, 1846.

105. Howard M. Cook, *Town Topics, Out of Town Topics, and Suburban Jottings* (Concord, N.H.: W. C. Gibson, 1912), pp. 53, 57; Lyford, *History of Concord*, 2:859; Secomb, *History of Amherst*, pp. 148-49; Lord, *History of Dartmouth College*, p. 273.

106. Ezra S. Stearns, *History of Plymouth, New Hampshire*, 2 vols. (Cambridge, Mass.: University Press, 1906), 1:344.

107. *Haverhill (Mass.) Weekly Bulletin*, November 14, 1874.

CHAPTER 8
Entertainment: Food and Drink

1. *New-Hampshire Gazette* (Portsmouth), August 3, 1782.

2. John Lambert, *Travels through Canada and the United States of North America in the Years 1806, 1807, & 1808*, 3d ed., 2 vols. (London: Baldwin, Cradock & Joy, 1816), 2:39.

3. James Birket, *Some Cursory Remarks Made by James Birket in His Voyage to North America, 1750-1751* (New Haven: Yale University Press, 1916), pp. 4-5.

4. Duke de La Rochefoucault-Liancourt, *Travels through the United States of North America, The Country of the Iroquois and Upper Canada in the Years 1795, 1796, and 1797, with an Authentic Account of Lower Canada* (London: R. Phillips, 1799; American Culture Series 2, reel 192.1, Ann Arbor, Mich.: University Microfilms, n.d.), p. 62.

5. Henry Wansey, *An Excursion to the United States of North America in the Summer of 1794*, 2d ed. (Salisbury, England: J. Easton, 1798), p. 20.

6. John Bernard, *Retrospections of America, 1797-1811*, ed. Mrs. Bayle Bernard, with an Introduction by Laurence Hutton and Brander Matthews (New York: Harper & Bros., 1887), p. 349.

7. P. Stansbury, *A Pedestrian Tour of Two Thousand Three Hundred Miles in North America to the Lakes, the Canadas, and the New England States Performed in the Autumn of 1821* (New York: J. D. Myers & W. Smith, 1822), p. 248.

8. Francis J. Grund, *The Americans in Their Moral, Social, and Political Relations*, 2 vols. in 1 (Boston: Marsh, Capen & Lyon, 1837), p. 328.

9. Anthony Trollope, *North America* (New York: Harper & Bros., 1862), p. 40.

10. Isaac Weld, *Travels through the States of North America and the Provinces of Upper and Lower Canada during the Years 1795, 1796, and 1797*, with an Introduction by Martin Roth, 2 vols. (London: John Stockdale, 1807; reprint ed., New York: Johnson Reprint Corporation, 1968), 1:28.

11. James Fenimore Cooper, *Notions of the Americans Picked up by a Travelling Bachelor*, with an Introduction by Robert E. Spiller, 2 vols. (London: H. Colburn, 1828; reprint ed., New York: Frederick Ungar Publishing Co., 1963), 1:50.

12. Robert Ferguson, *America during and after the War* (London: Longmans, Green, Reader, & Dyer, 1866), pp. 4-5.

13. Thomas Hamilton, *Men and Manners in America*, new ed. (Edinburgh: William Blackwood & Sons, 1843; reprint of [2d] ed., New York: Johnson Reprint Corporation, 1968), p. 90.

14. Charles Augustus Murray, *Travels in North America during the Years 1834, 1835, and 1836*, 2 vols. (London: Richard Bentley, 1839), 1:95.

15. Esther A. Parker, Memoirs, 1906, typewritten (privately owned); T. Hamilton, *Men and Manners in America*, pp. 89 and 145; Frederick Marryat, *A Diary in America with Remarks on Its Institutions*, ed. with an Introduction by Sydney Jackman, new ed., 1st pub. 1839 (New York: Alfred A. Knopf, 1962), p. 375; James O. Lyford, ed., *History of Concord, New Hampshire, from the Original Grant in Seventeen Hundred and Twenty-five to the Opening of the Twentieth Century*, 2 vols. (Concord, N.H.: Rumford Press, 1903), 2:865.

16. Rockingham County Probate Records, docket no. 6384; Seymour Dunbar, *A History of Travel in America*, 4 vols. (Indianapolis: Bobbs-Merrill Co., 1915), 1:211.

17. Ferguson, *America during and after the War*, p. 5.

18. Trollope, *North America*, p. 39.

19. Isaac Fidler, *Observations on Professions, Literature, Manners, and Emigration in the United States and Canada, Made during a Residence There in 1832* (London: Whittaker, Treacher, & Co., 1833), p. 177.

20. Wansey, *Excursion to the United States*, p. 21.

21. Joseph B. Walker, "Penacook House and the Old Time Taverns of the State," *Proceedings of the New Hampshire Historical Society*, 1 (1872-88):391.

22. John Grenville Cook, "An 1850 Journey to Sandwich," *Annual Excursions of the Sandwich Historical Society* 67 (August 1986):16.

23. J[ames] S[ilk] Buckingham, *The Eastern and Western States of America*, 3 vols. (London: Fisher, Son, & Co., [1842]; American Culture Series 2, reel 126.3, Ann Arbor, Mich.: University Microfilms, n.d.), 1:218.

24. Timothy Dwight, *Travels in New England and New York*, ed. Barbara Miller Solomon with the assistance of Patricia M. King,

new ed., 1st pub. 1821-22, 4 vols. (Cambridge: Harvard University Press, Belknap Press, 1969), 2:217; William Bentley, *The Diary of William Bentley, D.D., Pastor of the East Church, Salem, Massachusetts*, 4 vols. (Salem, Mass.: Essex Institute, 1907-14), 1:63.

25. Francisco de Miranda, *The New Democracy in America: Travels of Francisco de Miranda in the United States, 1783-84*, trans. Judson P. Wood, ed. John S. Ezell (Norman: University of Oklahoma Press, 1963), pp. 180 and 183.

26. Cook, "1850 Journey to Sandwich," p. 14.

27. Wansey, *Excursion to the United States*, p. 20; Cooper, *Notions of the Americans*, 1:50.

28. Ibid.

29. Francesco dal Verme, *Seeing America and Its Great Men: The Journal and Letters of Count Francesco dal Verme, 1783-1784*, trans. and ed. Elizabeth Cometti (Charlottesville: University Press of Virginia, 1969), p. 22.

30. Miranda, *The New Democracy in America*, pp. 179-80, 184.

31. Grund, *The Americans*, p. 327.

32. Murray, *Travels in North America*, 1:95.

33. Walker, "Penacook House," p. 391; see also Sarah F. McMahon, " 'A Comfortable Subsistence': A History of Diet in New England, 1630-1850" (Ph.D. dissertation, Brandeis University, 1981), pp. 191-92.

34. William Little, *The History of Weare, New Hampshire, 1735-1888* (Lowell, Mass.: S. W. Huse & Co., 1888), p. 650.

35. Aleksandr Borisovich Lakier, *A Russian Looks at America: The Journey of Aleksandr Borisovich Lakier in 1857*, trans. and ed. Arnold Schrier and Joyce Story (Chicago: University of Chicago Press, 1979), p. 22.

36. Lambert, *Travels through Canada and the United States*, 2:39-40.

37. Charles William Janson, *The Stranger in America* (London: Albion Press, 1807), p. 80.

38. Timothy Dwight, *Travels*, 4:249; Moreau de St. Méry, *Moreau de St. Méry's American Journey* [1793-1798], trans. and ed. Kenneth Roberts and Anna M. Roberts, with an Introduction by Stewart L. Mims (Garden City, N.Y.: Doubleday & Co., 1947), p. 265; Susan Baker Blunt, Memoir, 1913, Manchester Historic Association, typewritten transcript, p. 25; Lambert, *Travels through Canada and the United States*, 2:15; Buckingham, *Eastern and Western States*, 3:216-17, quoted in Peter B. Bulkley, "A History of the White Mountain Tourist Industry, 1818-1899" (M.A. thesis, University of New Hampshire, 1958), pp. 12-13.

39. Lakier, *A Russian Looks at America*, p. 21.

40. McMahon, "Comfortable Subsistence," pp. 215 and 229-30; Timothy Dwight, *Travels*, 4:249.

41. Moreau de St. Méry, *American Journey*, p. 265.

42. McMahon, "Comfortable Subsistence," p. 227.

43. Elizabeth Packer, Account for Entertaining Governor Dudley and his Guards, August 1704, New Hampshire Province Treasury Records, 1704, New Hampshire Division of Records Management and Archives.

44. Timothy Dwight, *Travels*, 4:249; Lambert, *Travels through Canada and the United States*, 2:29 and 39; Janson, *Stranger in America*, p. 444; and McMahon, "Comfortable Subsistence," p. 228.

45. Albert C. Koch, *Journey through a Part of the United States of North America in the Years 1844 to 1846*, trans. and ed. Ernst A. Stadler, with a Foreword by John Francis McDermott (Carbondale: Southern Illinois University Press, 1972), p. 12.

46. McMahon, "Comfortable Subsistence," p. 226; Janson, *Stranger in America*, p. 83.

47. McMahon, "Comfortable Subsistence," p. 227.

48. Timothy Dwight, *Travels*, 4:249.

49. Moreau de St. Méry, *American Journey*, p. 266; Trollope, *North America*, p. 40; Caroline Sloat, "Toasts & Tea," *Old Sturbridge Visitor* 27 (Winter 1987-88):10, quoting unidentified New Hampshire reminiscence.

50. Sarah Anna Emery, *Reminiscences of a Nonagenarian* (Newburyport, Mass.: William H. Huse & Co., 1879), p. 245.

51. Sarah Connell Ayer, *Diary of Sarah Connell Ayer: Andover and Newburyport, Massachusetts; Concord and Bow, New Hampshire; Portland and Eastport, Maine* [ed. Margaret H. Jewell], (Portland, Me.: Lefavor-Tower Co., 1910), p. 61.

52. Howard M. Cook, *Town Topics, Out of Town Topics and Suburban Jottings* (Concord, N.H.: W. C. Gibson, 1912), pp. 55-56.

53. Samuel Barnes, Daybook, Hillsborough, 1800-1810, privately owned; Hannah Osgood, Accounts, Concord, 1765-69, New Hampshire Historical Society; Paul Brooks, Account Book, Westmoreland, 1810-17, Historical Society of Cheshire County.

54. Lakier, *A Russian Looks at America*, p. 21; Ferguson, *America during and after the War*, p. 4; *Oxford English Dictionary*, s.v. "Luncheon."

55. Caroline Gilman, *The Poetry of Travelling in the United States* (New York: S. Colman, 1838), p. 134.

56. Timothy Dwight, *Travels*, 2:95.

57. Mary Jane Thomas, "Reminiscences of the White Mountains," ed. with Foreword by Harriet S. Lacy, *Historical New Hampshire* 28 (Spring 1973): 46 and 49; Asa McFarland, *An Outline of Biography and Recollection* (Concord, N.H.: Republican Press Association, 1880), p. 71.

58. Buckingham, *Eastern and Western States*, 1:218.

59. *New-Hampshire Gazette*, October 19, 1802; *New-Hampshire Patriot & State Gazette* (Concord), June 21, 1830; Catherine Fennelly, *Life in an Old New England Country Village* (New York: Thomas Y. Crowell Co., 1969), p. 103, quoting advertisement of Jacob Coffin, Londonderry, 1806.

60. McMahon, "Comfortable Subsistence," p. 92.

61. Daniel J. Boorstin, *The Americans: The National Experience* (New York: Random House, Vintage Books, 1965), pp. 10-16; Jane Whitehill, *Food, Drink, and Recipes of Early New England* (Sturbridge, Mass.: Old Sturbridge Village, 1963), p. 5.

62. McMahon, "Comfortable Subsistence," pp. 93-98.

63. Jeremy Belknap, "Tour to the White Mountains," *Collections of the Massachusetts Historical Society*, ser. 5, vols. 2-3 (1877): Belknap Papers, pt. 2, p. 181; McFarland, *Outline of Biography*, p. 71; Harriet Martineau, *Retrospect of Western Travel*, 3 vols. (London: Saunders & Otley, 1838), 3:69.

64. McMahon, "Comfortable Subsistence," pp. 189-90.

65. Joshua Atherton to his wife, Abigail Atherton, ca. 1800, in Anne M. Means, *Amherst and Our Family Tree* (Boston: By the Author, 1921), pp. 40-41.

66. McMahon, "Comfortable Subsistence," pp. 38, 41-43; Rockingham County Probate Records, docket no. 6384.

67. Lambert, *Travels through Canada and the United States*, 2:40.

68. Eliphalet Daniels, Account Books and Daybook, Portsmouth, 1764-93, New Hampshire Historical Society.

69. Rockingham County Probate Records, docket no. 6384; Jeremy Belknap, *The History of New-Hampshire*, 2d ed., vol. 3, ed. with an Introduction by G. T. Lord (Dover, N.H.: O. Crosby & J. Varney, 1812; reprint ed., Hampton, N.H.: Peter E. Randall, 1973), 3:158.

70. McFarland, *Outline of Biography*, p. 71.

71. Lucy Crawford, *The History of the White Mountains from the First Settlement of Upper Coos and Pequaket* (White Hills: n.p., 1846), pp. 7-8, 47-48, 59.

72. Thomas, "Reminiscences of the White Mountains," p. 49.

73. Timothy Dwight, *Travels*, 2:213, 224; Birket, *Some Cursory Remarks*, pp. 7, 14.

74. Rev. Stephen Peabody, quoted in Fennelly, *Life in a New England Country Village*, p. 94.

75. Ralph Stuart Wallace, "The Scotch-Irish of Provincial New Hampshire" (Ph.D. dissertation, University of New Hampshire, 1984), p. 322.

76. Matthew Patten, *The Diary of Matthew Patten of Bedford, N.H., 1754-1788* (Bedford, N.H.: By the Town, 1903), pp. 447-48.

77. Birket, *Some Cursory Remarks*, p. 7; Janson, *Stranger in America*, p. 20.

78. Moreau de St. Méry, *American Journey*, p. 266; *Oracle* (Portsmouth), November 2, 1805.

79. Steven R. Pendery, "The Archeology of Urban Foodways in Portsmouth, New Hampshire," *Foodways in the Northeast: The Dublin Seminar for New England Folklife Annual Proceedings, June 25 through 27, 1982*, ed. Peter Benes and Jane Montague Benes (Boston: Boston University, 1984), pp. 21-22.

80. Jeremy Belknap, *Jeremy Belknap's Journey to Dartmouth in 1774*, ed. Edward C. Lathem (Hanover: Dartmouth Publications, 1950), pp. 22 and [26]; Dwight, *Travels*, 2:88; see also p. 234.

81. Caroline M. Fitch, Diary, Old Sturbridge Village, transcribed by Dorothy W. Sears, Jr., 1986.

82. Crawford, *History of the White Mountains*, p. 48.

83. Birket, *Some Cursory Remarks*, p. 9.

84. Belknap, "Tour to the White Mountains," pt. 1, p. 387.

85. *New-Hampshire Patriot & State Gazette* (Concord), July 18, 1825.

86. McMahon, "Comfortable Subsistence," pp. 52-54, 105-112.

87. Birket, *Some Cursory Remarks*, p. 9.

88. Samuel Johnson, " 'Journal of a Tour to the White Hills': An 1842 Chronicle by Samuel Johnson," ed. with an Introduction by Bryant F. Tolles, Jr., *Essex Institute Historical Collections* 120 (January 1984):14.

89. Martineau, *Retrospect of Western Travel*, 3:61.

90. Belknap, "Tour to the White Mountains," pt. 2, p. 181.

91. Edward Augustus Kendall, *Travels through the Northern Parts of the United States in the Years 1807 and 1808*, 3 vols. (New York: I. Riley, 1809), 3:35.

92. Birket, *Some Cursory Remarks*, pp. 10-11; John Hughes to Jonathan Roberts, September 7, 1769, reprinted in Anna M. Holstein, *Swedish Holsteins in America from 1644 to 1892, Comprising Many Letters and Biographical Matter Relating to John Hughes, the "Stamp Officer"* (Norristown, Pa.: M. R. Wills, 1892), p. 56; Henry H. Saunderson, *History of Charlestown, New-Hampshire, The Old No. 4* (Claremont, N.H.: Claremont Manufacturing Co., 1876), pp. 716-17.

93. James Underwood, Account Book and Daybooks, Swanzey, 1814-32, Historical Society of Cheshire County; see also Crawford, *History of the White Mountains*, p. 36 and Patricia Riley, Background Research for Pitt Tavern Restoration, Strawbery Banke, Inc., Portsmouth, N.H., 1982-84 (typewritten), p. 7.

94. Parker, Memoirs of Esther A. Parker.

95. Koch, *Journey through Part of the United States*, p. 12.

96. Parker, Memoirs of Esther A. Parker; Martha McDanolds Frizzell, *A History of Walpole, New Hampshire*, 2 vols. (Walpole: Historical Society and the Town, 1963), 1:42.

97. Lyford, *History of Concord*, 1:305.

98. Seth Wyman, *The Life and Adventures of Seth Wyman, Embodying the Principal Events of a Life Spent in Robbery, Theft, Gambling, Passing Counterfeit Money, &c., &c.* (Manchester, N.H.: J. H. Cate, 1843), pp. 126-27.

99. William F. Whitcher, *History of the Town of Haverhill, New Hampshire* (Concord, N.H.: Rumford Press, 1919), p. 340.

100. New Hampshire Province Treasury Records, 1754.

101. Andrew McMillan, Account Book, Conway, 1774-1805, New Hampshire Historical Society.

102. *Farmer's Cabinet* (Amherst), June 19, 1810; *New-Hampshire Gazette*, February 3, 1846.

103. Nathaniel Bouton, *The History of Concord from Its First Grant in 1725 to the Organization of the City Government in 1853* (Concord, N.H.: Benning W. Sanborn, 1856), p. 373.

104. *A Journal of an Excursion Made by the Corps of Cadets of the American Literary, Scientific, and Military Academy under Capt. Alden Partridge, June 1822* (Concord, N.H.: Hill & Moore, 1822), p. 13.

105. James Underwood, Account Book and Daybooks, inserted bill.

106. Edgar Gilbert, *History of Salem, N.H.* (Concord, N.H.: Rumford Printing Co., 1907), p. 326; Alice K. Rice, "The Dover Hotel and the New Hampshire House," a lecture presented April 24, 1916, pp. 8-9.

107. New Hampshire Province Treasury Records, 1767.

108. Parker, Memoirs of Esther A. Parker.

109. Anne Royall, *The Black Book, or a Continuation of Travels in the United States*, 3 vols. (Washington, D.C.: By the Author, 1828-29), 2:386-87.

110. McMahon, "Comfortable Subsistence," p. 241; Sarah Josepha Hale, *Northwood; or, Life North and South: Showing the True Character of Both* (New York: H. Long & Bro., 1852), pp. 88-90.

111. Marcia Byrom Hartwell, "Researching Food in American History: Knowing What People Ate Can Tell You Who They Were," *History News* 42 (November/December 1987):20.

112. Thomas Jefferson to Lafayette, April 11, 1787, quoted in Rosemary Brandau, "A Taste of the Past," *Colonial Williamsburg: The Journal of the Colonial Williamsburg Foundation*, Summer 1987, p. 29.

113. Nathaniel Bouton, *History of the Temperance Reform in Concord: A Discourse Delivered on the Evening of December 10, 1843* (Concord, N.H.: Asa McFarland, 1843), p. 4, and Franklin McDuffee, *History of the Town of Rochester, New Hampshire, from 1722 to 1890*, 2 vols. (Manchester: John B. Clarke Co., 1892), 1:294.

114. Bouton, *Temperance Reform in Concord*, pp. 4-5.

115. W. J. Rorabaugh, *The Alcoholic Republic: An American Tradition* (New York: Oxford University Press, 1979), p. 17, based on Frost General Store, Durham, Day Books, 1810-33, Baker Library, Harvard University.

116. John R. Eastman, comp., *History of the Town of Andover, New Hampshire, 1751-1906* (Concord, N.H.: Rumford Printing Co., 1910), pt. 1, p. 183.

117. George Aldrich, *Walpole As It Was and As It Is, Containing the Complete Civil History of the Town from 1749 to 1879* (Claremont, N.H.: Claremont Manufacturing Co., 1880), pp. 82-83.

118. *The Records of the Town of Hanover, New Hampshire, 1761-1818* (Hanover, N.H.: By the Town, 1905), p. 222; Charles H. Bell, *History of the Town of Exeter, New Hampshire* (Boston: J. E. Farwell & Co., 1888), p. 76; and Peter L. Hoyt, *Hoyt's History of Wentworth, New Hampshire*, transcribed from original manuscript by Francis A. Muzzey (Littleton, N.H.: Courier Printing Co., 1976), p. 63; all citing town records.

119. Patten, *Diary*, pp. 305, 435, and *passim*.

120. Bouton, *Temperance Reform in Concord*, p. 4.

121. Christopher Daniel Chamberlin, "The Business of Robert Rand, Merchant at North Charlestown, New Hampshire, 1800-1810" (M.A. thesis, University of Missouri-St. Louis, 1985), p. 79.

122. Henry Clarke Wright, *Human Life: Illustrated in My Individual Experience as a Child, a Youth, and a Man* (Boston: Bela Marsh, 1849), quoted in McMahon, "Comfortable Subsistence," p. 67.

123. Rorabaugh, *Alcoholic Republic*, p. 16.

124. Julian Ursyn Niemcewicz, *Under Their Vine and Fig Tree: Travels through America in 1797-1799, 1805 with Some Further Account of Life in New Jersey*, trans. and ed. with an Introduction by Metchie J. E. Budka (Elizabeth, N.J.: Grassman Publishing Co., 1965), p. 169.

125. Rorabaugh, *Alcoholic Republic*, p. 18, quoting foreign visitor.

126. Samuel H. Edes, *Tales From the History of Newport* (Newport, N.H.: Argus-Champion, 1963), p. 29.

127. Royall, *Black Book*, 2:352.

128. Carl David Arfwedson, *The United States and Canada in 1832, 1833, and 1834*, with an Introduction by Marvin Fisher, 2 vols. (London: Richard Bentley, 1834, reprint ed., New York: Johnson Reprint Corporation, 1969), 2:242.

129. Lyman S. Hayes, *The Connecticut River Valley in Southern Vermont and New Hampshire: Historical Sketches* (Rutland, Vt.: Tuttle Co., 1929), pp. 253-54.

130. Wyman, *Life and Adventures of Seth Wyman*, p. 8.

131. Bouton, *Temperance Reform in Concord*, p. 3.

132. George Keith, *A Journal of Travels from New-Hampshire to Caratuck on the Continent of North-America* (London: Joseph Downing, 1706), p. 15.

133. C. C. Lord, *Life and Times in Hopkinton, N.H.* (Concord, N.H.: Republican Press Association, 1890), p. 256, citing Reverend Elijah Fletcher's account with Abel Kimball, 1783, and Charles Bell, *Facts Relating to the Early History of Chester, N.H., from the Settlement in 1720, until the Formation of the State Constitution in the Year 1784* (Concord, N.H.: G. Parker Lyon for the New Hampshire Historical Society, 1863), pp. 68-69, quoting Reverend Ebenezer Flagg's account with John Webster, 1752-58.

134. Eastman, *History of Andover*, pt. 1, p. 182.

135. See, for example, Jessie I. Beckley and Melvin E. Watts, comp. and ed., *The History of Londonderry*, vol. 2: *Excerpts from Willey's Book of Nutfield by George F. Willey* (Londonderry, N.H.: By the Town, 1975), p. 17, citing expense account for ordination of Reverend William Morrison, 1783.

136. Marryat, *Diary in America*, p. 129; Lakier, *A Russian Looks at America*, p. 22.

137. Henry Tufts, *The Autobiography of a Criminal*, ed. with an Introduction by Edmund Pearson, new ed., 1st pub. 1807, Dover, N.H. (New York: Duffield & Co., 1930), p. 233.

138. Records of Overseer of the Poor (1790-1890), Enfield, N.H., quoted in *Enfield Bicentennial, 1761-1961* (Canaan, N.H.: Reporter Press, 1961), pp. 30-31; Bell, *History of Exeter*, p. 76; Patten, *Diary*, p. 13; *NHPP*, 18:486-87; New Hampshire Province Treasury Records, 1759.

139. Belknap, *History of New-Hampshire*, 3:199.

140. W. R. Cochrane, *History of Francestown, N.H., from its Earliest Settlement, April 1758, to January 1, 1891* (Francestown, N.H.: By the Town, 1895), p. 172, quoting town records.

141. Ibid., p. 156.

142. New Hampshire Province Treasury Records, 1758, 1760, 1761, and 1766; Patten, *Diary*, p. 373.

143. J. Worth Estes and David M. Goodman, *The Changing Humors of Portsmouth: The Medical Biography of an American Town, 1623-1983* (Boston: Francis A. Countway Library of Medicine, 1986), p. 4; New Hampshire Province Treasury Records, 1766; William C. Wigglesworth, "Surgery in Massachusetts, 1620-1800," and J. Worth Estes, "Therapeutic Practice in Colonial New England," in *Medicine in Colonial Massachusetts, 1620-1820: A Conference Held 25 & 26 May 1978 by the Colonial Society of Massachusetts* (Boston: By the Society, 1980), pp. 222-26, 368; John King Lord, *A History of the Town of Hanover, N.H.* (Hanover, N.H.: By the Town, 1928), p. 157; Crawford, *History of the White Mountains*, pp. 29-30; John Duffy, *The Healers: A History of American Medicine* (Urbana: University of Illinois Press, 1976), pp. 146-54.

144. New Hampshire Province Treasury Records, 1766.

145. Ibid., 1758 and 1760.

146. *NHPP*, 8:500; New Hampshire, Laws, August 31, 1781, chapter 2.

147. Patten, *Diary*, p. 465.

148. Janson, *Stranger in America*, p. 81.

149. Eliphalet Daniels, Account Books and Daybook; James Underwood, Account Book and Daybooks; New Hampshire Province Treasury Records, 1703.

150. Lambert, *Travels through Canada and the United States*, 2:39-40.

151. Grund, *The Americans*, p. 327.

152. Wansey, *Excursion to the United States*, p. 20.

153. Birket, *Some Cursory Remarks*, pp. 9, 11.

154. Chamberlin, "Business of Robert Rand," p. 71.

155. James Underwood, Account Book and Daybooks, separate insert.

156. Rockingham County Probate Records, docket no. 6384.

157. Birket, *Some Cursory Remarks*, p. 10.

158. J. P. Brissot de Warville, *New Travels in the United States of America, 1788*, trans. Mara Soceanu Vamos and Durand Echeverria, ed. Durand Echeverria (Cambridge: Harvard University Press, Belknap Press, 1964), p. 369.

159. McMahon, "Comfortable Subsistence," pp. 64-66, 115-18, 165.

160. *New-Hampshire Gazette*, December 26, 1766.

161. Birket, *Some Cursory Remarks*, p. 11; Belknap, *History of New-Hampshire*, 3:199-200.

162. Advertisement, *New-Hampshire Gazette*, 1764, cited by Pendery, "Archeology of Urban Foodways in Portsmouth," p. 12; Wansey, *Excursion to the United States*, p. 224.

163. Chamberlin, "Business of Robert Rand," p. 71.

164. Belknap, *History of New-Hampshire*, 3:151.

165. Advertisement, *New Hampshire Sentinel* (Keene), November 5, 1803, quoted in Chamberlin, "Business of Robert Rand," p. 71; Edmund Wheeler, *The History of Newport, New Hampshire, from 1766 to 1878* (Concord, N.H.: Republican Press Association, 1879), p. 167.

166. Gerald Carson, *Rum and Reform in Old New England* (Sturbridge, Mass.: Old Sturbridge Village, 1966), p. 9.

167. Indenture between Erastus V. Freeman and Nathan Merrill, November 15, 1814 (privately owned).

168. Bouton, *History of Concord*, p. 521; Samuel Barnes, Daybook; McMahon, "Comfortable Subsistence," p. 118; [Theodore Dwight], *The Northern Traveller and Northern Tour with the Routes to the Springs, Niagara, Quebec, the Tour of New-England, and the Routes from the South*, 5th ed., rev. (New York: Goodrich & Wiley, 1834), p. 304.

169. Arfwedson, *The United States and Canada*, 1:144.

170. New Hampshire Province Treasury Records, 1729.

171. Patten, *Diary*, p. 464.

172. Bouton, *History of Concord*, p. 522.

173. Ibid., p. 523; Wyman, *Life and Adventures of Seth Wyman*, p. 12; Hayes, *Connecticut River Valley*, p. 257, quoting Lucia Maria Wheaton.

174. Bouton, *History of Concord*, p. 523; Benjamin Chase, *History of Old Chester from 1719 to 1869* (Auburn, N.H.: By the Author, 1869), p. 356.

175. Joseph B. Felt, *The Customs of New England* (Boston: T. R. Marvin, 1853), p. 43.

176. Estate Vendue, General Benjamin Butler, Deerfield, 1828-29, Butler Family Papers, New Hampshire Historical Society.

177. Felt, *Customs of New England*, p. 53.

178. Stansbury, *Pedestrian Tour*, p. 246.

179. Wyman, *Life and Adventures of Seth Wyman*, p. 12.

180. *Thomas's Massachusetts, Connecticut, Rhode-Island, New-Hampshire, & Vermont Almanack for 1792* (Worcester, Mass.; Isaiah Thomas, 1792), quoted in McMahon, "Comfortable Subsistence," p. 234.

181. Tufts, *Autobiography*, p. 158.

182. David A. Bundy, *100 Acres More or Less: The History of the Land and People of Bow, New Hampshire* (Canaan, N.H.: Phoenix Publishing for the Bow Town History Committee, 1975), pp. 176-77.

183. New Hampshire Province Treasury Records, 1704.

184. Thomas, "Reminiscences of the White Mountains," p. 46; Buckingham, *Eastern and Western States*, 3:216-17, quoted in Bulkley, "White Mountain Tourist Industry," p. 12.

185. Alexander Mackay, *The Western World; or, Travels in the United States in 1846-47*, 2 vols., from 2d London ed. (Philadelphia: Lea & Blanchard, 1849), p. 36.

186. Samuel Barnes, Daybook.

187. Wyman, *Life and Adventures of Seth Wyman*, p. 9.

188. *Farmer's Cabinet* (Amherst), December 18, 1810; Wyman, *Life and Adventures of Seth Wyman*, p. 41; *New-Hampshire Statesman* (Concord), November 17, 1823.

189. Amos Kendall, *Autobiography of Amos Kendall*, ed. William Stickney (Boston: Lee & Shepard, 1872), p. 19.

190. Richard Waldron to Nicholas Gilman, August 3, 1733, in *NHPP*, 18:50.

191. Belknap, *History of New-Hampshire*, 3:199.

192. Jeremy Belknap to Benjamin Rush, July 29, 1789, *Collections of the Massachusetts Historical Society*, ser. 6, vol. 4 (1891): *Belknap Papers*, pt. 3, p. 440.

193. Rorabaugh, *Alcoholic Republic*, pp. 43-45, quoting Benjamin Rush.

194. Belknap, *History of New-Hampshire*, 3:250.

195. Ibid.

196. New Hampshire, Laws, December 22, 1792, chapter 27.

197. G. M. Trevelyan, *English Social History: A Survey of Six Centuries, Chaucer to Queen Victoria* (New York: David McKay Co., 1942), pp. 323-25, 386-87; Kym S. Rice, *Early American Taverns: For the Entertainment of Friends and Strangers* (Chicago: Regnery Gateway in association with Fraunces Tavern Museum, 1983), pp. 38-41; *New-Hampshire Gazette*, December 19, 1766; March 20, 1767; November 13, 1767.

198. Jonathan Kittredge, *Address on the Effects of Ardent Spirits* and Charles H. Bell, *The Bench and Bar of New Hampshire, Including Biographical Notices of Deceased Judges of the Highest Court, and Lawyers of the Province and State* (Boston: Houghton, Mifflin & Co., Riverside Press, 1894), pp. 477-78.

199. Edwin Chamberlin et al., *Historical Notes of Bath, New Hampshire, 1765-1965* (Littleton, N.H.: Courier Printing Co., 1965), p. 139.

200. Bouton, *Temperance Reform in Concord*, p. 18.

201. Broadside, "Astounding Facts!" Dover, August 14, 1838, Dover Public Library, illustrated in *Dover, New Hampshire, 350th Anniversary, Commemorative Book, 1623-1973* (n.p., 1973), p. 109.

202. Washington Total Abstinence Society of Cheshire County, "Report of the Pauperism, Crime & Intemperance of Cheshire County," ca. 1846, Historical Society of Cheshire County, Keene, New Hampshire, p. 9.

203. Wheeler, *History of Newport*, p. 168.

204. Arfwedson, *The United States and Canada*, 1:147-48.

205. Rorabaugh, *Alcoholic Republic*, pp. 17-18, based on Frost Store, Durham, Day Books.

206. Belknap, *History of New-Hampshire*, 3:199.

207. Benjamin Chase, *History of Old Chester*, p. 357.

208. Cochrane, *History of Francestown*, p. 184.

209. J. L. Merrill, ed., *History of Acworth, with the Proceedings of the Centennial Anniversary, Genealogical Records, and Register of Farms* (Acworth, N.H.: By the Town, 1869), p. 133.

210. Cochrane, *History of Francestown*, pp. 365-66.

211. Bouton, *History of Concord*, p. 536.

212. [Frederic Kidder and Augustus Addison Gould], *The History of New Ipswich from Its First Grant in MDCCXXXVI to the Present Time* (Boston: Gould & Lincoln, 1852), p. 255, quoting town records; Newbury town records, transcribed by Ernest L. Sherman.

213. Benjamin Chase, *History of Old Chester*, p. 339, quoting church records.

214. *Proceedings of the Grand Lodge of New Hampshire, from July 8, 5789 [1789] to June 8, 5841 [1841], Inclusive* (Concord, N.H.: McFarland & Jenks, 1860), pp. 314, 336, 357, 363, and 373.

215. [Sarah Josepha Hale], "Editors' Table," *Godey's Magazine and Lady's Book* 33 (September 1846):141.

216. Charles Carleton Coffin, comp., *The History of Boscawen and Webster, from 1733 to 1878* (Concord, N.H.: Republican Press Association, 1878), p. 196.

217. [Sophia Hayes Wyatt], *The Autobiography of a Landlady of the Old School* (Boston: By the Author, 1854), pp. 31 and 116.

218. *Portsmouth Journal*, February 22, 1833.

219. Thomas J. Crawford to Reverend John G. Adams, June 30, 1845, New Hampshire Historical Society.

220. S. G. Griffin, *A History of the Town of Keene from 1732, When the Township Was Granted by Massachusetts, to 1874, When It Became a City* (Keene, N.H.: Sentinel Printing Co., 1904), p. 286, and Elise Lathrop, *Early American Inns and Taverns* (New York: Robert M. McBride & Co., 1926), p. 107, both quoting advertisement of Isaac Wyman, in *The New-Hampshire Recorder, and the Weekly Advertiser* (Keene), December 30, 1788.

221. *New-Hampshire Post* (Haverhill), February 24, 1830.

222. *New-Hampshire Gazette*, November 18, 1786.

223. *New-Hampshire Patriot & State Gazette* (Concord), June 11, 1832.

224. *New-Hampshire Gazette*, March 2, 1841.

225. Washington Total Abstinence Society of Cheshire County, "Report of Pauperism, Crime & Intemperance," p. 11.

226. Gordon F. Grimes, "A History of Dover, New Hampshire, 1790-1835," [Brunswick, Me.], 1971 (typewritten), pp. 148-49, citing resolution of anti-temperance group.

227. New Hampshire, Laws, July 6, 1849, chapter 846; July 14, 1855, chapter 1658; July 19, 1877, chapter 71; July 18, 1878, chapter 16.

228. James L. Garvin, *Historic Portsmouth: Early Photographs from the Collections of Strawbery Banke, Inc.* (Somersworth, N.H.: New Hampshire Publishing Co., 1974), pp. 67-68; Raymond A. Brighton, *Frank Jones: King of the Alemakers* (Hampton, N.H.: Peter E. Randall, 1976), *passim*; Stanley Baron, *Brewed in America: A History of Beer and Ale in the United States* (Boston: Little, Brown & Co., 1962), p. 198.

CHAPTER 9
Taverns in the Age of Tourism

1. James Duncan, "Journal Kept by James Duncan, Jr. of Haverhill, Mass. While on a Journey to Gilmanton, Warren, Haverhill and Lebanon, N.H., in November, 1806," with an Introduction by Stephen W. Phillips and James Duncan Phillips, *Essex Institute Historical Collections* 79 (January 1943):1-18.

2. Duke de La Rochefoucault-Liancourt, *Travels through the United States of North America, The Country of the Iroquois and Upper Canada in the Years 1795, 1796, and 1797, with an Authentic Account of Lower Canada* (London: R. Phillips, 1799; American Culture Series 2, reel 192.1, Ann Arbor, Mich.: University Microfilms, n.d.), p. 62.

3. Timothy Dwight, *Travels in New England and New York*, ed. Barbara Miller Solomon with the assistance of Patricia M. King, new ed., 1st pub. 1821-22, 4 vols. (Cambridge: Harvard University Press, Belknap Press, 1969), 2:232.

4. *Farmer's Weekly Museum* (Walpole), August 12, 1799.

5. Duncan, "Journal Kept by James Duncan," p. 12.

6. *Portsmouth Journal*, September 3, 1825.

7. Lucy Crawford, *The History of the White Mountains from the First Settlement of Upper Coos and Pequaket* (White Hills: n.p., 1846), p. 76.

8. Anne Royall, *The Black Book, or a Continuation of Travels in the United States*, 3 vols. (Washington, D.C.: By the Author, 1828-29), 2:383.

9. Harriet Martineau, *Retrospect of Western Travel*, 3 vols. (London: Saunders & Otley, 1838), 3:61; Samuel Johnson, " 'Journal of a Tour to the White Hills': An 1842 Chronicle by Samuel Johnson," ed. with an Introduction by Bryant F. Tolles, Jr., *Essex Institute Historical Collections* 120 (January 1984):22.

10. J. C. Myers, *Sketches on a Tour through the Northern and Eastern States, the Canadas & Nova Scotia* (Harrisonburg, Va.: J. H. Wartmann & Bros, 1849), p. 269.

11. Donald D. Keyes et al., *The White Mountains: Place and Perceptions* (Hanover, N.H.: University Press of New England for the University Art Galleries, University of New Hampshire, 1980).

12. Johnson, "Tour to the White Hills," p. 11.

13. Caroline Gilman, *The Poetry of Travelling in the United States* (New York: S. Colman, 1838), p. 134.

14. *Portsmouth Journal*, June 16, 1827; *New-Hampshire Patriot & State Gazette* (Concord), August 1, 1825.

15. *Dover State & Strafford Advertiser*, September 3, 1833, quoting *Democratic Republican* (Haverhill).

16. "Rye History as a Watering Place," *Portsmouth Journal*, September 13, 1862.

17. S. G. W. Benjamin, *The Atlantic Islands as Resorts of Health and Pleasure* (New York: Harper & Co., 1878), p. 272, quoted in Marie L. Ahearn, "Health Restoring Resorts on the New England Coast," in *Victorian Resorts and Hotels: Essays from a Victorian Society Autumn Symposium*, ed. Richard Guy Wilson, published as *Nineteenth Century* 8 (1982):42.

18. See, for example, *New-Hampshire Gazette* (Portsmouth), May 17, 1836; [Theodore Dwight], *The Northern Traveller and Northern Tour with the Routes to the Springs, Niagara, Quebec, the Tour of New-England, and the Routes from the South*, 5th ed., rev. (New York: Goodrich & Wiley, 1834), p. 299 and *passim*.

19. *Portsmouth Journal*, May 19, 1866.

20. Martineau, *Retrospect of Western Travel*, 3:61; *Portsmouth Journal*, September 4, 1852.

21. Peter B. Bulkley, "Identifying the White Mountain Tourist, 1853-1854: Origin, Occupation, and Wealth as a Definition of the Early Hotel Trade," *Historical New Hampshire* 35 (Summer 1980):107-62; *Portsmouth Journal*, August 9, 1851.

22. Henry David Thoreau, *Thoreau in the Mountains: Writings by Henry David Thoreau*, with Commentary by William Howarth (New York: Farrar, Straus, Giroux, 1982), p. 347; *Portsmouth Journal*, September 13, 1862.

23. *Portsmouth Journal*, July 29, 1865.

24. *New Hampshire Register*, 1842, pp. 118-19; 1845, pp. 100-102.

25. [Sarah Josepha Hale], "Editors' Table," *Godey's Magazine and Lady's Book* 33 (September 1846):140.

26. *New Hampshire Register*, 1859, pp. 152-55.

27. Thoreau, *Thoreau in the Mountains*, p. 295.

28. *New-Hampshire Patriot & State Gazette* (Concord), August 1, 1825.

29. *Dover Gazette & Strafford Advertiser*, September 3, 1833.

30. *Portsmouth Journal*, August 9, 1851; R. Stuart Wallace, "A Social History of the White Mountains," in Keyes et al., *The White Mountains: Place and Perceptions*, p. 28.

31. *Portsmouth Journal*, July 15, 1848; September 24, 1853.

32. Ibid., August 19, 1865.

33. Anthony Trollope, *North America* (New York: Harper & Bros., 1862), p. 35.

34. Thoreau, *Thoreau in the Mountains*, p. 363.

35. *Portsmouth Journal*, June 13, 1863.

36. William Little, *The History of Weare, New Hampshire, 1735-1888* (Lowell, Mass.: S. W. Huse & Co., 1888), p. 455; *Portsmouth Journal*, November 8 and 22, 1845.

37. [Frederick Kidder and Augustus Addison Gould], *The History of New Ipswich from Its First Grant in MDCCXXXVI to the Present Time* (Boston: Gould & Lincoln, 1852), p. 131.

38. Johnson, "Tour to the White Hills," p. 36.

39. *Portsmouth Journal*, February 22, 1833.

40. Nathaniel Bouton, *History of the Temperance Reform in Concord: A Discourse Delivered on the Evening of December 10, 1843* (Concord, N.H.: Asa McFarland, 1843), p. 13.

41. *Portsmouth Journal*, August 5, 1843.

42. John King Lord, *A History of Dartmouth College, 1815-1909: Being the Second Volume of A History of Dartmouth College and the Town of Hanover, New Hampshire, Begun by Frederick Chase* (Concord, N.H.: Rumford Press, 1913), pp. 268-69.

43. Washington Total Abstinence Society of Cheshire County, "Report of the Pauperism, Crime & Intemperance of Cheshire County," ca. 1846, Historical Society of Cheshire County, Keene, New Hampshire, pp. 3 and 9.

44. *Portsmouth Journal*, August 21, 1852.

45. S. G. Griffin, *A History of the Town of Keene from 1732, When the Township Was Granted by Massachusetts, to 1874, When It Became a City* (Keene, N.H.: Sentinel Printing Co., 1904), p. 441, quoting town resolution, September 1845.

46. *Portsmouth Journal*, August 10, 1833.

47. Ibid., August 25, 1855.

48. David A. Bundy, *100 Acres More or Less: The History of the Land and People of Bow, New Hampshire* (Canaan, N.H.: Phoenix Publishing for the Bow Town History Committee, 1975), pp. 280-81.

49. Edward L. Parker, *The History of Londonderry* (Boston: Perkins & Whipple, 1851; reprint ed., Londonderry, N.H.: By the Town, 1974), p. 63.

50. [Sophia Hayes Wyatt], *The Autobiography of a Landlady of the Old School* (Boston: By the Author, 1854), p. 31.

51. *Portsmouth Journal*, February 12, 1842 and October 3, 1845.

52. Edwin Chamberlin et al., *Historical Notes of Bath, New Hampshire, 1765-1965* (Littleton, N.H.: Courier Printing Co., 1965), p. 140.

53. *New-Hampshire Gazette*, January 28, 1840.

54. *New Hampshire Telegraph* (Nashua), May 1869, quoted in Emma P. Boylston Locke, comp., *Colonial Amherst: The Early History, Customs, and Homes* (Milford, N.H.: W. B. & A. B. Rotch, 1916), p. 57.

55. Joseph B. Walker, "Penacook House and the Old Time Taverns of the State," *Proceedings of the New Hampshire Historical Society*, 1 (1872-88):393.

56. George Wadleigh, *Notable Events in the History of Dover, New Hampshire from the First Settlement in 1623 to 1865* (Dover, N.H.: n.p., 1913), p. 261.

57. Walker, "Penacook House," p. 393 and *New Hampshire Telegraph* (Nashua), May 1869.

58. Peter L. Hoyt, *Hoyt's History of Wentworth, New Hampshire,* transcribed from original manuscript by Francis A. Muzzey (Littleton, N.H.: Courier Printing Co., 1976), pp. 152-53.

59. Stillman Moulton Hobbs and Helen Davis Hobbs, *The Way It Was in North Hampton: Some History, Sketches and Reminscences that Illuminate the Times of a New Hampshire Seacoast Town* (Seabrook, N.H.: Withey Press, 1978), p. 25 and conversation with coauthor, 1987.

60. William Allen Wallace, *The History of Canaan, New Hampshire* (Concord, N.H.: Rumford Press, 1910), p. 440.

61. Francis Lane Childs, ed., *Hanover, New Hampshire: A Bicentennial Book, Essays in Celebration of the Town's 200th Anniversary* (Hanover, n.p., 1961), pp. 132-34.

62. *New Hampshire Telegraph* (Nashua), May 1869.

63. New Hampshire, Laws, July 4, 1860, chapter 2424, and *passim.*

64. La Rochefoucault-Liancourt, *Travels through the United States,* p. 464.

65. Edmund Wheeler, *The History of Newport, New Hampshire from 1766 to 1878* (Concord, N.H.: Republican Press Association, 1879), pp. 78-79; John R. Eastman, comp., *History of the Town of Andover, New Hampshire, 1751-1906* (Concord, N.H.: Rumford Printing Co., 1910), pt. 1, p. 180.

66. C. C. Benton, "The Lafayette Hotel, with Memories of Earlier Days," *Granite State Free Press* (Lebanon), November 24, 1871, included in Allan Burritt Downs, comp., "Reminiscences of Lebanon," 1935 (typewritten), p. 17.

67. *Portsmouth Directory,* 1821; *Dover Directory,* 1837, 1843; *Portsmouth Journal,* March 28, 1840; *Nashua Directory,* 1843, pp. xvi-xvii; *The New-England Mercantile Union Business Directory,* 1849, p. 92; *The Farmers' Guide: A Description of the Business of Nashua and Nashville* (Nashua, N.H.: Kimball & Dodge, 1851), pp. 27 and 43.

68. William Bentley, *The Diary of William Bentley, D.D., Pastor of the East Church, Salem, Massachusetts,* 4 vols. (Salem, Mass.: Essex Institute, 1907-14), 2:389; Sarah Connell Ayer, *Diary of Sarah Connell Ayer: Andover and Newburyport, Massachusetts; Concord and Bow, New Hampshire; Portland and Eastport, Maine* [ed. Margaret H. Jewell] (Portland, Me.: Lefavor-Tower Co., 1910), p. 199; James Underwood, Account Book and Daybooks, Swanzey, 1814-32, Historical Society of Cheshire County; Crawford, *History of the White Mountains,* pp. 61, 70; *New-England Mercantile Union Business Directory,* 1849, p. 86.

69. Perry R. Duis, *The Saloon: Public Drinking in Chicago and Boston, 1880-1920* (Urbana: University of Illinois Press, 1983), p. 10; New Hampshire, Laws, 1903, chapter 95; Ronald Jager and Grace Jager, *New Hampshire: An Illustrated History of the Granite State* (Woodland Hills, Calif.: Windsor Publications in Cooperation with the New Hampshire Historical Society, 1983), p. 76.

70. John P. Adams, *Drowned Valley: The Piscataqua River Basin* (Hanover, N.H.: University Press of New England for the University of New Hampshire, 1976), p. 225; postcard collection, New Hampshire Historical Society, New Boston and Laconia.

71. Thomas Hamilton, *Men and Manners in America,* new ed. (Edinburgh: William Blackwood & Sons, 1843; reprint of [2d] ed., New York: Johnson Reprint Corporation, 1968), p. 89; Isabella Lucy Bird, *The Englishwoman in America,* with a Foreword by Andrew Hill Clark (London: John Murray, 1856; reprint ed., Madison: University of Wisconsin Press, 1966), p. 100.

72. Hale, "Editors' Table," p. 141.

73. Hoyt, *History of Wentworth,* p. 130; George L. Chindahl, *A History of the Circus in America* (Caldwell, Idaho: Caxton Printers, 1959), pp. 88 ff.; *Portsmouth Journal,* August 9, 1851.

74. Richard E. Winslow, III, *The Piscataqua Gundalow: Workhorse for a Tidal Basin Empire* (Portsmouth, N.H.: Portsmouth Marine Society, 1983), pp. 77 ff.

75. John B. Hill, *History of the Town of Mason, N.H. from the First Grant in 1749, to the Year 1858* (Boston: Lucius A. Elliot & Co., 1858), p. 247.

76. [Kidder and Gould], *History of New Ipswich,* pp. 130-31; *Portsmouth Journal,* August 12, 1837; November 3, 1838; *New-Hampshire Gazette,* January 28, 1840; March 8, 1841; *Portsmouth Journal,* May 26, 1849; Lyman S. Hayes, *The Connecticut River Valley in Southern Vermont and New Hampshire: Historical Sketches* (Rutland, Vt.: Tuttle Co., 1929), pp. 118-19, quoting *Bellows Falls* (Vt.) *Gazette,* June 1839.

77. Alice Morse Earle, *Stage-coach and Tavern Days* (New York: Macmillan Co., 1901), pp. 336-39; William F. Whitcher, *History of the Town of Haverhill, New Hampshire* (Concord, N.H.: Rumford Press, 1919), p. 345; Hayes, *Connecticut River Valley,* p. 124.

78. *New-Hampshire Gazette,* January 20, 1846.

79. Ibid., January 26, 1841.

80. Allan Forbes and Ralph M. Eastman, *Taverns and Stagecoaches of New England,* 2 vols. (Boston: State Street Trust Co., 1953-54), 1:105-107; Alden Hatch, *American Express: A Century of Service* (Garden City, N.Y.: Doubleday & Co., 1950), p. 89.

81. Caroline M. Fitch, Diary, Old Sturbridge Village, transcribed by Dorothy M. Sears, Jr., 1986.

82. Hale, "Editors' Table," p. 141.

83. *Portsmouth Journal,* July 15, 1848 and July 7, 1849.

84. Forbes and Eastman, *Taverns and Stagecoaches of New England* 2:30-41.

85. W. Dennis Chesley, "The New Hampshire Turnpike, 1796-1825," [Durham], 1982 (typewritten), pp. 48, 58.

86. W. R. Waterman, "The Fourth New Hampshire Turnpike," *Historical New Hampshire* 15 (November 1960): 21-22.

87. Harold S. Bryant, *History of Coos Turnpike* (Sarasota, Fla.: Aceto Bookmen, 1985), pp. 10, 17.

88. John Preston, "The [Fourth New Hampshire] Turnpike Road —Fortune or Folly," paper presented at the annual meeting of the New Ipswich Historical Society, August 1987 (typewritten), pp. 2-3.

89. John M. Shirley, "The Fourth New Hampshire Turnpike," *Granite Monthly* 4 (1881): 454.

90. Frederick Marryat, *A Diary in America with Remarks on Its Institutions,* ed. with an Introduction by Sydney Jackman, new ed., 1st pub. 1839 (New York: Alfred A. Knopf, 1962), p. 126.

91. Bryant, *History of Coos Turnpike,* p. 17.

92. "New Hampshire Turnpike Directors' Records," New Hampshire Historical Society, p. 108, quoted in Chesley, "The New Hampshire Turnpike," p. 42.

93. Frank West Rollins, "Roads and Road-Building in New Hampshire," typewritten, n.d., p. 13.

94. New Hampshire, Laws, June 29, 1826, chapter 29.

95. Shirley, "The Fourth New Hampshire Turnpike," pp. 454-59; Frederic J. Wood, *The Turnpikes of New England and Evolution of the Same through England, Virginia, and Maryland* (Boston: Marshall Jones Co., 1919), pp. 218-20, 227, 231-32.

96. Shirley, "The Fourth New Hampshire Turnpike," p. 459.

97. *Portsmouth Journal,* September 4, 1852; October 29, 1853.

98. Alonzo J. Fogg, comp., *The Statistics and Gazetteer of New-Hampshire* (Concord, N.H.: D. L. Guernsey, 1874), p. 498.

ON THE ROAD NORTH OF BOSTON

99. *Population of New Hampshire*, pt. 1: *Basic Data on Growth and Distribution since the Time of Settlement, 1623 to 1940* (Concord: New Hampshire State Planning and Development Commission, 1946).

100. Elliott C. Cogswell, *History of Nottingham, Deerfield*, and *Northwood* (Manchester, N.H.: John B. Clarke, 1878), pp. 319-21.

101. Fogg, *Statistics and Gazetteer of New-Hampshire*, pp. 403-4.

102. *Mirror and Farmer* (Manchester), September 26, 1889.

103. *Plymouth Record*, October 12, 1889.

104. Edgar O. Achorn, "To a Deserted New England Farmhouse," *New England Magazine* 24 (August 1901):605.

105. *Special Report of the Summer Boarding Business and Resorts in New Hampshire*, in *Third Biennial Report of the Bureau of Labor of the State of New Hampshire*, vol. 5 (Manchester, N.H.: Arthur E. Clarke, 1900), p. x. For statistics of 1905, see *Second Special Report . . . in Sixth Biennial Report*, vol. 8 (Nashua, N.H.: Telegraph Publishing Co., 1906).

106. *Plymouth Record*, September 6, 1890.

107. *Farmington News*, November 8, 1889.

108. *Concord Monitor*, August 23, 1890.

109. Ibid.

110. Ibid.

111. Ibid.

112. *Plymouth Record*, February 21, 1891; March 21, 1891.

113. Nahum J. Bachelder, *Reminiscences and Addresses* (East Andover, N.H.: By the Author, 1930), pp. 54-56.

114. Nahum J. Bachelder, *Secure a Home in New Hampshire, Where Comfort, Health, and Prosperity Abound* (Manchester, N.H.: John B. Clarke, 1890), pp. 7-8.

115. [Harlan C. Pearson, ed.], *New Hampshire Farms for Summer Homes* (Concord, N.H.: Rumford Press, 1902-13); *New Hampshire Farm Homes* (Concord, N.H.: Rumford Press, 1915-16).

116. *Granite State Magazine* 3 (June 1907):278-79.

117. Brochure, *Description of Fisher's Road Machine* (Walpole, N.H.: C.C. Davis, ca. 1875), New Hampshire Historical Society.

118. *Plymouth Record*, September 13, 1890.

119. James J. Flink, *America Adopts the Automobile, 1895-1910* (Cambridge, Mass.: MIT Press, 1970), pp. 204-5.

120. *Plymouth Record*, January 24, 1891.

121. Ibid., May 2, 1891.

122. Charles H. Pettee, "An Experiment with a Country Road," New Hampshire College Agricultural Experiment Station *Bulletin* 30 (July 1895); Pettee, "An Experiment with a Steam Drill," *Bulletin* 46 (August 1897); Pettee, "A Practical Study of Road Maintenance," *Bulletin* 46; Pettee, "Experiments in Road Surfacing," *Bulletin* 77 (September 1900).

123. John D. Quackenbos, "The Aesthetic Side of Farm Life," *Report of the Board of Agriculture from October 1, 1898 to January 1, 1901* (Manchester, N.H.: Arthur E. Clarke, 1901), pp. 445-46.

124. New Hampshire, Laws, 1903, chapters 54 and 133; 1905, chapter 35.

125. John W. Storrs, Address before the White Mountain Board of Trade, 1905, reprinted in *New Hampshire Highways* 6 (November 1928).

126. James O. Lyford, ed., *History of Concord, New Hampshire, from the Original Grant in Seventeen Hundred and Twenty-five to the Opening of the Twentieth Century*, 2 vols. (Concord, N.H.: Rumford Press, 1903), 2:865.

INDEX